13505

The enjoyment of literature /

3 0183 00820 0303

D1567949

DATE DUE

JAN 25 1979			

THE
ENJOYMENT
OF
LITERATURE

OTHER BOOKS BY BERNARD GREBANIER

The Uninhibited Byron: An Account of His Sexual Confusion
The Great Shakespeare Forgery
Thornton Wilder
Edwin Arlington Robinson
The Truth about Shylock
The Heart of Hamlet
Playwriting
Racine's Phaedra, *an English Acting Version in Verse*
Molière's The Misanthrope, *an English Acting Version*
Armenian Miniatures
Then Came Each Actor

POETRY

The Angel in the Rock
The Other Love
Mirrors of the Fire
Fauns, Satyrs and a Few Sages
Pegasus in the Seventies (editor)

THE
ENJOYMENT
OF
LITERATURE

Bernard Grebanier

CROWN PUBLISHERS, INC., NEW YORK

Printed in the United States of America
Published simultaneously in Canada by General Publishing Company Limited

Design by Nedda Balter

An earlier (considerably both truncated and enlarged) version of this book was published in 1960 as a portion of *Introduction to Imaginative Literature*.

Library of Congress Cataloging in Publication Data

Grebanier, Bernard D   N   1903–
  The enjoyment of literature.

  "An earlier version of this book was published in 1960 as a portion of Introduction to imaginative literature."
  Includes bibliographical references and index.
  1. Literature—History and criticism. I. Title.
PN523.G7   809   75–2176
ISBN 0–517–51893–7

ACKNOWLEDGMENTS

Acknowledgment is gratefully made as follows for permission to reprint copyrighted material:

Truman Capote, from *Other Voices, Other Rooms.* Copyright 1948 by Truman Capote. Reprinted by permission of Random House, Inc.

Willa Cather, "Neighbor Rosicky." Reprinted from *Obscure Destinies* by Willa Cather, by permission of Alfred A. Knopf, Inc. Copyright 1930, 1932 by Willa Cather.

G. K. Chesterton, "A Piece of Chalk." From *Tremendous Trifles* by G. K. Chesterton, Copyright, 1955, Sheed & Ward, Inc., New York. Reprinted by permission of Sheed & Ward, Inc. and Miss D. E. Collins.

e. e. cummings, "when faces called flowers." Copyright, 1950, by e. e. cummings. Reprinted from his volume, *Complete Poems 1913–1962,* by permission of Harcourt Brace Jovanovich, Inc. and Granada Publishing Limited. MacGibbon & Kee, Publisher.

Emily Dickinson, from "The Final Inch" in *Bolts of Melody* edited by Mabel Loomis Todd and Millicent Todd Bingham. Copyright, 1945, by The Trustees of Amherst College. Reprinted by permission of Harper & Row, Publishers, Inc.

Emily Dickinson, from "I never saw a Moor—." Reprinted by permission of the publishers and the Trustees of Amherst College from Thomas H. Johnson, Editor, *The Poems of Emily Dickinson,* Cambridge, Mass.: The Belknap Press of Harvard University Press, Copyright, 1951, 1955, by The President and Fellows of Harvard College.

Lord Dunsany, from *Fame and the Poet.* From *The Atlantic Monthly,* August, 1919. Copyright, 1919, by The Atlantic Monthly Company, Boston, Massachusetts.

Bernard Grebanier, "May Afternoon." Reprinted by permission of the author from *International Who's Who in Poetry.* Cambridge, England, 1974.

Thomas Hardy, "Ah, Are You Digging on My Grave?" From *Collected Poems of Thomas Hardy.* Copyright 1925 by The Macmillan Publishing Co., Inc. Reprinted by permission of The Macmillan Publishing Co., Inc., of New York, the Trustees of the Hardy Estate, Macmillan London and Basingstoke, and The Macmillan Company of Canada Limited.

Eric Hoffer, from *The True Believer* (pp. 62–64). Copyright, 1951, by Eric Hoffer. Reprinted by permission of Harper & Row, Publishers, Inc.

Gerard Manley Hopkins, from "Spring and Fall." From *The Poems of Gerard Manley Hopkins,* third edition 1948, published by Oxford University Press, Inc.

Oliver Jensen, from "The Forward Look and a Backward Glance." © 1958, American Heritage Publishing Co., Inc. Reprinted by permission from *Horizon* (September, 1958).

R. Prawer Jhabvala, "Better Than Dead." From *The New Yorker,* May 24, 1958. Copyright © 1968 by R. Prawer Jhabvala. Reprinted by permission of Russell & Volkening, Inc. as agents for the author.

by Bertha Georgia Yeats. Reprinted by permission of The Macmillan Publishing Co., Inc., of New York, M. B. Yeats, Miss Anne Yeats, and Macmillan of London & Basingstoke and The Macmillan Co. of Canada.

For
Stephen Pomerantz,
most select and generous, chief in that

CONTENTS

PREFACE-MANIFESTO

Quite apart from the pleasures which the reading of literature affords, literature may be said to bless us with a most precious gift: a sense of the continuity of human experience. It assures us that we are *not* alone. What we have experienced, enjoyed or suffered, we see that others, as far back as letters go, have experienced, enjoyed or suffered; and we know that the same will be true of those who live in the centuries to come. Modes change, each age has what it conceives to be its special tastes, yet literature continues to remind us that, despite such apparent alterations, men and women and children have always been fundamentally the same in their personal relationships. The changes of mode and the special characteristics of an era are in themselves interesting and sometimes exciting to contemplate, but the priceless proof by literature of the continuity of human experience is not thereby affected. No doubt, all the arts have this in common, together with the concern of each art as to how much and what can be done because of the limitations of the medium. Each art has its own special function in what it can express, but literature, operating as it does through language, has the particular privilege (as music and painting do not) of dealing with ideas and the specifics of human relationships. Ludwig Wittgenstein, philosopher of Cambridge, says profoundly: "The limits of my language mean the limits of my world."

The limits of anyone's language are indeed the limits of his world. That truth should make us realize that we are suddenly faced with a grave crisis. As a result of its peculiar history, Britain by the seventeenth century had already by far the largest language in the world, which is to say it had the richest vehicle of expression among world languages. The result has been that the English language has the world's richest and most varied literature. (It is not strange that the piano, possessing as it does the largest compass for musical expression of any solo instrument, has had by far the vastest amount of great music written for it.) But within the last few decades there has developed what one must almost call a movement: a movement to debase, deliberately to diminish and narrow the vast resources of English. The causes are manifold: the reducing of great books to the rubbish of comic books; the obsession of watching any and all TV programs (where nothing has to be read), the idiotic repetitions and poverty-stricken vocabulary of rock 'n' roll, all eventuating in a narrowing of the limits of most people's world, as shown by the laziness which has made a ritual of obscenity in books, movies, TV, and the theatre—in itself not so morally disgusting as intellectually so, for it betrays an inability to use the word called for, as well as by the maddening growth of the "y'know," "y'know," between every two spoken phrases (of this legislators, popular authors, and, of course, the man in the street are increasingly guilty), even though the phrase "y'know" means absolutely nothing.

Everyone's speech is likely to encompass a smaller vocabulary than his writing vocabulary; his writing vocabulary, if he is a reader, is likely to be much smaller than his reading vocabulary. It is upon one's reading vocabulary, then, that one's command of the language and of an understanding of the world depend. The sad fact is that literature is being read less and less. The official position of the country on the subject of pornography is not the question of whether a book has literary value, but only whether it has "social" usefulness —whatever *that* may mean. *Women in Love,* which years ago was stupidly banned on moral grounds, is a fine novel, which has a great deal to say about human relationships. Nowadays, even chic magazines in their reviews of plays and movies speak of hard-core pornography as though pornography were a merit, a new Declaration of Independence—from what? The fact is that *anything* can be said if the author has the vocabulary; bawdry is always welcome (outside of a church) if it is witty—Shakespeare has enough of such delightful passages— but pornography ought to the man or woman with a mind be as stimulating as a piece of raw, bleeding beef.

But this book is an introduction to literature and what literature is concerned with, not a work devoted to vocabulary-building (though that should be an unsought-for dividend in what follows). This book is intended for the general reader, which in this case includes college students too. For ever since colleges have become places where social problems are supposed to be solved instead of institutions where every individual may have doors opened for him to enrich his own personal life, literary studies have not only been dropped on a wholesale scale, but the students themselves often come to college with the greatest ignorance as to how one must read.

There are in existence a number of books which generously tell the reader what to think about various poems, other books about various pieces of prose. The present work has no such intent. Moreover, most of those books indulge the prejudices of the commentators; those written by the so-called New Critics—by this time they are very old New Critics— for instance, take the opportunity to ridicule Shelley, for that is *their* mode; poets like Browning are, in their eyes, hardly worth mentioning. Yet surely the domain of literature is wide enough to admit every kind of excellence. And if Shelley is no poet, then there are no poets. I do not have to despise Debussy or Schumann because I love Bach, Mozart and Beethoven; and if I admire Dryden and Pope at their best, there is no reason why I must dismiss Shelley.

But, as I have intimated, my object is not to equip the reader with security-proof opinions; I desire that when he reads literature he form his own. With that end in view I have had to strike out on my own, in order to equip the reader with sufficient cargo to adventure into literature like a pioneer. The only satisfactory way to accomplish such a purpose, I decided, is to make him aware of what to look for, and step by step make him more sensitive to what the author puts into his work, what, in short, literature is made of. I am interested in discovering principles, not in pronouncing particular judgments.

For that reason I discuss the "content" of the selections quoted only on the occasions when an analysis of the "content" is necessary to the matter under consideration—as, for example, in the discussion of structure or what is now known as "ambiguity."

My method of procedure is something of an innovation. I have, as far as possible, presented the principles of literary appreciation inductively. Using each piece of writing quoted to illustrate but *one* point, I ask the reader to go over the piece first, so that he may react spontaneously to it, and then only do I make the one point I wish to consider. In this way I hope to avoid the impression that authors work by "rules."

As for the principles of literary appreciation which I undertake to inculcate, I have gladly availed myself of what I find best in the New Criticism without discarding what is best in traditional modes of looking at literature. The New Criticism has had the invaluable effect of turning the reader back to the work itself and of riveting attention on values which are literary. But much of the New Criticism's contribution tends either to be clouded in terminology or else to repel the honest reader because its findings stand in danger of degenerating into a new pedantry. The New Critic is sometimes too ready to espouse one school of writing at the expense of another. Result: all the dangers of cultism—writers who are "in" and writers who are "out"—whatever their literary worth. There are treasures enough in all periods of our poetry and prose, and that much the reader must understand before he can presume to judge. Without enrolling myself as a New Critic, I should like to do New Criticism the service of bringing what in it is valid out of the "learned" periodicals and out-of-print books to within the reach of the general reader.

I have used twentieth-century writings liberally among established pieces for my illustrations. At the same time I have deliberately used selections from all important periods of British and American literature, and, on other occasions (when the point did not particularly involve nuances of language) translations from other literatures. I have done all this because I believe it a serious error to restrict the cultivation of taste and study of literary principles to a narrow range of literary accomplishment. And everywhere, except when poetry or prose is under particular consideration, I have shown the principles operating in both prose and poetry.

My opening chapters, to involve the interest of the reader, have been written in a light tone, sometimes in a jocular vein. I do not hold that learning need be tedious. It has indeed been a conviction of mine that when one is writing about a highly serious subject one need not wear a long white beard; it was for that reason that my books on Hamlet and Shylock cut many a caper and do not hesitate to provoke laughter—just because the subjects are so grave—and it has pleased me that my readers have delighted in the interspersed fun. This is a serious book and I have therefore performed similarly. In the later chapters when merriment was less possible, I have tried to use literary examples which would inject some amusement into the discussion.

In two important fields of inquiry I have been forced to break new ground: verse technique and prose rhythm. As a practicing poet I found, many years ago, that the available handbooks on verse rhythms might have been invaluable to me if I were writing poetry in Latin or Greek, but were useless to anyone writing in English. I therefore was obliged to analyze poetic practice in English—and came to the unheard-of conclusion that, because of the nature of our language as it is spoken, there are, besides accentual verse only four feet in English, not the dozen or more spoken of in textbooks. As for prose rhythm there is, to my knowledge, no study of it which makes any sense or which is not, to quote Lewis Carroll, "harder than Bézique!" I trust that both of my efforts on these topics will prove real (and readily understandable) contributions.

I wish to thank especially the encouragement of my good friend, Mr. John Hawes, and equally my dear friend, Mr. Philip Winsor, who has proved to me Prince of Editors, for their encouragement and enthusiasm in *my* pioneering.

Bernard Grebanier
1975

BEFORE THE BEGINNING: THE AUTHOR AND HIS WORK

1

The White Rabbit put on his spectacles. "Where shall I begin, please your Majesty?" he asked.
"Begin at the beginning," the King said, very gravely, "and go on till you come to the end: then stop."

THIS ADVICE of Lewis Carroll's monarch is very sage, and we are of a mind to follow it. Well, then, where do we begin?

Clearly, a piece of literature begins to exist as its words come into being. We are therefore tempted to begin with a consideration of words. But the account in Genesis, which has as its subject beginnings, opens: "In the beginning God created . . ."—a reminder that there is always a Creator before the creating.

We had better first consider, then, the author who existed before the work of literature, the author who was there to summon or choose or find the words of which the work is made. As for the words, we shall, as the older novelists used to say, deal with them in our next chapter.

THE CREATIVE MOOD

The author? We are not going to try characterizing him. The number of his traits is doubtless greater than the number of men and women who have created literature, since no creator is single-minded. (As Allen Tate has said: "Poets may be expected to write more than one kind of poetry.") Nor are we going to try gauging the motives which impel the author's creating. With many writers the motives may vary with each new attempt at composition. We shall not even try to describe the author's state of mind when he begins creating—beyond a guess that he is then probably in a state of considerable intellectual excitement—probably, even if he is creating in the midst of sorrow, in a state of exhilaration. As Coleridge knew, Joy

> is the spirit and the power,
> Which, wedding Nature to us, gives in dower
> A new Earth and a new Heaven . . .
> And thence flows all that charms or ear or sight,
> All melodies the echoes of that voice,
> All colors a suffusion from that light.*

With the creator, even in the creating of an expression of sorrow there is likely to be some measure of joy.

*From "Dejection: an Ode."

1

Beyond this, we must be satisfied to say only that the great author is one who, for private reasons, finds it irresistible to write. Nobody makes him do it. There are far easier and less frustrating ways to earn his bread and butter. His urge is partly play, partly compulsion, partly the mood of a pole-vaulter who must try an apparently impossible leap, partly the mood of a prophet who feels commissioned to say what he has to say.

THE SUBJECTS AND BASIC CRITERION OF LITERATURE

What does he write about? About life as it is, as it has been, as it might have been, as he feels it should be—about other people, about his relation to them, about himself, about his God, about Nature, and about the things Man himself has created. The degree to which he can illuminate these relationships will always be a criterion of his greatness.

This is the most important criterion by which *The Iliad* has survived as a great book, and it is the criterion by which *For Whom the Bell Tolls* will either prove long-lived too or be forgotten. With most readers now Ernest Hemingway would seem to have the advantage over Homer. Hemingway is both a contemporary and a modern. The average reader assumes that in the works of his own contemporaries he will find a greater sense of reality than could be expected of books of the past, particularly in books of such antiquity as Homer's. And, on the face of it, we should have to grant that in *The Iliad* the gods are indeed not our gods, the customs are not our customs, the warfare is not our kind of warfare, whereas in *For Whom the Bell Tolls* the gods are our gods, the customs are our customs, the kind of warfare our kind of warfare.

We do not belittle Hemingway's accomplishment, nor deny the excellence of some of his books. Many critics would rate this one among his very best. Nevertheless, it is fair to inquire whether or not there is in *For Whom the Bell Tolls* any passage of such universality as one finds in deathless passages of *The Iliad*—like that in which Hector takes leave of his wife, for instance, or that in which Priam comes to beg for his son's remains. In these two passages we find all the sorrowful leave-taking that has ever been, and all the inconsolable loss men have ever known over the death of loved ones.

Here is the passage from Book VI of *The Iliad* (in the Lang-Leaf-Myers translation) where Hector says farewell to his wife and son:

Hector hastened from his house back by the same way down the well-builded streets. When he had passed through the great city and was come to the Skaian gates, whereby he was minded to issue upon the plain, then came his dear-won wife, running to meet him, even Andromache daughter of great-hearted Eëtion, Eëtion that dwelt beneath wooded Plakos, in Thebe under Plakos, and was king of the men of Kilikia; for his daughter was wife to bronze-harnessed Hector. So she met him now, and with her went the handmaid bearing in her bosom the tender boy, the little child, Hector's loved son, like unto a beautiful star. Him Hector called Skamandrios, but all the folk Astyanax;[1] for only Hector guarded Ilios. So now he smiled and gazed at his boy silently, and Andromache stood by his side weeping, and clasped her hand in his, and spake and called upon his name. "Dear my lord, this thy hardihood will undo thee, neither hast thou any pity for thine infant boy, nor for me forlorn that soon shall be thy widow; for soon will the Achaians all set upon thee and slay thee. But it were better for me to go down to the grave if I lose thee; for never more will any comfort be mine, when once thou, even thou, hast met thy fate, but only sorrow. Moreover I have no father nor lady mother: my father was slain of goodly Achilles, for he wasted the populous city of the Kilikians, even high-gated Thebe, and slew Eëtion; yet he despoiled him not, for his soul had shame of that, but he burnt him in his inlaid armor and raised a barrow over him; and all about were elm-trees planted by the mountain nymphs, daughters of ægis-bearing Zeus. And the seven brothers that were mine within our halls, all these on the self-

---

[1]Astyanax means "City King"—a compliment to his father.

same day went within the house of Hades; for fleet-footed goodly Achilles slew them all amid their kine of trailing gait and white-fleeced sheep. And my mother, that was queen beneath wooded Plakos, her brought he hither with the other spoils, but afterward took a ransom untold to set her free; but in her father's halls was she smitten by the Archer Artemis. Nay, Hector, thou art to me father and lady mother, yea and brother, even as thou art my goodly husband. Come now, have pity and abide here upon the tower, lest thou make thy child an orphan and thy wife a widow. And stay thy folk beside the fig-tree, where best the city may be scaled and the wall is assailable. Thrice came thither the most valiant that are with the two Aiantes and famed Idomeneus and the sons of Atreus and Tydeus' valiant son, and essayed to enter; whether one skilled in soothsaying revealed it to them, or whether their own spirit urgeth and biddeth them on."

Then great Hector of the glancing helm answered her: "Surely I take thought for all these things, my wife; but I have very sore shame of the Trojans and Trojan dames with trailing robes, if like a coward I shrink away from battle. Moreover mine own soul forbiddeth me, seeing I have learnt ever to be valiant and fight in the forefront of the Trojans, winning my father's great glory and mine own. Yea of a surety I know this in heart and soul; the day shall come for holy Ilios to be laid low, and Priam[2] and the folk of Priam of the good ashen spear. Yet doth the anguish of the Trojans hereafter not so much trouble me, neither Hekabe's[3] own, neither king Priam's, neither my brethren's, the many and brave that shall fall in the dust before their foemen, as doth thine anguish in the day when some mail-clad Achaian shall lead thee weeping and rob thee of the light of freedom. So shalt thou abide in Argos and ply the loom at another woman's bidding, and bear water from fount Messeis[4] or Hypereia,[5] being grievously entreated, and sore constraint shall be laid upon thee. And then shall one say that beholdeth thee weep: 'This is the wife of Hector, that was foremost in battle of the horse-taming Trojans when men fought about Ilios.' Thus shall one say hereafter, and fresh grief will be thine for

lack of such an husband as thou hadst to ward off the day of thraldom. But me in death may the heaped-up earth be covering, ere I hear thy crying and thy carrying into captivity."

So spake glorious Hector, and stretched out his arm to his boy. But the child shrunk crying to the bosom of his fair-girdled nurse, dismayed at his dear father's aspect, and in dread at the bronze and horsehair crest that he beheld nodding fiercely from the helmet's top. Then his dear father laughed aloud, and his lady mother; forthwith glorious Hector took the helmet from his head, and laid it, all gleaming, upon the earth; then kissed he his dear son and dandled him in his arms, and spake in prayer to Zeus and all the gods, "O Zeus and all ye gods, vouchsafe ye that this my son may likewise prove even as I, preeminent amid the Trojans, and as valiant in might, and be a great king of Ilios. Then may men say of him, 'Far greater is he than his father,' as he returneth home from battle; and may he bring with him blood-stained spoils from the foeman he hath slain, and may his mother's heart be glad."

So spake he, and laid his son in his dear wife's arms; and she took him to her fragrant bosom, smiling tearfully. And her husband had pity to see her, and caressed her with his hand, and spake and called upon her name: "Dear one, I pray thee be not of oversorrowful heart; no man against my fate shall hurl me to Hades; only destiny, I ween, no man hath escaped, be he coward or be he valiant, when once he hath been born. But go thou to thine house and see to thine own tasks, the loom and distaff, and bid thine handmaidens ply their work; but for war shall men provide and I in chief of all men that dwell in Ilios."

So spake glorious Hector, and took up his horsehair-crested helmet; and his dear wife departed to her home oft looking back, and letting fall big tears. Anon she came to the well-stablished house of man-slaying Hector, and found therein her many handmaidens, and stirred lamentation in them all. So bewailed they Hector, while yet he lived, within his house: for they deemed that he would no more come back to them from battle, nor escape the fury of the hands of the Achaians.

At such moments the strangeness of gods, customs, methods of warfare is dissipated, seems merely a matter of external equipment to the plot, and we find ourselves participating in what is basic to human experience. In comparison with Hector and Priam, the people in many modern novels, though the equipment is all familiar, appear to be made only of paper.

[2]Hector's father, King of Troy.
[3]Hector's mother's.

[4]In Thessaly.
[5]In Lakonia.

In such books we may recognize the things being done as familiar—in our minds we may even see the things being done—but if we cannot feel that we are participating in the doing, or if we cannot get inside the people involved in the doing, the work fails to achieve what is demanded of literature of rank, universality.

For it is the *values* of human experience which are fundamentally the subject matter of literature, not the mere events through which characters may move. Literature is concerned with the quintessences of human experience, not with the bare facts of experience. That is why the bulk of great literature has to do with ideas, aspirations, and emotions which can find an echo in most readers. On the whole, great books do not deal with freaks or oddities—though now and then it becomes diverting, for a change, to read of them. But when a literary master does deal with deviators from the norm it is usually in a way that diminishes their apartness from common humanity. Thus, if Shakespeare had made Macbeth seem only an ambitious murderer, his play would have been merely an unimportant melodrama; but because, murderer though he becomes, Macbeth is depicted as all too human, we feel compassion for him and, innocent of murder ourselves, can put ourselves in his place.

There is a whole world of material for the writer, then, in the endless combinations of human experience, and he can hope to evoke a response in us as long as he writes as a member of the human race and addresses us as members too.

It is not true, of course, that the man of letters will find material in everything that happens. Here is a piece of straight forward writing:

> Any day now, the dredges and tugs of the Great Lakes Dredge & Dock Co., of Chicago, and the Arundel Corp., of Baltimore, will chug out into Boston Harbor, and start scooping out the bottom for an extension to the President Roads anchorage. Both companies, Great Lakes as prime contractor and Arundel as sub-contractor, are happy about this prospect. Only a few weeks ago, further work on the $2 million project seemed to have been abandoned indefinitely, as the Budget Bureau clamped down on non-defense Government spending in the wake of the sputniks. . . .*

The author of this article was certainly not writing as a man of letters; his material—that is, what he found important in his material—is not put to literary use. As prose his is efficient enough for its modest purpose, which is to inform. It was not written to evoke excitement of sympathy in the reader—though conceivably stockholders in Great Lakes Dredge & Dock or in Arundel might be "happy about this prospect,"—or a Bostonian devoted to Boston Harbor might, on the other hand, be upset by that same prospect. The end of such prose, to inform, is outside literature.

Every year many hundreds of books and thousands of articles are published with this same laudable end. Thre is no need to deny the usefulness of such compositions. But it is somewhat overwhelming to think of those very very serious folk who avow that they "have no time for reading novels and that sort of light stuff," and who conscientiously devote their precious eyesight to "heavier," "really important" reading about such grave matters as the currency situation in Abyssinia or the sex habits of the Australian aborigines.

Without disparaging the importance of currency situations or sex habits anywhere in the world, we merely point out that writing which only informs has a very limited usefulness, and is not in the province of literature. Literature has more important ends than this disseminating of factual information. It enlarges our horizons, helps explain us to ourselves, deepens our comprehension and compassion for our fellow human beings. It enables us to live within the span of one lifetime the equivalent of many lifetimes. Through it we can encompass the universe from an armchair. And, not least of all, it can provide us the pleasures which come from literature and from no other of our experiences. What these

*From *Barron's National Financial Weekly*. April 7, 1958.

pleasures are need not be explained to the book-lover; to the uninitiate, however, these pleasures would be as hard to explain, without seeming fatuous, as it would be to explain the joys of swimming to one who cannot swim. All one can say is, Jump in! The effort expended learning will be more than justified in the rewards.

The prospects for the Great Lakes Dredge & Dock Company are not material for the man of letters—unless he can connect those prospects with meaningful values of human experience. If he can, for instance, conceive of an individual whose love, friendship, or hate is significantly involved in those prospects, he begins to have possible literary material. (E.g., John Smith's wife is about to leave him; she reads in *Barron's* about the prospects of the Great Lakes Dredge & Dock Company, in which her husband has large holdings which have been in jeopardy because of the clamping down of the Budget Bureau "on non-defense Government spending"; she decides to stay, and so on.) Thus, it is only when the writer's vision sees a human meaning (beyond mere information) in things or events or people that they become his proper material. He may range the whole world, actively or imaginatively, for such meaning.

In writing of the world he has all sorts of choices.

SUBJECTIVITY AND OBJECTIVITY

He may, to begin with, deal with the world in terms of his own experience or in terms which exclude himself. This is Edgar Allan Poe's (1809–1849) "A Dream within a Dream":

> Take this kiss upon the brow!
> And, in parting from you now,
> Thus much let me avow—
> You are not wrong, who deem
> That my days have been a dream;
> Yet if hope has flown away
> In a night, or in a day,
> In a vision, or in none,
> Is it therefore the less *gone?*
> *All* that we see or seem   10
> Is but a dream within a dream.
>
> I stand amid the roar
> Of a surf-tormented shore,
> And I hold within my hand
> Grains of the golden sand—
> How few! yet how they creep
> Through my fingers to the deep,
> While I weep—while I weep!
> O God! can I not grasp
> Them with a tighter clasp?   20
> O God! can I not save
> *One* from the pitiless wave?
> Is *all* that we see or seem
> But a dream within a dream?

The poem is highly personal in feeling and in approach to the ideas it conveys; it is openly *subjective*. This passage from Shakespeare's (1564–1616) *Measure for Measure* (III/i/19 seq.) holds a similar view of life:

> Happy thou art not;
> For what thou hast not, still thou striv'st to get,
> And what thou hast, forget'st. Thou art not certain;

> For thy complexion shifts to strange effects,[1]
> After the moon. If thou art rich, thou'rt poor;
> For, like an ass whose back with ingots[2] bows,
> Thou bear'st thy heavy riches but a journey,
> And Death unloads thee. . . .
> . . . . Thou hast nor youth nor age,
> But, as it were, an after-dinner's sleep,
> Dreaming on both. . . .

Here the speaker is not the author but a character in a play; and that character is thinking neither of himself nor the person addressed, but of the world at large. The passage is deliberately *objective* in approach to the ideas expressed. Poe was plainly thinking of Poe and his experiences; Shakespeare, or rather his character, of the experiences common to humanity.

It is possible to become perverse over this distinction between the subjective and objective approaches in art. You can, of course, split hairs and say: "Isn't it true that each of us can view the world only through his own pair of spectacles? Isn't it impossible to understand the world except as we are taught by our own experiences? And doesn't that make all artistic creation subjective?" It is undeniable that we can view the world only through our own pair of spectacles, or our own particular experiences. It will not have escaped you, for instance, that, as objective as the passage from Shakespeare is, the intense warmth of the expression penetrates to us with an irresistible immediacy of conviction which makes *us,* at least, feel personally addressed, as though the author were talking directly to us. Yet Shakespeare does not claim that he is presenting his own experiences. Poe, on the other hand, is openly speaking in his own person. There remains, therefore, a considerable difference between writing about one's self, as Poe wrote, and leaving out one's own concerns to write of the world at large, as Shakespeare did.

In music, for example, you are aware that in his *Preludes* and *Nocturnes* Chopin was talking almost exclusively about Chopin, and that in his *St. Matthew Passion* Bach was not talking to you about Bach. So, too, in poetry you become aware that Keats is Keats's favorite subject while Browning usually prefers to leave Browning out so that he may concentrate on the rest of the world (as he saw it). In the plays of Christopher Marlowe you are very much aware of the author behind the dramas. His contemporary Shakespeare, however, is so objective a creator that in his plays the man himself escapes you.

When Keats (1795 1821) thought of Homer as a subject for tribute the important thing to him was the great personal revelation he himself had experienced the first time he read him in Chapman's English translation; this he has recorded in a celebrated sonnet, "On First Looking into Chapman's Homer":

> Much have I traveled in the realms of gold,
> And many goodly states and kingdoms seen:
> Round many western islands have I been
> Which bards in fealty to Apollo hold.
> Oft of one wide expanse had I been told,
> That deep-browed Homer ruled as his demesne:
> Yet did I never breathe its pure serene
> Till I heard Chapman[1] speak out loud and bold:
> Then felt I like some watcher of the skies
> When a new planet swims into his ken;   10

[1]I.e., thou art inconstant.

[2]Bars of gold.

[1]George Chapman (d. 1634), Elizabethan dramatist and poet, who made translations of the *Iliad* and the *Odyssey*.

Or like stout Cortez[2] when with eagle eyes
He stared at the Pacific—and all his men
Looked at each other with a wild surmise—
Silent, upon a peak in Darien.[3]

Here again is a tribute from one poet to another, Matthew Arnold's (1822–1888) sonnet, "Shakespeare":

Others abide our question. Thou art free.
We ask and ask—thou smilest and art still,
Out-topping knowledge. For the loftiest hill,
Who to the stars uncrowns his majesty,
Planting his steadfast footsteps in the sea,
Making the heaven of heavens his dwelling-place,
Spares but the cloudy border of his base
To the foiled searching of mortality;
And thou, who didst the stars and sunbeams know,
Self-schooled, self-scanned, self-honored, self-secure,   10
Didst tread on earth unguessed at.—Better so!
All pains the immortal spirit must endure,
All weakness which impairs, all griefs which bow,
Find their sole speech in that victorious brow.

To Arnold the important thing was what Shakespeare had meant not to him alone but to the whole world because of the great dramatist's universality. Keats in his sonnet was highly subjective; Arnold, in his, objective.

Is it essential that when we read we be aware of this difference? Well, let us consider Robert Browning's (1812–1889) amusing "Up at a Villa—Down in the City":

Had I but plenty of money, money enough and to
spare,
The house for me, no doubt, were a house in the
city-square;
Ah, such a life, such a life, as one leads at the
window there!

Something to see, by Bacchus, something to hear,
at least!
There, the whole day long, one's life is a perfect
feast;
While up at a villa one lives, I maintain it, no
more than a beast.
Well now, look at our villa! stuck like the horn of
a bull
Just on a mountain edge as bare as the creature's
skull,
Save a mere shag of a bush with hardly a leaf to
pull!
I scratch my own, sometimes, to see if the hair's
turned wool!   10

But the city, oh the city—the square with the
houses! Why?
They are stone-faced, white as a curd, there's
something to take the eye!

Houses in four straight lines, not a single front
awry;
You watch who crosses and gossips, who saun-
ters, who hurries by;
Green blinds, as a matter of course, to draw when
the sun gets high;
And the shops with fanciful signs which are
painted properly.

What of a villa? Though winter be over in March
by rights,
'Tis May perhaps ere the snow shall have withered well off the heights:
You've the brown ploughed land before, where
the oxen steam and wheeze,
And the hills over-smoked behind by the faint
gray olive-trees.   20

Is it better in May, I ask you? You've summer all
at once;
In a day he leaps complete, with a few strong
April suns.
'Mid the sharp short emerald wheat, scarce risen
three fingers well,
The wild tulip, at the end of its tube, blows out
its great red bell

[2]Keats was in error; the Pacific was discovered by Balboa.
[3]In Panama.

Like a thin clear bubble of blood, for the children to pick and sell.

Is it ever hot in the square? There's a fountain to spout and splash!
In the shade, it sings and springs; in the shine, such foam-bows flash
On the horses with curling fish-tails, that prance and paddle and pash
Round the lady atop in her conch—fifty gazers do not abash,
Though all that she wears is some weeds round her waist in a sort of sash.   30

All the year long at the villa, nothing to see, though you linger!
Except yon cypress that points like death's lean lifted forefinger.
Some think fireflies pretty, when they mix i' the corn and mingle,
Or thrid the stinking hemp till the stalks of it seem a-tingle.
Late August or early September, the stunning cicala is shrill,
And the bees keep their tiresome whine round the resinous firs on the hill.
Enough of the seasons! I spare you the months of the fever and chill.

Ere you open your eyes in the city, the blesséd church-bells begin.
No sooner the bells leave off than the diligence rattles in:
You get the pick of the news, and it costs you never a pin.   40
By-and-by there's the traveling doctor gives pills, lets blood, draws teeth;
Or the Pulcinello-trumpet[1] breaks up the market beneath.
At the post-office, such a scene-picture—the new play, piping hot!
And a notice how, only this morning, three liberal thieves[2] were shot.

Above it, behold the Archbishop's most fatherly of rebukes,
And beneath, with his crown and his lion, some little new law of the Duke's!
Or a sonnet with flowery marge, to the Reverend Don So-and-so,
Who is Dante, Boccaccio, Petrarca, Saint Jerome, and Cicero,[3]
"And moreover," (the sonnet goes rhyming), "the skirts of Saint Paul has reached,
Having preached us those six Lent-lectures more unctuous than ever he[4] preached."   50

Noon strikes—here sweeps the procession! our Lady borne smiling and smart
With a pink gauze gown all spangles, and seven swords[5] stuck in her heart!
Bang-whang-whang goes the drum, *tootle-te-tootle* the fife;
No keeping one's haunches still: it's the greatest pleasure in life.

But bless you, it's dear—it's dear! fowls, wine, at double the rate.
They have clapped a new tax upon salt, and what oil pays passing the gate[6]
It's a horror to think of. And so, the villa for me, not the city!
Beggars can scarcely be choosers: but still—ah, the pity, the pity!
Look, two and two go the priests, then the monks with cowls and sandals,
And the penitents dressed in white shirts, a-holding the yellow candles;   60
One, he carries a flag up straight, and another a cross with handles,
And the Duke's guard brings up the rear, for the better prevention of scandals:
Bang-whang-whang goes the drum, *tootle-te-tootle* the fife.
Oh, a day in the city-square, there is no such pleasure in life!

This outburst, presumably by "an Italian person of Quality," because of its very liveliness and tone of conviction might easily, if we knew no better, lead us to suppose that the speaker was delivering Browning's own feelings about the annoying disadvantages of living in the country. Nothing could be further from the truth. This oversophisticated, quite heartless product of the Renaissance, who is bored to death with Nature, has nothing in common with Robert Browning, horseman, indefatigable walker, lover of the outdoors, and, above all,

[1]Announcing the beginning of a Punch-and-Judy performance.
[2]I.e., political radicals.
[3]I.e., the sonnet attributes the abilities of all these great men to the Reverend Don So-and-so.
[4]I.e., St. Paul.
[5]The seven swords symbolize the seven sorrows of Mary.
[6]The city gate. The commodities were taxable upon conveyance to the city.

compassionate observer of his fellow human beings. Browning was so much the artist that he could make all kinds of human beings, including the most villainous, talk in their own voice. In this poem he portrayed the temperament of a typical pleasure-loving gentleman of the late Italian Renaissance, living only for the delight of his senses, and quite indifferent to humaneness or the meaning of true religion.

In reading a poet, then, it becomes quite important to gauge quickly whether or not he is talking in his own person. In a poem such as this, until we know that it is perfectly objective in its presentation we cannot grasp the full import of its meaning. When we understand its objectivity we begin to arraign the speaker in our thoughts, as the author intended us to do. We then can allow our "person of Quality" to condemn himself.

It must be obvious that if we wish to procure the maximum from any given work of art, we must try to recapture as nearly as we can what its author was consciously doing with it and in it while he was creating it. We must try to see it as he saw it and hear it as he heard it. For this reason an awareness of the difference between a subjective and an objective attitude on his part becomes of importance to his audience. But important though this distinction be, it is perhaps even more essential that we remember what the two approaches have in common, for therein lies the nature of artistic creation itself. All artistic expression is a form of communication; hence the need of universality in every work that lays claim to our esteem. The most subjective of creators, therefore, must so deal with his own experiences as to enable us to share them. If what he has to say about himself can have meaning and significance only to himself, he need not expect an audience of so much as one. The very fact of his publishing his work, exhibiting it, or having it performed on a stage or in a hall necessarily implies that he is not creating only for his own satisfaction, no matter how he may pretend otherwise.

If it were not so, poets would die of despair at the thought that anyone else might read their works; painters and sculptors would cover their works with heavy cloths so that no chance visitor might see them; and composers would flee to another country at the invitation of some leading musician or conductor to perform their music. The facts are: composers follow every trail that may lead to such a musician or conductor; painters and sculptors will invite you to tea so that you may view their works lying about the studio; and as for poets —! Run into one of them in a café and the chances are that, digging his hand into his pocket, he will say, "Oh, I just happen to have a recent poem of mine with me. Care to hear it?" It would be risking your life to say, "No." And it is natural that they behave in this way. Creators need an audience, no matter how small.

And since they do, they must, we repeat, so deal with their own experience as to enable us to share it. Subjective as Chopin is, it is his ability to make us feel what he has felt which makes him a great composer. Thus, too, with Poe and Keats. While Poe does record his own anguish and while it is himself he depicts on the "surf-tormented shore," it is nonetheless true that he concludes with a universal idea, not a personal one, when he asks:

> Is *all* that we see or seem
> But a dream within a dream?

Thus, the poem, for all its subjectivity, has something to say of concern to the reader. (So much so, indeed, that it was a reading of this poem which inspired Tschaikovsky to write his *Sixth Symphony*.) And Keats, however intense his purpose to re-create his own awesome encounter with Homer, by comparing it to the wonder and excitement of the "watcher of the skies" who discovers a new planet and to the rapturous astonishment of the first European to gaze upon the Pacific, causes *us* to know what he knew and to feel what he felt.

In short, if it is only too obvious that all objectivity is to some degree limited by the author's own pair of spectacles, it is no less true that to attain the dignity of art all subjectivity must be to some degree enlarged—by implying the universal.

This stricture may explain why some personal correspondence has passed into our literary heritage, while most has not. What people write to each other in letters is likely to have no interest for anyone other than the writer, the individual addressed, or (later) a biographer. But here and there we find a letter-writer who rises above the merely subjective level; when such a one writes with charm or distinction, his letters become literature. Indeed, there are instances when an author's professional works are of no greater interest to us than his correspondence. There are even a few in which the interest in his correspondence exceeds that in his works.

Philip Stanhope, Earl of Chesterfield (1604–1773), is known to the world of literature, aside from his connection with Samuel Johnson, only for the letters he wrote to his son. Here is an excerpt from his letter of September 5, 1748:

As women are a considerable, or at least a pretty numerous, part of company, and as their suffrages go a great way toward establishing a man's character in the fashionable part of the world (which is of great importance to the fortune and figure he proposes to make in it), it is necessary to please them. I will therefore, upon this subject, let you into certain *arcana*, [1] that will be very useful for you to know, but which you must with the utmost care conceal, and never seem to know. Women, then, are only children of a larger growth; they have an entertaining tattle and sometimes wit, but for solid reasoning good sense, I never in my life knew one that had it, or acted consequentially for four-and-twenty hours together. Some little passion or humor always breaks in upon their best resolutions. Their beauty neglected or controverted, their age increased, or their supposed understandings depreciated, instantly kindles their little passions, and overturns any system of consequential conduct that in their most reasonable moments they might have been capable of forming. A man of sense only trifles with them, plays with them, humors and flatters them, as he does with a sprightly, forward child: but he neither consults them about, nor trusts them with, serious matters, though he often makes them believe that he does both,—which is the thing in the world that they are proud of; for they love mightily to be dabbling in business (which, by the way, they always spoil), and, being justly distrustful that men in general look upon them in a trifling light, they almost adore that man who talks more seriously to them, and who seems to consult them:—I say, who seem, for weak men really do, but wise ones only seem to do it. No flattery is either too high or too low for them. They will greedily swallow the highest, and gratefully accept the lowest; and you may safely flatter any woman, from her understanding down to the exquisite taste of her fan. Women who are either indisputably beautiful or indisputably ugly are best flattered upon the score of their understandings; but those in a state of mediocrity are best flattered upon their beauty, or at least their graces; for every woman who is not absolutely ugly thinks herself handsome, but, not hearing often that she is so, is the more grateful and the more obliged to the few who tell her so; whereas a decided and conscious beauty looks upon every tribute paid to her beauty only as her due, but wants to shine and to be considered on the side of her understanding; and a woman who is ugly enough to know that she is so, knows that she has nothing left but her understanding, which is consequently—and probably in more senses than one—her weak side.

Chesterfield is an extreme case of objectivity in letter-writing—so much so, that his very impersonality makes us feel that as he wrote he must already have seen his words between the covers of a book. The polish of his cynicism is so perfectly contrived that it is hard to believe that Chesterfield was so much addressing his son as his future readers. In any event, he avoids indulging a single autobiographical touch in the passage.

Not so with Byron when writing to John Murray from Venice (May 30, 1817) about a public execution he has witnessed:

The day before I left Rome I saw three robbers guillotined. The ceremony —including the *masqued* priests; the half-naked executioners; the bandaged criminals; the black Christ and his banner; the scaffold; the soldiery; the slow

[1] Secrets (Latin).

procession, and the quick rattle and heavy fall of the axe; the splash of the blood, and the ghastliness of the exposed heads—is altogether more impressive than the vulgar and ungentlemanly dirty "new drop," and dog-like agony of infliction upon the sufferer of the English sentence. Two of these men behaved calmly enough, but the first of the three died with great horror and reluctance, which was very horrible. He would not lie down; then his neck was too large for the aperture, and the priest was obliged to drown his exclamation by still louder exhortations. The head was off before the eye could trace the blow; but from an attempt to draw back the head, notwithstanding it was held forward by the hair, the first head was cut off close to the ears; the other two were taken off more cleanly. It is better than the oriental way, and (I should think) than the axe of our ancestors. The pain seems little; and yet the effect to the spectator, and the preparation to the criminal, are very striking and chilling. The first turned me quite hot and thirsty, and made me shake so that I could hardly hold the opera-glass (I was close, but determined to see, as one should see every thing, once, with attention); the second and third (which shows how dreadfully soon things grow indifferent), I am ashamed to say, had no effect on me as a horror, though I would have saved them if I could.

Byron seems as much preoccupied with himself (as was his habit) as with the spectacle. Nevertheless, despite its highly subjective presentation, the account of the execution is objectively given, and there is therefore more for us to be interested in than merely Byron's personal reactions to them. Byron's reactions become our reactions.

REALISM AND ROMANTICISM

The author, we have said, is a man devoted to quintessences of human experience. Now, in presenting to his readers these quintessences, he may prefer to create a sense of everyday actuality—what is loosely called the *realistic*—or, on the other hand, he may prefer to create a feeling far removed from everyday living and a sense of the contemporary—what is usually called the *romantic*.

Edna St. Vincent Millay (1892–1950) is the author of this poem, "The Return from Town":

> As I sat down by Saddle Stream
>   To bathe my dusty feet there,
> A boy was standing on the bridge
>   Any girl would meet there.
>
> As I went over Woody Knob
>   And dipped into the hollow,
> A youth was coming up the hill
>   Any maid would follow.
>
> Then in I turned at my own gate,—
>   And nothing to be sad for—
> To such a man as any wife
>   Would pass a pretty lad for.

10

She chooses, we see, to write about love in a realistic setting and gives us the sense of everyday living. John Lyly (d. 1606) in this song sings about love in a different strain:

> Cupid and my Campaspe played
> At cards for kisses; Cupid paid.
> He stakes his quiver, bow, and arrows,

His mother's doves and team of sparrows.[1]
Loses them too; then down he throws
The coral of his lip, the rose
Growing on's cheek (but none knows how);
With these the crystal of his brow,
And then the dimple of his chin;
All these did my Campaspe win.   10
At last he set her both his eyes;
She won, and Cupid blind did rise.
O Love, has she done this to thee?
What shall, alas! become of me?

Here the poet romantically avoids the kind of homely reality we found in the Millay poem. He is deliberately indulging his fancy in graceful artifice, though with the completest artistic sincerity. In such moods his fancy is as real a realm to the poet as the farmland is to the farmer. Despite the differences in their manner—the firm homely warmth of Miss Millay's and the bright airiness of Lyly's—it would be impossible to say that one is less honestly meant or less touching than the other. A poet may find thoughts of love in his kitchen or in the colorful world of his imagination, and both may be equally real, each in its own way.

It would have to be conceded that some of the differences between these two love poems are a consequence of the fact that Miss Millay wrote in the twentieth century and Lyly in the sixteenth. That kind of sprightly elegance and wit turning upon mythological reference which we find in Lyly's song (e.g., Cupid is blind) was very popular in Elizabethan court circles; and a preoccupation with the homely actualities of everyday life has certainly been one of the prevailing modes of twentieth-century literature. As Gertrude Stein has observed of "any sort of creative artist," he cannot help expressing "imperceptibly" what is contemporary; "He can't live in the past, because it is gone. He can't live in the future, because no one knows what it is."*

Sometimes, indeed, the writer quite consciously writes as a man of his own time. Matthew Arnold, for instance, was well aware of contemporary issues when he wrote "Dover Beach":

The sea is calm tonight,
The tide is full, the moon lies fair
Upon the straits—on the French coast the light
Gleams and is gone; the cliffs of England stand,
Glimmering and vast, out in the tranquil bay.
Come to the window; sweet is the night-air!
Only, from the long line of spray
Where the sea meets the moon-blanched land,
Listen! you hear the grating roar
Of pebbles which the waves draw back, and
    fling,   10
At their return, up the high strand,
Begin, and cease, and then again begin,
With tremulous cadence slow, and bring
The eternal note of sadness in.

Sophocles[1] long ago
Heard it on the Ægean, and it brought
Into his mind the turbid ebb and flow
Of human misery; we
Find also in the sound a thought,
Hearing it by this distant northern sea.   20
The Sea of Faith[2]
Was once, too, at the full, and round earth's shore
Lay like the folds of a bright girdle furled,[3]
But now I only hear
Its melancholy, long, withdrawing roar,
Retreating, to the breath
Of the night-wind, down the vast edges drear
And naked shingles[4] of the world.

[1]Cupid's mother, the goddess of love, Aphrodite, was said to have her chariot drawn by sparrows. (Some writers say the birds were doves.)

*From *How Writing Is Written*.

[1]Great Greek tragic poet (496–406 B.C.), whom Arnold admired for his "even-balanc'd" vision, a man "who saw life steadily, and saw it whole."

[2]I.e., religious belief.

[3]The early Greeks believed that the earth was a flat circle engirdled by the River Oceanus.

[4]Pebbled beaches.

Ah, love, let us be true
To one another! for the world, which seems   30
To lie before us like a land of dreams,
So various, so beautiful, so new,
Hath really neither joy, nor love, nor light,

Nor certitude, nor peace, nor help for pain;
And we are here as on a darkling plain
Swept with confused alarms of struggle and
    flight,
Where ignorant armies clash by night.

This poem was published in 1867; it could not have been written so much as thirty-five years earlier, for it is somewhat the product of mid-nineteenth-century scientific speculation. Sir Charles Lyell's *Principles of Geology* (1830–1833) routed long-held ideas as to the age of the world; and Charles Darwin's *The Origin of Species* (1859) marshaled an imposing array of facts to vindicate new theories of organic evolution at seeming variance with the account of man's origin in Genesis. The effect of these concepts was to undermine the religious faith of many Victorians. Arnold's poem frankly admits his uncertainty, and attempts to find a new basis for faith and hope.

These geological and evolutionary theories have now been long incorporated into the tissue of our thinking. Neither they nor the authority of the Bible is a topic of dispute; everyone has more or less taken his stand. No poet today would feel himself torn between the two; if he were writing upon a subject touching upon man's origin, he would "imperceptibly" reveal himself a son of our times by his allegiances. He would not argue his convictions about Darwin or the Bible—since we no longer do so. And since we no longer do so, it becomes necessary to recapture the Victorian anguish over the issue if we are to understand the full force of Arnold's poem.*

It is on such considerations, therefore, that the student of literature is also always a student of literary history. It is very important to see the author in his contemporary setting. A knowledge of the life of the times and current literary trends could only enrich the appreciation of the poetry we have already quoted from Poe, Shakespeare, Keats, Arnold, Browning, Lyly, and Millay.

However, the study of literary history is important for a quite different reason. A knowledge of current literary trends will also make clear to what extent a writer is more than just a reflection of his times. One must be careful not to push too far the notion that the creator is only his epoch's mirror. It is safe to say that unless any writer were better than his times, there would be not much point in reading him now. Shakespeare was certainly an Elizabethan in a thousand ways; in what is most valuable in his work, there was no Elizabethan like him. (It was to take centuries, for example, for any other writer to exhibit Shakespeare's profound comprehension of the female character. No one has remotely approached yet his lightning-swift imagination. No English writer has as much as half the richness of his vocabulary.) It is not even possible to insist that because an author lived in an age preponderantly romantic, he was therefore forced always to be romantic too. Consider the instances of Sir Walter Scott (1771–1832) and Jane Austen (1775–1817), who were contemporaries. Observe how Scott depicts the heroine of his novel, *The Bride of Lammermoor:*

In passing through a large Gothic anteroom, Sir William Ashton heard the sound of his daughter's lute. Music, when the performers are concealed, affects us with a pleasure mingled with surprise, and reminds us of the natural concert of birds among the leafy bowers. The statesman, though little accustomed to give way to emotions of this natural and simple class, was still a man and a father. He stopped, therefore, and listened, while the silver tones of Lucy Ashton's voice mingled with the accompaniment in an ancient air, to which some one had adapted the following words:—

    "Look not thou on beauty's charming,—
    Sit thou still when kings are arming,—

---

*Of course, "Dover Beach" can speak to us to a degree without our recapturing the Victorian perspective; if it could not, it would not be worth anything to us. The poem pictures a collapsing world in which love is the only solid rock on which to stand. Our own world may seem to be collapsing for other reasons; and perhaps the same solution might offer itself.

Taste not when the wine-cup glistens,
Speak not when the people listens,—
Stop thine ear against the singer,—
From the red gold keep thy finger,
Vacant heart, and hand, and eye,—
Easy live and quiet die."

The sounds ceased, and the Keeper entered his daughter's apartment.

The words she had chosen seemed particularly adapted to her character; for Lucy Ashton's exquisitely beautiful, yet somewhat girlish features, were formed to express peace of mind, serenity and indifference to the tinsel of worldly pleasure. Her locks, which were of shadowy gold, divided on a brow of exquisite whiteness, like a gleam of broken and pallid sunshine upon a hill of snow. The expression of the countenance was in the last degree gentle, soft, timid, and feminine, and seemed rather to shrink from the most casual look of a stranger, than to court his admiration. Something there was of a Madonna cast, perhaps the result of delicate health, and of residence in a family where the dispositions of the inmates were fiercer, more active, and energetic, than her own.

Yet her passiveness of disposition was by no means owing to an indifferent or unfeeling mind. Left to the impulse of her own taste and feeling. Lucy Ashton was peculiarly accessible to those of a romantic cast. Her secret delight was in the old legendary tales of ardent devotion and unalterable affection, checkered as they so often are with strange adventures and supernatural horrors. This was her favored fairy realm, and here she erected her aërial palaces. But it was only in secret that she labored at this delusive, though delightful architecture.

The sharp-witted Miss Austen, however, had little patience with the trappings of romantic idealization, and her career as a novelist is largely that of a quietly satirical antiromantic. How different is this portrait of her heroine in *Northanger Abbey:*

No one who had ever seen Catherine Morland in her infancy would have supposed her born to be a heroine. Her situation in life, the character of her father and mother, her own person and disposition, were all equally against her. Her father was a clergyman, without being neglected or poor, and a very respectable man, though his name was Richard, and he had never been handsome. He had a considerable independence, besides two good livings, and he was not in the least addicted to locking up his daughters. Her mother was a woman of useful plain sense, with a good temper, and, what is more remarkable, with a good constitution. She had three sons before Catherine was born; and instead of dying in bringing the latter into the world, as anybody might expect, she still lived on—lived to have six children more—to see them growing up around her, and to enjoy excellent health herself. A family of ten children will be always called a fine family, where there are heads, and arms, and legs enough for the number; but the Morlands had little other right to the word, for they were in general very plain, and Catherine, for many years of her life, as plain as any. She had a thin awkward figure, a sallow skin without colour, dark lank hair, and strong features: so much for her person, and not less unpropitious for heroism seemed her mind. She was fond of all boys' plays, and greatly preferred cricket, not merely to dolls, but to the more heroic enjoyments of infancy, nursing a dormouse, feeding a canary bird, or watering a rosebush. Indeed she had no taste for a garden, and if she gathered flowers at all, it was chiefly for the pleasure of mischief, at least so it was conjectured from her always preferring those which she was forbidden to take. Such were her propensities; her abilities were quite as extraordinary. She never could learn or understand anything before she was taught, and sometimes not even then, for she was often inattentive, and occasionally stupid. Her mother was three months in teaching her only to repeat the "Beggar's Petition," and after all, her next sister Sally could say it better than she did. Not that Catherine was always stupid; by no means; she learnt the fable of "The Hare and Many Friends" as quickly as any girl in England. Her mother wished her to learn music; and Catherine was sure she should like it, for she was very fond of tinkling the keys of the old forlorn spinet, so at eight years old she began. She learnt a year and could not bear it: and Mrs. Morland, who did not insist on her daughters being accomplished in spite of incapacity or distaste, allowed her to leave off. The day which dismissed the music-master was one of the happiest of Catherine's life. Her taste for drawing was not superior; though whenever she could obtain the outside of a letter from her mother, or seize upon any other odd piece of paper, she did what she could in that way by drawing houses and trees, hens and chickens, all very much like one another. Writing and accounts she was taught by her father; French by her mother. Her proficiency in either was not remarkable, and she shirked her lessons in both whenever she could. What a strange unaccountable character! for with all these symptoms of profligacy at ten years old, she had neither a bad heart nor a bad temper, was seldom stubborn, scarcely ever quarrelsome, and very kind to the little ones, with few interruptions of tyranny. She was, moreover, noisy and wild, hated confinement and cleanliness, and loved nothing so well in the world as rolling down the green slope at the back of the house.

Such was Catherine Morland at ten. At fifteen appearances were mending; she began to curl her hair and long for balls, her complexion improved, her features were softened by plumpness and col-our, her eyes gained more animation, and her figure more consequence. Her love of dirt gave way to an inclination for finery, and she grew clean as she grew smart. She had now the pleasure of sometimes hearing her father and mother remark on her personal improvement. "Catherine grows quite a good-looking girl; she is almost pretty to-day," were words which caught her ears now and then; and how welcome were the sounds! To look *almost* pretty is an acquisition of higher delight to a girl who has been looking plain the first fifteen years of her life, than a beauty from her cradle can ever receive.

Miss Austen's interests were in the life about her. The character of the girl is almost remorselessly realistic in its honesty, stripped as it is of any suggestion of illusion.

We should now be able to enlarge our notions of the romantic and the realistic. The reflections of the English novelist Hugh Walpole (1884–1941) in his study of Joseph Conrad are apposite. He defines the romantic as "the study of life with the faculties of the imagination"; the realistic as "the study of life with all the rational faculties of observation, reason, and reminiscence." The realistic may certainly be emotional, poetic, even lyrical (qualities usually associated with the romantic); however its foundation is always "truth perceived and recorded—it is the essence of observation." The romantic, on the other hand, cannot be merely vague and confused in conception or outline, it must be equally accurate and defined" in its own world: its spirit is "the spirit of the imagination." Sometimes the imagination works upon observation too; sometimes it works only on "inspiration." The romantic, of course, is not divorced from the world of fact, nor is the realistic occupied with a "detailed and dusty preference" for "unagreeable subjects." The romantic can be as honest and clear as the realistic in the perception of the world, but it cannot easily be so because the imagination is harder to discipline than is observation. The romantic can more easily be eloquent, since it is less subject to the discipline of facts. On the other hand, the realistic can be as eloquent as the romantic, but it cannot easily be so because "of its fear of deserting truth."

In the light of these observations, let us reexamine some of our quoted passages. In "Cupid and My Campaspe" the notions are presented not as the essence of observation, but clearly as the product of an imagination working on inspiration; the conception is sharply defined; the analogy of the card-game, though taking every liberty with fact (Cupid's staking the coral of his lip, the dimple of his chin), is consistently and logically maintained; the eloquence of the whimsical conclusion is made possible by the very extravagance of the whole analogy. In Scott's romantic portrait of Lucy Ashton, while a minimum of observation may be conceded the author, the spirit of the whole is again the spirit of the imagination; girls whose features express "indifference to the tinsel of worldly pleasure," whose locks are of "shadowy gold, divided on a brow of exquisite whiteness, like a gleam of broken and pallid sunshine" are rarely found; her "secret delight" in the lore of the past places her more out of the world than in it; but her traits have been organized into a logically defined whole, consonant with the mood set by the author's imagination. Both these romantic creations are, characteristically, removed from the world of fact; yet both are in their own way studies of life in that, through idealization of women, they sharpen our awareness of the possibilities of beauty in women. (Of course, Scott's passage, exhibiting less imagination and too much sentimentality, is the inferior of the two.)

Now let us look at our two realistic pieces. "The Return from Town" studies life with the faculties of observation and reason; it is emotional and lyrical, but its foundation is truth perceived and recorded; its details summon the realities of everyday observation (the homely country names, Saddle Stream and Woody Knob; "dusty feet"; "turned at my own gate"); its eloquence at the end is involved with a sturdy apprehension of truth. The portrait of Catherine Morland seems conceived almost in defiance of such idealizations of a heroine as Scott's; her father "was not in the least addicted to locking up his daughters" (we can well imagine Lucy Ashton being kept under lock and key submissively!); unlike Lucy, Catherine had an awkward figure, "a sallow skin without colour, dark lank hair, and strong [not angelic!] features"; she seems to have preferred cricket to reading the old legends; while Lucy was proficient at the lute, Catherine gave up the spinet after a year; she was "noisy and wild, hated confinement and cleanliness"; everything about her seems normal, and her portrait is clearly the product of close observation as to what young girls are usually like; the sum-total gives one the impression of cheerful good sense and well-being. Both these realistic creations have their roots in the world of fact; and both are studies of life in that they interpret that world and therefore sharpen our awareness of its possibilities.

In our own time the enormous advances of science have inevitably made for a strong emphasis in literature on the world of fact. Among our leading literary critics, as is perhaps natural, the romantic view has therefore come into great disfavor, and many poets (as, for instance, Shelley) who until recently were considered giants are now treated with scarely concealed contempt. One of the best of our critics, John Crowe Ransom, admits that a "stigma" must attach to the romantic. Professor Fairchild has defined romanticism as "the endeavor, in the face of growing factual obstacles, to achieve, to retain, or to justify that illusioned view of the universe and of human life which is produced by an imaginative fusion of the familiar and the strange, the known and the unknown, the real and the ideal, the finite and the infinite, the material and the spiritual, the natural and the supernatural." Ransom, accepting this delineation, concludes from it that the romantic is a "morbid indulgence," a deliberate "retreat from reality," a childish defiance of the best "revelations of science."*

It is not necessary to take sides in the current war against romanticism. The world of art is capacious enough to have room for both a Shelley and a Pope (a current idol), a Swinburne and a T. S. Eliot; and it is not truly required that we disparage one in order to appreciate the other. The student of independent mind, particularly when he is busy developing his literary taste, will do well to keep clear of being unduly influenced against the Romantics just because at the moment they are out of favor. One ought, in any era, to be chary of being too entirely *à la mode*. Nothing becomes outdated as swiftly as extreme new fashions. The criteria which are summoned these days to discredit Wordsworth and Shelley only recently held to be far the superior of poets now adored—are the criteria of today, and are not necessarily the criteria of tomorrow. Quite conceivably today's divinities will in a few decades be the object of withering scorn—for we have romantics among contemporary poets too who may be the ones to win out (e.g., Dylan Thomas)—and the now-neglected idols of an earlier day will be raised to a new eminence. That would mean, of course, only a new set of fanaticisms. Perhaps it will seem to another generation that to "achieve . . . that illusioned view of the universe and of human life which is produced by an imaginative fusion of the . . . real and the ideal, the finite and the infinite, the material and the spiritual, the natural and the supernatural" is the highest kind of wisdom. Such violent alterations of criteria are what constitute a good part of the history of literature.

It is hard to keep above the hue and cry of contemporary fashions in any era. But one cannot go too far wrong if one remembers that, first and last, an informed reader reacts spontaneously to a work of art, and only secondly does he begin to analyze further what he has read; and, consequently, when our criteria banish works of irresistible quality, we must assume that the trouble is not with the works but with our criteria. Tolstoi evolved a theory which forced him to discredit the music of Beethoven. That was Tolstoi, the theorist. Nevertheless, after he had proved the inadequacy of Beethoven's piano sonatas, Tolstoi's

*The *New Criticism,* p. 41.

friends used to find him playing those sonatas with tears running down his cheeks. That was Tolstoi, the artist, the author of *War and Peace* and of *Anna Karenina.*

If Romanticism is wrong, then not only is Shelley wrong but Shakespeare is wrong too. And many thousands of the simplest people of the world who read Shakespeare in their native tongue know better than that. Their love and knowledge are enough to confute so extreme a position.

Anyhow, it is far more worth anyone's time and effort to concern himself with understanding and enjoying literature rather than merely appraising it. The important thing about all the arts is to learn how to *experience them, not merely discuss or judge them.*

ROMANTICISM AND CLASSICISM

The romantic is often also distinguished from the classic approach to life. The classic was the typical mode of early eighteenth-century England. In Joseph Addison's (1672–1719) "Spectator #44," the author is reflecting on various conventions peculiar to the stage:

For the moving of pity, our principal machine is the handkerchief; and indeed in our common tragedies, we should not know very often that the persons are in distress by anything they say, if they did not from time to time apply their handkerchiefs to their eyes. Far be it from me to think of banishing this instrument of sorrow from the stage: I know a tragedy could not subsist without it: all that I contend for, is to keep it from being misapplied. In a word, I would have the actor's tongue sympathize with his eyes.

A disconsolate mother, with a child in her hand, has frequently drawn compassion from the audience, and has therefore gained a place in several tragedies. A modern writer, that observed how this had took in other plays, being resolved to double the distress, and melt his audience twice as much as those before him had done, brought a princess upon the stage with a little boy in one hand and a girl in the other. This too had a very good effect. A third poet, being resolved to outwrite all his predecessors, a few years ago introduced three children with great success. And, as I am informed, a young gentleman, who is fully determined to break the most obdurate hearts, has a tragedy by him, where the first person that appears upon the stage is an afflicted widow in her mourning-weeds, with half a dozen fatherless children attending her, like those that usually hang about the figure of Charity. . . .

There is an air of calmness and lucidity pervading Addison's lines, a sense that what was written was intellectually controlled to achieve order and clarity, that the author moved from idea to idea in a highly rational way. First the use of the handkerchief to arouse pity, then the child. Then two children. Then three. Then half a dozen.

The classic spirit is devoted to order, clarity, and moderation as the chief artistic virtues.

A century later these qualities were held in small esteem by the leading writers. How utterly different is the atmosphere we breathe in this passage from Thomas De Quincey's (1785–1859) "The Vision of Sudden Death." The incident recorded here by the author occurred, he tells us, "in the dead of night," when he was the "solitary spectator, . . . seated on the box of the Manchester and Glasgow" mail-coach, during the summer of 1817 or 1818:

Suddenly, from thoughts like these I was awakened to a sullen sound, as of some motion on the distant road. It stole upon the air for a moment; I listened in awe; but then it died away. Once roused, however, I could not but observe with alarm the quickened motion of our horses. Ten years' experience had made my eye learned in the valuing of motion; and I saw that we were now running thirteen miles an hour. I pretend to no presence of mind. On the contrary, my fear is that I am miserably and shamefully deficient in that quality as regards action. The palsy of doubt and distraction hangs like some guilty weight of dark unfathomed remembrances upon my energies when the signal is flying for *action.* But, on the other hand, this accursed gift I have, as regards *thought,* that in the first step towards the possibility of a misfortune I see its total evolution; in the radix of the series I see too certainly and too instantly its entire expansion; in the first syllable of the dreadful sentence I read already the last. It was not that I feared for ourselves. *Us* our bulk and impetus charmed against peril in any collision. And I had ridden through too many hundreds of perils that were frightful to approach, that were matter of laughter to look back upon, the first face of which was horror, the parting face a jest—for any anxiety to rest upon *our* interests. The mail was not built, I felt assured, nor bespoke, that could betray *me* who trusted to its protection. But any carriage that we could meet would be frail and light in comparison of ourselves. And I remarked this ominous accident of our situation,—we were on the wrong side of the road. But then, it may be said, the other party, if other there was, might also be on the wrong side; and two wrongs might make a right. *That* was not likely. The same motive which had drawn *us* to the right-hand side of the road—viz., the luxury of the soft beaten sand as contrasted with the paved centre—would prove attractive to others. The two adverse carriages would therefore, to a certainty, be travelling on the same side; and from this side, as not being ours in law, the crossing over to the other would, of course, be looked for from *us*.[1] Our lamps, still lighted, would give the impression of vigilance on our part. And every creature that met us would rely upon *us* for quartering. All this, and if the separate links of the anticipation had been a thousand times more, I saw, not discursively, or by effort, or by succession, but by one flash of horrid simultaneous intuition.

Under this steady though rapid anticipation of the evil which *might* be gathering ahead, ah! what a sullen mystery of fear, what a sigh of woe, was that which stole upon the air, as again the far-off sound of a wheel was heard! A whisper it was—a whisper from, perhaps, four miles off—secretly announcing a ruin that, being foreseen, was not the less inevitable; that, being known, was not therefore healed. What could be done—who was it that could do it—to check the storm-flight of these maniacal horses? Could I not seize the reins from the grasp of the slumbering coachman? You, reader, think that it would have been in *your* power to do so. And I quarrel not with your estimate of yourself. But, from the way in which the coachman's hand was viced between his upper and lower thigh, this was impossible. Easy was it? See, then, that bronze equestrian statue. The cruel rider has kept the bit in his horse's mouth for two centuries. Unbridle him for a minute, if you please, and wash his mouth with

water. Easy was it? Unhorse me, then, that imperial rider; knock me those marble feet from those marble stirrups of Charlemagne.

The sounds ahead strengthened, and were now too clearly the sounds of wheels. Who and what could it be? Was it industry in a taxed cart? Was it youthful gaiety in a gig? Was it sorrow that loitered, or joy that raced? For as yet the snatches of sound were too intermitting, from distance, to decipher the character of the motion. Whoever were the travellers, something must be done to warn them. Upon the other party rests the active responsibility, but upon *us*—and, woe is me! that *us* was reduced to my frail opium-shattered self —rests the responsibility of warning. Yet, how should this be accomplished? Might I not sound the guard's horn? Already, on the first thought, I was making my way over the roof of the guard's seat. But this, from the accident which I have mentioned, of the foreign mails being piled upon the roof, was a difficult and even dangerous attempt to one cramped by nearly three hundred miles of outside travelling. And, fortunately, before I had lost much time in the attempt, our frantic horses swept round an angle of the road which opened upon us that final stage where the collision must be accomplished and the catastrophe sealed. All was apparently finished. The court was sitting; the case was heard; the judge had finished; and only the verdict was yet in arrear.

Before us lay an avenue straight as an arrow, six hundred yards, perhaps, in length; and the umbrageous trees, which rose in a regular line from either side, meeting high overhead, gave to it the character of a cathedral aisle. These trees lent a deeper solemnity to the early light; but there was still light enough to perceive, at the further end of this Gothic aisle, a frail reedy gig, in which were seated a young man, and by his side a young lady. Ah, young sir! what are you about? If it is requisite that you should whisper your communications to this young lady— though really I see nobody, at an hour and on a road so solitary, likely to overhear you—is it therefore requisite that you should carry your lips forward to hers? The little carriage is creeping on at one mile an hour; and the parties within it, being thus tenderly engaged, are naturally bending down their heads. Between them and eternity,

[1] "It is true that, according to the law of the case as established by legal precedents, all carriages were required to give way before royal equipages, and therefore before the mail as one of them. But this only increased the danger, as being a regulation very imperfectly made known, very unequally enforced, and therefore often embarrassing the movements on both sides."—De Quincey.

to all human calculation, there is but a minute and a half. Oh heavens! what is it that I shall do? Speaking or acting, what help can I offer? Strange it is, and to a mere auditor of the tale might seem laughable, that I should need a suggestion from the *Iliad* to prompt the sole resource that remained. Yet so it was. Suddenly I remembered the shout of Achilles, and its effect. But could I pretend to shout like the son of Peleus, aided by Pallas? No: but then I needed not the shout that should alarm all Asia militant; such a shout would suffice as might carry terror into the hearts of two thoughtless young people and one gighorse. I shouted—and the young man heard me not. A second time I shouted—and now he heard me, for now he raised his head.

Here, then, all had been done that, by me, *could* be done; more on *my* part was not possible. Mine had been the first step; the second was for the young man; the third was for God. If, said I, this stranger is a brave man, and if indeed he loves the young girl at his side—or, loving her not, if he feels the obligation, pressing upon every man worthy to be called a man, of doing his utmost for a woman confided to his protection—he will at least make some effort to save her. If *that* fails, he will not perish the more, or by a death more cruel, for having made it; and he will die as a brave man should, with his face to the danger, and with his arm about the woman that he sought in vain to save. But, if he makes no effort,—shrinking without a struggle from his duty,—he himself will not the less certainly perish for this baseness of poltroonery. He will die no less: and why not? Wherefore should we grieve that there is one craven less in the world? No; *let* him perish, without a pitying thought of ours wasted upon him; and, in that case, all our grief will be reserved for the fate of the helpless girl who now, upon the least shadow of failure in *him,* must by the fiercest of translations—must without time for a prayer—must within seventy seconds—stand before the judgment-seat of God.

But craven he was not: sudden had been the call upon him, and sudden was his answer to the call. He saw, he heard, he comprehended, the ruin that was coming down: already its gloomy shadow darkened above him; and already he was measuring his strength to deal with it. Ah! what a vulgar thing does courage seem when we see nations buying it and selling it for a shilling a-day: ah! what a sublime thing does courage seem when some fearful summons on the great deeps of life carries a man, as if running before a hurricane, up to the giddy crest of some tumultuous

crisis from which lie two courses, and a voice says to him audibly, "One way lies hope; take the other, and mourn for ever!" How grand a triumph if, even then, amidst the raving of all around him, and the frenzy of the danger, the man is able to confront his situation—is able to retire for a moment into solitude with God, and to seek his counsel from *Him!*

For seven seconds, it might be, of his seventy, the stranger settled his countenance steadfastly upon us, as if to search and value every element in the conflict before him. For five seconds more of his seventy he sat immovably, like one that mused on some great purpose. For five more, perhaps, he sat with eyes upraised, like one that prayed in sorrow, under some extremity of doubt, for light that should guide him to the better choice. Then suddenly he rose; stood upright; and, by a powerful strain upon the reins, raising his horse's fore-feet from the ground, he slewed him round on the pivot of his hind-legs, so as to plant the little equipage in a position nearly at right angles to ours. Thus far his condition was not improved; except as a first step had been taken towards the possibility of a second. If no more were done, nothing was done; for the carriage still occupied the very centre of our path, though in an altered direction. Yet even now it may not be too late: fifteen of the seventy seconds may still be unexhausted; and one almighty bound may avail to clear the ground. Hurry, then, hurry! for the flying moments—*they* hurry. Oh, hurry, hurry, my brave young man! for the cruel hoofs of our horses—*they* also hurry! Fast are the flying moments, faster are the hoofs of our horses. But fear not for *him,* if human energy can suffice; faithful was he that drove to his terrific duty; faithful was the horse to *his* command. One blow, one impulse given with voice and hand, by the stranger, one rush from the horse, one bound as if in the act of rising to a fence, landed the docile creature's fore-feet upon the crown or arching centre of the road. The larger half of the little equipage had then cleared our overtowering shadow: *that* was evident even to my own agitated sight. But it mattered little that one wreck should float off in safety if upon the wreck that perished were embarked the human freightage. The rear part of the carriage—was *that* certainly beyond the line of absolute ruin? What power could answer the question? Glance of eye, thought of man, wing of angel, which of these had speed enough to sweep between the question and the answer, and divide the one from the other? Light does not tread upon the steps of light more indivisibly than did our all-conquering arrival upon the escaping efforts of the gig. *That* must the young man have felt too plainly. His back was now turned to us; not by sight could he any longer communicate with the peril; but, by the dreadful rattle of our harness, too truly had his ear been instructed that all was finished as regarded any effort of *his*. Already in resignation he had rested from his struggle; and perhaps in his heart he was whispering, "Father, which are in heaven, do Thou finish above what I on earth have attempted." Faster than ever millrace we ran past them in our inexorable flight. Oh, raving of hurricanes that must have sounded in their young ears at the moment of our transit! Even in that moment the thunder of collision spoke aloud. Either with the swinglebar, or with the haunch of our near leader, we had struck the off-wheel of the little gig; which stood rather obliquely, and not quite so far advanced as to be accurately parallel with the near-wheel. The blow, from the fury of our passage, resounded terrifically. I rose in horror, to gaze upon the ruins we might have caused. From my elevated station I looked down, and looked back upon the scene; which in a moment told its own tale, and wrote all its records on my heart for ever.

For the terror which De Quincey wishes to evoke, and which he evokes so well, moderation and order are not especially useful virtues. What he requires is not the lucid light of reasonableness but the many-hued shadows now of the brooding, now of the wildly exciting. He is here the true romantic, exhibiting excess rather than moderation, excited imagination rather than intellectual orderliness.

When we compare his prose with Addison's, we can understand that the classic spirit emanates from a writer's inner harmony which enables him to speak out as part of his social milieu, at peace with the best of what is traditional and contemporary to him; the romantic spirit, on the other hand, breathes a sense of the author's feeling of isolation in personality and experience, a sense of his being apart.

In the twentieth century we are inheritors of both traditions. Let us compare two poems by contemporary American poets. This is Edwin Arlington Robinson's (1869–1935) "Miniver Cheevy":

> Miniver Cheevy, child of scorn,
>   Grew lean while he assailed the seasons;
> He wept that he was ever born,
>   And he had reasons.
>
> Miniver loved the days of old
>   When swords were bright and steeds were prancing;
> The vision of a warrior bold
>   Would set him dancing.
>
> Miniver sighed for what was not,
>   And dreamed and rested from his labors;
> He dreamed of Thebes and Camelot,
>   And Priam's neighbors.
>
> Miniver mourned the ripe renown
>   That made so many a name so fragrant;
> He mourned Romance, now on the town,
>   And Art, a vagrant.
>
> Miniver loved the Medici,
>   Albeit he had never seen one;
> He would have sinned incessantly
>   Could he have been one.
>
> Miniver cursed the commonplace
>   And eyed a khaki suit with loathing;
> He missed the medieval grace
>   Of iron clothing.

10

20

Miniver scorned the gold he sought,
    But sore annoyed was he without it;
Miniver thought, and thought, and thought,
    And thought about it.

Miniver Cheevy, born too late,
    Scratched his head and kept on thinking;   30
Miniver coughed, and called it fate,
    And kept on drinking.

And here is a song by e. e. cummings (1894–1962):

when faces called flowers float out of the ground
and breathing is wishing and wishing is having—
but keeping is downward and doubting and never
—it's april (yes, april; my darling) it's spring!
yes the pretty birds frolic as spry as can fly
yes the little fish gambol as glad as can be
(yes the mountains are dancing together)

when every leaf opens without any sound
and wishing is having and having is giving—
but keeping is doting and nothing and nonsense
—alive; we're alive, dear: it's (kiss me now) spring!   10
now the pretty birds hover so she and so he
now the little fish quiver so you and so i
(now the mountains are dancing, the mountains)

when more than was lost has been found has been found
and having is giving and giving is living—
but keeping is darkness and winter and cringing
—it's spring (all our night becomes day) o, it's spring!
all the pretty birds dive to the heart of the sky
all the little fish climb through the mind of the sea
(all the mountains are dancing; are dancing)   20

The poem by e. e. cummings has the traits which we have associated with the romantic, the product of an imagination working on inspiration; in contrast to Robinson's it has an air of mystery and wonder; it is an "imaginative fusion of the familiar and the strange, . . . the real and the ideal, . . . the material and the spiritual." Robinson's poem, on the other hand, has an air of calmness and lucidity; the emotion behind the poem is well under control in the interest of order and clarity.

One would be tempted, also, to say that "Miniver Cheevy" appears to be fairly realistic in approach. Commonly the classic spirit prefers the realistic approach, for the record of experience is more easily arranged in lucid order than the products of the imagination.

It is not unusual in modern writings to find the classic and the romantic blended. The opening of Oliver Jensen's (1914—) essay "The Forward Look and a Backward Glance" has something in common with both Addison and De Quincey:

Every year, indeed almost every month, it seems, man, driven by some wild longing, finds ways to move faster. Speed in our time begins at the breakneck and then moves on to an ever dizzier pace. We have left sound behind, and the rotation of the earth. Only the speed of light remains to be overcome—and a few terrifying questions. Where does it all stop? Will speed vanquish time? What happens, for example, to a pilot who constantly circles the earth westward, losing a day every few hours? As the calendar rushes backward each time he passes the International Date Line, will he grow younger and younger, shrinking in his space suit until finally he vanishes back into the womb? What will his mother think?

Perhaps there is a flaw in that reasoning, but

what happens on a space ship hurtling away from earth so much faster than sound that it overtakes the faint traces of words spoken in millennia past? Allow that modern electronics can detect and amplify the most attenuated signal. Will those voyagers between galaxies tune in the click of bowling balls on Plymouth Hoe, and the distant gunfire of the Spanish Armada? Will they catch the chant of Roman legions on the march? The voice of Demosthenes? The grunt of cave men? The roar of Creation?

The mind boggles.

There are, however, a few certainties we may cling to, although without enthusiasm. The easier it becomes to reach the moon, let us say, the harder it will be to get from New York to the Westchester suburbs. The more roads we build, the slower traffic will creep along them. The longer automobiles, the less space they will have inside. The more we have of the "forward look," the more deponent glances back with affection at earlier looks in travel.

TONE, SUBJECT AND THEME

Now, you will have remarked in the pieces we have thus far quoted certain qualities quite apart from their being subjective or objective; realistic, classic, or romantic—though these qualities are not easily to be separated from those which we have thus categorized. We have hinted at these qualities, which you must have felt while you were reading each piece, when we spoke of the anguish of Poe's poem, the awesomeness in Keats's, the over-sophistication of the speaker in Browning's, the polished cynicism of Chesterfield's letter, the homely warmth of Miss Millay's "The Return from Town," the bright airiness of Lyly's song, the quietly satirical antiromanticism of Jane Austen's portraiture, the calmness of Addison's prose, the alternate brooding and excitement of De Quincey's, the self-control in Robinson's lines, the wonder in e. e. cummings's. Each of these qualities, peculiar to the composition in question, is a matter of *tone*.

In music a tone is a sound of definite pitch; in painting it refers to the prevailing effect produced in a picture by the use of color. In literature the word, though distantly allied to these two ideas, is harder to define with equal precision because it refers to a quality which must be *felt*. We shall have to be content with a loose definition, such as "attitude," "mood," or "state of mind." But, though harder to define, like most matters connected with our feelings, it is not a whit the less present—as it is present in every work of literature. *Tone is a product of the author's attitude toward his subject and his reader.*

To illustrate: two books could be written on the same *subject*—for example, the search for the knowledge which brings happiness. Now, *the theme of a work is its basic idea.* These two books could be written on the same subject and on the same theme—for example, the theme could be that the knowledge which brings happiness need not be sought in far-off places since it can be found close to one's own home. But despite identity of subject and affinity of theme, these two books would be very different if they were written in quite different tones. As a matter of fact, in the late eighteenth century two books on this subject and this theme actually were written and appeared in print at almost the same time. This is a passage from one, Voltaire's (1694–1778) *Candide* (Chapter VI):

> After the earthquake had destroyed three-fourths of Lisbon, the sages of that country could think of no means more effectual to prevent utter ruin than to give the people a beautiful *auto-da-fé*;[1] for it had been decided by the University of Coimbra that the burning of a few people alive by a slow fire, and with great ceremony, is an infallible secret to hinder the earth from quaking.
>
> In consequence hereof, they had seized on a Biscayner, convicted of having married his godmother, and on two Portuguese, for rejecting the bacon which larded a chicken they were eating; after dinner, they came and secured Dr. Pangloss, and his disciple Candide, the one for speaking his mind, the other for having listened with an air of approbation. They were conducted to separate apartments, extremely cold, since they were never incommoded by the

[1]Public burning of heretics.

sun. Eight days after, they were dressed in *san-benitos*[2] and their heads ornamented with paper mitres. The mitre and *san-benito* belonging to Candide were painted with reversed flames and with devils that had neither tails nor claws; but Pangloss' devils had claws and tails, and the flames were upright. They marched in procession thus habited and heard a very pathetic sermon, followed by fine church music. Candide was whipped in cadence while they were singing; the Biscayner, and the two men who had refused to eat bacon, were burnt; and Pangloss was hanged, though that was not the custom. The same day the earth sustained a most violent concussion.

Short though this excerpt is, it exhibits well enough the wittiness, gaiety and flippancy which is characteristic of *Candide* throughout. This is a passage from the other book on the same theme, Samuel Johnson's (1709–1784) *Rasselas* (Chapter XVIII):

As he was one day walking in the street, he saw a spacious building which all were, by the open doors, invited to enter. He followed the stream of people, and found it a hall or school of declamation, in which professors read lectures to their auditory. He fixed his eye upon a sage raised above the rest, who discoursed with great energy on the government of the passions. His look was venerable, his action graceful, his pronunciation clear, and his diction elegant. He showed, with great strength of sentiment and variety of illustration, that human nature is degraded and debased when the lower faculties predominate over the higher; that when fancy, the parent of passion, usurps the dominion of the mind, nothing ensues but the natural effect of unlawful government, perturbation, and confusion; that she betrays the fortresses of the intellect to rebels, and excites her children to sedition against reason, their lawful sovereign. He compared reason to the sun, of which the light is constant, uniform, and lasting; and fancy to a meteor, of bright but transitory lustre, irregular in its motion and delusive in its direction.

He then communicated the various precepts given from time to time for the conquest of passion, and displayed the happiness of those who had obtained the important victory, after which man is no longer the slave of fear nor the fool of hope; is no more emaciated by envy, inflamed by anger, emasculated by tenderness, or depressed by grief, but walks on calmly through the tumults or privacies of life, as the sun pursues alike his course through the calm or the stormy sky.

He enumerated many examples of heroes immovable by pain or pleasure, who looked with indifference on those modes or accidents to which the vulgar give the names of good and evil. He exhorted his hearers to lay aside their prejudices, and arm themselves against the shafts of malice or misfortune, by invulnerable patience; concluding that this state only was happiness, and that this happiness was in everyone's power.

Rasselas listened to him with the veneration due to the instructions of a superior being, and, waiting for him at the door, humbly implored the liberty of visiting so great a master of true wisdom. The lecturer hesitated a moment, when Rasselas put a purse of gold into his hand, which he received with a mixture of joy and wonder.

"I have found," said the prince at his return to Imlac, "a man who can teach all that is necessary to be known; who, from the unshaken throne of rational fortitude, looks down on the scenes of life changing beneath him. He speaks, and attention watches his lips. He reasons, and conviction closes his periods. This man shall be my future guide; I will learn his doctrines and imitate his life."

"Be not too hasty," said Imlac, "to trust or to admire the teachers of morality: they discourse like angels, but they live like men."

This selection from *Rasselas* will illustrate the gravity, high seriousness and indifference to mirth of the entire work. One book is full of laughter, skeptical and light; the other is solemn, religious, and often melancholy. As a result of their difference in tone, *Candide* and *Rasselas* will strike any reader as being far more unlike each other than similar.

Differences in tone in various works on similar subjects make for the endless variety possible to literature. Consider two estimates, written within a year of each other, of Samuel Johnson's biographer, James Boswell (1740–1795). Thomas Babington Macaulay (1800–1859) in 1831 had this to say of him:

[2]Yellow garments worn by penitents at the *auto-da-fé*.

The "Life of Johnson"[1] is assuredly a great, a very great work. Homer is not more decidedly the first of dramatists. Demosthenes is not more decidedly the first of orators, than Boswell is the first of biographers. He has no second. He has distanced all his competitors so decidedly that it is not worth while to place them. Eclipse is first, and the rest nowhere.

We are not sure that there is in the whole history of the human intellect so strange a phenomenon as this book. Many of the greatest men that ever lived have written biography. Boswell was one of the smallest men that ever lived, and he has beaten them all. He was, if we are to give any credit to his own account or to the united testimony of all who knew him, a man of the meanest and feeblest intellect. Johnson described him as a fellow who had missed his only chance of immortality by not having been alive when the "Dunciad"[2] was written. Beauclerk[3] used his name as a proverbial expression for a bore. He was the laughing-stock of the whole of that brilliant society which has owed to him the greater part of its fame. He was always laying himself at the feet of some eminent man, and begging to be spit upon and trampled upon. He was always earning some ridiculous nickname, and then "binding it as a crown unto him," not merely in metaphor, but literally. He exhibited himself, at the Shakespeare Jubilee, to all the crowd which filled Stratford-on-Avon, with a placard round his hat bearing the inscription of Corsica Boswell.[4] In his Tour, he proclaimed to all the world that at Edinburgh he was known by the appellation of Paoli Boswell. Servile and impertinent, shallow and pedantic, a bigot and a sot, bloated with family pride, and eternally blustering about the dignity of a born gentleman, yet stooping to be a talebearer, and eavesdropper, a common butt in the taverns of London, so curious to know everybody that was talked about, that, Tory and High Churchman as he was, he manœuvered, we have been told, for an introduction to Tom Paine;[5] so vain of the most childish distinctions, that when he had been to Court, he drove to the office where his book was printing without changing his clothes, and summoned all the printer's devils to admire his new ruffles and sword; such was this man, and such he was content and proud to be. Everything which another man would have hidden, everything the publication of which would have made another man hang himself, was matter of gay and clamorous exultation to his weak and diseased mind. What silly things he said, what bitter retorts he provoked, how at one place he was troubled with evil presentiments which came to nothing, how at another place, on waking from a drunken doze, he read the prayer-book and took a hair of the dog that had bitten him, how he went to see men hanged and came away maudlin, how he added five hundred pounds to the fortune of one of his babies because she was not scared at Johnson's ugly face, how he was frightened out of his wits at sea, and how the sailors quieted him as they would have quieted a child, how tipsy he was at Lady Cork's one evening and how much his merriment annoyed the ladies, how impertinent he was to the Duchess of Argyle and with what stately contempt she put down his impertinence, how Colonel Macleod sneered to his face at his impudent obtrusiveness, how his father, and the very wife of his bosom laughed and fretted at his fooleries—all these things he proclaimed to all the world, as if they had been subjects for pride and ostentatious rejoicing. All caprices of his temper, all the illusions of his vanity, all his hypochondriac whimsies, all his castles in the air, he displayed with a cool self-complacency, a perfect unconsciousness that he was making a fool of himself, to which it is impossible to find a parallel in the whole history of mankind. He had used many people ill; but assuredly he has used nobody so ill as himself. . . .

This entertaining piece of character-assassination, written in the highly paradoxical witty style for which Macaulay was celebrated, is more libelous, we know now, than truthful. Macaulay was quite ready to sacrifice veracity by exaggerating some facts and omitting others, in the interest of being amusing. The black and white contrasts of the opening paragraphs are characteristic of his flair for the startling. We perhaps forget to note his indifference to being just to his victim, and do not stop to consider that no one could be quite

[1]Boswell's great biography.

[2]A blistering satire written by Pope against literary foes.

[3]A friend of Johnson's.

[4]Boswell had visited Corsica, where he came to know the Corsican patriot, General Paoli.

[5]Noted radical, prominent in the American Revolution, and author of works considered "dangerous" in England.

so deplorable as Boswell is here depicted. Partly as a result of Macaulay's popularity, Boswell's reputation as a human being was in eclipse for the better part of a century.

Nevertheless, entertained though they were, Macaulay's readers ought to have reflected that there is something preposterous in the point of view of a critic who maintains that the meanest of the world's men could have written one of the world's greatest books. Thomas Carlyle (1795–1881) was quick to hear this note of falsity, and the next year published his own view of Boswell's character:

We next have a word to say of James Boswell. Boswell has already been much commented upon; but rather in the way of censure and vituperation than of true recognition. He was a man that brought himself much before the world; confessed that he eagerly coveted fame, or if that were not possible, notoriety; of which latter as he gained far more than was his due, the public were incited, not only by their natural love of scandal, but by a special ground of envy, to say whatever ill of him could be said. Out of the fifteen millions that then lived, and had bed and board in the British islands, this man has provided us a greater pleasure than any other individual, at whose cost we now enjoy ourselves; perhaps has done us a greater *service* than can be especially attributed to more than two or three yet, ungrateful that we are, no written or spoken eulogy of James Boswell anywhere exists; his recompense in solid pudding (so far as copyright went) was not excessive; and for the empty praise, it has altogether been denied him. Men are unwiser than children; they do not know the hand that feeds them.

Boswell was a person whose mean or bad qualities lay open to the general eye; visible, palpable to the dullest. His good qualities, again, belonged not to the time he lived in; were far from common then; indeed, in such a degree, were almost unexampled; not recognizable therefore by every one; nay, apt even (so strange had they grown) to be confounded with the very vices they lay contiguous to and had sprung out of. That he was a wine-bibber and gross liver; gluttonously fond of whatever would yield him a little solacement, were it only of a stomachic character, is undeniable enough. That he was vain, heedless, a babbler; had much of the sycophant, alternating with the braggadocio, curiously spiced too with an all-pervading dash of the coxcomb; that he gloried much when the tailor, by a court-suit, had made a new man of him; that he appeared at the Shakespeare Jubilee with a ribbon, imprinted "Corsica Boswell," round his hat; and in short, if you will, lived no day of his life without doing and saying more than one pretentious ineptitude: all this unhappily is evident as the sun at noon. The very look of Boswell seems to have signified so much. In that cocked nose, cocked partly in triumph over his weaker fellow-creatures, partly to snuff up the smell of coming pleasure, and scent it from afar; in those bag-cheeks, hanging like half-filled wineskins, still able to contain more; in that coarsely protruded shelf-mouth, that fat dew-lapped chin: in all this, who sees not sensuality, pretension, boisterous imbecility enough; much that could not have been ornamental in the temper of a great man's overfed great man (what the Scotch name *flunky*), though it had been more natural there? The under part of Boswell's face is of a low, almost brutish character.

Unfortunately, on the other hand, what great and genuine good lay in him was nowise so self-evident. That Boswell was a hunter after spiritual notabilities, that he loved such, and longed, and even crept and crawled to be near them; that he first (in old Touchwood Auchinleck's[1] phraseology) "took on with Paoli"; and then being off with "the Corsican landlouper,"[2] took on with a schoolmaster,[3] "ane that keeped a schule, and ca'd it an academy"; that he did all this, and could not help doing it, we account a very singular merit. The man, once for all, had an "open sense," an open loving heart, which so few have: where excellence existed, he was compelled to acknowledge it; was drawn towards it, and (let the old sulphur-brand of a laird say what he liked) *could not but* walk with it—if not as superior, if not as equal, then as inferior and lackey, better so than not at all. If we reflect now that this love of excellence had not only such an evil *nature* to triumph over; but also what an *education* and social position withstood it and weighed it down, its innate strength, victorious over all these things, may astonish us. Consider what an inward impulse there must have been, how many mountains of impediment hurled aside, before the Scottish laird could, as humble servant, embrace the knees (the bosom was not permitted him) of the English dominie! Your Scottish laird, says an English naturalist of these days, may be defined as the hungriest and vainest of all bipeds yet known.

[1] Alexander Boswell, Laird of Auchinleck, Boswell's father.

[2] Adventurer.

[3] Johnson had once taught school.

Boswell too was a Tory, of quite peculiarly feudal, genealogical, pragmatical temper; had been nurtured in an atmosphere of heraldry, at the feet of a very Gamaliel[4] in that kind; within bare walls, adorned only with pedigrees, amid serving-men in threadbare livery; all things teaching him, from birth upwards, that a laird was a laird. Perhaps there was a special vanity in his very blood: old Auchinleck had, if not the gay, tail-spreading, peacock vanity of his son, no little of the slow stalking, contentious, hissing vanity of the gander; a still more fatal species. Scottish advocates will tell you how the ancient man, having chanced to be the first sheriff appointed (after the abolition of "hereditary jurisdiction") by royal authority, was wont, in dull-snuffling pompous tone, to preface many a deliverance from the bench with these words: "I, the first king's sheriff in Scotland."

And now behold the worthy Bozzy, so prepossessed and held back by nature and by art, fly nevertheless like iron to its magnet with what enclosures and encumbrances you please—with wood, with rubbish, with brass: it matters not, the two feel each other, they struggle restlessly towards each other, they *will* be together. The iron may be a Scottish squirelet, full of gulosity[5] and "gigmanity";[6] the magnet an English plebeian, and moving rag-and-dust mountain, coarse, proud, irascible, imperious: nevertheless, behold how they embrace, and inseparably cleave to one another!

The subject of both authors is the same: the relationship of Boswell's accomplishment as a biographer to his personal character. This time the themes are in opposition. Macaulay's theme is that Boswell became the world's greatest biographer because he was the most contemptible of men. Carlyle's theme is that Boswell became a great biographer because his extraordinary spiritual gifts triumphed brilliantly over personal defects which were obvious and unimportant.

As you may have noted, Carlyle does not disdain the appeal of wit in his prose, but since he is anxious to be just to what is admirable in Boswell, he is less preoccupied than Macaulay with the feat of amusing us. He wishes, above all, to understand Boswell the man. His prose, therefore, if less bright and less fluid than Macaulay's, is far warmer, richer, and, without ever becoming soft-minded, radiant with human compassion.

In the case of Voltaire and Johnson, differences of tone emanated from differences of attitude toward the same subject and theme. Here the differences of tone begin with a difference of theme on the same subject. With such fundamental differences as those of Macaulay and Carlyle on the possible relationship of a man's character to his work, a radical difference of tone was inevitable.

Tone is, then, an essential part of what an author is saying to us. Different tones make different meanings.

For example, sometime around A.D. 200 a Greek writer of love letters (in prose) composed a passage with a graceful allusion to a drinking cup. The lines so fired the imagination of the English poet Ben Jonson (1573–1637), friend and admirer of Shakespeare, that he paraphrased them in an exquisite song now known everywhere in the English-speaking world:

> Drink to me only with thine eyes,
>   And I will pledge with mine;
> Or leave a kiss but in the cup
>   And I'll not look for wine.
> The thirst that from the soul doth rise
>   Doth ask a drink divine;
> But might I of Jove's nectar sup,
>   I would not change for thine.

[4]The teacher of St. Paul.

[5]Gluttony.

[6]Shallow respectability (coined from gig, a carriage—making *gigmanity* instead of *humanity*—i.e., those people who judge others according to such possessions).

I sent thee late a rosy wreath,
 Not so much honoring thee   10
As giving it a hope that there
 It could not withered be;
But thou thereon didst only breathe,
 And sent'st it back to me;
Since when it grows, and smells, I swear,
 Not of itself but thee!

But the pleasures of drinking and of sharing the cup with the beloved had associations quite different from these for an earlier Elizabethan. This is a song from *Gammer Gurton's Needle* (c. 1560):

Back and side, go bare, go bare,
 Both foot and hand go cold;
But, belly, God send thee good ale enough,
 Whether it be new or old.

I cannot eat but little meat,
 My stomach is not good;
But, sure, I think that I can drink
 With him that wears a hood.
Though I go bare, take ye no care,
 I am nothing a-cold;   10
I stuff my skin so full within
 Of jolly good ale and old.

Back and side, go bare, go bare, etc.

I love no roast, but a nut-brown toast,
 And a crab[1] laid in the fire;
A little bread shall do me stead,
 Much bread I not desire.
No frost nor snow, no wind, I trow,
 Can hurt me if i[t] would,
I am so wrapt and thoroughly lapt 20
 Of jolly good ale and old.

Back and side, go bare, go bare, etc.

And Tib, my wife, that as her life
 Loveth well good ale to seek,
Full oft drinks she till ye may see
 The tears run down her cheek;
Then doth she trowl[2] to me the bowl,
 Even as a malt-worm[3] should,
And saith, "Sweetheart, I took my part
 Of this jolly good ale and old." 30

Back and side, go bare, go bare, etc.

Now let them drink till they nod and wink
 Even as good fellows should do;
They shall not miss to have the bliss
 Good ale doth bring men to.
And all poor souls that have scoured[4] bowls,
 Or have them lustily trowled,
God save the lives of them and their wives,
 Whether they be young or old.

Back and side, go bare, go bare, etc. 40

The tone of one is delicate grace, that of the other noisy lustiness.

THE COMPLEXITY AND SUBTLETY OF TONE

It must already be clear that it would be impossible to list all the tones to be found in literature. Each emotional shade, an emanation of the author's temperament or emotional bent at the time of composition, is in itself a distinct tone. If we observe that literary tones include the satirical, reflective, compassionate, playful, angry, cold, elegant, gentle, noble, whimsical, cynical—we do not begin to exhaust the list.

We may profitably examine the complexity and subtlety of tone by considering the satirical. The satirical itself is capable of all sorts of shadings. This is Arthur Hugh Clough's (1819–1861) "The Latest Decalogue."

   Thou shalt have one God only; who
   Would be at the expense of two?
   No graven images may be
   Worshiped, except the currency.

[1] Apple.
[2] Pass.

[3] A lover of drink.
[4] Emptied.

> Swear not at all; for, for thy curse
> Thine enemy is none the worse.
> At church on Sunday to attend
> Will serve to keep the world thy friend.
> Honor thy parents; that is, all
> From whom advancement may befall.   10
> Thou shalt not kill; but need'st not strive
> Officiously to keep alive.
> Do not adultery commit;
> Advantage rarely comes of it.
> Thou shalt not steal; an empty feat,
> When it's so lucrative to cheat.
> Bear not false witness; let the lie
> Have time on its own wings to fly.
> Thou shalt not covet, but tradition
> Approves all forms of competition.   20

It is a bitter adaptation of the Ten Commandments to the code of Victorian materialism—a fine example of *irony*—its intent being the opposite of the literal meaning of the words.

Francis Jeffrey's (1773–1850) epitaph-couplet "On Peter Robinson" is also satirical:

> Here lies the preacher, judge and poet, Peter,
> Who broke the laws of God, and man, and metre.

The lines are personal and malicious—tones not uncommon in a lampoon. But satire need not be bitter or ill-natured. Here is an anonymous limerick on "Relativity":

> There was a young woman named Bright
> Who traveled much faster than light.
>   She started one day
>   In a relative way,
> And returned on the previous night.

The satire is totally impersonal, and the jesting is only with an idea. Oliver Goldsmith's (1728–1774) portrait of the schoolmaster in *The Deserted Village* is, of course, satirical:

> Well had the boding tremblers learn'd to trace
> The day's disasters in his morning face;
> Full well they laugh'd with counterfeited glee
> At all his jokes, for many a joke had he;
> Full well the busy whisper, circling round,
> Convey'd the dismal tidings when he frown'd;
> Yet he was kind, or if severe in aught,
> The love he bore to learning was in fault; ...
> In arguing, too, the parson own'd his skill,
> For e'en though vanquish'd, he could argue still;   10
> While words of learned length and thundering sound
> Amazed the gazing rustics ranged around;
> And still they gazed, and still the wonder grew
> That one small head could carry all he knew.

But the satire is in a most affectionate vein, devoid of any but the kindliest feelings. Consider another anonymous jingle:

> See the happy moron,
> He doesn't give a damn!
> I wish I were a moron—
> My God! Perhaps I am!

The tone is light and merry, and comes close to a kind of satirical writing in which English literature is peculiarly rich, nonsense. *Nonsense,* as a literary type, might be defined as a kind of satire where nothing is being attacked beyond excessive solemnity and gravity. It is *fun for its own sake.* Even Samuel Johnson, for all his high seriousness and melancholy, was capable of indulging in such fun:

> If the man who turnip cries[1]
> Cry not when his father dies,
> 'Tis proof that he had rather
> Have a turnip than his father.

Nonsense is a field in which Edward Lear, Lewis Carroll and W. S. Gilbert made themselves notable careers. And the cheery blooms of nonsense flourish in many major English novels.

The fun in Johnson's quatrain depends, of course, upon the pun on the word *cry.* Such manipulation of language is a characteristic of *wit,* which we may define as the expression of a swift perception of the incongruous. Wit, which gives its own tone to literature, itself has many shadings.

The Earl of Rochester (1648–1680) wrote an epigram "On Charles II":

> Here lies our sovereign Lord the King,
> Whose word no man relies on,
> Who never said a foolish thing
> Nor ever did a wise one.

It is an accurate portrait painted with witty cold precision. There is wit too in Francis Quarles's (1592–1644) epigram "Respice Finem":*

> My soul, sit thou a patient looker-on;
> Judge not the play before the play is done:
> Her plot hath many changes; every day
> Speaks a new scene; the last act crowns the play.

But the little poem shows how wit may be allied to dignity and loftiness, even though it result from a swift perception of the incongruous. Quarles brilliantly seizes on the incongruous notion of life as a play, its progress the plot of the play, and entrance into the Hereafter as the last act—and carries out the analogy without faltering. Of the use of wit in the service of sublimity in poetry, the works of John Donne (1573–1631) will furnish many instances.

In our discussion of tone we have been freely using some words concerning which there exists considerable confusion. In his valuable *A Dictionary of Modern English Usage,* H. W. Fowler lists eight such words: *sarcasm, the sardonic, invective, wit, humor, irony, satire,* and *cynicism.* It is to him that we are indebted for each of the illuminating differentiations which follow our examples below. In addition to countless other tones, these eight can all be found in Shakespeare's *As You Like It:*

1. *Sarcasm.* In Act I, scene ii, Rosalind and Celia are informed by the courtier Le Beau that they "have lost much good sport": Charles the wrestler has just finished off three fine brothers; Charles in one move threw the eldest "and broke three of his ribs, that there is little hope of life in him; so he served the second, and so the third. Yonder they lie; the poor old man, their father, making such pitiful dole over them that all the beholders take his part with weeping." Where upon Touchstone asks: "But what is the sport, monsieur, that the ladies have lost?"

Sarcasm is addressed, for the purpose of wounding, to the intended victim and bystanders, deals with "faults and foibles," and employs an inversion of the facts as its device.

[1]I.e., while he is selling turnips.
*Consider the end carefully (Latin).

2. *The Sardonic.* In Act II, scene iv, Rosalind, Celia, and Touchstone, escaping from the Court, after a weary journey, arrive at the forest of Arden in search of Rosalind's father. They are depressed from fatigue, but Rosalind, in an effort to cheer the spirits of the other two, says bravely: "Well, this is the forest of Arden." Touchstone appends: "Ay, now am I in Arden; the more fool I! when I was at home, I was in a better place."

The Sardonic is addressed, for the purposes of "self-relief," to one's self, deals with adversity, and is pessimistic in its outlook.

3. *Invective.* In Act II, scene vii, the "melancholy Jaques" tells the banished Duke, after meeting the jester Touchstone, that he himself yearns for the profession of court-jester, and concludes that if the Duke will permit him henceforth to speak his mind, he will completely "cleanse the foul body of the infected world." The Duke, who knows his courtier well, comments in the presence of his followers:

> Most mischievous foul sin, in chiding sin:
> For thou thyself hast been a libertine,
> As sensual as the brutish sting[1] itself;
> And all the embossed[2] sores and headed[3] evils,
> That thou with license of free foot[4] has caught,
> Wouldst thou disgorge into the general world.

Invective is addressed, for the purpose of discrediting someone or something, to the world at large, deals with misconduct, and employs direct statement as its method.

4. *Wit.* In Act IV, scene i, Jaques meets Rosalind (disguised as the boy, Ganymede) and speaks proudly of the jaundiced view he has of the world; it is a product of his observation during his wide travels, he explains. "A traveler!" echoes Rosalind. "Yes," continues Jaques, "I have gained my experience." Rosalind, too much in love to countenance misanthropy, retorts: "And your experience makes you sad![5] I had rather have a fool to make me merry than experience to make me sad; and to travel for it too!"

Wit is addressed, for the purpose of "throwing light," to the intelligent, deals with words and ideas, and employs surprise as its device.

5. *Humor.* Rosalind and Orlando have met but once, and then at Court, and have fallen in love at first sight. When they meet again in the forest of Arden, Rosalind is disguised as Ganymede, a boy, and Orlando does not recognize her. Because he is disconsolate over his frustrated love for Rosalind, she promises to cure him of his love if he will practice the art of wooing Rosalind on her. When in Act IV, scene i, Orlando courts Ganymede half in jest, calling the youth "Rosalind," and not recognizing Ganymede to be indeed Rosalind, that is a scene of humor.

Humor is addressed, for the purpose of revealing human traits, to the sympathetic, deals with human nature, and employs observation in the use of its material.

6. *Irony.* In that same scene (IV/i) Ganymede promises to be suspicious of Orlando, "clamorous," "new-fangled," and "giddy"; and to weep for nothing when Orlando wishes to be merry, and to laugh like a hyena when he wishes to sleep. Orlando demands, "But will my Rosalind do so?" She answers, "By my life, she will do as I do."

Irony is addressed, with the aim of being exclusive, to the one or the few who can follow it, deals with facts, and employs "mystification" as its device.

7. *Satire.* In Act V, scene iv, Touchstone the jester is introduced to the banished Duke by Jaques, who bids that he be welcomed. Jaques adds: "He hath been a courtier, he swears." Touchstone proceeds to prove the fact: "If any man doubt that, let him put me to my purgation.[6] I have trod a measure;[7] I have flattered a lady; I have been politic with my friend,

---

[1]Carnal desire.
[2]Swollen.
[3]Grown to a head.
[4]I.e., during his irresponsible travels.

[5]Sober.
[6]I.e., challenge me to prove it.
[7]A stately court dance.

smooth with mine enemy; I have undone three tailors; I have had four quarrels, and like to have[8] fought one."

Satire is addressed, for the purpose of improving, to the "self-satisfied," deals with morals and manners, and employs a heightening of the facts as its device.

8. *Cynicism.* In the same scene (V/iv) Touchstone is accompanied by a stupid country girl, Audrey, whom he has promised to marry. He introduces her to everyone: "A poor virgin, sir, an ill-favored[9] thing, sir, but mine own; a poor humor of mine, sir, to take that that no man else will."

Cynicism is addressed, with the aim of self-justification, to the respectable, deals with manners and morals, and employs a seemingly ruthless candor as its means.

Of course, some of these terms overlap. *Satire* is a general word; examples, 1, 3, and 4, above, are all satirical. In the aim to improve one may employ humor, wit or irony. Wit is often ironic; humor may be so too. Perhaps the sharpest distinction is between humor and wit: *humor is a matter of situation, wit a matter of language and ideas.*

It is perhaps true enough that in most works an intelligent reader can hardly fail to be aware of the tone of what he is reading. This is particularly true of works which are undisguisedly subjective, where the author's intrinsic meaning will impart to the reader quite directly and inevitably the tone in which the piece was conceived (e.g., Millay's "The Return from Town"). And even in objective writing the tone, which is indeed inseparable from the meaning, will often be clear at once—as the two pieces on Boswell by Macaulay and Carlyle will each witness.

Sometimes, however, the tone of a work is not clear at once. Take, for example, the brilliant "Soliloquy of the Spanish Cloister" by Robert Browning (1812–1889):

Gr-r-r—there go, my heart's abhorrence!
    Water your damned flower-pots, do!
If hate killed men, Brother Lawrence,
    God's blood, would not mine kill you!
What? your myrtle-bush wants trimming?
    Oh, that rose has prior claims—
Needs its leaden vase filled brimming?
    Hell dry you up with its flames!

At the meal we sit together:
    Salve tibi![1] I must hear   10
Wise talk of the kind of weather,
    Sort of season, time of year:
Not a plenteous cork-crop: scarcely
    Dare we hop oak-galls,[2] *I doubt:*
What's the Latin name for "Parsley"?
    What's the Greek name for Swine's
Snout?

Whew! We'll[3] have our platter burnished,
    Laid with care on our own shelf!
With a fire-new spoon we're furnished,
    And a goblet for ourself,   20

Rinsed like something sacrificial
    Ere 'tis fit to touch our chaps—
Marked with L for our initial!
    (He-he! There his lily snaps!)

Saint, forsooth! While brown Dolores
    Squats outside the Convent bank
With Sanchicha, telling stories,
    Steeping tresses in the tank,
Blue-black, lustrous, thick like horsehairs;
    —Can't I see his dead eye glow,   30
Bright as 'twere a Barbary corsair's?
    (That is, if he'd let it show!)

When he finishes refection,
    Knife and fork he never lays
Cross-wise, to my recollection,
    As do I, in Jesu's praise.
I the Trinity illustrate,
    Drinking watered orange-pulp—
In three sips the Arian[4] frustrate;
    While he drains his at one gulp.   40

[8]I.e., very nearly.

[9]A pun. *Favor* also means "face."

[1]A greeting (Latin).

[2]Swellings on the tissues of the oak, caused by certain parasites. The galls contain tannic acid and are important in commerce.

[3]I.e., Brother Lawrence.

[4]The Arians were a heretical sect who denied that Christ was of the same substance as God. The speaker in the soliloquy publicly proves his belief in the Trinity.

Oh, those melons! If he's able
    We're to have a feast! so nice!
One goes to the Abbot's table,
    All of us get each a slice.
How go on your flowers? None double?
    Not one fruit-sort can you spy?
Strange!—And I, too, at such trouble
    Keep them close-nipped on the sly!

There's a great text in Galatians,[5]
    Once you trip on it, entails   50
Twenty-nine distinct damnations,
    One sure, if another fails:
If I trip him just a-dying,
    Sure of heaven as sure can be,
Spin him round and send him flying
    Off to hell, a Manichee?[6]

Or, my scrofulous French novel
    On gray paper with blunt type!
Simply glance at it, you grovel
    Hand and foot in Belial's gripe: 60
If I double down its pages
    At the woeful sixteenth print,
When he gathers his greengages,
    Ope a sieve and slip it in't?

Or, there's Satan!—one might venture
    Pledge one's soul to him, yet leave
Such a flaw in the indenture
    As he'd miss till, past retrieve,
Blasted lay that rose-acacia
    We're so proud of! *Hy, Zy, Hine*[7] ...   70
'St, there's Vespers! *Plena gratiâ,*
    Ave, Virgo![8] Gr-r-r—you swine!

The tone of this little masterpiece is deliberately one of blistering hatred. But you must read to the end before you understand the author's intentions. Then it becomes clear that the speaker in this monologue is a lost soul: it is horrifying that such a creature should ever have become a monk. He is one who observes all the external ceremonies of his religion and knows nothing of its spirit. And despite his self-righteous fury against Brother Lawrence, who is innocently tending his flowers and plants and is totally unaware of the venom he has inspired, we are made to see the beauty and sweetness of the latter's character. Thus, after a reading of this poem, we must relate its tone to the author's literary intentions; a second reading will place its hate in true perspective as not the author's point of view, but as a tone adopted for literary purposes that is highly dramatic in effect.

Now suppose that you, an intelligent reader, without any preface or warning were suddenly confronted by the following paragraphs:

It is a melancholy object to those who walk through this great town[1] or travel in the country, when they see the streets, the roads, and cabin doors, crowded with beggars of the female sex, followed by three, four, or six children, all in rags and importuning every passenger for an alms. These mothers, instead of being able to work for their honest livelihood, are forced to employ all their time in strolling to beg sustenance for their helpless infants: who as they grow up either turn thieves for want of work, or leave their dear native country to fight for the Pretender in Spain,[2] or sell themselves to the Barbadoes. . . .

There is likewise another great advantage in my scheme, that it will prevent those voluntary abortions, and that horrid practice of women murdering their bastard children, alas! too frequent among us! sacrificing the poor innocent babes I doubt more to avoid the expense than the shame, which would move tears and pity in the most savage and inhuman breast.

The number of souls in this kingdom being usually reckoned one million and a half, of these I calculate there may be about two hundred thousand couple whose wives are breeders; from which number I subtract thirty thousand couple who are able to maintain their own children, although I apprehend there cannot be so many, under the present distresses of the kingdom; but this being granted, there will remain an hundred

---

[5]The Epistle to the Galatians in the *New Testament.*

[6]A believer in the teachings of Manes, a Persian who propounded a faith in which Zoroastrian doctrines were combined with the Christian.

[7]Possibly "the words echo the ringing of the vesper bell, which causes the monk to cross himself and begin his 'Hail, Mary' " (De Vane).

[8]Hail, Virgin, full of grace (Latin).

[1]Dublin.

[2]Son of James II, who was anxious to secure the British throne.

and seventy thousand breeders. I again subtract fifty thousand for those women who miscarry, or whose children die by accident or disease within the year. There only remains one hundred and twenty thousand children of poor parents annually born. The question therefore is, how this number shall be reared and provided for, which, as I have already said, under the present situation of affairs, is utterly impossible by all the methods hitherto proposed. For we can neither employ them in handicraft or agriculture; we neither build houses (I mean in the country) nor cultivate land: they can very seldom pick up a livelihood by stealing, till they arrive at six years old, except where they are of towardly parts, although I confess they learn the rudiments much earlier, during which time, they can however be properly looked upon only as probationers, as I have been informed by a principal gentleman in the county of Cavan, who protested to me that he never knew above one or two instances under the age of six, even in a part of the kingdom so renowned for the quickest proficiency in that art.

I am assured by our merchants, that a boy or a girl before twelve years old is no salable commodity; and even when they come to this age they will not yield above three pounds, or three pounds and half-a-crown at most on the exchange; which cannot turn to account either to the parents or kingdom, the charge of nutriment and rags having been at least four times that value.

I shall now therefore humbly propose my own thoughts, which I hope will not be liable to the least objection.

I have been assured by a very knowing American of my acquaintance in London, that a young healthy child well nursed is at a year old a most delicious, nourishing, and wholesome food, whether stewed, roasted, baked, or boiled; and I make no doubt that it will equally serve in a fricassee or a ragout.

I do therefore humbly offer it to public consideration that of the hundred and twenty thousand children already computed, twenty thousand may be reserved for breed, whereof only one-fourth part to be males; which is more than we allow to sheep, black cattle or swine; and my reason is, that these children are seldom the fruits of marriage, a circumstance not much regarded by our savages, therefore one male will be sufficient to serve four females. That the remaining hundred thousand may, at a year old, be offered in the sale to the persons of quality and fortune through the kingdom; always advising the mother to let them suck plentifully in the last month, so as to render them plump and fat for a good table. A child will make two dishes at an entertainment for friends; and when the family dines alone, the fore or hind quarter will make a reasonable dish, and seasoned with a little pepper or salt will be very good boiled on the fourth day, especially in winter.

I have reckoned upon a medium that a child just born will weigh 12 pounds, and in a solar year, if tolerably nursed, increaseth to 28 pounds.

Taken at their face value, these words might well puzzle you. How are you to take this author? His first paragraph would lead you to believe that he writes with some compassion. But in the second a chill creeps in, for suddenly he seems to be a little too much disinterested when he swerves into a concern for the commonwealth; his commiseration seems to be evaporating. The third and fourth become still colder because of their statistical air. By the end of the fifth his "tears and pity" seem less felt than unctuously stated. The sixth and the seventh begin to be repellent in their preoccupation with the arithmetic of the situation; but in the midst of the calculations there is a brief, apparently irrelevant passage:

> For we can neither employ them in handicraft or agriculture; we neither build houses (I mean in the country) nor cultivate land . . .

—which makes you wonder still further. Why cannot the offspring of the poor be employed in manufacture or on farms? Why cannot houses be built or the land cultivated? Would not such measures alleviate the distresses of which the author is writing? Is he truly the friend of the poor that he professes to be? And what can he mean by stressing the fact that it is in the country that houses are not built? And why does he stand so frigidly aloof at the end of the seventh paragraph with his concentration on the profit "to the parents or kingdom"? But it is when he comes at length to revealing his great philanthropic proposal that he really stuns you:

> ... a young healthy child well nursed is at a year old a most delicious,
> nourishing, and wholesome food, whether stewed, roasted, baked, or boiled;
> and I make no doubt that it will equally serve in a fricassee or a ragout.

You may very likely ask with some indignation—for after all here, unlike Browning, the author seems to be speaking out in his own person—"Who is this cannibal? Does he dare number himself among civilized men?" Nor is your blood less frozen when he proceeds to apportion the 120,000 "children of poor parents annually born" in Ireland, as though he were talking of so many head of cattle.

Cannibals, of course, do not usually write this perfect, chiseled English; but the easy cultivation of the man's prose would appear to make his offensiveness all the more disgusting.

The author, however, in the next paragraph after his reckoning of a child's weight suddenly reveals his hand:

> I grant this food will be somewhat dear, and therefore very proper for
> landlords, who, as they have already devoured most of the parents, seem to
> have the best title to the children.

The bitter sarcasm of that sentence at last gives the clue. You now have the author's point of view. In the light of it, as you reread all that has preceded, you realize that he has purposefully mystified you, and deliberately led you on with some confusion as to his intent. Now you understand what he meant by the apparent irrelevancy of the sixth paragraph; it was written with the same indignation as this one. And you gather, too, that it is only for the poor in the country that houses are not built; in town the wealthy are building to their heart's desire.

The paragraphs we have quoted are the opening of "A Modest Proposal," written by the greatest of English satirists, Jonathan Swift (1667–1745), whose distress at the extreme poverty of the Irish caused him to compose in icy fury his indictment of the callousness of the rich. You will wish to read further:

Infant's flesh will be in season throughout the year, but more plentiful in March, and a little before and after; for we are told by a grave author, an eminent French physician, that fish being a prolific diet, there are more children born in Roman Catholic countries about nine months after Lent than at any other season; therefore, reckoning a year after Lent, the markets will be more glutted than usual, because the number of popish infants is at least three to one in this kingdom: and therefore it will have one other collateral advantage, by lessening the number of papists among us.

I have already computed the charge of nursing a beggar's child (in which list I reckon all cottagers, laborers, and four-fifths of the farmers) to be about two shillings per annum, rags included; and I believe no gentleman would repine to give ten shillings for the carcass of a good fat child, which, as I have said, will make four dishes of excellent nutritive meat, when he hath only some particular friend or his own family to dine with him. Thus the squire will learn to be a good landlord, and grow popular among his tenants; the mother will have eight shillings net profit, and be fit for work till she produces another child.

Those who are more thrifty (as I must confess the times require) may flay the carcass; the skin of which artificially dressed will make admirable gloves for ladies, and summer boots for fine gentlemen. ...

I can think of no one objection that will possibly be raised against this proposal, unless it should be urged that the number of people will be thereby much lessened in the kingdom. This I freely own, and it was indeed one principal design in offering it to the world. I desire the reader will observe, that I calculate my remedy for this one individual kingdom of Ireland and for no other that ever was, is, or I think ever can be upon earth. Therefore let no man talk to me of other expedients: of taxing our absentees at five shillings a pound; of using neither clothes nor household furniture except what is of our own growth and manufacture; of utterly rejecting the materials and instruments that promote foreign luxury; of curing the expensiveness of pride, vanity, idleness, and gaming in our women; of introducing a vein of parsimony, prudence, and temperance; of learning to love our country, wherein we differ even from Laplanders and the inhabitants of Topinamboo;[3] of quitting our animosities and factions, nor act any longer like the Jews, who were murdering one another at the very moment their city[4] was taken; of being a little cautious not to sell our country and conscience for nothing; of teaching landlords to have at least one degree of mercy toward their tenants; lastly, of putting a spirit of honesty, industry, and skill into our shopkeepers; who, if a resolution could now be taken to buy only our native goods, would immediately unite to cheat and exact upon us in the price, the measure, and the goodness, nor could ever yet be brought to make one fair proposal of just dealing, though often and earnestly invited to it.

Therefore I repeat, let no man talk to me of these and the like expedients, till he hath at least some glimpse of hope that there will be ever some hearty and sincere attempt to put them in practice.

But as to myself, having been wearied out for many years with offering vain, idle, visionary thoughts, and at length utterly despairing of success I fortunately fell upon this proposal; which, as it is wholly new, so it hath something solid and real, of no expense and little trouble, full in our own power, and whereby we can incur no danger in disobliging England. For this kind of commodity will not bear exportation, the flesh being of too tender a consistence to admit a long continuance in salt, although perhaps I could name a country which would be glad to eat up our whole nation without it.

After all, I am not so violently bent upon my own opinion as to reject any offer proposed by wise men, which shall be found equally innocent, cheap, easy, and effectual. But before something of that kind shall be advanced in contradiction to my scheme, and offering a better, I desire the author or authors will be pleased maturely to consider two points. First, as things now stand, how they will be able to find food and raiment for an hundred thousand useless mouths and backs. And secondly, there being a round million of creatures in human figure throughout this kingdom, whose whole subsistence put into a common stock would leave them in debt two millions of pounds sterling, adding those who are beggars by profession to the bulk of farmers, cottagers, and laborers, with their wives and children who are beggars in effect: I desire those politicians who dislike my overture, and may perhaps be so bold as to attempt an answer, that they will first ask the parents of these mortals, whether they would not at this day think it a great happiness to have been sold for food at a year old in the manner I prescribe, and thereby have avoided such a perpetual scene of misfortunes as they have since gone through by the oppression of landlords, the impossibility of paying rent without money or trade, the want of common sustenance, with neither house nor clothes to cover them from the inclemencies of the weather, and the most inevitable prospect of entailing the like or greater miseries upon their breed for ever.

I profess, in the sincerity of my heart that I have not the least personal interest in endeavoring to promote this necessary work, having no other motive than the public good of my country, by advancing our trade, providing for infants, relieving the poor, and giving some pleasure to the rich. I have no children by which I can propose to get a single penny; the youngest being nine years old, and my wife past child-bearing.

This is one of the finest examples of irony in the whole range of our literature. The social situation which evoked it belongs to history; but while the poor are with us "A Modest Proposal" will continue to sting the conscience of the honorable.

Naturally, the informed among Swift's contemporaries would have more rapidly understood the ironic device of mystification—and not only because they may have been aware of the condition of Ireland. Some of them had read, five years earlier, his *Letters* of *M. B. Drapier,* written in a similar vein as an attack on a plan, after hundreds of years of English depredation, to exploit further the conquered Irish. Many of his readers would have recognized that matchlessly precise style, and were familiar with its trenchant satire. They knew that one of Swift's favorite devices was to attack an evil by pretending to advocate an even more monstrous one.

[3]In Brazil.   [4]Jerusalem.

We may pause to reflect that a modern reader can never know too much about any given author and the circumstances connected with his work. It is perfectly fair to say that we need not especially concern ourselves with any piece of writing that has nothing to say to us today. But our understanding of any work that has stood the test of time can only be enriched by knowing all we can of the author's epoch, his literary career, and his biography.* We must be careful, however, not to confuse in our minds what we may have learned of these facts with what the work in itself has actually to say.

A knowledge of Swift's literary career would certainly have prepared us better to understand him more readily. The tone of some writings is not always what it at first appears to be—sometimes because of such tricks as Swift plays. The true focus of the author of "A Modest Proposal" is hidden at first in that single sentence which we have isolated. A too hasty reader might even miss it. A bigoted reader might misinterpret it. It is not until near the end of the essay that Swift ironically indicates the things which could be done to save Ireland, in the paragraph beginning "I can think of no one objection":

1. Tax the absentee landlords.
2. Encourage domestic industries.
3. Manufacture for the needs of Ireland.
4. Cut down the foolish extravagances of fashionable women.
5. Learn economy, thrift and moderation.
6. Encourage pride in Ireland and love for it.
7. Cease mutual cutting of throats among Irishmen.
8. Teach the evil of treason and other such acts.

But even these are stated as though they were impossible and unreasonable expedients. Again the bigot and oppressor might think that Swift was conceivably supporting the impoverishment of Ireland.

Sometimes the reader will miss the meaning of the author's tone because of the fact that he brings to his reading his own prejudices. There is on record a highly amusing illustration. During the first years of the eighteenth century the Tories, the party in power, were using highly repressive measures against those who refused to worship in the Church of England. Daniel Defoe (1660–1731) wrote "The Shortest Way with Dissenters," in which he ironically suggested that the laws were not severe enough, and proposed the severest possible persecution against the Dissenters from the Established Church. The Tories missed the irony, were delighted with Defoe, and heaped rewards upon him. When the politicians found themselves the object of ridicule for having misread Defoe, they rewarded him further—with the pillory, fine, and imprisonment! The incident will demonstrate the role of prejudice in ascertaining an author's tone.

Naturally, in any given work there need not be uniformity of tone. We have seen how the opening paragraphs of Swift's satire seemed to veer from compassion to coldness—until at the revealing sentence the whole suddenly was unified by our awareness of his irony. But the tone of a piece may actually vary—perhaps imperceptibly, perhaps plainly, perhaps abruptly, as we move from passage to passage. Such variations will be noted in pieces already quoted. The Poe poem moves from anguish to meditation in the last lines; the liveliness and enthusiasm of the speaker in "Up at a Villa—Down in the City" when he is evoking the delights of the town are throughout contrasted with his boredom or his fury when he tells us of life in the country; in "The Return from Town" the change in tone from the first two stanzas to the last makes the chief point of the poem; there is a sharp change in tone in the last paragraph of our quotation from Jane Austen; in the third paragraph of his piece on Boswell, Carlyle passes from merciless condemnation to warm approval.

*These important matters are, of course, outside the province of the present study, and are touched upon only when relevant to what is being discussed. There is a vast library available in the fields of biography and literary history.

Whether he make such changes in tone or maintain a uniform tone, an author must give considerable attention to the artistic problem of keeping his tone right. In the dialogue of his delicious comedy, *The Importance of Being Earnest,* Oscar Wilde (1856–1900) never once employs a syllable out of keeping with the delicate and arch gaiety of plot, characterization and dialogue. Here is a little specimen:

GWENDOLEN. ... Of course you are quite, quite sure that it is not Mr. Ernest Worthing who is your guardian?

CECILY. Quite sure. [*A pause.*] In fact, I am going to be his.

GWEND. [*enquiringly*]. I beg your pardon?

CECIL. [*rather shy and confidingly*]. Dearest Gwendolen, there is no reason why I should make a secret of it to you. Our little county newspaper is sure to chronicle the fact next week. Mr. Ernest Worthing and I are engaged to be married.

GWEND. [*quite politely, rising*]. My darling Cecily, I think there must be some slight error. Mr. Ernest Worthing is engaged to me. The announcement will appear in the *Morning Post* on Saturday at the latest.

CECIL. [*very politely, rising*]. I am afraid you must be under some misconception. Ernest proposed to me exactly ten minutes ago. [*Shows diary.*]

GWEND. [*examines diary through lorgnette carefully*]. It is certainly very curious, for he asked me to be his wife yesterday afternoon at 5:30. If you would care to verify the incident, pray do so. [*Produces diary of her own.*] I never travel without my diary. One should always have something sensational to read in the train. I am so sorry, dear Cecily, if it is any disappointment to you, but I am afraid *I* have the prior claim.

CECIL. It would distress me more than I can tell you, dear Gwendolen, if it caused you any mental or physical anguish, but I feel bound to point out that since Ernest proposed to you he clearly has changed his mind.

GWEND. [*meditatively*]. If the poor fellow has been entrapped into any foolish promise I shall consider it my duty to rescue him at once, and with a firm hand.

CECIL. [*thoughtfully and sadly*]. Whatever unfortunate entanglement my dear boy may have got into, I will never reproach him with it after we are married.

GWEND. Do you allude to me, Miss Cardew, as an entanglement? You are presumptuous. On an occasion of this kind it becomes more than a moral duty to speak one's mind. It becomes a pleasure.

CECIL. Do you suggest, Miss Fairfax, that I entrapped Ernest into an engagement? How dare you? This is no time for wearing the shallow mask of manners. When I see a spade I call it a spade.

GWEND. [*satirically*]. I am glad to say that I have never seen a spade. It is obvious that our social spheres have been widely different.

Now suppose one of these elegant young ladies should have interpolated some such phrase as "O.K.!" or "Gosh!" or "You're kidding." Though they are expressions one hears every day, and therefore admissible on the stage, any one of them would utterly annihilate the whole passage—perhaps, indeed, the whole play! On the audience it would have the effect of a sudden dousing in ice water. (It is interesting to note, in passing, that the elegance of Wilde's dialogue is attained without the shadow of a pompous or long-winded word. The vocabulary, though elevated, is entirely simple and unostentatious.)

An author's good intentions may not always be productive of lucky results, if his ear is insensitive. Here, for example, is a ballad sold in the streets of London soon after King Edward VII's death (1910):

> The will of God we must obey.
> Dreadful—our King taken away!
> The greatest friend of the nation,
> Mighty monarch and protection!
>
> Heavenly Father, help in sorrow
> Queen-Mother, and then to follow,
> What to do without him who has gone!
> Pray help! help! and do lead us on.
>
> Greatest sorrow England ever had
> When death took away our dear Dad;

A king was he from head to sole,
Loved by his people one and all.

His mighty work for the Nation,
Making peace and strengthening Union—
Always at it since on the throne:
Saved the country more than one billion.

It is not necessary to conclude from the oddity of the rhymes and the strangeness of the grammar that this anonymous author was less than completely patriotic. We cannot impugn his intentions. But his tone is, to say the least, confusing. The religious resignation of the first line is at odds with the sorrow of the second and the enthusiasm of the third and fourth lines. There is perhaps too sudden an anguish in the "help! help!" of the second stanza, and perhaps too much familiarity in the "Dad" of the third. Then "from head to sole" seems a little too prosaic for the occasion, even though the author needed "sole" to rhyme with "all"—which it doesn't quite do. Then there is a note of solidity in the first two lines of the last stanza, somewhat weakened by the colloquial "always at it" of the next line. And the very last line is perhaps not quite dignified enough, though it states a fact of unchallengeable importance.

Why are we forced, despite the author's good heart, to pronounce his elegy a failure, while the following, of far more ancient date, written by William Browne (1591–1643?), "On the Countess Dowager of Pembroke," is a success?

Underneath this sable hearse
Lies the subject of all verse:
Sidney's sister, Pembroke's[1] mother:
Death, ere thou hast slain another
Fair and learn'd and good as she,
Time shall throw a dart at thee.

The tone of the modern balladeer is chaotic, the tone of Browne's little poem is beautifully unified. The failure of the one and the success of the other can be identified in the misuse (in the first) and exquisite use (in the second) of language. For as we read, the tone of a work is communicated to us by the kinds of words an author employs and the way he employs them.

The author must be sensitive to the suitability of every word he uses to the tone he requires. Just so, no experienced painter would permit one daub of scarlet on his canvas to stand in disconcerting isolation; it would throw off the whole tone of his picture. What he will do, if he wishes a touch of scarlet on a woman's dress, for instance, will be to work in hints of scarlet in the background of the painting, possibly even in her face or hands, to balance it. In the street ballad, the phrase "dear Dad" is unthinkable in a solemn composition, and certainly is at odds with such phrases as "the will of God," "Heavenly Father," "mighty monarch." "Dear Dad" would be in tone in the company of such phrases as perhaps "us kids," "blokes" or "the old lady." It introduces a tone that should never have been allowed to enter.

From the reader's point of view, tone, like much else in literature, is a matter of language. And to language we turn our attention in the next chapter.

THE "MEANING" OF A LITERARY WORK

But before we do so, let us settle one thing more. We have made reference here and there to the "meaning" of a given work or to the "author's meaning." Where are we to look for this meaning?

[1]Sidney and Pembroke were both outstanding men of the period.

It is certainly not identical with what is loosely called "the author's purpose." Very often the only way that could be determined would be from the lips of the author himself. In the midst of the confusion of tone in the street ballad, for instance, how are we to guess at the author's "purpose" beyond a general benevolent intention to pay tribute to the deceased Edward VII? The ballad itself, however, is not much of a tribute as written; and even if we were privately informed by the author of his "purpose," we should still be at a loss concerning the meaning of his ballad. Clearly, then, the meaning of a work must be found in the work itself.

But where in the work? The meaning is not the subject, nor is it the theme. For example, the meaning of *Candide* and of *Rasselas* is neither "the search for the knowledge which brings happiness" (the subject) nor "the search for the knowledge which brings happiness is a search most wisely conducted near home" (the theme). The reading of even the excerpts we have quoted makes eloquently evident how different is the meaning of each from the other. This much, then, we may at present conclude: meaning has more to do with tone than with subject or theme.

Tone, however, is only one of the aspects of meaning. To pursue further what is involved in meaning, let us consider Shakespeare's magnificent "Sonnet CXVI":

> Let me not to the marriage of true minds
> Admit impediments. Love is not love
> Which alters when it alteration finds,
> Or bends with the remover to remove.
> Oh, no! it is an ever-fixèd mark
> That looks on tempests and is never shaken;
> It is the star to every wandering bark,
> Whose worth's unknown, although his height be
>   taken.
> Love's not Time's fool, though rosy lips and cheeks
> Within his bending sickle's compass come;   10
> Love alters not with his brief hours and weeks,
> But bears it out even to the edge of doom.
>   If this be error and upon me proved,
>   I never writ, nor no man ever loved.

From its position in the sequence of sonnets by Shakespeare, this poem, it is generally believed, is addressed to a man. The love of which the poet is speaking is the deep affection which can exist in the friendship of two men.

The subject, then, is True Friendship. The theme is: "True Friendship is eternal." But that, of course, is not the meaning of the sonnet; if it could be, there would be no need of reading the sonnet, and all we should have to do, to digest the author's meaning, would be to read the bald statement contained in these four words, which, indeed, is no more than a cliché—although no one will respond to the poem as to a cliché.

Let us next examine fairly closely what is known as the "content" of the sonnet by paraphrasing in prose each passage:

Let me not to the marriage of true minds/ Admit impediments.
> Do not allow me to admit that there could be any obstacles (also: Do not allow me to permit the entrance of obstacles)* to the union of persons who are faithful, honorable, steadfast, constant—human beings fit to be called men.†

*This doubleness of possible interpretation connected with the word *admit* which enriches the significance of the line is known in critical terminology as *ambiguity*. It will be discussed more fully in the next chapter. Other examples of such ambiguity, it will be noted, abound in the sonnet.

†In Shakespeare's day the word *true* could have implied any or all of these interpretations.

Love is not love/ Which alters when it alteration finds,
> That is not real love which can cease when it finds affection no longer reciprocated or when the person who is loved has changed,

Or bends with the remover to remove.
> or can incline to cooperate with the terminator of the affection in terminating that affection.

Oh, no! it is an ever-fixèd mark/ That looks on tempests and is never shaken;/ It is the star to every wandering bark,/ Whose worth's unknown, although his height be taken.
> Oh no! Love is like the North Star, fixed in its place in the heavens, the guide to every ship in the boundless sea. The mariner knows nothing of the worth or power of the star, and yet because it is fixed, he can chart by its altitude his ship's position, and come safely to port. So, too, all we can know of love is that it is constant, and by its constancy, unaffected by the tempests of life, we too are able to ride the storms of life and come safely home.

Love's not Time's fool, though rosy lips and cheeks/ Within his bending sickle's compass come;
> Love cannot be the sport of Time, even though the beauty of youth is subject to the ravages of passing time; beauty dies but love does not die with it;

Love alters not with his brief hours and weeks,/ But bears it out even to the edge of doom.
> Love does not seek a new object or become indifferent with the passage of time, but is constant until the Day of Judgment, to the end of time.

If this be error and upon me proved,/ I never writ, nor no man ever loved.
> If what I have said here is untrue, and can be proved so, then I have never written a line worth the writing, nor is there such a thing as love.

We have just examined the "contents" of the sonnet. The "contents," too, are not identical with the meaning of the poem, but a knowledge of the contents is essential to getting to the meaning. But this prose paraphrase, by necessity, omits all sorts of associations attaching to the original, and therefore part of the meaning of the original. To sample just a few of these omissions: The words *marriage* and *impediment* are probably suggested by the language of the Marriage Service: "If any of you know cause or just impediment. . . ." The reference to the star is likely to have an astrological significance too; the fact that the star's "worth's unknown" probably involves the idea of the influence of the stars upon individual destiny. Reference is possibly also made to the significance of the star in the scheme of the universe. The word *fool* applies, of course, to one whose business it is to amuse the court or the world of the theatre; this association gives another dimension to the phrase, "Love's not Time's fool." And so on. Even at the very end there enters a host of associations with the Day of Judgment, when everyone's reckoning must be made.

Besides the many facets of these ideas, the meaning of the poem is also involved in its structure. Read the poem again, and note its powerful architecture. There is a strong pause in sense and rhythm at the end of the fourth and eighth lines. At the end of the twelfth line, where the main division of the thought of the poem occurs, the pause is particularly emphatic (partly too because the pattern of the rhyme scheme changes after this line), the concluding two lines are thereby rendered the more solemn and impressive.

There are several well-considered patterns in the structure. As is usual in the Shakespearean sonnet,* there is, first of all, the pattern of the rhymes at the end of the line—what we call the *rhyme scheme.* Every four lines, of the first twelve, have two sets of interlocking rhymes:† *minds* and *finds, love* and *remove; mark* and *bark, shaken* and *taken; cheeks* and

---

*See the chapters below on "Musical Attributes" and "Verse Techniques" for a full discussion of metre, rhyme, and the sonnet-form.

†*Love* and *remove, come* and *doom, proved* and *loved* were pronounced in a fashion that made each pair rhymes in Shakespeare's day.

weeks, come and *doom.* The concluding lines, which make the final affirmation, are in rhyme: *proved* and *loved.*

Then we may observe a grammatical pattern in the poem. The third, fifth, and seventh lines each begin with a modifying clause: *Which alters . . ., That looks . . ., Whose worth's. . . .* There is, further, a rhetorical pattern. The fourth, eighth, and twelfth lines each contain an antithesis: *Or bends . . ., although his height . . ., But bears it out. . . .* *

This perfectly wrought architecture, moreover, which gives solidity of design to the poem, is wonderfully wedded to the ideas, to the inner experience which makes its way from doubt to certainty. Beginning in uncertainty, the first four lines deal with what love is not; with growing assurance, the next four lines deal with what love is; the next three lines dismiss false ideas about love; the twelfth, strongest of all these, asserts firmly what love is capable of sustaining. The concluding two lines are staunch in the confidence won by the preceding lines.

This sort of analysis is necessary if one is to procure the maximum from a literary work.[†] What did the author mean, then, in this sonnet? His meaning is a many-faceted combination of the aspects of the poem: its subject; its theme; its tone; its contents; the multiple associations of its imagery; its structure; its music. When the reader has realized all these (and understood, too, that it is actually impossible to catch everything in one's net), he may read the poem again and again, and discover the meaning of the poem in the synthesis he can make only after such an analysis. The meaning of the poem *is* the poem.

It is interesting to reflect that if we had any incontestable information about Shakespeare's private life which could be brought to bear upon this sonnet, it would probably help us hardly at all in extracting more meaning from the poem. It is, naturally, stimulating to know all we can about the biography of a creator. In the case of highly subjective writers (like Byron) it may even be valuable to know a great deal. But with so objective an artist as Shakespeare, biographical interest has little to contribute to our understanding of the man's works, and tends to become an end in itself. We know a great deal about Shakespeare, but what we know throws little light on his lines. As for the Sonnets, there is evidence that Shakespeare may have been addressing no particular persons in them; he may have imagined them for artistic purposes just as he imagined the men and women in his plays. But even if we could positively identify someone as the man addressed in the sonnet we have quoted and knew what the author's relationship to him was, that knowledge could not very much enrich what the lines say—if it could, indeed, enrich their meaning at all.

Even writers as autobiographical as Byron, once we have related what we know of their biography to a given work, must still be understood as writers and they can be understood as writers only through what their lines tell us. As we must see the work in its own lights, it becomes, at the end, actually necessary to detach what we have learned about an author's private life from what the work itself has to say. Otherwise we may see the poem in a false light and misjudge either its meaning or its quality as a poem. Byron's life was fairly public property in the nineteenth century, and the confusion between it and his work resulted in his being rather overrated as a poet. Because we view his life with quite different spectacles today, that same confusion has resulted in his being in our own time probably underrated. Such confusion between biography and a given work itself is a temptation to readers of any author.

*There is another antithesis in the ninth line, *though rosy lips . . .,* which is not part of the geometrical design involving lines four, eight and twelve. (An antithesis is an opposition of thoughts.)

[†]It is, of course, beyond the scope of the present work to make such an analysis of the various pieces we cite. That kind of inspection, it is hoped, the reader will choose to make for himself. Our business is to point out what is capable of analysis in works of literature. Our selections are used to illustrate literary principles. Here we have seen how structure operates in the meaning of a poem. But the analysis of structure depends on the analysis of the contents of a piece. There are therefore as many structures as there are works of literature, and the analysis of content must be a regular exercise for the reader.

A newspaper informs us that an unemployed plasterer, who had come five years earlier from Atlanta to settle in Chicago, has written a "eulogy" entitled "To One Whose Place Can Never Be Taken"—the reporter presumably meant "elegy"—to his wife, who had just died after giving birth to twins, "the couple's 22nd and 23rd children":

> As mother of 23 children,
> Your championship stands out bold;
> The toil of your hands and your worries—
> Of this not a half could be told.
>
> Let's pray you're over your suffering,
> Let's pray your worries are done.
> While in your sleep we all miss you,
> May this temper our own selfish fun.
>
> You guarded the lives of the little ones,
> So that death stayed away from our home,   10
> Yet still young in your forties, you leave us—
> On a trip to God's mystery dome.*

The newspaper account provides a number of affecting details concerning the condition of this author. He wrote his "tragic ode" (*sic*) in a "dim, dingy basement apartment." We are told that he is ailing himself, ever since he drank some "polluted water on a construction job" twelve years ago; "he has supported his family on $414 a month," a sum provided by welfare agencies, and with the additional help provided by his son-in-law; his married daughter "has vowed to care for" the fourteen youngsters still at home "along with her own four children." This daughter, twenty-two years of age, is firm in that intention and declares, "I'll fight anyone who comes to the door to take them. Because Mom begged me on her deathbed with her dying breath and tears in her eyes, 'Marie,' she cried, 'Marie— keep them together!' "

These biographical details might evoke an assortment of reactions among various readers: pity for the author, pity for the dead wife, pity for her possible successor, pity for the son-in-law, pity for Chicago's taxpayers, congratulations for Atlanta's taxpayers, wonder at the ailing author's stamina, admiration for his applied economics, recognition of Marie's respect for family tradition. But none of these reactions helps us with the "ode" itself. Nor are we helped by any of the wealth of biographical information surrounding its composition; we know, for example, rather more about this Marie than we do about either of Shakespeare's daughters.

This elegy also brings up the much-talked-about question of "sincerity." The sincerity of the author's feelings has been well documented by the newspaper article. We are informed not only about the dinginess of the place where the piece was written, but also that the author wrote "painfully, carefully," "hunched over his eulogy, his eyes still damp with his loss." We possess nothing remotely like this fullness of knowledge concerning the circumstances in which Shakespeare wrote his sonnet. Alas, after all, the sincerity of the former's emotions are irrelevant; the only kind of sincerity that can concern his readers is, as always, his artistic sincerity, the integrity with which he has spared himself no pains in shaping the work. Here both authors must stand the test of what the lines themselves reveal, whatever the originating intentions. Shakespeare's sonnet, by its success as a poem and as a sonnet, meets that test. We have only to consult the rightness of the work to be certain of its artistic sincerity.

What of "To One Whose Place Can Never Be Taken"? If we allow them to, certain of its expressions do bring up associations of meaning—*our own selfish fun,* for example. Here is ambiguity, it is conceded—but of the wrong kind, the kind that confuses, not

---

The New York World-Telegram and Sun, Nov. 10, 1958, Final Edition, p. 14.

enriches, the meaning. The associations conjured up by that phrase are rather unfortunate for the occasion. And *God's mystery dome,* although an unusual expression, presents an even more unlucky kind of ambiguity, for it defies all attempts at associated meanings. At the end, it seems more opaque than ambiguous. Despite all that we know of the author and the circumstances surrounding his lines, these two expressions are so unconvincing that they deprive the piece of artistic sincerity. The author was perhaps a little too quickly satisfied with that *dome.*

These two examples might lead one to conclude that everything outside a work is irrelevant to its meaning. So, indeed, do many contemporary critics insist. And we have considerable sympathy with their position, for it operates to emphasize the work itself, and to remind us that the meaning of the work is the work. But it is a view too extreme to be entirely true. There are occasions when one vastly enriches the lines by bringing certain information to the work itself. Let us take as an eloquent example this sonnet by John Milton (1608–1674):

> When I consider how my light is spent
> Ere half my days, in this dark world and wide,
> And that one talent which is death to hide
> Lodged with me useless, though my soul more bent
> To serve therewith my Maker, and present
> My true account, lest he returning chide;
> "Doth God exact day-labor, light denied?"
> I fondly ask. But Patience, to prevent
> That murmur, soon replies, "God doth not need
> Either man's work or his own gifts. Who best   10
> Bear his mild yoke, they serve him best. His state
> Is kingly; thousands at his bidding speed,
> And post o'er land and ocean without rest;
> They also serve who only stand and wait."

To begin with, even the most rigid excluder of biographical data from the appreciation of a work would have to admit that to understand this sonnet it is absolutely essential that the reader know

1. that the poet was blind when he wrote this sonnet and
2. that he took his calling as poet to be of cardinal importance, to be, indeed, the reason for his existence.

Without this information the first and third lines, respectively, could not be understood.

Moreover, although with this knowledge the reader can procure some meaning from the poem, he is nonetheless missing the most vital import of the first six lines unless he knows the Parable of the Talents, as told in Matthew 25:14, and also realizes that the allusion is to that parable. This is the little story itself:

For the kingdom of heaven is as a man traveling into a far country, who called his own servants, and delivered unto them his goods. And unto one he gave five talents, to another two, and to another one; to every man according to his several ability; and straightway took his journey. Then he that had received the five talents went and traded with the same, and made them other five talents. And likewise he that had received two, he also gained other two. But he that had received one went and digged in the earth, and hid his lord's money.

After a long time the lord of those servants cometh, and reckoneth with them. And so he that had received five talents came and brought other five talents, saying, Lord, thou deliveredst unto me five talents: behold, I have gained beside them five talents more. His lord said unto him, Well done, thou good and faithful servant; thou hast been faithful over a few things, I will make thee ruler over many things: enter thou into the joy of thy lord.

He also that had received two talents came and said, Lord, thou deliveredst unto me two talents:

behold, I have gained two other talents beside them. His lord said unto him, Well done, good and faithful servant: thou hast been faithful over a few things: enter thou into the joy of thy lord.

Then he which had received the one talent came and said, Lord, I knew thee that thou art an hard man, reaping where thou hast not sown, and gathering where thou hast not strawed: And I was afraid, and went and hid thy talent in the earth: lo, there thou hast that is thine.

His lord answered and said unto him, Thou wicked and slothful servant, thou knewest that I reap where I sowed not, and gather where I have not strawed: Thou oughtest therefore to have put my money to the exchangers, and then at my coming I should have received mine own with usury. Take therefore the talent from him, and give it unto him which hath ten talents. For unto every one that hath shall be given, and he shall have abundance: but from him that hath not shall be taken away even that which he hath. And cast ye the unprofitable servant into outer darkness: there shall be weeping and gnashing of teeth.

It is of the third servant, who hid his lord's money in the earth, that Milton is thinking; the analogy is with Milton's poetic gift, lying, because of his blindness, unused and useless within him. Our rigid critic would counter that this meaning is *in* Milton's lines by allusion; Milton, the critic would say quite validly, assumes, as is his right, that the reader is familiar with the story of the Talents. It would be, however, more accurate to say that Milton assumes that the reader knows the parable's details intimately; the poet's phraseology re-creates the details of the narrative in Matthew: "that *one* talent *which is death to hide*—Lodged with me *useless*—and *present my true account—lest he returning chide.*" It would be fair, in short, to counter in return that to know the parable that well is to bring something to the lines that is not in them. And to bring that much is to go away the richer, for the lines are made deeper in meaning by what one has brought to them.

Now, the subject of this sonnet having to do with Milton's blindness, let us cull some facts about that blindness from Milton's biography. Blindness is a dreadful affliction to any man; to Milton it must have been beyond calculation. This man was the greatest reader among world poets. By the time he became blind, at forty-four, he had at his command the Bible, the biblical commentaries, the writings of the Church Fathers, the literatures of England, Italy and France, as well as those of ancient Greece and Rome. He was, in addition, a skilled organist. As a brilliant poet, he was plainly a keen observer of the beauties of life. What must blindness have meant to such a man!

But more than all this, was the crucial issue of his career as a poet. His masterpiece, *Paradise Lost,* was a work planned for, prepared for, thought of ever since his youth. When only nineteen, Milton had decided to write an English poem in which the "deep transported mind" would soar to and "look in" at "Heaven's door," and that it should be on a subject equal in dignity to Homer's epics. Two years later he had begun to formulate principles of living such a stainless life as would prepare him for writing such an important poem. When composing on request his great lyric poem "Lycidas," at the age of twenty-nine, he complained of having to write before he was ready, but in its concluding lines promised again that the great poem to come would yet be written:

Tomorrow to fresh woods and pastures new.

However, beginning with his thirty-third year, Milton became enmeshed in important issues of religious, political, and personal liberty, and turned out a long series of prose writings on matters of urgency to the Puritans. For the next eleven years he gave his best energies to the Puritan cause, eventually holding office in Cromwell's government. Naturally, these labors gave him no time for the projected great poem—though passages in his pamphlets show that it was never absent from his thoughts. Finally, even his eyesight went in service to his political beliefs. Though warned of impending total blindness, he kept at his governmental tasks. At length it was that blindness which, forcing him to diminish his political labors, gave him time for himself again.

This sonnet was written three years after blindness had struck him. One gathers from it, by implication, the dismay and misery of those three years.

And now, turning again to both sonnet and parable, we realize that Milton in his poem was probing his conscience and examining the future. All his life had been a consecration to the great poem—even the pamphleteering for the Puritan cause to which he had devoted his eyes, for it had been an article of faith with him that the great poem could not be written if he ever turned his back on what he knew to be his duty. Now he was blind, and his great gift as a poet seemed buried useless within the darkness of his blindness just as that talent had been buried in the darkness of the earth. Would not God, asking for an accounting like the lord of the parable, chide him for having put that talent to no use? Would he be condemned like the foolish servant?

The noble conclusion of the sonnet turned out, in a few years, to have been justified. Regaining his self-assurance, somewhat through the writing of this sonnet, Milton began to dictate his great poem *Paradise Lost,* the fruit of all he knew, had experienced, believed, suffered and triumphed over.

It would be manifestly absurd to deprive oneself of the perspectives which these truths open for one when one brings them to a rereading of the sonnet. In the light of this knowledge, the connection with the parable means more, and the sonnet takes on a greater pathos and dignity. To deny oneself the added light that can be cast on a great work by the creator's biography is to be perverse indeed.

Obviously Milton's sonnet is a far different case from Shakespeare's. The more personal reference in Milton's makes biographical study for it inevitable; otherwise, because the poet makes no open statement of his blindness in the poem, we do not have the knowledge with which to understand fully the situation the sonnet describes. The more objective point of view in Shakespeare's sonnet makes such biographical study fairly superfluous.

But in Milton's case, no less than in Shakespeare's, it is to the lines themselves we must return. Carrying with us all that we have learned, we must seek for the author's meaning in his words. Not to do this is to treat him as less than an author; the literary values to which we ought to respond are in his work, not in his biography. From the reader's point of view the writer becomes in the last analysis only the agent through whom the meaning of the lines came into being. And that meaning, we repeat, is in the author's words and the form in which they are molded.

Let us now turn to them.

THE BEGINNING: LANGUAGE

∞ 2 ∞

IN THE BEGINNING is the word.

A sculptor begins with stone or clay; a painter with pigments and with canvas, panel or wall. The material with which the writer begins and must work is words. It is with words only that he can shape his thought, with words only that he as a writer can communicate.

Stone or clay, pigments, canvas, panel, wall, and words are realities in themselves. They have their own existence before the creator has need of them. If he is to "use" them, he can do so only because he comes to grips with them, because he understands clearly their own terms of existence.

A sculptor is limited in what he can carve out of stone by the size and shape of the given piece of stone; many sculptors will assure you that the size and shape of the stone will suggest the subject to the sculptor, and will direct the form of the finished work. If he is working in clay, the sculptor is limited in what he shapes by the extent to which clay can be massed into one piece without falling apart. A painter is limited in the picture he can paint by the size and shape of the canvas, panel, or wall on which he is painting; he could not, obviously, paint the identical picture on a rectangular, a square, or an oval space. He is further limited by the fact that certain colors will harmonize with others, while certain colors will clash with one another.

THE WRITER'S MEDIUM

A writer is similarly limited by words. Though there are, indeed, some words whose associated meanings are beyond count, every word is circumscribed by that vast number of meanings with which it cannot be or resists being associated.* Each word seems more or less planted on the territory of its possible meanings and associations. With these the writer either comes to terms or wrestles.

Every word, too, has its own size, shape, color, and potential music. Some words—in English they are legion—are one-syllabled; others have two, three, four or more syllables. Some monosyllables are bound to sound unemphatic (*a, the, of*) except under unusual circumstances; others are bound to sound important (*sword, true, straight*); many could be one or the other. Words of more than one syllable have an inevitable stress on a particular syllable. Various vowels and consonants have varying effects upon the ear; their arrangement

---

*The attempt to bring words into associations which they seem to resist is, of course, an inviting challenge to writers. For a remarkable example of such a challenge met, see the sonnet by John Donne, page 63.

46

in a word gives the word its own character. Such considerations have to do with what is part of the word itself, and must be accepted by the writer as part of the word not subject to change—and these are all matters of consequence to him.

Much more vital still is what happens to a word in combination with other words. The true significance of a word is conditioned by the other words with which it keeps company in a given piece of writing. The word *arise,* for instance, is of little interest by itself; it takes on a wealth of meaning in the combinations of this line from Isaiah 60:1:

> Arise, shine, for thy light is come, and the glory of the Lord is risen upon thee.

Now the meaning of the word is conditioned and expanded by the words following it; its meaning is further amplified by the effect of the four long *i*'s in succession (*Arise, shine, thy light*) which help impart a wonderful radiance to the whole line. Again, the words *bought, sold,* and *mansion* when thought of in combination suggest a situation in real estate of no literary excitement; nevertheless, Shakespeare thought otherwise while he was writing *Romeo and Juliet,* III/ii/26–28. Juliet, after her marriage to Romeo, is waiting impatiently for her lover, and cries:

> O, I have bought the mansion of a love,
> But not possessed it; and though I am sold,
> Not yet enjoyed.

In such a setting these words take on completely new significance, and become a source of great imaginative energy. It is in combination, then, that words are the writer's medium.

DENOTATION AND CONNOTATION

Words have various attributes. Let us consider one of these attributes.

The poet Alexander Pope (1688–1744) once gave a royal friend the gift of a dog, and composed for its collar a malicious little inscription. One can imagine the astonishment of the courtier who, bending to stroke the pet, read Pope's epigram:

> I am his Highness' dog at Kew;
> Pray tell me, sir, whose dog are you?

The first line, with its calm statement of fact, surely ill prepared the reader for the shocker in the second. The effect was achieved by putting the word *dog* to two different uses.

In the first line Pope plainly used the word to mean a four-footed "carnivorous domesticated mammal"—as the dictionary defines it. But in the second line the same word means something quite different—the various associations which experience has attached to the position of the domesticated mammal in a household: its fawning, subservience, anxiety to please, readiness to obey orders, and eagerness for stray crumbs and bones.

Language, thus, can be used in one of these two ways. In the first line *dog* is used in a *denotative* fashion—that is, in its basic dictionary meaning. In the second line it is used in a connotative fashion—that is, for its associational values.

The denotative use of a word calls upon our knowledge of what object or concept is precisely signified by the word; its connotative use evokes associations from our experience (real or imagined) with that object or concept.

When Emily Dickinson (1830–1886) wrote:

> I never saw a Moor—
> I never saw the Sea—
> Yet I know how the Heather looks
> And what a Billow be . . .

she was employing *moor, sea, heather* and *billow* in the basic meanings the dictionary allots them, their denotative meanings. On the other hand, the author of these lines:

> Although his discourse was a barren moor,
> It left me all at sea. . . .

meant by *moor* not (as Emily Dickinson did) an "extensive area of waste ground," but rather the desolateness and dreariness one finds in such an area of waste ground; by *at sea* he did not mean that he was physically on "one of the larger bodies of salt water," but rather that he was suffering the lack of direction, the sense of being lost which one has when cast adrift on such a body of water.

Even such concepts as Heaven and Hell are capable of either treatment in words. The scientist Whitehead remarks that

> in the early medieval times, Heaven was in the sky, and Hell was underground;
> volcanoes were the jaws of Hell.

—clearly a denotative use of the words. But when the historian Green records of England's Elizabeth I that

> No adulation was too fulsome for her, no flattery of her beauty too gross. To
> see her was Heaven, Hatton told her; the lack of her was Hell.

—he is quoting Hatton's connotative use of the same words.

Again, when Carlyle affectionately spoke of Samuel Johnson as a "moving rag-and-dust mountain," he was not using language in the denotative sense with which a meticulous young lady, Miss Harriet Fogg of Wilmington, Vermont—an outdoor girl if ever there was one! —wrote that

> when Euphemia said she was at last ready for our mountainclimb up old
> Hogback, I tore up a pillowcase as a rag to wipe the dust from our food-
> hamper.

In *The Merchant of Venice* when Portia exclaims:

> That light we see is burning in my hall.
> How far that little candle throws his beams!

Shakespeare is employing the denotative meaning of *candle,* "a cylindrical mass of tallow or wax with a wick through its centre, which gives light when burned." However, when Macbeth, tired and disenchanted with life, cries:

> . . . all our yesterdays have lighted fools
> The way to dusty death. Out, out, brief candle!

—he is made to use the same word connotatively with a host of associated meanings.

As we have seen, any given author may in different places use language now one way, now the other. Some writers, however, tend toward one manner because of temperamental preference. Jonathan Swift, perhaps our greatest master of the denotative style, is likely to use words almost exclusively in their basic dictionary meanings. This little passage from *Gulliver's Travels* exhibits his preference:

> The two horses came up close to me, looking with great earnestness upon my
> face and hands. The grey steed rubbed my hat all round with his right forehoof,
> and discomposed it so much that I was forced to adjust it better, by taking it
> off and settling it again; whereat both he and his companion (who was a brown
> bay) appeared much surprized.

It is to be noted that although the subject matter of this piece, as indeed of all of *Gulliver's Travels,* shows an exercise of fancy, there is nothing fanciful in the use of the words. The effect of such language is to make us feel that we are being addressed logically, that our reason is called upon to function actively. Everything is clear, nothing needs to be reconsidered for overtones we may have missed. There are no overtones. Everything stands sharply revealed in an unwavering light, without shadow.

For certain kinds of literary expression this denotative language is perfect. It has the great virtues of clarity, precision, and directness—qualities highly prized by classic taste—and there are occasions when these are the qualities any author absolutely requires. But denotative language has its very real limitations too.

There are times when the writer wishes to call less upon our rational faculties than upon our imaginations—as the romanticist characteristically prefers to do—times when he has no need of the clear light, the precision, the directness of denotative language. On such occasions he may require shadow as well as light, innuendo rather than directness. His best meaning, indeed, may now be communicated chiefly by overtones: we may be asked to read him more between his lines than in them. Such are the times when a writer will be employing the connotative resources of language.

Thus, Truman Capote gives us a picture of the journey through night made by a lonely boy in an old wagon drawn by a mule and driven by a "gnomish little Negro," Jesus Fever; the thought occurs to the boy, bound for a new and unknown home, that all the people he had met today

> were perhaps what he'd first imagined: apparitions. He touched his cheek, the corn-husks, glanced at the sleeping Jesus—the old man was trance-like but for his body's rubbery response to the wagon's jolting—and was reassured. The guide reins jangled, the hoofbeats of the mule made a sound as drowsy as a fly's bzzz on a summer afternoon. A jungle of stars rained down to cover him in blaze, to blind and close his eyes. Arms akimbo, legs crumpled, lips vaguely parted—he looked as if sleep had struck him with a blow.*

In the first lines the boy is trying to establish for himself the reality of his surroundings; it is not surprising, therefore, that the author begins with using words for the most part in their basic dictionary sense. *Apparitions, cheek, corn-husks, old man, wagon's jolting, guide reins jangled, hoofbeats of the mule, fly's bzzz, summer afternoon* are all used in their sharp denotative sense. But the actual hoofbeats of the mule do make a drowsy sound, and the drowsiness begins to change the tone, begins to bring back the wonder, mystery, and magic with which the passage opened. To recapture those tones, Capote suddenly employs a powerful language of connotation: *a jungle of stars, rained down, to cover him, in blaze, to blind . . . his eyes, legs crumpled, sleep had struck him with a blow.* How distant is the use of this last group of words from what would be their basic dictionary meanings:

jungle of stars: land covered with dense growth of trees and tall vegetation, etc.—in this case, such an area in the stars.

rained down: descended in the form of water falling to the earth in drops that have been condensed from the moisture in the atmosphere.

to cover him: to place over him in order to hide or protect him.

in blaze: in a brilliant mass or burst of flame.

to blind . . . his eyes: to take away his eyesight.

legs crumpled: legs crushed together into creases or wrinkles.

sleep had struck him with a blow: sleep had hit him with the hand or with a tool or weapon in the hand, with a sudden forcible effort.

To read these beautiful phrases denotatively as above, is to make them absurd. As the author has composed them, we are called upon to take them wholly in their associational values. And how marvelously, so read, do they stir our imagination! Suddenly we become the awestruck boy himself, and feel what he has felt. Such can be the power of connotative language in literature.

*From *Other Voices, Other Rooms*, Part I, Chap. I.

Let us now banish the magic of that star-bathed night, and alter the mood. We are of a mind, let us say, to inveigh against the inconvenience of having poor relations. Let us begin an essay on the subject:

> A poor relation is the most useless object in the world. He annoys you with his impudent and unasked-for letters. He is forever calculating the cost of your modest possessions. His own condition makes you constantly feel guilty about his poverty. When you have achieved a little security or success, his presence is enough to rob you of your pleasure in them. Without any suggestion from you he is always recollecting the family's past. His every visit is embarrassing. He constantly applies to you for a loan. He challenges any claims to pride you may feel. He is a hindrance to your success and seems forever to be calling it into question. He is a disgrace to your family and your common forebears. He makes it utterly impossible to cut a figure before the world or to be merry in it. He is a reminder of everything you prefer to forget. He is a busybody in all your concerns. He is an unending threat to your peace of mind, contentment, joy; a disturbance to your conscience; a source of glee to your foes and a nuisance to your well-wishers. He is utterly superfluous and ruinous.

Now see what a master-stylist can do with such notions through a brilliant use of connotative language. This is the opening paragraph of Charles Lamb's (1775–1834) essay on "Poor Relations":

> A poor Relation—is the most irrelevant thing in nature,—a piece of impertinent correspondency,—an odious approximation,—a haunting conscience,—a preposterous shadow, lengthening in the noontide of our prosperity,—an unwelcome remembrancer,—a perpetually recurring mortification,—a drain upon your purse,—a more intolerable dun upon your pride,—a drawback upon success,—a rebuke to your rising,—a stain in your blood,—a blot on your scutcheon,—a rent in your garment,—a death's head at your banquet,—Agathocles' pot,[1]—a Mordecai in your gate,[2]—a Lazarus at your door,[3]—a lion in your path,—a frog in your chamber,—a fly in your ointment,—a mote in your eye,—a triumph to your enemy,—an apology to your friends,—the one thing not needful,—the hail in harvest,—the ounce of sour in a pound of sweet.

It will be noted that these lines say a vast deal more than those of our own flat paragraph. Every expression evokes a flood of related notions. More, the connotative qualities of every expression cause the paragraph to assume a merrier and merrier tone as it proceeds, until it ends in a mounting rhythm of hilarity. Our own paragraph might conceivably be thought faintly amusing in intention, though one could never be sure; certainly there is no mirth in the lines themselves. In Lamb's prose we quickly perceive that he is having fun with his subject; as a consequence, its rising thunder becomes deliberately absurd, and we understand that his anger is all simulated—that there is no callousness in the pretended attack.

Lamb's whimsical temperament inevitably directed him to this connotative use of language, which, moreover, gave him scope to indulge his delight in puns and quibbles. There is a droll play on words at the beginning, between *relation* and *irrelevant* (unrelated)—a quibble that invites us to a number of amusing thoughts and images. Such too is the case with "odious approximation." With *approximation* Lamb may very well be invoking all these meanings at once:

[1] Agathocles, tyrant of ancient Sicily, could not bear the sight of a pot because it was a reminder that his father had been only a potter.

[2] In order to keep track of what was happening to his relative Esther, Mordecai hung about the palace-gates of King Ahasuerus. (Esther 3:1–2; 5:11–12)

[3] This is a reference to the beggar who stood by the portals of a wealthy man to beg for the crumbs from the table. (Luke 16:20)

1. The action of coming near or close to
2. (In medicine) communication of a disease by contact
3. An approach to a correct estimate
4. A process of solving problems in mathematics

Though the first is the word's basic meaning, since the poor relation is not an "action" but a man or a woman, this becomes a figurative and connotative use of language. Calling a human being an action, a communication, an approach, or a process is in itself comic. The fact that the medical definition is obsolete would only have recommended it to Lamb.

Such many-sided use of language—an artistic ambiguity which invites several interpretations at once—of course adds dimension to the passage. So do the pictures which Lamb flashes in rapid succession before us: the stain, the blot, the rent, the death's head, the frog, the fly, the mote, the hail—all of them, since the poor relation is *in fact* none of these, connotations. And not the least effective of the pictures are those furnished by the brilliant literary allusions—effective, that is, to those either well informed enough to know or else eager enough to look up the reference—: Agathocles, turning away with a shudder every time anyone crosses his horizon with a pot in hand; Mordecai, forever lingering about the King's gates, eavesdropping on everything being said within earshot; Lazarus the beggar, full of leprous sores, lying at the rich man's door, daring to be ignored.

There is, naturally, no question here of respective merit between denotative and connotative language. It is the *differences* (between language which appeals to the rational and language which appeals to the imaginative apprehension of words) which we are emphasizing. Indeed, in the last two quotations we have cited we find both kinds, and both have their own kind of power. *He touched his cheek, the guide reins jangled, the hoofbeats of the mule, a fly's bzzz on a summer afternoon, a jungle of stars rained down to cover him in blaze, arms akimbo, legs crumpled, sleep had struck him with a blow, a stain in your blood, a death's head at your banquet, a fly in your ointment*— some of these are denotative, some connotative, yet both have also some *equal* source of power. What is this source? Why, too, are we likely to be equally impressed, once we associate the man hounded by a poor relation with Agathocles turning away shudderingly from a slave crossing the room, pot in hand? The answer is obvious. All of these expressions make a strong appeal to our senses. A picture is flashed before us in which we *see* the boy touch his cheek, see the stars rain down to cover the old man in a blaze, see the arms akimbo and legs crumpled, see the death's head at a banquet, see the fly in the ointment, see Agathocles turn away with a shudder. So too we *hear* the reins jangle, hear the hoofbeats of the mule, hear the fly's bzzz. Our apprehension of what we are reading thus becomes immediate, vivid, and therefore powerful.

ABSTRACT AND CONCRETE LANGUAGE

Let us consider the following passage from William Dean Howells (1837–1920):

> I would have our American novelists be as American as they consciously can. Matthew Arnold complained that he found no "distinction" in our life, and I would gladly persuade all artists intending greatness in any kind among us that the recognition of the fact pointed out by Mr. Arnold ought to be a source of inspiration to them, and not discouragement. We have been now some hundred years building up a state on the affirmation of the essential equality of men in their rights and duties, and whether we have been right or been wrong the gods have taken us at our word, and have responded to us with a civilization in which there is no "distinction" perceptible to the eye that loves and values it. Such beauty and grandeur as we have is common beauty, common grandeur, or the beauty and grandeur in which the quality of solidarity so prevails that neither distinguishes itself to the disadvantage of

anything else. It seems to me that these conditions invite the artist to the study and the appreciation of the common, and to the portrayal in every art of those finer and higher aspects which unite rather than sever humanity, if he would thrive in our new order of things.*

Certainly this piece lacks the immediacy and vividness of the passages from Swift, Lamb and Capote. Here Howells, addressing himself to American novelists, is talking exclusively in the realm of intellectual concepts. He has nothing to depict or paint, and consequently it does not occur to him to use the kind of language we have seen in Swift, Capote or Lamb. Examining his passage, we perceive that the differences between it and the others is once more a matter of language. But this time it is not a question of the *way* words are used but rather of the *kind* of words which are chosen.

Looking at words from this point of view now, we note that there are two kinds from which an author may select his vocabulary. One class may be represented by such words as *truth, beauty, idea, loyalty;* the other by such words as *chair, desk, tree, Charles Lamb, boy.* The first class consists of words which express a concept apart from any particular or material instance; we call such words *abstract.* The second class consists of words which designate a thing or happening or class of things or happenings which can be perceived by our senses; we call such words *concrete.* The abstract word *truth* presents nothing to our senses; the concrete word *chair* does.

If we take a closer look at the passage from Howells, we shall find a considerable number of abstract words: *distinction, life, greatness, kind, recognition, fact, source, inspiration, discouragement, state, affirmation, equality, rights, duties, right, wrong, civilization, beauty, grandeur, solidarity, distinguishes, disadvantage, conditions, study, appreciation, the common, portrayal, art, aspects, order.* For abstract ideas the author has chosen abstract words. We commonly meet with this kind of language in books of philosophy and economics; in literature, as in the present instance, we sometimes find it dominant in critical discussions. The effect of such abstract language is to keep us in a region of pure, non-experiential thought.

In certain kinds of scientific speculation, no doubt, abstract language is demanded. But it would be wrong to suppose that this is universally the case. Consider, for instance, this meditation of the scientist Charles Darwin (1809–1882):

The main conclusion arrived at in this work, namely that man is descended from some lowly organized form, will, I regret to think, be highly distasteful to many. But there can hardly be a doubt that we are descended from barbarians. The astonishment I felt on first seeing a party of Feugians on a wild and broken shore will never be forgotten by me, for the reflection at once rushed into my mind—such were our ancestors. These men were absolutely naked and bedaubed with paint, their long hair was tangled, their mouths frothed with excitement, and their expression was wild, startled, and distrustful. They possessed hardly any arts, and like wild animals lived on what they could catch; they had no government, and were merciless to every one not of their own small tribe. He who has seen a savage in his native land will not feel much shame, if forced to acknowledge that the blood of some more humble creature flows in his veins. For my own part I would as soon be descended from that heroic little monkey, who braved his dreaded enemy to save the life of his keeper, or from that old baboon, who descending from the mountains, carried away in triumph his young comrade from a crowd of astonished dogs—as from a savage who delights to torture his enemies, offers up bloody sacrifices, practices infanticide without remorse, treats his wives like slaves, knows no decency, and is haunted by grossest superstitions.†

In Darwin's lines we again find expressions at the opposite pole from Howells'. The language is mostly concrete throughout: *descended, regret, highly distasteful, astonishment, first seeing, party of Feugians, wild, broken, shore, rushed, naked, bedaubed with paint, long hair, tangled, mouths frothed, wild animals, catch, merciless, not of their own small tribe, feel*

*From *Criticism and Fiction.*   †From *The Descent of Man,* Conclusion.

much shame, blood, flows, veins, heroic little monkey, braved, dreaded, save, keeper, old baboon, mountains, carried away in triumph, young, crowd, astonished dogs, torture, offers up bloody sacrifices, practices infanticide without remorse, treats his wives like slaves, haunted. Such concrete language refers the train of ideas presented to our sensuous experience; once more, what is being said takes on considerable vividness and immediacy for us. We are likely to have to wrestle more with abstract writing like Howells' just because our senses are left out. That is why a textbook written in abstract language—as for instance a textbook on economics—is for most of us the hardest kind to digest; there is so little for us to sink our teeth into.

We may further note that the concreteness of an expression can be more or less intense. For instance, *mind* and *rushed* are both concrete words; but *rushed into my mind* is much more specific than *thought* would have been (or, perhaps, *occurred to me*), and therefore more vivid than the other possible alternatives.

Conversely, the following expressions beginning Howells' paragraph, though concrete, are too general to be very vivid: *American novelists, American, as they consciously can, artists.* None of these enables us to see or feel much. That is not necessarily an objection to his passage since his purpose was to be strictly logical. Nevertheless, if it were true that this paragraph were quite representative of Howells' prose, we should be prone to declare Darwin more the literary man of the two. For literature is primarily concerned, as we have said, with recording the complex experiences of Man in relation to his God, Nature, other human beings, and/or himself; and in such experiences our sensuous perceptions play an important role. The truth about Howells is that, able novelist as he is, the vocabulary of this particular passage is not characteristic of his prose. Rather, it is typical of any writer advancing an abstract argument. Yet even the author of a textbook on economics, the very nature of which is abstract, after speaking about capital, labor, wages, and marginal returns, will, if he is wise, take pity on his reader and insert some concrete passage like "When I bring a piece of cloth to a tailor—." Such an expression recaptures the wavering attention, and makes us sigh with relief, "Ah, at last!" with something of the gratitude felt by a lost wanderer in the desert on sighting an oasis. A judicious sprinkling of concrete expressions which instantly flash pictures upon the mind—the language, as it is called in literary terms, of *imagery*—in the midst of long sections of abstract discussion helps us renew our concentration. It is interesting to note that Darwin, scientist though he was, was writing in the selection quoted like a man of letters.

COMMUNICATION THROUGH IMAGERY

Concrete language is indispensable to the man of letters, for concrete words are the stuff out of which images are made; and images in literature are the source of vividness, power, and immediacy of meaning. From abstract expression no images emerge.

Imagery can be either of two kinds: *literal* or *figurative.* Imagery is literal when the images are to be taken in their natural or strict meaning; imagery is figurative when the meaning is an extension of the image presented.

Clever news reporters are also aware of the value of imagery in capturing our imagination. Here is a lively summary of the problems of New York City in the illegal importation of murder weapons in 1974:

> About a half-mile out of Greenville, S.C., a sign proclaims "Discounts on Guns, Ammo, Fireworks." The sign draws attention to a one-story stucco-and-brick store called Roberts Trading Post. On February 15, 1972, Richard Thrift, Jr., a fair-haired, 22-year-old native of South Carolina, did some shopping at Roberts Trading Post. At about nine o'clock that morning, he walked through the screen door and put six crisp hundred-dollar bills and four twenties on the glass display counter. He chatted with the owner's son, Blakely,

then got busy signing a pile of federal forms. In the meantime, Blakely went to the back storeroom, took out 5 cartons containing 90 handguns and loaded them into Thrift's station wagon. [After 6 more visits Thrift that day bought "a total of 241 handguns." 42 states do not restrict such sales; nothing of Thrift's transactions "was illegal." But Thrift "had friends."] In the early morning of February 9, 1973, a man was shot and killed in the South Bronx in a dispute. . . . On March 3, 1973, the police picked up a 17-year-old youth in Harlem because they thought he was selling heroin. . . . They found a handgun in his boot. On March 27, 1973, a man was arrested [in Brooklyn] . . . after he allegedly threatened someone with a handgun . . . 8 days after that, someone used a handgun to put 2 bullets into a police officer [in the Bronx]. . . . The next day, another kid was picked up carrying a handgun in a school-yard . . . in the South Bronx. Each of the weapons . . . [and those involved in 10 similar actions in New York] Thrift had bought from Roberts Trading Post, February 15, 1972.*

Composed largely of concrete expression (*half-mile, sign, one-story stucco-and-brick store, fair-haired, shopping, nine o'clock, screen door, six crisp, etc.*) that vividly creates imagery, this account stirs our imagination (and indignation), and ends by causing us to be gravely concerned, as is plainly the writer's intention.

"Our imaginations are stirred. Well and good," we can hear certain readers prepared to ask, "but is there any need of analyzing *why* they are stirred? What is the value of your insistence on every page of this book that we must learn to identify the literary stimulus occasioning our response? Isn't it enough that we do respond?"

Well, I reply, the response is certainly the important thing. But there is also a question as to whether you, the reader, may not be overlooking treasures right under your nose just because you may not recognize them for what they are. We can commend the enthusiast who eagerly picks up a pretty colored stone among pebbles and rocks; but we are bound to deplore his blindness if, in his excitement over the obvious, he overlooks a diamond or an emerald close at hand only because he has not learned what they look like.

If you develop the habit of understanding what it is that evokes imaginative excitement, and, further, what it is that evokes feebler and what it is that evokes more powerful reaction to words you are reading, you inevitably will become more alert to the potentialities of literature—and hence to the potentialities of literature for becoming rewarding to you.

And when you have attained that alertness you can, moreover, part company with the ignorant who think to corner you with a supercilious, "How can you *tell* that a work (or a passage) is good?" For you will be on the road to answering for yourself what is not so impossible to answer after all. To those who have acquired it, literary taste is no mythical possession; it is as real as their good right arm. But it takes patience and thought to come by it. You are, we hope, already en route.

Apart, too, from sheer esthetic pleasure, it might be of considerable intellectual value to recognize in such writing as the news analysis quoted and in such orations as we hear from politicians, just how much of our excitement has been purely literary. When we know why we are stimulated, we are less likely to fall into the errors of mob hysteria. This is not to suggest that we object to the comments of the news analyst, but only that we are in the best possible relation to them when, in the midst of our approval or pleasure, we recognize literary devices for what they are.

Poetry and prose, particularly literary prose, as we have seen, both use imagery. But since, generally speaking, ideas in prose are presented more or less with some kind of logical sequence, imagery is somewhat less generic to prose than to poetry. With most poets imagery has been the very lifeblood of their poetry. The long history of great poetry has been the

*From *New York Magazine*, April 8, 1974.

history of a species of communication much more intense, more condensed, more compact, more vivid, more stirring to the imagination than is possible in prose. And that kind of communication is achieved only by communication through imagery. In consequence, while in prose the image is often the riveter of our attention or the welcome oasis in the desert —in poetry the image becomes the tissue itself of the poet's thought. On the whole, the best prose is content to give us much to dwell upon; the best poetry aims to afford a revelation.

Consciously or unconsciously Shakespeare may have had in mind these distinctions between poetry and prose and between abstractions and concreteness when he wrote the celebrated Forum Scene in *Julius Caesar* (III/ii). In that scene both Brutus and Mark Antony have their turns in trying to sway the minds of the crowd collected in the Forum after the assassination of Caesar. Brutus has killed Caesar, despite their close friendship, because he believed Caesar to be an enemy to the ancient liberties of Rome; his act was committed in defiance of personal feelings, on purely ideological grounds. He is confident of having acted with reason and justice, and he is equally certain that that reason and justice have only to be announced to the crowd to be understood. When he addresses the crowd it is in the words of a man conscious of his own integrity, appealing to the intelligence of his hearers. Though most of the play is in verse, Shakespeare has cast this speech of his hero in prose.

> Romans, countrymen, and lovers![1] hear me for my cause, and be silent, that you may hear: believe me for mine honor, and have respect to[2] mine honor, that you may believe: censure[3] me in your wisdom, and awake your senses that you may the better judge. If there be any in this assembly, any dear friend of Caesar's, to him I say that Brutus' love to Caesar was no less than his. . . . As Caesar loved me, I weep for him; as he was fortunate, I rejoice at it: as he was valiant I honor him: but as he was ambitious, I slew him. There is tears for his love; joy for his fortune; honor for his valor; and death for his ambition.

It is as though Brutus disdained to make other than a philosophical appeal. Hence the prose. And hence the abstractions: *cause, honor, assembly* (less abstract in effect because of *this*), *love, fortunate, valiant, ambitious, fortune, valor, ambition.* The effect is what Brutus intends: a reasonable man addressing reasonable men.

However, when Antony takes his place to speak it is no philosopher but a skilled politician who addresses the crowd. His purposes are not to convince but to inflame:

> Friends, Romans, countrymen, lend me your ears:
> I come to bury Caesar, not to praise him . . .
> You all did see that on the Lupercal
> I thrice presented him a kingly crown,
> Which he did thrice refuse: was this ambition? . . .
> My heart is in the coffin there with Caesar,
> And I must pause till it come back to me . . .
> But yesterday the word of Caesar might
> Have stood against the world: now lies he here,
> And none so poor to do him reverence . . .   10
> But here's a parchment with the seal of Caesar;
> I found it in his closet;[1] tis his will:
> Let but the commons hear this testament—
> Which, pardon me, I do not mean to read—
> And they would go and kiss dead Caesar's wounds,
> And dip their napkins[2] in his sacred blood,

[1]Friends.   [1]Private chamber.

[2]Think over well.   [2]Handkerchiefs.

[3]Judge.

Yea, beg a hair of him for memory,
And, dying, mention it within their wills . . .
You are not wood, you are not stones, but men;
And being men, hearing the will of Caesar,
It will inflame you, it will make you mad . . .   20
I have o'ershot myself to tell you of it:
I fear I wrong the honorable men
Whose daggers have stabbed Caesar; I do fear it . . .
You will compel me, then, to read the will?
Then make a ring about the corpse of Caesar,
And let me show you him that made the will . . .
If you have tears prepare to shed them now.
You all do know this mantle: I remember
The first time ever Caesar put it on;   30
'Twas on a summer's evening, in his tent,
The day he overcame the Nervii.[3]
Look, in this place ran Cassius' dagger through:
See what a rent the envious Casca made:[4]
Through this the well-beloved Brutus stabbed;
And as he plucked his cursed steel away,
Mark how the blood of Caesar followed it,
As rushing out of doors, to be resolved[5]
If Brutus so unkindly[6] knocked, or no;
For Brutus, as you know, was Caesar's angel;[7]   40
Judge, O you gods, how dearly Caesar loved him!
This was the most unkindest[8] cut of all;
For when the noble Caesar saw him stab,
Ingratitude, more strong than traitor's arms,
Quite vanquished him: then burst his mighty heart;[9]
And, in his mantle muffling up his face,
Even at the base of Pompey's statue,
Which all the while ran blood, great Caesar fell.

He has spoken in verse studded with powerful images. This is perhaps the most brilliant piece of demagoguery in literature. When Antony began, his hearers were muttering, after Brutus' oration, "This Caesar was a tyrant"; "We are blest that Rome is rid of him." But the wily Antony so manages to turn the crowd against its own self-interest, that before he is through he has his audience screaming, "Most noble Caesar! We'll revenge his death": "Go fetch fire!"

Brutus had called upon his hearers to reflect, to take a philosophic stand on the question of liberty. His speech was not, of course, without its own emotional appeal—largely due to the rhythmic balance of his phrases. But his argument was in the realm of the abstract.

Resourceful Antony, on the other hand, overlooks no opportunity to capitalize on the tangible and the immediate. He uses, like props in a theatre, everything available: the coffin,

[3]The three preceding lines with their apparent irrelevancy about Caesar's mantle and the summer evening seem to call for soft music. But they are shrewdly calculated to lead up to the reference to Caesar's great victory over the Nervii, for which all Rome had occasion to be jubilant.

[4]The concreteness here causes his hearers to forget to wonder how Antony could possibly identify the wounds made by the various conspirators!

[5]To be assured.

[6]Inhumanly.

[7]Caesar's guardian angel; his better self.

[8]Most inhuman.

[9]Apparently none of the many other wounds had taken effect, according to Antony!

the parchment containing the will, Caesar's mantle, the various rents made by the daggers —singled out, one by one—Pompey's statue, and finally Caesar's uncovered corpse itself. Though not one of these refutes Brutus' argument, all of them are concrete beyond the power of any words over the mob, for they are there to be seen.

And in Antony's words there is no more pretense to reason or logical argument than in those tangibles. He plays upon the emotions of the crowd, employing the stronger rhythms of poetry, and, for his own ends, puts imagery to more energetic use than Brutus did through the use of a higher proportion of concrete words: *lend me your ears, I come to bury Caesar, I thrice presented him, a kingly crown, he did thrice refuse, my heart is in the coffin there, I must pause, till it come back to me, the word of Caesar might have stood against the world, now lies he here* [*etc. etc.*]. These words are also accompanied by powerful movements and gestures, inflaming his audience by their visual incitements—waving the will before the mob, bidding them make a ring about Caesar's body, plucking up a corner of Caesar's mantle, and at last throwing off the cloak to disclose the bleeding corpse. He has little title to his hypocritical claim of being

> no orator, as Brutus is.

He is not the "plain blunt man" he pretends to be. He is a dangerous politician, complete master of the image and theatrical effects, and very adept in wielding their power well for his own ends. (These ends do not include acts friendly to the liberties of Rome!)

Of course, his speech is not devoid of abstractions; with mounting sarcasm, for example, he reiterates the idea that

> Brutus is an honorable man

and reminds the crowd of Brutus' declaration that

> Caesar was ambitious.

The very indefiniteness of such abstractions, which supply nothing to disprove the truth of the first or deny that of the second, allows the mob to be led by the tone of his voice, and reinforces the emotional fever of his theatrical props and gestures—an indefiniteness which all the more forces attention upon the concretenesses surrounding it. For the scant, but highly effective, abstractions in his oration are completely overshadowed by the imagery with which he wins over the mob.

On the other hand, the oration of Brutus contains a number of concrete expressions. We should not have expected him to employ a textbook prose; and since his is a literary style of high order we meet inevitably with concrete phrases: *Romans, countrymen, lovers; hear me; be silent; have respect to; I weep; I rejoice.* The effect of these is to lend vivacity to the prose, which is still distant from the emotional sweep of Antony's verse. It might be said in conclusion that the concretenesses in Brutus' oration help the apprehension of his abstract presentation, and that the abstractions in Antony's seem to give an air of reasonableness to the rabble-rousing emotionalism of his imagery.

Now, images vary considerably in their intrinsic power. Some images can overwhelm us. The effect of some, however, can be quite pallid. Let us consider "Song LXX" of Susanna Harrison:

> Lord, is it not my soul's desire
> To honor thee in all my ways?
> O let thy grace my heart inspire,
> So shall thy grace have all the praise.
>
> Thou know'st I'm ignorant and weak,
> Prone to prefer the thing that's wrong;

> I often think, and often speak,
> And then reprove my heart and tongue. . . .*

If you were asked to describe the tone of this piece you might say, as we do, that it is anemic. In assessing the energy of literature there is never a question of the sincerity of the author or speaker involved. We must not infer from the example of Antony's oration that there is any connection between his indifference to logic or sincerity and his use of imagery; our point was merely that Antony was using the persuasive power of imagery to its fullest. In the case of Miss Susanna Harrison, the reader is assured by her publisher of her complete sincerity. "Suffice it to say of this publication," he tells us, "that the author of it is a very obscure young woman, and quite destitute of the advantages of education, as well as under great bodily affliction." She worked as a domestic until she became a victim of disorders which have baffled physicians. But God "has been instructing her from that time in the things pertaining to his kingdom," as the poems in the volume "witness. But such is her modesty, they would never have appeared to the world in her lifetime, if it had not been that some months ago she thought she was actually in dying circumstances." (Preface to the 1st Edition, Jan. 6, 1780.)

This settles the question of Miss Harrison's honest intentions. As a poet, however, she is certainly "ignorant and weak." Her language is diluted with images so feeble (*I often think, often speak, reprove my heart and tongue*) that we can well believe she was a sickly girl—though literary success seems to have improved her health.

There is no escaping the criterion: in poetry a basic requirement for excellence is power and energy of imagery. It is difficult to be deeply moved by Miss Harrison's lines, even though there is a sprinkling of concrete expressions, because her imagery is so flat. Compare her verses with the well-known Negro spiritual:

> Swing low, sweet chariot,
> Comin' for to carry me home.
>
> I looked over Jordan and what did I see,
> Comin' for to carry me home?
> A band of angels comin' after me,
> Comin' for to carry me home. . . .

Lacking any editorial testimonial in this instance, we cannot certify the religious sincerity of the anonymous author or authors of this song. But we can be sure of one thing: the lines reveal the mastery and instinct of a true poet. Miss Harrison's well-meant effusion leaves us out of her religious experience; the Negro spiritual, by the energy of its imagery, invites us into the very heart of one.

LITERAL AND FIGURATIVE IMAGERY

We now wish to return to the matter of literal and figurative imagery. Imagery is *literal,* it will be remembered, when the images are to be taken in their natural or strict meaning. Please consult the excerpt from the concluding passage of Charles Darwin's epochal *The Descent of Man* on page 52. After the abstractions of the opening, Darwin presents us with a series of lively pictures, *literal* images which are to be taken in their natural meaning. *A party of Fuegians, a wild and broken shore, absolutely naked, bedaubed with paint, long hair tangled, mouths frothed with excitement,* mean precisely, and no more than, what the expressions indicate. So, too, with the accounts of the heroic little monkey and the old baboon.

*From *Songs in the Night* by "A Young Woman under Heavy Afflictions," 1st ed. 1780. By 1819 some 10 or 11 English editions and 4 American editions had appeared.

This lovely song by Christina Rossetti (1830–1894) presents a series of images:

> When I am dead, my dearest,
>   Sing no sad songs for me;
> Plant thou no roses at my head,
>   Nor shady cypress tree:[1]
> Be the green grass above me
>   With showers and dewdrops wet:
> And if thou wilt, remember,
>   And if thou wilt, forget.
>
> I shall not see the shadows,
>   I shall not feel the rain;
> I shall not hear the nightingale
>   Sing on as if in pain:
> And dreaming through the twilight
>   That doth not rise nor set,
> Haply I may remember,
>   And haply may forget.

10

Most of the images of this song are to be taken literally. *Plant, roses, at my head, shady cypress tree, green grass, above me, with showers and dewdrops wet,* and so on are all used in their natural meaning. It is clear from this example that literal imagery in no way is necessarily divorced from strong feelings. It must be obvious that, despite the apparent lightness of tone, Miss Rossetti's feelings are not gay—that she intends a sadness, perhaps a bitterness, beyond the sweetness of the imagery. Indeed, it is the contrast between the lightness of the manner and the seriousness of the poet's feelings which gives this song its peculiarly moving quality.

But images can be figurative rather than literal. A *figurative* image is one which is not to be read literally, but for a meaning which is an extension of the image. This extension is achieved by presenting or suggesting an analogy, so that one concept is represented in terms of another. Thus, when Richard, the hero-king of England, was nicknamed "the Lion-Hearted," it was not intended that people imagine some miracle of surgery had been accomplished upon his vital organs; rather, the epithet intends a tribute to Richard's courage, and does so by drawing an analogy with the fearlessness of the lion. The lion, on the other hand, has been called "King of the Beasts," not because he wears a crown and owns an empire, but for the sake of the analogy between his relation to other animals and that of a mighty monarch to his subjects. The use of figurative language is known as *trope*.

William Blake (1757–1827) is able to condense limitless meaning into the four lines which stand as a motto to *Auguries of Innocence:*

> To see the world in a grain of sand,
>   And a heaven in a wild flower;
> Hold infinity in the palm of your hand,
>   And eternity in an hour.

These lines contain the mystic truth that the understanding, majesty and wonder of the macrocosm are to be found in the microcosm—that the understanding, majesty and wonder of the universe are waiting to be discovered, by those with imagination, in every one of its parts. And these truths are conveyed to us by trope. The world is made of grains of sand, and the marvel of the Creation is in each of its grains. A handful of sand held up to the sun at the seashore will reveal all the colors of the rainbow. Many people cannot bear the thought of enduring the span of mortal life without the assurance of a life in the hereafter; yet with their few allotted years on earth they are bored, they know little delight; they expect heaven

[1]Cypress trees are to be seen in cemeteries all over Europe.

will at last supply the joy they have missed here. Nonetheless, the little wild flower by the roadside could afford them intense joy if they had the eyes to see it, a joy that in itself Blake implies must be as great as any that heaven could offer. Even the infinity of the interstellar spaces is no greater an infinity than the infinity crossing the palm of one's hand. And as for time! What would those who are bored with a brief life-span do with an eternity of time? Some people can condense more of life in a short space than others could in a century. And all of us know that a certain twenty minutes of living has compressed for us more of experience than other barren stretches of weeks and months.—All this and very much more do Blake's four lines of figurative language suggest to the imagination. Such is the power of the trope.

Certain tropes, or figures of speech, are more common than others. Wordsworth (1770–1850) in one of his *Lucy* poems says that Lucy, a simple country girl, was

> A violet by a mossy stone
> Half-hidden from the eye!
> —Fair as a star, when only one
> Is shining in the sky.

1. *A violet by a mossy stone* is a *metaphor. A metaphor provides an analogy by declaring that one object or idea* is *another.* Here Lucy is said *to be* a violet.

2. *Fair as a star, when only one/Is shining in the sky* is a *simile. A simile provides an analogy by stating that one object* is like *another. Here Lucy is said to be* like *a star.* * A metaphor *asserts the identity* of two objects or ideas; a simile *compares* them.

Here is a passage from Jeremy Taylor's (1613–1667) *Holy Dying:* Man, he says,

> comes into the world like morning mushrooms, soon thrusting up their heads into the air, and conversing[1] with their kindred of the same production, and as soon they turn into dust and forgetfulness: some of them without any other interest in the affairs of the world, but that they made their parents a little glad and very sorrowful; others ride longer in the storm; it may be until seven years of vanity be expired, and then peradventure the sun shines hot upon their heads, and they fall into the shades below, into the cover of death and darkness of the grave to hide them. But if the bubble stands the shock of a bigger drop, and outlives the chances of a child, of a careless nurse, of drowning in a pail of water, of being overlaid[2] by a sleepy servant, or such little accidents, then the young man dances like a bubble, empty and gay, and shines like a dove's neck, or the image of a rainbow, which hath no substance; and so he dances out the gaiety of his youth, and is all the while in a storm, and endures, only because he is not knocked on the head by a bigger drop of rain, or crushed by the pressure of a load of indigested meat.

This powerful passage opens with a simile: *comes into the world like morning mushrooms;* the analogy is made more elaborate by being carried out further: *thrusting up their heads . . . they turn into dust.* Other similes are here too: *the young man dances like a bubble; shines like a dove's neck; or* [like] *the image of a rainbow. If the bubble stands the shock of a bigger drop* presents two metaphors: man is identified with a bubble, and Fate or Chance with a bigger drop of rain. *Others ride longer in the storm* is metaphorical too; *storm* is here identified with living. There is a great deal of figurative language present: *they fall into the shades below; into the cover of death . . . to hide them; dances out the gaiety of his youth;* and so on. Some of the imagery is not figurative but literal: *they made their parents a little glad*

---

*It is perhaps worthwhile recalling here a point made earlier in the chapter. Had Wordsworth merely said that Lucy was *fair,* he would have been using an abstraction, more generic to prose. But when he adds *as a star when only one is shining in the sky,* he converts the abstraction to a brilliant figure of speech.

[1]Consorting.

[2]I.e., suffocated by having too many bedclothes laid over him.

and very sorrowful; the sun shines hot upon their heads; drowning in a pail of water. And, of course, there is a certain minimum of abstract language too: *any other interest in the affairs of the world; vanity; the chances.*

Metaphors and similes are the most important figures of speech. There are others met with fairly frequently. These lines are from Shelley's (1792–1822) *Prometheus Unbound* (IV):

> Spectres we
> Of the dead Hours be,
> We bear Time to his tomb in eternity.

3. *Hours* and *Time* are *personifications. A personification ascribes personality to the inanimate. Hours* and *Time* are spoken of as though they were persons.

These lines are from Althea Urn's (1903–1969) "The Most Foolish Virgin of Them All Is Spring":

> Each year she dresses, a pale bride
> In palest green, with blossoms in her hair;
> Small cowslips and wild crocus
> Bind her waist;
> While in her face reflected
> Are centuries of grace.
> In flushed expectancy she awaits
> The bridegroom who can only bring
> Disaster with his wedding ring.

Throughout this poem Spring is a personification, and is spoken of as a maiden. The *bridegroom,* another personification, is, of course, Summer.

In *The Merchant of Venice* this song is sung (III/ii/63):

> Tell me, where is fancy[1] bred,
> Or in the heart or in the head? . . .

4. *Heart* and *head* are each an example of *metonymy. Metonymy is the use of a word for another which it suggests*—i.e., using the effect for the cause, or the cause for the effect; the sign for the thing signified; or the container for the thing contained (e.g., "he is addicted to the *bottle*"—i.e., alcohol"; "he knows his *Shakespeare*"—i.e., the works of Shakespeare). In the song we have cited, the *heart,* seat of the emotions, suggests the emotions; the *head,* seat of reason, suggests reason.

Here are four lines from FitzGerald's (1809–1883) *Rubáiyát of Omar Khayyám:*

> For some we loved, the loveliest and the best
> That from his Vintage rolling Time has prest,
>   Have drunk their Cup a Round or two before,
> And one by one crept silently to rest.

Cup is used as metonymy; the container here signifies the thing contained (i.e., wine). (*Time* is another personification.)

5. In Tennyson's (1809–1902) "Locksley Hall" occurs the line:

> Saw the heavens fill with commerce, argosies of magic sails . . .

Sails is an example of *synecdoche. Synecdoche is the substitution of the part for the whole or the whole for the part.* Here *sails* are spoken of as representing the idea of the whole ship or of a fleet of ships.

In Matthew Arnold's (1882–1888) "Shakespeare" we have met with these lines:

> All pains the immortal spirit must endure,

[1] Love.

> All weakness which impairs, all griefs which bow
> Find their sole speech in that victorious brow.

Here *brow* is a use of synecdoche. Shakespeare's *brow* is made to stand for the poet himself.

CERTAIN RHETORICAL DEVICES

There are, of course, other methods of achieving telling effects with words besides the use of figurative language: through devices such as puns and quibbles, understatement, hyperbole (overstatement), paradox, ambiguity, and irony.

We may illustrate both pun and understatement by an anecdote told of Walter Pater (1839–1894), Oxford don, and philosopher of a new estheticism during the latter part of the nineteenth century. Among his student-disciples was Oscar Wilde (1854–1900), who decided to popularize Pater's teachings that life could be an art, and that art could be a life. Setting himself up as "Professor of Aesthetics," young Wilde made many appearances on the lecture-platforms of America and England. It was generally understood that Pater was disgusted with the notoriety Wilde was giving his cherished ideas by vulgarizing them. At last Wilde came to Oxford with his lecture. At its conclusion, Wilde brushed aside the compliments of his admirers, and rushed to the back of the room, eager to win the approval of his old teacher. "You were sitting so far back!" he cried. "Could you at all hear me?" "Oh yes," Pater answered coolly, "we heard you, Oscar. In fact, we *overheard* you." Wilde had Pater's opinion. *A pun is the use of a word in two or more meanings, or of two words which sound alike in such a way as to imply different meanings.*

A *quibble is any play upon words.* Shakespeare's plays frequently illustrate how puns and quibbles may be used for dramatic, rather than comic, effect. An unforgettable instance occurs when, in the last scene, Othello, his heart full of love for his wife, enters, taper in hand, to put an end to what he believes her adulterous life; and says:

> Put out the light, and then put out the light.

The whole tragedy of his position is eloquent in that play of words. The first *light* refers to the taper; the second refers to the light of life—her life, as well as his own; and he continues:

> If I quench thee, thou flaming minister,
> I can again thy former light restore,
> Should I repent me; but once put out thy light,
> Thou cunning'st pattern of excelling nature,
> I know not where is that Promethean heat
> That can thy light relume.

> > —V/ii/7 seq.

Another rhetorical device may be illustrated by Bernard Grebanier's epigram, "The Medico":

> Doctor Marcus on his way
> Touched this statue yesterday.
> Now, although a god and clay,
> Its funeral will be today.

Here we find *hyperbole,* or *overstatement for effect.* On the face of it, nothing could be killed by a passing touch. Moreover, a god is conceived of as not subject to death, and clay statues do not have funerals. But the exaggerations are justified because they make the point of the satire—that Doctor Marcus' merest attentions are always fatal to his patients.

Again in *Hamlet* (III/ii/308) we find this instance of hyperbole:

> GUILDENSTERN. Good my lord, vouchsafe me a word with you.
> HAMLET. Sir, a whole history.

A whole history by its very exaggeration expresses Hamlet's dislike and distrust of Guildenstern.

In W. S. Gilbert's (1836–1911) comic opera *The Pirates of Penzance,* much of the plot hinges upon a "most ingenious paradox." The hero was born on February 29 in a leap year. He has been indentured to the pirates until his twenty-first birthday, and looks forward eagerly to his release from a profession he loathes. The day arrives when he is twenty-one. He takes leave of his fellow-pirates, but suddenly his hopes for a respectable life are thwarted. Someone has looked up the language of the contract, and it turns out that he has had only five birthdays. He must serve as a pirate until his twenty-first birthday, when he will be eighty-one! His being twenty-one and still only five is a *paradox. A paradox is an assertion or an attitude apparently contradictory or opposed to common sense.*

This "Holy Sonnet" of John Donne (1573–1631) shows an astonishing use of paradox:

> Batter my heart, three-personed God; for you
> As yet but knock, breathe, shine, and seek to mend.
> That I may rise and stand, o'erthrow me and bend
> Your force to break, blow, burn and make me new.
> I, like an usurped town, to another due,
> Labour to admit you, but Oh, to no end;
> Reason, your viceroy in me, me should defend,
> But is captived and proves weak or untrue.
> Yet dearly I love you and would be loved fain,
> But am betrothed unto your enemy: 10
> Divorce me, untie or break that knot again,
> Take me to you, imprison me, for I
> Except you enthrall me, never shall be free,
> Nor ever chaste, except you ravish me.

Paradox is the very life blood of this poem. Donne prays to be overthrown so that he may rise and stand, to be broken and burned that he may be made whole. Like a besieged town belonging to the Devil, he is eager to prove traitor in order to be good. He is betrothed to Satan and wishes to break the contract. He begs to be taken prisoner so that he may be free. He knows he can never be chaste until God ravish him. These paradoxes make for sublimity in the tone of the poem. Through apparent contradictions Donne, whose passionate intellectuality is perfectly at home in the realm of paradox, reveals the burning truth about his soul and its yearning for God. As we have observed, the kind of language an author uses and the way he uses it are often an extension of his own temperament.

Paradox as a literary device—the revelation of truth through apparent contradictions—is in close affinity with irony—the phrasing of meaning in apparent opposition to what the reader is actually to understand. (See, for example, Swift's "A Modest Proposal," page 32.)

And these, in turn, are related to what contemporary criticism calls *ambiguity.* In William Collins' (1721–1759) "Ode to Evening," the poet personifies Evening; we begin at the sixth stanza:

> For when thy[1] folding-star[2] arising shows
> His paly circlet, at his warning lamp
>   The fragrant Hours, and elves
>   Who slept in buds the day,
>
> And many a nymph who wreathes her brows with
>   sedge,
> And sheds the freshening dew, and, lovelier still,
>   The pensive Pleasure sweet,
>   Prepare thy shadowy car.

[1]Evening's.
[2]The star that bids the shepherds bring their flocks back to the fold.

> Then lead, calm votaress, where some sheety lake
> Cheers the lone heath, or some time-hallowed pile[3]
> Or upland fallows gray
> Reflect its last cool gleam. . . .

Now, the music of these lines expresses perfectly the tone and the mood of early twilight —none more than the last line quoted. But it is this same last line which renders it impossible to know precisely what the poet is talking about. The confusion results from the uncertainty of meaning in the words *reflect* and *its*. *Reflect* is a plural; if we allow the poet the grammatical license of collecting a series of singular subjects separated by *or,* it would seem that only the lone heath, the time-hallowed ruin or, possibly, the upland fallows, which *is* plural, can be doing the reflecting. If so, the *its* must refer to the sheety lake. But that is obviously nonsense. The heath, the ruin and the fallows cannot reflect a lake. On the other hand, if *reflect* is a grammatical slip for *reflects,* and it is the lake, as we should expect, which is doing the reflecting, to what does *its* now refer? The lone heath, the time-hallowed pile, and the upland fallows gray are each incapable of having a last cool gleam to be reflected in the lake. The only conceivable candidate as the word to which *its* refers is the folding-star, in the first line we have quoted. And that is so far removed in position from *its* that the likelihood is equally remote; moreover, it is doubtful whether one would think of the star as shedding a "cool gleam." The mind is likely to insist that the last cool gleam must be the lake's. If that is what the poet meant, he certainly has failed to say so.

Here is ambiguity, then, of a kind which no poet aware of what he is doing would permit himself to indulge. But ambiguity can also be a deliberate device employed by a writer to enrich his meaning. William Empson defines *ambiguity* as *"any verbal nuance . . . which gives room for alternative reactions to the same piece of language."** A pun would be an obvious example of such ambiguity. Perhaps the most important kind, however, to consider is the ambiguity which involves several effective meanings at once without resort to pun or quibbles. Empson enlarges on the fourth line of Shakespeare's "Sonnet LXXIII," which opens:

> That time of year thou may'st in me behold
> When yellow leaves, or none, or few, do hang
> Upon those boughs which shake against the cold,
> Bare ruined choirs, where late the sweet birds sang.

Although a comparison between boughs and choirs may at first seem startling, it is, Empson shows at some length, more than appropriate. Birds sing on boughs, choirs were built to sing in; birds often sit in rows, as do singers in a choir; boughs and choirs are both made of wood; boughs are often knotted, choirs are "carved into knots"; boughs are found in a forest, choirs are sheltered by a building "crystallized out of the likeness of a forest" with colors provided by stained glass windows and "painting like flowers and leaves"; the wintry skies above the naked boughs are like the gray moldering walls about the ruined choirs.

Such analysis of the imagery of any piece of writing can be very much enriching to our apprehension. But it is also likely that to seek associations as extensive as these Empson brings to bear upon a single line is to exaggerate the author's actual meaning. Moreover, to force so many meanings upon one line (and we have omitted others suggested by Empson which we cannot accept as remotely possible) is inevitably to obscure the structure of the work as a whole. It is obvious that were we to extract so many meanings from every line of a poem, we should indeed not see the forest for the trees. Another distinguished contemporary critic, John Crowe Ransom, protests that Empson's is an "over-reading," and assures us that his own associations with the same line do not go beyond envisioning "the soiled wood and broken stones, both intricate, of an edifice whose roof has come off, once a sacred

---

[3]The ruin of some medieval building.
*Seven Types of Ambiguity, rev. ed. (1947), pp. 1–3.

edifice." For the rest, this critic avers, since it is impossible to "attend to all the meaning behind any poem," it is better to put first things first, and not allow the logic of the whole to be lost in a mass of alternate meanings for various lines. Still, if this sort of excess is a fault, it is not the worst sort of fault of which a reader can be guilty. "It is better to have too much imagination than to have too little."* Indulged within the limits suggested by Ransom, the analysis of the possibilities inherent in deliberate ambiguity can only add dimension to our understanding of a given work. Such analyzing is a good habit to cultivate, besides, because it keeps us attentive to what the work undertakes to say.

Let us now reexamine Donne's "Holy Sonnet" (see page 63).

It opens with an imperious command to the Trinity (though the ruler of a city would hardly be expected to command his walls to be battered). As the sonnet unfolds, that command is understood to be a cry of despair. Indeed, before the first line ends the poet begins to explain himself in a descending scale; the words in that descending scale, *knock, breathe, shine, and seek to mend,* are full of ambiguity, the precise meaning depending on whether the word is looking back or ahead. To look back: God has only been knocking for admittance to mend the poet (i.e., to remove his defects, faults or evil); and has only given utterance to His wish; has only looked favorably on the poet; has only looked for the poet.

The statement in the third and fourth lines is not imperative in tone. Since he is defective, the poet wants God to *bend* (i.e., incline and strain) His power to *break* the poet to pieces and in a furnace re-create him (*blow, burn, and make me new*) purged of his evils so that he can *stand* (i.e., not fall to Satan). There are also sexual connotations in these third and fourth lines: *rise and stand, break* (i.e., do violence to), *blow* (excite), *burn* (inflame). The effect derives not from the defined meanings of these words, but from the tone established and the image implied by them; their tone flows back to the second line, infusing it with a delicate but real sexual suggestiveness.

There are still other meanings to be wrested from some of the words in these four lines, meanings which point ahead to the central warfare imagery. *Batter* begins the warfare imagery, suggesting a ram to break down the gates and walls of the town. *Knock* in such a context means "hard blows"; *breathe,* "to take breathing space" in the battle; *seek,* "to attack"; *bend,* "to dispose one's force, bring to bear"; *force,* "army"; *break,* "to break upon the enemy." All of this language is directed against the poet: not being with God, he is against Him.

For the poet, though *due* to God (in lines 5 and 6) has been *usurped* by Satan, and labors in vain *to admit* God. Again, *labor* and *admit* have sexual connotations too. In *usurped town* Donne unites the imagery of warfare and the sexual imagery; a woman was commonly likened, in Renaissance poetry, to a fortress or embattled town when a man was trying to win her.

The seventh and eighth lines conclude with the culminating idea of the first part of the poem, and explain why the poet cannot let God enter his heart. Reason, which should rule man for God, is captured, and is proving weak or faithless. The tone of the first eight lines of this sonnet shifts from the imperative to the declarative to the explanatory, with an undertone of hopelessness beneath all.

In the last six lines the poet implores God as a mistress might her lover. Though *Reason* in him has proved *untrue* (the suggestion in the seventh line was that since Reason is God's *viceroy* and *should defend* the poet, God was perhaps to blame), the poet has *dearly* loved God and wishes to be loved in return. But since he is *betrothed* to Satan—the word *break* in the fourth line looks forward to the last four lines, in its meanings "to dissolve or annul a marriage" and "to do violence to"—let God *divorce* him, free him from his captive bonds, or annul the union with Satan since the poet's original bond was with God. Let God *take*

The New Criticism (1941), pp. 128–131.

the poet, *imprison* him, for unless God reduces him to thralldom, he *never shall be free* (for man is truly free only in God's service); unless God *ravish* him, he never will be *chaste*. The poet cannot surrender himself, yet desires to be entirely God's. He has the faith of love, but not the strength of reason to choose God, though he as one of mankind must make his choice. In despair the poet cries out to God to make him His; the despair erupts as violent desire.

The sexual connotations in the first eight lines turn into the explicit imagery of the union between man and woman in the last six, culminating in a plea to be violated. The motif of conquest by war in the first eight is made part of the conquest by union in the last six lines.

This analysis of Donne's "Holy Sonnet" attempts no more than an intellectual understanding of its meanings. But the poem is essentially mystical, and no such analysis can completely capture the ultimate meaning of the sonnet.*

Ambiguity is, then, a device which makes for irony. For ambiguity is found when there are two or more possible opposing ways in which to understand an expression, and the author refrains from endorsing one of these meanings rather than another. Irony has been defined as "the bringing in of the opposite, the complementary impulses."† It is the vogue in contemporary critical theory to rate irony as one of the highest of literary accomplishments. André Breton has gone so far as to say that "to compare two objects, as remote from one another as possible, or by any other method put them together in a sudden and striking fashion, this remains the highest task to which poetry can aspire."‡ Against this extreme position one might quote, for the sake of a balanced judgment, the opinion of the great Greek critic, Longinus, that one of the chief obstacles to achieving sublimity in literature is a "puerile" preoccupation with novelty: "Men slip into this kind of error because, while they aim at the uncommon and the elaborate and most of all at the attractive, they drift unawares into the tawdry and affected."ſ It is, however, true that irony is the source of some of the most inspired and inspiring moments in literature.

SYMBOLISM

There is another use of language which can vastly enrich the meaning of a work. When Stendhal entitled his novel *The Red and the Black,* he was employing the word *red* to signify the military, and the word *black* the priesthood. To use words this way is to employ them as symbols. A symbol is something used to represent or to stand for something else. Studies such as mathematics and chemistry, of course, employ symbols. The x in mathematics and H_2O in chemistry are used, characteristically of the sciences, to *denote* or *indicate* a quantity or thing. But symbols in language can serve a different end. The lion is a symbol of courage; the sceptre, of power; the Cross, of Christianity. Here the symbol itself *portrays* or *suggests* the thing signified by the associations of experience. However, the man of letters does not have much use for such public symbols since they tend to triteness. An author who wishes to deepen the meaning of his lines will invent for a particular work the symbol or symbols which will be of significance to the meaning of that work. When Stendhal used "the red" to symbolize the military, he was evoking not only the color of the soldier's uniform but also the blood that must be spilled and the courage required by the profession; by "the black" he was evoking not only the priestly garb but also the gravity, sombreness, and high solemnity of that profession.

Again, in Enid Bagnold's play, *The Chalk Garden,* the title is a literary symbol. The drama takes place on the estate of Mrs. St. Maugham, a woman of intellect but of no affections, who has managed to alienate her daughter and to confuse the life of her young

*We may give an example of all we are enforced to omit: since it is the Trinity which is addressed in the first line, is it not Christ who is asked to *knock,* the Holy Spirit who is asked to *breathe,* and God the Father who is asked to *shine?*

†I. A. Richards, *Principles of Literary Criticism* (1938), p. 250.

‡Quoted by I. A. Richards, *The Philosophy of Rhetoric* (1936), p. 123.

ſ*On the Sublime,* III (translated by W. Rhys Roberts).

granddaughter. A chalk garden is one whose soil, lacking the necessary nutritive elements, will permit nothing to grow. The title symbolizes the fact that all of Mrs. St. Maugham's general benevolence is in vain; the aridness of her heart makes her intended goodness a soil in which nothing can thrive. The symbol is further strengthened when Madrigal, the girl's governess, in exasperation at length (in the last act) exclaims: "You have not a green thumb, Mrs. St. Maugham." Anything confided to Mrs. St. Maugham's care can only die.

Let us take note of some of the imagery in Shakespeare's *Romeo and Juliet*. When Romeo first sees Juliet he murmurs (I/v/46 seq.):

> Oh, she doth teach the torches to burn bright!
> It seems she hangs upon the cheek of night
> Like a rich jewel in an Ethiop's ear ...
> So shows a snowy dove trooping with crows.

Shortly after, in the Balcony Scene (II/ii), he cries as he looks up from the garden:

> But, soft! What light through yonder window breaks?
> It is the east, and Juliet is the sun!
> Arise, fair sun. ...
> Two of the fairest stars in all the heaven,
> Having some business, do entreat her eyes
> To twinkle in their spheres till they return.
> What if her eyes were there, they in her head?
> The brightness of her cheek would shame those stars
> As daylight doth a lamp; her eyes in heaven
> Would through the airy region stream so bright
> That birds would sing and think it were not night.

Presently, after he has vowed his love for her, Juliet fears that his love is

> too sudden,
> Too like the lightning.

It will be remarked that the lovers, from their first encounter, speak of each other and of their love in images which have to do with light and radiance, and that this light and this radiance are set against a background of darkness. The concept is continued intermittently throughout the play. Juliet, waiting impatiently for the Nurse's return from her embassy to Romeo, says (II/v/4 seq.):

> Love's heralds should be thoughts,
> Which ten times faster glide than the sun's beams,
> Driving back shadows over lowering hills.

After the lovers have been secretly married, Juliet, anticipating Romeo's coming to consummate their union, murmurs ecstatically (III/iii/17 seq.):

> Come, night, come, Romeo, come, thou day in night,
> For thou wilt lie upon the wings of night
> Whiter than new snow on a raven's back.
> Come, gentle night, come, loving, black-browed night,
> Give me my Romeo; and when he shall die,
> Take him and cut him out in little stars,
> And he will make the face of heaven so fine
> That all the world will be in love with night
> And pay no worship to the garish sun.

In the last scene, Romeo cries as he enters Juliet's tomb:

> A grave? Oh, no, a lantern ...
> For here lies Juliet, and her beauty makes
> This vault a feasting presence full of light. ...

How oft when men are at the point of death
Have they been merry! Which their keepers call
A lightning before death. Oh, how may I
Call this a lightning!

This persistence of images of light set against darkness is an enrichment of the meaning. Shakespeare has the lovers use these images because their love is all light against the black hate of their families' feud. Such recurrence of the same symbol in a work constitutes *symbolism* in literature. A literary symbol is one which contains a relationship between the sign and the thing signified, and thus becomes the means of an imaginative experience for the reader. *When a literary symbol recurs or persists* in a work, *the author is using symbolism* as a device to deepen the imaginative meaning.

Virginia Woolf's (1882–1941) short story "The New Dress" exhibits a skillful use of symbolism. The two literary symbols appearing in this story are marked respectively with two asterisks and two daggers.

Mabel had her first serious suspicion that something was wrong as she took her cloak off and Mrs. Barnet, while handing her the mirror** and touching the brushes and thus drawing her attention, perhaps rather markedly, to all the appliances for tidying and improving hair, complexion, clothes, which existed on the dressing table, confirmed the suspicion—that it was not right, not quite right, which growing stronger as she went upstairs and springing at her with conviction as she greeted Clarissa Dalloway, she went straight to the far end of the room, to a shaded corner where a looking-glass** hung and looked. No! It was not right. And at once the misery which she always tried to hide, the profound dissatisfaction—the sense she had had, ever since she was a child, of being inferior to other people —set upon her, relentlessly, remorselessly, with an intensity which she could not beat off, as she would when she woke at night at home, by reading Borrow or Scott; for, oh, these men, oh, these women, all were thinking—"What's Mabel wearing? What a fright she looks! What a hideous new dress!"—their eyelids flickering as they came up and then their lids shutting rather tight. It was her own appalling inadequacy; her cowardice; her mean, water-sprinkled blood that depressed her. And at once the whole of the room where, for ever so many hours, she had planned with the little dressmaker how it was to go, seemed sordid, repulsive; and her own drawing-room so shabby, and herself, going out, puffed up with vanity as she touched the letters on the hall table and said: "How dull!" to show off—all this now seemed unutterably silly, paltry, and provincial. All this had been absolutely destroyed, shown up, exploded, the moment she came into Mrs. Dalloway's drawing-room.

What she had thought that evening when, sitting over the teacups, Mrs. Dalloway's invitation came, was that, of course, she could not be fashionable. It was absurd to pretend to even—fashion meant cut, meant style, meant thirty guineas at least—but why not be original? Why not be herself, anyhow? And, getting up, she had taken that old fashion book of her mother's, a Paris fashion book of the time of the Empire, and had thought how much prettier, more dignified, and more womanly, they were then, and so set herself —oh, it was foolish—trying to be like them, pluming herself in fact upon being modest and old-fashioned and very charming, giving herself up, no doubt about it, to an orgy of self-love which deserved to be chastised, and so rigged herself out like this.

But she dared not look in the glass**. She could not face the whole horror—the pale yellow, idiotically old-fashioned silk dress with its long skirt and its high sleeves and its waist and all the things that looked so charming in the fashion book, but not on her, not among all these ordinary people. She felt like a dressmaker's dummy standing there for young people to stick pins into.

"But my dear, its perfectly charming!" Rose Shaw said, looking her up and down with that little satirical pucker of the lips which she expected—Rose herself being dressed in the height of the fashion, precisely like everybody else, always.

"We are all like flies†† trying to crawl over the edge of the saucer," Mabel thought, and repeated the phrase as if she were crossing herself, as if she were trying to find some spell to annul this pain, to make this agony endurable. Tags of Shakespeare, lines from books she had read ages ago, suddenly came to her when she was in agony, and she repeated them over and over again. "Flies†† trying to crawl," she repeated. If she could say that over often enough and make herself see the flies††, she would become numb, chill, frozen, dumb. Now she could see flies†† crawling slowly out of a saucer of milk with their wings stuck together; and she strained and strained (standing in front of the looking-glass**, listening to Rose Shaw) to make herself see Rose Shaw and all the other people there as flies††, trying to hoist themselves out of something, or into something, meager, insignificant, toiling flies††. But she could not see them like that, not other people. She saw herself like that—she was a fly††, but the others were dragonflies, butterflies, beautiful insects, dancing, fluttering, skimming, while she alone dragged herself up out of the saucer††. (Envy and spite, the most detestable of the vices, were her chief faults.)

"I feel like some dowdy, decrepit, horribly dingy old fly††," she said, making Robert Haydon stop just to hear her say that, just to reassure herself by furbishing up a poor weak-kneed phrase and so showing how detached she was, how witty, that she did not feel in the least out of anything. And, of course, Robert Haydon answered something quite polite, quite insincere, which she saw through instantly, and said to herself, directly he went (again from some book), "Lies, lies, lies!" For a party makes things either much more real or much less real, she thought; she saw in a flash to the bottom of Robert Haydon's heart; she saw through everything. She saw the truth. This was true, this drawing-room, this self, and the other false. Miss Milan's little workroom was really terribly hot, stuffy, sordid. It smelt of clothes and cabbage cooking; and yet, when Miss Milan put the glass** in her hand, and she looked at herself with the dress on, finished, an extraordinary bliss shot through her heart. Suffused with light, she sprang into existence. Rid of cares and wrinkles, what she had dreamed of herself was there—a beautiful woman. Just for a second (she had not dared look longer, Miss Milan wanted to know about the length of the skirt), there looked at her, framed in the scrolloping mahogany**, a gray-white, mysteriously smiling, charming girl, the core of herself, the soul of herself; and it was not vanity only, not only self-love that made her think it good, tender, and true. Miss Milan said that the skirt could not well be longer; if anything the skirt, said Miss Milan, puckering her forehead, considering with all her wits about her, must be shorter; and she felt, suddenly, honestly, full of love for Miss Milan, much, much fonder of Miss Milan than of anyone in the whole world, and could have cried for pity that she should be crawling on the floor with her mouth full of pins and her face red and her eyes bulging—that one human being should be doing this for another, and she saw them all as human beings merely, and herself going off to her party, and Miss Milan pulling the cover over the canary's cage, or letting him pick a hemp-seed from between her lips, and the thought of it, of this side of human nature and its patience and its endurance and its being content with such miserable, scanty, sordid, little pleasures filled her eyes with tears.

And now the whole thing had vanished. The dress, the room, the love, the pity, the scrolloping looking-glass**, and the canary's cage—all had vanished, and here she was in a corner of Mrs. Dalloway's drawing-room, suffering tortures, woken wide awake to reality.

But it was all so paltry, weak-blooded, and petty-minded to care so much at her age with two children, to be still so utterly dependent on people's opinions and not have principles or convictions, not to be able to say as other people did, "There's Shakespeare! There's death! We're all weevils in a captain's biscuit"—or whatever it was that people did say.

She faced herself straight in the glass**; she pecked at her left shoulder; she issued out into the room, as if spears were thrown at her yellow dress from all sides. But instead of looking fierce or tragic, as Rose Shaw would have done—Rose would have looked like Boadicea[1]—she looked foolish and self-conscious and simpered like a schoolgirl and slouched across the room, positively slinking, as if she were a beaten mongrel, and looked at a picture, an engraving. As if one went to a party to look at a picture! Everybody knew why she did it—it was from shame, from humiliation.

"Now the fly's†† in the saucer," she said to herself, "right in the middle, and can't get out, and the milk," she thought, rigidly staring at the picture, "is sticking its wings together††."

"It's so old-fashioned," she said to Charles Burt, making him stop (which by itself he hated) on his way to talk to someone else.

She meant, or she tried to make herself think that she meant, that it was the picture and not her dress, that was old-fashioned. And one word of praise, one word of affection from Charles would have made all the difference to her at the moment. If he had only said, "Mabel, you're looking charming tonight!" it would have changed her life. But then she ought to have been truthful and direct. Charles said nothing of the kind, of course. He was malice itself. He always saw

---

[1] British queen (died A.D. 62) who revolted unsuccessfully against the Roman rulers of Britain.

through one, especially if one were feeling particularly mean, paltry, or feeble-minded.

"Mabel's got a new dress!" he said, and the poor fly†† was absolutely shoved into the middle of the saucer. Really, he would like her to drown††, she believed. He had no heart, no fundamental kindness, only a veneer of friendliness. Miss Milan was much more real, much kinder. If only one could feel that and stick to it, always. "Why," she asked herself—replying to Charles much too pertly, letting him see that she was out of temper, or "ruffled" as he called it ("Rather ruffled?" he said and went on to laugh at her with some woman over there)—"Why," she asked herself, "can't I feel one thing always, feel quite sure that Miss Milan is right, and Charles wrong and stick to it, feel sure about the canary and pity and love and not be whipped all round in a second by coming into a room full of people?" It was her odious, weak, vacillating character again, always giving at the critical moment and not being seriously interested in conchology,[2] etymology, botany, archeology, cutting up potatoes and watching them fructify like Mary Dennis, like Violet Searle.

Then Mrs. Holman, seeing her standing there, bore down upon her. Of course a thing like a dress was beneath Mrs. Holman's notice, with her family always tumbling downstairs or having the scarlet fever. Could Mabel tell her if Elmthorpe was ever let for August and September? Oh, it was a conversation that bored her unutterably!—it made her furious to be treated like a house agent or a messenger boy, to be made use of. Not to have value, that was it, she thought, trying to grasp something hard, something real, while she tried to answer sensibly about the bathroom and the south aspect and the hot water to the top of the house; and all the time she could see little bits of her yellow dress in the round looking-glass** which made them all the size of boot-buttons or tadpoles; and it was amazing to think how much humiliation and agony and self-loathing and effort and passionate ups and downs of feeling were contained in a thing the size of a threepenny bit. And what was still odder, this thing, this Mabel Waring, was separate, quite disconnected; and though Mrs. Holman (the black button) was leaning forward and telling her how her eldest boy had strained his heart running, she could see her, too, quite detached in the looking-glass**, and it was impossible that the black dot, leaning forward, gesticulating, should make the yellow dot, sitting solitary, self-centered, feel

[2]The study of shells.

what the black dot was feeling, yet they pretended.

"So impossible to keep boys quiet"—that was the kind of thing one said.

And Mrs. Holman, who could never get enough sympathy and snatched what little there was greedily, as if it were her right (but she deserved much more for there was her little girl who had come down this morning with a swollen knee-joint), took this miserable offering and looked at it suspiciously, grudgingly, as if it were a halfpenny when it ought to have been a pound and put it away in her purse, must put up with it, mean and miserly though it was, times being hard, so very hard; and on she went, creaking, injured Mrs. Holman, about the girl with the swollen joints. Ah, it was tragic, this greed, this clamor of human beings, like a row of cormorants, barking and flapping their wings for sympathy—it was tragic, could one have felt it and not merely pretended to feel it!

But in her yellow dress tonight she could not wring out one drop more; she wanted it all, all for herself. She knew (she kept on looking into the glass**, dipping into that dreadfully showing-up blue pool) that she was condemned, despised, left like this in a backwater, because of her being like this—a feeble, vacillating creature; and it seemed to her that the yellow dress was a penance which she had deserved, and if she had been dressed like Rose Shaw, in lovely, clinging green with a ruffle of swansdown, she would have deserved that; and she thought that there was no escape for her—none whatever. But it was not her fault altogether, after all. It was being one of a family of ten; never having money enough, always skimping and paring; and her mother carrying great cans, and the linoleum worn on the stair edges, and one sordid little domestic tragedy after another—nothing catastrophic, the sheep farm failing, but not utterly; her eldest brother marrying beneath him but not very much—there was no romance, nothing extreme about them all. They petered out respectably in seaside resorts; every watering-place had one of her aunts even now asleep in some lodging with the front windows not quite facing the sea. That was so like them—they had to squint at things always. And she had done the same—she was just like her aunts. For all her dreams of living in India, married to some hero like Sir Henry Lawrence, some empire builder (still the sight of a native in a turban filled her with romance), she had failed utterly. She had married Hubert, with his safe, permanent underling's job in the Law Courts, and they managed tolerably in a smallish house, without proper maids, and hash when she was alone or just bread and butter, but now and then—Mrs. Holman was off, thinking her the most dried-up, unsympathetic twig she had ever met, absurdly dressed, too, and would tell everyone about Mabel's fantastic appearance—now and then, thought Mabel Waring, left alone on the blue sofa, punching the cushion in order to look occupied, for she would not join Charles Burt and Rose Shaw, chattering like magpies and perhaps laughing at her by the fireplace—now and then, there did come to her delicious moments, reading the other night in bed, for instance, or down by the sea on the sand in the sun, at Easter—let her recall it—a great tuft of pale sand-grass, standing all twisted like a shock of spears against the sky, which was blue like a smooth china egg, so firm, so hard, and then the melody of the waves—"Hush, hush," they said, and the children's shouts paddling—yes, it was a divine moment, and there she lay, she felt, in the hand of the Goddess who was the world; rather a hard-hearted, but very beautiful Goddess, a little lamb laid on the altar (one did think these silly things, and it didn't matter so long as one never said them). And also with Hubert sometimes she had quite unexpectedly—carving the mutton for Sunday lunch, for no reason, opening a letter, coming into a room—divine moments, when she said to herself (for she would never say this to anybody else), "This is it. This has happened. This is it!" And the other way about it was equally surprising—that is, when everything was arranged—music, weather, holidays, every reason for happiness was there—then nothing happened at all. One wasn't happy. It was flat, just flat, that was all.

Her wretched self again, no doubt! She had always been a fretful, weak, unsatisfactory mother, a wobbly wife, lolling about in a kind of twilight existence with nothing very clear or very bold, more one thing than another, like all her brothers and sisters, except perhaps Herbert—they were all the same poor water-veined creatures who did nothing. Then in the midst of this creeping, crawling life suddenly she was on the crest of a wave. That wretched fly††—where had

she read the story that kept coming into her mind about the fly and the saucer?††—struggled out. Yes, she had those moments. But now that she was forty, they might come more and more seldom. By degrees she would cease to struggle any more. But that was deplorable! That was not to be endured! That made her feel ashamed of herself!

She would go to the London Library tomorrow. She would find some wonderful, helpful, astonishing book, quite by chance, a book by a clergyman, by an American no one had ever heard of; or she would walk down the Strand and drop, accidentally, into a hall where a miner was telling about the life in the pit, and suddenly she would become a new person. She would be absolutely transformed. She would wear a uniform; she would be called Sister Somebody; she would never give a thought to clothes again. And forever after she would be perfectly clear about Charles Burt and Miss Milan and this room and that room; and it would be always, day after day, as if she were lying in the sun or carving the mutton. It would be it!

So she got up from the blue sofa, and the yellow button in the looking-glass** got up too, and she waved her hand to Charles and Rose to show them she did not depend on them one scrap, and the yellow button moved out of the looking-glass**, and all the spears were gathered into her breast as she walked towards Mrs. Dalloway and said, "Good night."

"But it's too early to go," said Mrs. Dalloway, who was always so charming.

"I'm afraid I must," said Mabel Waring. "But," she added in her weak, wobbly voice which only sounded ridiculous when she tried to strengthen it, "I have enjoyed myself enormously."

"I have enjoyed myself," she said to Mr. Dalloway, whom she met on the stairs.

"Lies, lies, lies!" she said to herself, going downstairs, and "Right in the saucer††!" she said to herself as she thanked Mrs. Barnet for helping her and wrapped herself, round and round and round, in the Chinese cloak she had worn these twenty years.

The symbolism here is achieved through the recurrence of two symbols:

1. The looking-glass image (marked by the editor with **). Mabel's whole concern is for the figure she is cutting before everyone at the gathering. She feels utterly on display, and is sure that what everyone sees is only her contemptible appearance. All their conversation, gestures, intonations, private thoughts have, she is sure, to do with the sorry show she is making. The persistence of the looking-glass symbol is an intensification of her sense of being miserably on public exhibition—everything but reflects her failure. The looking-glass

image is also meaningful in another way. Mabel shrinks from direct contact with the world, and her life is one chiefly of her own visions, always once-removed from reality, like reflections in a mirror.

There are other touches in the story which cooperate with this symbol—the looking at the picture, for example. A picture, like a mirror, is in a frame, and is to be looked at too. Nevertheless, one doesn't go "to a party to look at a picture!" The picture, like the mirror, is also for Mabel an escape from the people present. The passage in which Mabel hopes for "one word of praise, one word of affection" from Charles Burt also reinforces the mirror-symbol. That word of praise or affection, which is not forthcoming, would have altered what the mirror had revealed to Mabel; it would have reflected a quite different picture of her.

2. The fly and the fly-in-the-saucer image (marked by the editor with ††). Mabel feels herself to be completely insignificant; her life has been a tale of petty boredom without the dignity of a major catastrophe. The persistence of the fly and the fly-in-the-saucer image is an intensification of her sense of inferiority. She is like a fly crawling slowly out of a saucer of milk, its wings stuck together, trying to hoist itself from one insignificance to something else equally insignificant. She would like to think of the others the same way, but cannot; they are beautiful—if insects, not less than butterflies or dragonflies.

The repetition of "Lies, lies, lies!"—near the beginning and at the end of the story—cooperates with the fly image because the word will associate itself by rhyme with *flies*.

This story well exemplifies the power of symbolism to charge with emotion the meaning of a work.

ALLEGORY

Symbols, whether used for their figurative power in isolation or in the more sophisticated fashion of symbolism, are a technique rather than a form. When symbolic actions are tied together to make a narrative, they become a literary form: allegory. In such a narrative, characters, things and places, as well as happenings, have another meaning.

Here are passages of political and church allegory turned to satirical purposes in Jonathan Swift's (1667–1745) *Gulliver's Travels*. The shipwrecked Gulliver is living in the country of Lilliput, whose taller inhabitants are somewhat longer than his middle finger (trees, houses, cattle are to scale); their littleness is a mirror of human pettiness.

My gentleness and good behavior had gained so far on the Emperor and his court, and indeed upon the army and people in general, that I began to conceive hopes of getting my liberty in a short time. I took all possible methods to cultivate this favorable disposition. The natives came by degrees to be less apprehensive of any danger from me. I would sometimes lie down, and let five or six of them dance on my hand. And at last the boys and girls would venture to come and play at hide and seek in my hair. I had now made a good progress in understanding and speaking their language. The Emperor had a mind one day to entertain me with several of the country shows, wherein they exceed all nations I have known, both for dexterity and magnificence. I was diverted with none so much as that of the ropedancers, performed upon a slender white thread, extended about two foot, and twelve inches from the ground. Upon which I shall desire liberty, with the reader's patience, to enlarge a little.

This diversion is only practiced by those persons who are candidates for great employments, and high favor, at court.[1] They are trained in this art from their youth, and are not always of noble birth, or liberal education. When a great office is vacant, either by death or disgrace, (which often happens) five or six of those candidates petition the Emperor to entertain his Majesty and the court with a dance on the rope, and whoever jumps the highest without falling, succeeds in the office. Very often the chief ministers themselves are commanded to show their skill, and to convince the Emperor that they have not lost their faculty. Flimnap, the Treasurer, is allowed to cut a caper on the straight rope, at least an inch higher than any other lord in the whole empire.

[1]Here the actions stand for the devious means used by politicians to get power.

I have seen him do the summerset several times together upon a trencher fixed on the rope, which is no thicker than a common packthread in England. My friend Reldresal, principal Secretary for private Affairs, is, in my opinion, if I am not partial, the second after the Treasurer; the rest of the great officers are much upon a par.

These diversions are often attended with fatal accidents, whereof great numbers are on record. I myself have seen two or three candidates break a limb. But the danger is much greater when the ministers themselves are commanded to show their dexterity; for, by contending to excel themselves and their fellows, they strain so far, that there is hardly one of them who hath not received a fall, and some of them two or three. I was assured that a year or two before my arrival, Flimnap would have infallibly broke his neck, if one of the King's cushions, that accidently lay on the ground, had not weakened the force of his fall.

There is likewise another diversion, which is only shown before the Emperor and Empress, and first minister, upon particular occasions. The Emperor lays on the table three fine silken threads of six inches long. One is blue, the other red, and the third green.[2] These threads are proposed as prizes for those persons whom the Emperor hath a mind to distinguish by a peculiar mark of his favor. The ceremony is performed in his Majesty's great chamber of state, where the candidates are to undergo a trial of dexterity very different from the former, and such as I have not observed the least resemblance of in any other country of the old or the new world. The Emperor holds a stick in his hands, both ends parallel to the horizon, while the candidates advancing one by one, sometimes leap over the stick, sometimes creep under it backwards and forwards several times, according as the stick is advanced or depressed. Sometimes the Emperor holds one end of the stick, and his first minister the other; sometimes the minister has it entirely to himself. Whoever performs his part with most agility, and holds out the longest in leaping and creeping, is rewarded with the blue-colored silk; the red is given to the next, and the green to the third, which they all wear girt twice round about the middle; and you see few great persons about this court, who are not adorned with one of these girdles.

One morning, about a fortnight after I had obtained my liberty, Reldresal, principal Secretary (as they style him) of private Affairs, came to my house attended only by one servant. He ordered his coach to wait at a distance, and desired I would give him an hour's audience; which I readily consented to, on account of his quality and personal merits, as well as the many good offices he had done me during my solicitations at court. I offered to lie down, that he might the more conveniently reach my ear; but he chose rather to let me hold him in my hand during our conversation. He began with compliments on my liberty; said he might pretend to some merit in it: but, however, added, that if it had not been for the present situation of things at court, perhaps I might not have obtained it so soon. For, said he, as flourishing a condition as we may appear to be in to foreigners, we labor under two mighty evils; a violent faction at home, and the danger of an invasion by a most potent enemy from abroad. As to the first, you are to understand, that for about seventy moons past there have been two struggling parties in this empire, under the names of *Tramecksan* and *Slamecksan*, from the high and low heels on their shoes,[3] by which they distinguish themselves. It is alleged indeed, that the high heels are most agreeable to our ancient constitution: but however this be, his Majesty hath determined to make use of only low heels in the administration of the government, and all offices in the gift of the Crown, as you cannot but observe; and particularly, that his Majesty's Imperial heels are lower at least by a *drurr* than any of his court; (*drurr* is a measure about the fourteenth part of an inch). The animosities between these two parties run so high, that they will neither eat nor drink, nor talk with each other. We compute the *Tramecksan,* or High-Heels, to exceed us in number; but the power is wholly on our side. We apprehend his Imperial Highness, the Heir to the Crown, to have some tendency towards the High-Heels; at least we can plainly discover one of his heels higher than the other, which gives him a hobble in his gait.[4] Now, in the midst of these intestine disquiets, we are threatened with an invasion from the Island of Blefuscu, which is the other great empire of the universe, almost as large and powerful as this of his Majesty. For as to what we have heard you affirm, that there are other kingdoms and states

[2]These stand for the ribbons of the Garter, the Bath, and the Thistle, for which the "great persons about this court" degrade themselves "leaping and creeping."

[3]The high heels are the Tories or High Church party; the low heels, the Whigs or Low Church party.

[4]A reference to the intrigues with both parties conducted by the Prince of Wales, later George II.

in the world inhabited by human creatures as large as yourself, our philosophers are in much doubt, and would rather conjecture that you dropped from the moon, or one of the stars; because it is certain, that an hundred mortals of your bulk would, in a short time, destroy all the fruits and cattle of his Majesty's dominions. Besides, our histories of six thousand moons make no mention of any other regions, than the two great empires of Lilliput and Blefuscu. Which two mighty powers have, as I was going to tell you, been engaged in most obstinate war for six and thirty moons past. It began upon the following occasion. It is allowed on all hands, that the primitive way of breaking eggs before we eat them, was upon the larger end: but his present Majesty's grandfather,[5] while he was a boy, going to eat an egg, and breaking it according to the ancient practice, happened to cut one of his fingers. Whereupon the Emperor his father published an edict, commanding all his subjects, upon great penalties, to break the smaller end of their eggs.[6] The people so highly resented this law, that our histories tell us there have been six rebellions raised on that account; wherein one Emperor lost his life, and another his crown.[7] These civil commotions were constantly fomented by the monarchs of Blefuscu; and when they were quelled, the exiles always fled for refuge to that empire. It is computed, that eleven thousand persons have, at several times, suffered death, rather than submit to break their eggs at the smaller end. Many hundred large volumes have been published upon this controversy: but the books of the Big-Endians have been long forbidden, and the whole party rendered incapable by law of holding employments. During the course of these troubles, the Emperors of Blefuscu did frequently expostulate by their ambassadors, accusing us of making a schism in religion, by offending against a fundamental doctrine of our great prophet Lustrog, in the fifty-fourth chapter of the Brundecral (which is their Alcoran). This, however, is thought to be a mere strain upon the text: for the words are these; *That all true believers break their eggs at the convenient end:* and which is the convenient end, seems, in my humble opinion, to be left to every man's conscience, or at least in the power of the chief magistrate to determine. Now the Big-Endian exiles have found so much credit in the Emperor of Blefuscu's court, and so much private assistance and encouragement from their party here at home, that a bloody war has been carried on between the two empires for six and thirty moons with various success; during which time we have lost forty capital ships, and a much greater number of smaller vessels, together with thirty thousand of our best seamen and soldiers; and the damage received by the enemy is reckoned to be somewhat greater than ours. However, they have now equipped a numerous fleet, and are just preparing to make a descent upon us; and his Imperial Majesty, placing great confidence in your valor and strength, has commanded me to lay this account of his affairs before you.

I desired the Secretary to present my humble duty to the Emperor, and to let him know, that I thought it would not become me, who was a foreigner, to interfere with parties; but I was ready, with the hazard of my life, to defend his person and state against all invaders.

In the great medieval tradition of allegory, types and personifications of virtues and vices often became characters in the story. In the fifteenth-century play *Everyman,* God, impatient with the worldliness of mankind, commands Death to summon Everyman on a pilgrimage to judgment.

GOD. I perceive here in my majesty,
How that all creatures be to me unkind,
Living without dread in worldly prosperity:
Of ghostly[1] sight the people be so blind,
Drowned in sin, they know me not for their God;
In worldly riches is all their mind,
They fear not my rightwiseness, the sharp rod;
My law that I showed, when I for them died,
They forgot clean, and shedding of my blood
    red;   30

I hanged between two, it cannot be denied;
To get them life I suffered to be dead;
I healed their feet, with thorns hurt was my head:
I could do no more than I did truly,
And now I see the people do clean forsake me.
They use the seven deadly sins damnable;
As pride, covetise, wrath, and lechery,
Now in the world be made commendable;
And thus they leave of angels the heavenly company;

[5]Henry VIII, who withdrew from the Church of Rome and established the English Church.
[6]The Big-Endians are the Catholics; the Little-Endians the Protestants.
[7]Charles I lost his life and James II his crown.
[1]Spiritual.

Everyman liveth so after his own pleasure, 40
And yet of their life they be nothing sure:
I see the more that I them forbear
The worse they be from year to year;
All that liveth appaireth[2] fast,
Therefore I will in all the haste
Have a reckoning of *Everyman's* person;
For and I leave the people thus alone
In their life and wicked tempests,
Verily they will become much worse than beasts,
For now one would by envy another up eat; 50
Charity they all do clean forget.
I hoped well that *Everyman*
In my glory should make his mansion,
And thereto I had them all elect;
But now I see, like traitors deject,
They thank me not for the pleasure that I to them
meant,
Nor yet for their being that I them have lent;
I proffered the people great multitude of mercy,

And few there be that asketh it heartily;
They be so cumbered with worldly riches, 60
That needs on them I must do justice,
On *Everyman* living without fear.
Where art thou, *Death,* thou mighty messenger?
DEATH. Almighty God, I am here at your
will,
Your commandment to fulfil.
GOD. Go thou to *Everyman,*
And show him in my name
A pilgrimage he must on him take,
Which he in no wise may escape;
And that he bring with him a sure reckoning 70
Without delay or any tarrying.
DEATH. Lord, I will in the world go run
over all,
And cruelly outsearch both great and small;
Every man will I beset that liveth beastly
Out of God's laws, and dreadeth not folly.

When *Death* will not consent to spare him even until the morrow, *Everyman* cries out:

How shall I do now for to excuse me?
I would to God I had never be gete![3]
To my soul a full great profit it had be; 190
For now I fear pains huge and great.
The time passeth; Lord, help that all wrought;
For though I mourn it availeth nought.
The day passeth, and is almost a-go;
I wot not well what for to do.
To whom were I best my complaint to make?
What, and I to *Fellowship* thereof spake,
And showed him of this sudden chance?
For in him is all mine affiance;
We have in the world so many a day 200
Be on good friends in sport and play.
I see him yonder, certainly;
I trust that he will bear me company;
Therefore to him will I speak to ease my sorrow.
Well met, good *Fellowship,* and good morrow!
FELLOWSHIP SPEAKETH. *Everyman,* good
morrow by this day.
Sir, why lookest thou so piteously?
If any thing be amiss, I pray thee, me say,
That I may help to remedy.
EVERYMAN. Yea, good *Fellowship,* yea, 210
I am in great jeopardy.
FELLOWSHIP. My true friend, show to me
your mind;
I will not forsake thee, unto my life's end,
In the way of good company.
EVERYMAN. That was well spoken, and lov-
ingly.

FELLOWSHIP. Sir, I must needs know your
heaviness;
I have pity to see you in any distress;
If any have you wronged ye shall revenged be,
Though I on the ground be slain for thee,—
Though that I know before that I should die.220
EVERYMAN. Verily, *Fellowship,* gramercy.[4]
FELLOWSHIP. Tush! by thy thanks I set not
a straw.
Show me your grief, and say no more.
EVERYMAN. If I my heart should to you
break,
And then you to turn your mind from me,
And would not me comfort, when you hear me
speak,
Then should I ten times sorrier be.
FELLOWSHIP. Sir, I say as I will do in deed.
EVERYMAN. Then be you a good friend at
need:
I have found you true here before. 230
FELLOWSHIP. And so ye shall evermore;
For, in faith, and thou go to Hell,
I will not forsake thee by the way!
EVERYMAN. Ye speak like a good friend; I
believe you well;
I shall deserve it, and I may.
FELLOWSHIP. I speak of no deserving, by
this day.
For he that will say and nothing do
Is not worthy with good company to go;
Therefore show me the grief of your mind,

[2]Degenerates.
[3]Been born.

[4]Thanks.

As to your friend most loving and kind.   240
  EVERYMAN. I shall show you how it is;
Commanded I am to go a journey,
A long way, hard and dangerous,
And give a strait count without delay
Before the high judge Adonai.
Wherefore I pray you, bear me company,
As ye have promised, in this journey.
  FELLOWSHIP. That is matter indeed! Promise is duty,
But, and I should take such a voyage on me,
I know it well, it should be to my pain: 250
Also it make me afeard, certain.
But let us take counsel here as well as we can,
For your words would fear a strong man.
  EVERYMAN. Why, ye said, If I had need,
Ye would me never forsake, quick[5] nor dead,
Though it were to hell truly.
  FELLOWSHIP. So I said, certainly,
But such pleasures be set aside, thee sooth to say:
And also, if we took such a journey,
When should we come again?   260
  EVERYMAN. Nay, never again till the day of doom.
  FELLOWSHIP. In faith, then will not I come there!
Who hath you these tidings brought?
  EVERYMAN. Indeed, *Death* was with me here.
  FELLOWSHIP. Now, by God that all hath bought,
If *Death* were the messenger,
For no man that is living to-day
I will not go that loath journey—
Not for the father that begat me!
  EVERYMAN. Ye promised other wise, pardie.[6]   170
  FELLOWSHIP. I wot well I say so truly;
And yet if thou wilt eat, and drink, and make good cheer,
Or haunt[7] to women, the lusty company,
I would not forsake you, while the day is clear,
Trust me verily!
  EVERYMAN. Yes, thereto ye would be ready;
To go to mirth, solace, and play,

Your mind will sooner apply
Than to bear me company in my long journey.
  FELLOWSHIP. Now, in good faith, I will not that way.   280
But and thou wilt murder, or any man kill,
In that I will help thee with a good will!
  EVERYMAN. O that is a simple advice indeed!
Gentle fellow, help me in my necessity;
We have loved long, and now I need,
And now, gentle *Fellowship,* remember me.
  FELLOWSHIP. Whether ye have loved me or no,
By Saint John, I will not with thee go.
  EVERYMAN. Yet I pray thee, take the labor, and do so much for me
To bring me forward, for saint charity,   290
And comfort me till I come without the town.
  FELLOWSHIP. Nay, and thou would give me a new gown,
I will not a foot with thee go;
But and you had tarried I would not have left thee so.
And as now, God speed thee in thy journey,
For from thee I will depart as fast as I may.
  EVERYMAN. Whither away, *Fellowship?* Will you forsake me?
  FELLOWSHIP. Yea, by my fay, to God I betake thee.
  EVERYMAN. Farewell, good *Fellowship;* for this my heart is sore;
Adieu for ever, I shall see thee no more.   300
  FELLOWSHIP. In faith, *Everyman,* farewell now at the end;
For you I will remember that parting is mourning.
  EVERYMAN. Alack! shall we thus depart indeed?
Our Lady, help, without any more comfort,
Lo, *Fellowship* forsaketh me in my most need:
For help in this world whither shall I resort?
Fellowship herebefore with me would merry make;
And now little sorrow for me doth he take.
It is said, in prosperity men friends may find,
Which in adversity be full unkind.   310

Others also desert him. He knows he can turn to *Good-Deeds,*

But alas, she is so weak,
That she can neither go[8] nor speak;
Yet will I venture on her now.—
My *Good-Deeds,* where be you?

  GOOD-DEEDS. Here I lie cold in the ground;
Thy sins hath me sore bound,
That I cannot stir.

[5]Alive.
[6]Fr. *par dieu,* an oath.

[7]Resort.
[8]Walk.

Knowledge, the sister of *Good-Deeds,* takes *Everyman* to *Confession,* "that cleansing river," who gives him the "precious jewel of penance." *Everyman* then prays:

> EVERYMAN. O eternal God, O heavenly fig-
> ure,
> O way of rightwiseness, O goodly vision,
> Which descended down in a virgin pure
> Because he would *Everyman* redeem,
> Which *Adam* forfeited by his disobedience;
> O blessed Godhead, elect and high-divine,
> Forgive my grievous offense;
> Here I cry thee mercy in this presence.
> O ghostly treasure, O ransomer and redeemer
> Of all the world, hope and conductor,   590
> Mirror of joy, and founder of mercy,
> Which illumineth heaven and earth thereby,
> Here my clamorous complaint, though it late be;
> Receive my prayers; unworthy in this heavy life,
> Though I be, a sinner most abominable,
> Yet let my name be written in *Moses'* table;
> O *Mary,* pray to the Maker of all thing,
> Me for to help at my ending,
> And save me from the power of my enemy,
> For *Death* assaileth me strongly;   600
> And, Lady, that I may by means of thy prayer
> Of your Son's glory to be partaker,
> By the means of his passion I it crave,
> I beseech you, help my soul to save.—

After the "scourge of penance," *Good-Deeds* becomes "whole and sound." In *Everyman's* death-hour *Beauty* refuses to smother in the grave, not for all his gold, although she promised to live and die with him; *Strength* tells him he is old enough to travel alone; *Discretion* runs to follow *Strength;* even his *Five-Wits,* whom he took for his best friend, forsakes him. Only *Good-Deeds* accompanies him to *Death;* the others, going their own way, are earthly vanities—worthless to the soul.

Sometimes moral abstractions are embodied in an allegory and given other names, as in the passage we reproduce in our next chapter from Edmund Spenser's (1552?–1599) epic, *The Faerie Queene.* Here the Red Crosse Knight is holiness; the lady Una travelling with him is truth and equally the Church of England; she rides a white ass, humility; and so forth.

In allegory the artist faces the difficulty of making such characters as the Knight and the lady credibly human, who by definition are not. To put it another way, the allegory must be, as it were, completely dissolved in the story, and the story must catch us up. The story cannot be simply a transparent window for the allegorical meaning. When we speak of the story, we do not refer merely to the sequence of happenings; the language, the structure, and other elements are crucial to our experience of the allegory as a work of art. One of the greatest successes in this form is John Bunyan's (1628–1688) *The Pilgrim's Progress* "from this world to that which is to come, delivered under the similitude of a dream, wherein is discovered the manner of his setting out, his dangerous journey, and his safe arrival at the desired country." This Protestant allegory has probably been better known in the English-speaking world than any other book besides the Bible of 1611. Those of our readers who know the book will remember the excitement and humanity of the story, the vividness of the characters, and the unaffected mastery of the prose.

"SIMPLICITY" AND "COMPLEXITY"

In addition to the aspects of language we have discussed, there is one other for us to consider, though it is a matter that sometimes has as much to do with stylistic structure as with vocabulary.

One of the inanities one frequently hears is that "all great art is really simple." We call it inane because it is rather meaningless. What does simplicity imply with respect to art? For example, would you call our Jeremy Taylor passage simple? If you think that a normal English prose style must consist of brief sentences, you may call Taylor's complicated. Yet, surely you had no difficulty in understanding him. If you had no trouble following him, you must hesitate to pronounce his prose difficult.

Ask a trained musician or music-lover, "Is a Bach fugue simple or complicated?"—and he will hardly know how to answer. "Yes," he will probably say, "a Bach fugue is very simple to follow—if it is being well-played, and if you know how to listen to it." Then he might add, "However, it is also true that simple as a Bach fugue is to follow, the *means* employed in its composition are quite complicated." You would run into similar answers if you sought professional opinion about the simplicity of the cathedral at Chartres or Leonardo da Vinci's "Mona Lisa."

To consider the case in literature let us take William Blake's "A Poison Tree":

> I was angry with my friend:
> I told my wrath, my wrath did end.
> I was angry with my foe:
> I told it not, my wrath did grow.
>
> And I watered it in fears
> Night and morning with my tears,
> And I sunnèd it with smiles
> And with soft deceitful wiles.
>
> And it grew both day and night,
> Till it bore an apple bright,
> And my foe beheld it shine,
> And he knew that it was mine,—   10
>
> And into my garden stole
> When the night had veiled the pole;
> In the morning, glad, I see
> My foe outstretched beneath the tree.

The language of this poem is undeniably simple; the words are in the vocabulary of a grammar-school child. Yet you would hesitate to call the *poem* simple. Indeed, you will probably have to ponder it before you understand the poem's meaning. It would even be no disgrace to you if you decided you need help with it.* This work of art eludes being described as either simple or difficult.

On the other hand, here is a passage from the first book of Milton's (1608–1674) *Paradise Lost.* The poet is telling how God hurled the rebel Satan out of Heaven through Chaos and down to Hell:

> Him the Almighty Power
> Hurled headlong flaming from the ethereal sky,
> With hideous ruin and combustion, down

*In case you do, we suggest you answer for yourself the following questions about it, to clarify your notions: Why did he feel compelled to tell his friend his wrath? Why did he refuse to do the same with his foe? What is this "poison tree" which he watered day and night with tears and which he sunned with deceitful wiles? What was the apple that the tree bore? What happened to his foe in the last line? Why was he glad to find his foe that way? Is the foe the only victim here?

> To bottomless perdition; there to dwell
> In adamantine chains and penal fire.

Here the simplicity-complexity is exactly opposite to that of Blake. These words are undeniably not simple; they will not be found in a child's vocabulary. (If they could be, it would be good cause for a parent's alarm!) Yet if you will take the trouble to look them up in a dictionary, you will—despite a certain complexity in the word order too—have no impediment to arriving precisely and with no further help at Milton's meaning. (This would be an experience comparable to preparing yourself for following the lines of a Bach fugue.) This work of art also eludes the labels.

Rather than deciding about the simplicity of Blake or Milton, it is wiser to say, as we can readily enough, that Blake's language is simple, Milton's not; Milton's thought is clear, Blake's more shadowy. It is the contrast between Blake's simplicity of language and the subtlety of his thought which imparts an electric quality to his poetry. In Milton the combination of strong-minded clear thought and grandeur of expression helps make him one of the very noblest poets in any language.

Simplicity, then, is in itself neither virtue nor vice. However, it is quite another matter when we turn from Blake and Milton to writing which is grandiose in manner while its subject is on an elementary level. If you were standing in a country graveyard looking at the headstones of the unlettered and unknown good folk who lie buried there, it would do you credit if you paused to feel sympathy for their humble lot. Their lives were without event, without importance to their country, you might reflect; yet they were human, they had their own joys and sorrows, and therefore their own dignity. Such thoughts would do you credit, we repeat, and they did Thomas Gray (1716–1771) credit when he wrote the celebrated "Elegy Written in a Country Churchyard." But these thoughts, though creditable, can be deemed neither profound nor startlingly original. Obviously if you chose to record them, it ought to occur to you that the less ornate you were, the better. Listen, however, to Gray:

> Let not Ambition mock their useful toil,
>   Their homely joys and destiny obscure;
> Nor Grandeur hear with a disdainful smile,
>   The short and simple annals of the poor.

There is surely something absurd in the disparity here between the pomposity of the expression and the thing being said. "Homely joys" no longer appear so when discussed in the language of the first two lines. And nothing could seem less "short and simple" than the "annals" of the poor.* It is one thing to unite simple words, as Blake does, to complicated thoughts. It is quite another to attempt swelling simple thoughts by complicated words.

On the other hand, there is no particular virtue in simple expression when nothing much is being said.

> I turned the knob, and opened the door. I came into the room, and the door
> shut behind me. It was closed.

This kind of simplicity we meet with only too often among some contemporary novelists, who prefer not to be men of letters. It is easy to be simple when you are being dull or obvious. Such simplicity, easily acquired, would seem to imply simplicity of mind in author and admirer.

Possibly what people have in mind when they talk about "the simplicity of all great art"

---

*We are here treading on many toes in disparaging an old favorite. We even remember that General Wolfe, before taking Quebec, is supposed to have remarked that he would have preferred being the author of one of the *Elegy*'s (poorest) stanzas, "The boast of heraldry, the pomp of power," etc.,to being the greatest of military heroes. This would only prove General Wolfe a better soldier than literary critic. We are, however, in good company. It was Wordsworth who said (not of Pope! but) of Gray that he "was more than any other man curiously elaborate in the structure of his own poetic diction."

is really comprehensibility. It would be hard to limit writers to a vocabulary of two hundred words so that every moron can be sure to follow. There is no reason why an author should not be as elaborate in his language as Milton is, if he finds that necessary to express his exalted ideas. No writer need compromise with his audience's laziness or illiteracy. But a good case could be made for the obligation of an author to be comprehensible, if we make all the effort required to follow him. We ought not to be left, at the end, having to guess what was in his mind when he wrote. Literature *is* a form of communication.

Apparently, however, this is an opinion not universally accepted. The question is still unsettled among critics as to whether there is any artistic justification for the language of James Joyce's (1882–1941) *Finnegans Wake:*

> ... nor had topsawyer's rocks by the stream Oconee exaggerated themselves to Laurens County's gorgios while they went doublin their mumper all the time.

This is one of the easier moments!

STRUCTURE AND THE DOMINIONS OF PROSE AND POETRY

ᴆᴆ **3** ᴆᴆ

WE HAVE SEEN what an author can do with words. But striking individual words or a collection of striking phrases cannot suffice to make a work of literature. In a musical composition a particular phrase may seem, at the moment it occurs, to lift the work to the skies; but the presence of such a phrase or of several such phrases, if they are unrelated to the composition as a whole, cannot qualify the work as a masterpiece. In literature at its best any expression, no matter how arresting or moving the words may be, must be relevant to the structure of the whole. The harmony and unity of a literary work are of primary importance to the achievement of meaning.

STRUCTURE AND ARTISTIC APPREHENSION

James Joyce (1882–1941) has brilliantly discoursed on unity and harmony as corresponding to "phases of artistic apprehension." In *A Portrait of the Artist as a Young Man* the hero Stephen Dedalus is speaking to a classmate:

> Stephen pointed to a basket which a butcher's boy had slung inverted on his head.
> —Look at that basket—he said.
> —I see it—said Lynch.
> —In order to see that basket—said Stephen—your mind first of all separates the basket from the rest of the visible universe which is not the basket. The first phase of apprehension is a bounding line drawn about the object to be apprehended. An esthetic image is presented to us either in space or in time. What is audible is presented in time, what is visible is presented in space. But temporal or spatial, the esthetic image is first luminously apprehended as selfbounded and selfcontained upon the immeasurable background of space or time which is not it. You apprehended it as *one* thing. You see it as one whole. You apprehend its wholeness. That is *integritas.*—
> —Bull's eye!—said Lynch, laughing—Go on.—
> —Then—said Stephen—you pass from point to point, led by its formal lines; you apprehend it as balanced part against part within its limits; you feel the rhythm of its structure. In other words, the synthesis of immediate perception is followed by the analysis of apprehension. Having first felt that it is *one* thing you feel now that it is a *thing.* You apprehend it as complex, multiple, divisible, separable, made up of its parts, the result of its parts and their sum, harmonious. That is *consonantia.*—

81

Thus, how a literary work comes to us depends on its structure. Every successfully written piece, since it has its own meaning to convey, has its own structure, its own unity and harmony. Regarding the matter in this light, we see that there are as many structures as there are literary works. But if we focus on the manner in which the work comes to us, we can understand certain general principles of structure. Understanding these principles puts us in a better position to gather in the meaning of the work; for, if we do not realize by what route a work is coming to us, we may, as it were, see it as it passes by but have no real meeting with it, no real apprehension of what it can mean to us.

STRUCTURE AND CONTENT

The structure of a work is conditioned by all the elements that go into making the meaning of the work. Of all the elements, however, the "content" of the work most basically determines the structure.* Therefore it is wise to begin with a clear notion as to what the "content" is—always remembering, of course, that "content" is only part of the meaning. Once the "content" can be firmly stated, the reader can take a nearer view of the structure.

Let us discover what we can concerning the last complete work quoted, William Blake's "A Poison Tree." The speaker in the poem is a person with an intense hatred for a man he considers his enemy, and the poem itself deals with the growth and culmination of that hate. We shall paraphrase the "content":

Stanza 1. Because I loved my friend, when I was angry with him, love urged me to tell him of my anger; and as I told it, the anger vanished. Because I hated my enemy, when I was angry with him, hate urged me to keep my anger secret, and to allow it to grow.

Stanza 2. Night and day I fed my anger with my fears and my wretchedness, and I encouraged its growth with smiles and deceit. (The figurative language amplifies the idea: I concealed my hate from my enemy by fawning on him—"smiles"—and encouraged him to think me harmless by my gentle ways—"soft deceitful wiles." Like an anxious parent, I nurtured my anger and hate lest they wane from inattention—"sunnèd it with smiles/ And with soft deceitful wiles.")

Stanza 3. My tree of hate grew and bore a shining fruit. My enemy saw the fruit, and knew it to be mine. (My hate grew and grew until it gave birth to a beautiful trap with which I might undo my enemy. My enemy was deceived by the outward attractiveness of my stratagem—"apple bright," "beheld it shine"—and imagined that a new occasion was afforded him to do me injury—"And he knew that it was mine.")

Stanza 4. My enemy stole the fruit of my hate one night. The next morning I rejoiced to find him dead. (He thought himself quite secure, and so walked right into the snare I had prepared for him. I had so contrived my scheme that it was his own deed—"And into my garden stole"—which proved his undoing. My hate triumphed. With mad delight I witnessed the success of my plot. I had killed my enemy.)

Our paraphrase makes clear that the subject of the poem is Hate. *The subject of a work is what the work is about.* It is possible, of course, to have various ideas on any subject; *the central or governing idea in a work is its theme.* The theme of Blake's poem may be stated as: Hate is an obsession which ends by destroying both the hater and the hated. The "content" of a work elaborates and brings into the world of particular experience the work's subject and theme.

Now we are ready to examine the relationship between "content" and structure. The word *stanza* (literally, in Italian, "the stopping place") *means a group of lines which form*

*Writers would add that, on the other hand, the other elements contributing to meaning will also condition the "content."

one of the divisions of a poem. The stanza is therefore one of the elements involved in the structure of a poem when the work employs stanzaic form. Note how each of Blake's four stanzas begins a new turn in the procession of thoughts. The first differentiates between love and hate when under the incitement of anger. The second shows the cultivation of hate. The third tells of hate's fruit. The last shows the end toward which hate moves: the destruction of hater and hated alike; the hated is dead, the hater has become a murderer. The progress to that end is felt to be the steadier and surer because of the regular recurrence of the four-line stanza as the form employed, and of the pattern of rhyming in pairs (*friend, end; foe, grow; fears, tears; smiles, wiles*). Both stanzaic form and rhyme-pattern contribute to the solidity and symmetry of the structure. In this instance a solid, symmetrical structure renders the "content" the more startling.

Of course, a writer may find this kind of symmetrical structure undesirable for his meaning. D. H. Lawrence's (1885–1930) "Snake" is such an instance:

A snake came to my water-trough
On a hot, hot day, and I in pyjamas for the heat,
To drink there.

In the deep, strange-scented shade of the great
    dark carob-tree
I came down the steps with my pitcher
And must wait, must stand and wait, for there he
    was at the trough before me.

He reached down from a fissure in the earth-wall
    in the gloom
And trailed his yellow-brown slackness soft-bel-
    lied down, over the edge of the stone trough
And rested his throat upon the stone bottom,
And where the water had dripped from the tap,
    in a small clearness,   10
He sipped with his straight mouth,
Softly drank through his straight gums, into his
    slack long body,
Silently.

Some one was before me at my water-trough,
And I, like a second comer, waiting.

He lifted his head from his drinking, as cattle do,
And looked at me vaguely, as drinking cattle do,
And flickered his two-forked tongue from his lips,
    and mused a moment,
And stooped and drank a little more,
Being earth brown, earth golden from the burn-
    ing bowels of the earth   20
On the day of Sicilian July, with Etna[1] smoking.

The voice of my education said to me
He must be killed,
For in Sicily the black, black snakes are innocent,
    the gold are venomous.
And voices in me said, If you were a man
You would take a stick and break him now, and
    finish him off.

But I must confess how I liked him,
How glad I was he had come like a guest in quiet,
    to drink at my water-trough
And depart peaceful, pacified, and thankless,
Into the burning bowels of this earth.   30

Was it cowardice, that I dared not kill him?
Was it perversity, that I longed to talk to him?
Was it humility, to feel so honored?
I felt so honored.

And yet those voices:
If you were not afraid, you would kill him!

And truly I was afraid, I was most afraid,
But even so, honored still more
That he should seek my hospitality
From out the dark door of the secret earth.   40
He drank enough
And lifted his head, dreamily, as one who has
    drunken,
And flickered his tongue like a forked night on
    the air, so black,
Seeming to lick his lips,
And looked around like a god, unseeing, into the
    air,
And slowly turned his head,
And slowly, very slowly, as if thrice adream,
Proceeded to draw his slow length curving round
And climb again the broken bank of my wall-
    face.

And as he put his head into that dreadful hole,
And as he slowly drew up, snake-easing his shoul-
    ders, and entered farther,   51
A sort of horror, a sort of protest against his
    withdrawing into that horrid black hole,
Deliberately going into the blackness, and slowly
    drawing himself after,
Overcame me now his back was turned.

[1] A volcano in Sicily.

I looked round, I put down my pitcher,
I picked up a clumsy log
And threw it at the water-trough with a clatter.
I think it did not hit him,
But suddenly that part of him that was left behind
    convulsed in undignified haste,
Writhed like lightning, and was gone   60
Into the black hole, the earth-lipped fissure in the
    wall-front,
At which, in the intense still noon, I stared with
    fascination.

And immediately I regretted it.
I thought how paltry, how vulgar, what a mean
    act!

I despised myself and the voices of my accursed
    human education.

And I thought of the albatross,[2]
And I wished he would come back, my snake.

For he seemed to me again like a king,
Like a king in exile, uncrowned in the under-
    world,
Now due to be crowned again.   70

And so, I missed my chance with one of the lords
Of life.
And I have something to expiate;
A pettiness.

The structure of this poem is conditioned by the simple but striking incident Lawrence relates. With the second stanza the poem follows the incident in chronological sequence. The divisions of the work are fixed by the details of the experience and of the reflections arising in the narrator, in order of their original occurrence. First, the characters (the snake, the narrator) and the setting (the water-trough); next, the introduction of the narrator; next, the introduction of the snake; next, the feelings of the narrator at the first encounter ("like a second comer"); next, the actions of the snake; next, the promptings of the narrator's learning ("the gold are venomous"); next, the promptings of his manhood ("If you were a man"); next, the promptings of his better judgment ("How glad I was"); next, his self-questionings ("Was it cowardice,"); next, the voice of his manhood again ("If you were not afraid"); next, the return of his higher judgment ("honored"); next, the end of the snake's drinking; next, the snake's slow retreat; next, the narrator's deed; next, the disappearance of the snake; next, the narrator's reaction to his deed ("how paltry . . ."); next, his regrets ("I thought of the albatross"); next, the reason for his regrets ("he seemed . . . Like a king in exile"); last, his evaluation of the experience ("I missed my chance").

For his purposes Lawrence preferred a verse form that does not call for rhyme, meter, or regularity of stanza—* what is called *free verse.* In free verse every line, ideally, takes on the contour of the "content" of that line. In "Snake" the structure admirably cooperates with the incident, the setting, the movements of the snake, and the thoughts of the narrator —to give harmony and unity to the whole.

STRUCTURE IN NARRATIVE LITERATURE

"A Poison Tree" and "Snake" are both *narrative* poems, for they both relate happenings—or, roughly put, tell a story. They both illustrate structure typical of a narrative, one that follows the outline of the story to be told.

There was probably never a time when human beings did not relish hearing a story. Primitive literature abounds in narratives. The narrative is, in fact, one of three characteristic ways in which writers tend to present their visions of life, the other two being the *reflective* and the *lyrical.* Each of these ways has its structure. And, as we have said, the structure determines how the vision in a literary work comes to us.

Of course, while agreeing to call "Snake" a narrative, one might well hesitate to apply that designation to "A Poison Tree." The materials of literature being life, we are forever rediscovering the vanity of taking literary analyses too strictly. Life resists categorizing, and

[2]In Coleridge's "The Rime of the Ancient Mariner."
*Rhyme, meter, stanzaic forms, and so forth are fully dealt with, below, in the chapters on Musical Attributes and Verse Techniques.

literature does too. We no sooner arrive at a fairly reasonable category than we find it overlapping with another. "Snake," for example, is plainly a narrative; nevertheless, the story is told only because of what the narrator can conclude from it; it therefore is also somewhat reflective too. That is, we associate the development of ideas primarily with reflective literature, the structure of which we shall discuss later in this chapter. And as for "A Poison Tree"—! It tells a story—a fairly complete one, too. Well and good; that makes it narrative. But the events in the story are merely symbolic—events can be symbolic even as words can be—and not to be taken literally as are the events in "Snake"; they are presented only for the theme, the pervading idea of the work; they show us how hate destroys both hater and hated; the poem is therefore also reflective. Moreover, "A Poison Tree" was published in a volume called *Songs of Experience;* the musical element is strong in a song, and certainly strong in Blake's poem; a song, typically, is connected with the lyrical; Blake's song therefore also partakes of the qualities which we must presently associate with the lyrical.

Nevertheless, if we remember not to take our demarcations too literally, and to observe how the limits of categories frequently disappear, we may say that writings on the whole tend to be shaped according to the structural principles characteristic of the narrative, reflective or lyrical. We may say this because each of these three ways in which an author can present his vision of life has its characteristic structure. It was probably reflection (or even, possibly, the lyrical impulse) which originated the composition of "A Poison Tree." But as it comes to us, the finished poem does tell us a story. And its structure is the structure characteristic of the narrative, one dictated by the outlines of the story to be told.

It is indeed not unusual that an author prefers to compel his readers to make their own inferences concerning his interpretation of life by presenting it to them in the guise of a story. This was true, of course, of Virginia Woolf's "The New Dress" (see page 68). Thomas Hardy (1840–1928) wrote a series of great novels exhibiting his pessimistic and fatalistic view of man's place in the world; later in life he chose to relate his stories in a number of concise poems. This one, "Ah, Are You Digging on My Grave?," is characteristic of its author's point of view:

"Ah, are you digging on my grave
   My loved one?—planting rue?"
—"No: yesterday he went to wed
One of the brightest wealth has bred.
'It cannot hurt her now,' he said,
   'That I should not be true.' "

"Then who is digging on my grave?
   My nearest dearest kin?"
—"Ah, no: they sit and think, 'What use!
What good will planting flowers produce?   10
No tendance of her mound can loose
   Her spirit from Death's gin.' "

"But some one digs upon my grave?
   My enemy?—prodding sly?"
—"Nay: when she heard you had passed the
   Gate
That shuts on all flesh soon or late,
She thought you no more worth her hate,
   And cares not where you lie."

"Then, who is digging on my grave?
   Say—since I have not guessed!"   20
—"O it is I, my mistress dear,
Your little dog, who still lives near,
And much I hope my movements here
   Have not disturbed your rest?"

"Ah yes! *You* dig upon my grave . . .
   Why flashed it not on me
That one true heart was left behind!
What feeling do we ever find
To equal among human kind
   A dog's fidelity!"   30

"Mistress, I dug upon your grave
   To bury a bone, in case
I should be hungry near this spot
When passing on my daily trot.
I am sorry, but I quite forgot
   It was your resting-place."

Hardy's poem is, of course, saying something about life; nor is there absent an implication of strong feelings of bitterness. But as the poem comes to us it has first of all a story to tell. When the heart of the work is a story, we call such a work narrative. If the events of the story are presented by way of narration, the narrative will be in the form of a narrative poem, short story and so forth; if they are presented by way of action, the narrative will be in the form of a play.

The subject of the poem is Loyalty after Death. The theme is: when one dies one is utterly forgotten.* The structure of the poem is conditioned by the action of the story it relates. First, we are told of what the loved one is doing; next, of what the nearest of kin are thinking; next, of what the enemy is feeling. Next the digger is identified; next, we hear the gratitude of his mistress. Finally, we are given the digger's true motive. The first half of the poem places the dead woman in the setting of those who knew her; the second half deals with her relationship to her little dog. The first half makes plain how quickly the dead are forgotten by loved one, kin and enemy; the second half denies the love of even the devoted pet.

Most modern readers, of course, are more familiar with narratives written in prose. The following amusing little story is by the twentieth-century Englishman, Hector Hugh Munro (1870–1916), who wrote under the pen-name of "Saki." It is entitled "Reginald's Choir Treat."

"Never," wrote Reginald to his most darling friend, "be a pioneer. It's the Early Christian that gets the fattest lion."

Reginald, in his way, was a pioneer.

None of the rest of his family had anything approaching Titian hair or a sense of humour, and they used primroses as a table decoration.

It follows that they never understood Reginald, who came down late to breakfast, and nibbled toast, and said disrespectful things about the universe. The family ate porridge, and believed in everything, even the weather forecast.

Therefore the family was relieved when the vicar's daughter undertook the reformation of Reginald. Her name was Amabel; it was the vicar's one extravagance. Amabel was accounted a beauty and intellectually gifted; she never played tennis, and was reputed to have read Maeterlinck's *Life of the Bee.* If you abstain from tennis *and* read Maeterlinck in a small country village, you are of necessity intellectual. Also she had been twice to Fécamp to pick up a good French accent from the Americans staying there; consequently she had a knowledge of the world which might be considered useful in dealings with a worldling.

Hence the congratulations in the family when Amabel undertook the reformation of its wayward member.

Amabel commenced operations by asking her unsuspecting pupil to tea in the vicarage garden; she believed in the healthy influence of natural surroundings, never having been in Sicily, where things are different.

And like every woman who has ever preached repentance to unregenerate youth, she dwelt on the sin of an empty life, which always seems so much more scandalous in the country, where people rise early to see if a new strawberry has happened during the night.

Reginald recalled the lilies of the field, "which simply sat and looked beautiful, and defied competition."

"But that is not an example for us to follow," gasped Amabel.

"Unfortunately, we can't afford to. You don't know what a world of trouble I take in trying to rival the lilies in their artistic simplicity."

"You are really indecently vain of your appearance. A good life is infinitely preferable to good looks."

"You agree with me that the two are incompatible. I always say beauty is only sin deep."

Amabel began to realize that the battle is not always to the strong-minded. With the immemorial resource of her sex, she abandoned the frontal attack and laid stress on her unassisted labours in parish work, her mental loneliness, her discouragements—and at the right moment she produced strawberries and cream. Reginald was obviously affected by the latter, and when his preceptress suggested that he might begin the strenuous life by helping her to supervise the annual outing of the bucolic infants who composed the local choir, his eyes shone with the dangerous enthusiasm of a convert.

Reginald entered on the strenuous life alone, as far as Amabel was concerned. The most virtuous women are not proof against damp grass, and Amabel kept her bed with a cold. Reginald called

---

*It would be possible, of course, to write a narrative with exactly the opposite theme on the same subject —e.g., One is never forgotten after death by either those who have loved one or those who have hated one. It is perhaps also worth observing here that, writing on Hardy's subject and theme, another poet—Pope, for instance—might have used a light, flippant tone instead of the dry, bitter one we find in Hardy, and so communicated a different meaning.

it a dispensation; it had been the dream of his life to stage-manage a choir outing. With strategic insight, he led his shy, bullet-headed charges to the nearest woodland stream and allowed them to bathe; then he seated himself on the discarded garments and discoursed on their immediate future, which, he decreed, was to embrace a Bacchanalian procession[1] through the village. Forethought had provided the occasion with a supply of tin whistles, but the introduction of a he-goat from a neighbouring orchard was a brilliant afterthought. Properly, Reginald explained, there should have been an outfit of panther skins; as it was, those who had spotted handkerchiefs were allowed to wear them, which they did with thankfulness. Reginald recognized the impossibility in the time at his disposal, of teaching his shivering neophytes a chant in honour of Bacchus, so he started them off with a more familiar, if less appropriate, temperance hymn. After all, he said, it is the spirit of the thing that counts. Following the etiquette of dramatic authors on first nights, he remained discreetly in the background while the procession, with extreme diffidence and the goat, wound its way lugubriously towards the village. The singing had died down long before the main street was reached, but the miserable wailing of pipes brought the inhabitants to their doors. Reginald said he had seen something like it in pictures; the villagers had seen nothing like it in their lives, and remarked as much freely.

Reginald's family never forgave him. They had no sense of humour.

Again, the structure is conditioned by the outline of the story to be told. It will not be news to learn that "Reginald's Choir Treat" is a short story. The short story and the novel form with the drama the three most important forms of modern prose storytelling. We shall analyze and discuss all three further in Chapters 5 and 6.

PROSE AND POETRY IN DRAMA

At the moment it seems opportune to correct a popular misimpression. For a long time now audiences have largely assumed that prose is the normal medium for drama. But this was not always so. The history of the world's greatest drama is part of the history of the world's greatest poetry. In some epochs, such as the Golden Age of Athens, Elizabethan England, and Louis XIV's France, the normal medium for drama was poetry. Aeschylus, Sophocles, Shakespeare and Racine are no less incomparable as poets than as dramatists. As poets we must rank very high such great dramatists, too, as Aristophanes, Marlowe, Webster, Ford, Otway and Corneille. In our own times dramatists like Maxwell Anderson and Christopher Fry have made notable attempts to restore poetry to the English-speaking stage; other playwrights, particularly Tennessee Williams, have written a prose for their plays very close to the language of poetry. It may be that the future will see a renaissance of poetic drama in English.

Certainly poetry can stir our senses and compress much in little to a degree of which prose is incapable. Witness this passage from Shakespeare's *Othello* (III/iii). At its opening the Moor, Othello, is an open-hearted, heroic man, with the completest confidence in the love and loyalty of his wife, Desdemona. In a mere two hundred lines we see, horror-struck, how the villain Iago can so subtly by devilish innuendo inoculate him with the poison of jealousy, that Othello, noble and generous pillar of the Venetian state, is irretrievably lost as a man. Prose could never create the illusion of such a volcanic change in so brief a span:

IAGO.   My noble lord,—
OTH.   What dost thou say, Iago?
IAGO.   Did Michael Cassio, when you
    woo'd my lady,
Know of your love?
OTH.   He did, from first to last: why dost
    thou ask?
IAGO.   But for a satisfaction of my thought;
No further harm.
OTH.   Why of thy thought,

    Iago?   110
IAGO.   I did not think he had been ac-
    quainted with her.
OTH.   O, yes; and went between us very oft.
IAGO.   Indeed!
OTH.   Indeed! ay, indeed: discern'st thou
    aught in that?
Is he not honest?
IAGO.   Honest, my lord!
OTH.   Honest! ay, honest.

[1]In worship of Bacchus, the god of wine.

IAGO.   My lord, for aught I know.

OTH.   What dost thou think?

IAGO.   Think, my lord!   120

OTH.   Think, my lord!

By heaven, he echoes me,
As if there were some monster in his thought
Too hideous to be shown. Thou dost mean some-
thing:
I heard thee say even now, thou lik'dst not that,
When Cassio left my wife: what didst not like?
And when I told thee he was of my counsel
In my whole course of wooing, thou criedst 'In-
deed!'
And didst contract and purse thy brow together,
As if thou then hadst shut up in thy brain   130
Some horrible conceit:[1] if thou dost love me,
Show me thy thought.

IAGO.   My lord, you know I love you.

OTH.   I think thou dost;
And, for I know thou'rt full of love and honesty,
And weigh'st thy words before thou giv'st them
breath,
Therefore these stops of thine fright me the more:
For such things in a false disloyal knave
Are tricks of custom, but in a man that's just
They are close delations,[2] working from the heart
That passion cannot rule.   141

IAGO.   For Michael Cassio,
I dare be sworn I think that he is honest.

OTH.   I think so too.

IAGO.   Men should be what they seem;
Or those that be not, would they might seem
none!

OTH.   Certain, men should be what they
seem.

IAGO.   Why, then, I think Cassio's an honest man.

OTH.   Nay, yet there's more in this:
I prithee, speak to me as to thy thinkings,   150
As thou dost ruminate, and give thy worst of
thoughts
The worst of words.

IAGO.   Good my lord, pardon me:
Though I am bound to every act of duty,
I am not bound to that all slaves are free to.
Utter my thoughts? Why, say they are vile and
false;
As where's that palace whereinto foul things
Sometimes intrude not? who has a breast so pure,
But some uncleanly apprehensions
Keep leets[3] and law[4]-days and in session sit 160
With meditations lawful?

OTH.   Thou dost conspire against thy
friend, Iago,
If thou but think'st him wrong'd and mak'st his
ear
A stranger to thy thoughts.

IAGO.   I do beseech you—
Though I perchance am vicious in my guess,
As, I confess, it is my nature's plague
To spy into abuses, and oft my jealousy[5]
Shapes faults that are not—that your wisdom yet,
From one that so imperfectly conceits,[6]   170
Would take no notice, nor build yourself a trou-
ble
Out of his scattering and unsure observance.
It were not for your quiet nor your good,
Nor for my manhood, honesty, or wisdom,
To let you know my thoughts.

OTH.   What dost thou mean?

IAGO.   Good name in man and woman,
dear my lord,
Is the immediate jewel of their souls;
Who steals my purse steals trash; 'tis something,
nothing;
'Twas mine, 'tis his, and has been slave to thou-
sands;
But he that filches from me my good name   180
Robs me of that which not enriches him
And makes me poor indeed.

OTH.   By heaven, I'll know thy thoughts.

IAGO.   You cannot, if my heart were in
your hand;
Nor shall not, whilst 'tis in my custody.

OTH.   Ha!

IAGO.   O, beware, my lord, of jealousy;[7]
It is the green-ey'd monster which doth mock
The meat it feeds on: that cuckold lives in bliss
Who, certain of his fate, loves not his wronger;
But, O, what damned minutes tells[8] he o'er   192
Who dotes, yet doubts, suspects, yet strongly
loves!

OTH.   O misery!

IAGO.   Poor and content is rich and rich
enough.
But riches fineless[9] is as poor as winter
To him that ever fears he shall be poor.
Good heaven, the souls of all my tribe defend
From jealousy!

OTH.   Why, why is this?   200
Think'st thou I'ld make a life of jealousy,
To follow still[10] the changes of the moon

[1]Conception.
[2]Secret accusations.
[3]Law-courts.
[4]Court.

[5]Suspicion.
[6]Imagines.
[7]Suspicion.
[8]Counts.
[9]Without end.
[10]Always.

With fresh suspicions? No; to be once in doubt
Is once to be resolv'd: exchange me for a goat,
When I shall turn the business of my soul
To such exsufflicate[11] and blown surmises,
Matching thy inference. 'Tis not to make me jealous
To say my wife is fair, feeds well, loves company,
Is free of speech, sings, plays and dances well;
Where virtue is, these are more virtuous: 210
Nor from mine own weak merits will I draw
The smallest fear or doubt[12] of her revolt;
For she had eyes, and chose me. No, Iago;
I'll see before I doubt; when I doubt, prove;
And on the proof, there is no more but this,—
Away at once with love or jealousy!
    IAGO.   I am glad of it; for now I shall have
      reason
To show the love and duty that I bear you
With franker spirit: therefore, as I am bound,
Receive it from me. I speak not yet of proof. 220
Look to your wife; observe her well with Cassio;
Wear your eyes thus, not jealous nor secure:
I would not have your free and noble nature,
Out of self-bounty,[13] be abus'd; look to 't·
I know our country disposition[14] well;
In Venice they do let heaven see the pranks
They dare not show their husbands; their best
    conscience
Is not to leave't undone, but keep't unknown.
    OTH.   Dost thou say so?
    IAGO.   She did deceive her father, marrying
      you;   230
And when she seem'd to shake and fear your
    looks,
She lov'd them most.
    OTH.   And so she did.
    IAGO.   Why, go to then;
She that, so young, could give out such a seeming,
To seel her father's eyes up close as oak[15] —
He thought 'twas witchcraft—but I am much to
    blame;
I humbly do beseech you of your pardon
For too much loving you.
    OTH.   I am bound to thee for ever.
    IAGO.   I see this hath a little dash'd your
      spirits.
    OTH.   Not a jot, not a jot.   242
    IAGO.   I' faith, I fear it has.
I hope you will consider what is spoke
Comes from my love. But I do see you're mov'd:

I am to pray you not to strain my speech
To grosser issues nor to larger reach
Than to suspicion.
    OTH.   I will not.
    IAGO.   Should you do so, my lord,   250
My speech should fall into such vile success[16]
As my thoughts aim not at. Cassio's my worthy
    friend—
My lord, I see you're mov'd.
    OTH.   No, not much mov'd:
I do not think but Desdemona's honest.
    IAGO.   Long live she so! and long live you
      to think so!
    OTH.   And yet, how nature erring[17] from
      itself,—
    IAGO.   Ay, there's the point: as—to be bold
      with you—
Not to affect[18] many proposed matches   260
Of her own clime, complexion, and degree,[19]
Whereto we see in all things nature tends—
Foh! one may smell in such, a will most rank,
Foul disproportion, thoughts unnatural.
But pardon me; I do not in position[20]
Distinctly speak of her, though I may fear
Her will, recoiling to her better judgment,
May fall to match you with her country forms
And happily[21] repent.
    OTH.   Farewell, farewell: 270
If more thou dost perceive, let me know more;
Set on thy wife to observe: leave me, Iago.
    IAGO [going]. My lord, I take my leave.
    OTH.   Why did I marry? This honest crea-
      ture doubtless
Sees and knows more, much more, than he un-
    folds.
    IAGO [returning]. My lord, I would I
      might entreat your honour
To scan this thing no further; leave it to time:
Though it be fit that Cassio have his place,
For, sure, he fills it up with great ability,
Yet, if you please to hold him off awhile,   280
You shall by that perceive him and his means:
Note, if your lady strain his entertainment[22]
With any strong or vehement importunity;
Much will be seen in that. In the mean time,
Let me be thought too busy in my fears—
As worthy cause I have to fear I am—
And hold her free,[23] I do beseech your honour.

[11]Blown-up.

[12]Suspicion.

[13]Natural goodness.

[14]Disposition of our people.

[15]The grain of the oak.

[16]Results.

[17]Wandering.

[18]Like.

[19]Rank.

[20]Positiveness.

[21]Perhaps.

[22]Regaining his position.

[23]Innocent.

OTH.   Fear not my government.
IAGO.   I once more take my leave. [*Exit.*]
OTH.   This fellow's of exceeding honesty, 290
And knows all qualities, with a learned spirit,
Of human dealings. If I do prove her haggard,[24]
Though that her jesses[25] were my dear heart-
    strings,
I'ld whistle her off and let her down the wind,
To prey at fortune. Haply, for I am black
And have not those soft parts of conversation
That chamberers[26] have, or for I am declin'd
Into the vale of years,—yet that's not much—
She's gone. I am abus'd; and my relief

Must be to loathe her. O curse of marriage, 300
That we can call these delicate creatures ours,
And not their appetites! I had rather be a toad,
And live upon the vapour of a dungeon,
Than keep a corner in the thing I love
For others' uses. Yet, 'tis the plague of great ones;
Prerogativ'd are they less than the base;
'Tis destiny unshunnable, like death:
Even then this forked plague[27] is fated to us
When we do quicken.[28] Desdemona comes:
    [*Reenter Desdemona and Emilia.*]
If she be false, O, then heaven mocks itself! 310
I'll not believe 't.

Only poetry of impassioned figurative language and compelling rhythms, making our imagination ardent and swift, could convince us, as does this scene, that so violent a change in
a man's life could take place in a matter of minutes.

There are many things to be said concerning drama as a literary form. We shall speak
of them in Chapter 6.

KINDS OF NARRATIVE POETRY

Of narrative poetry, there are several kinds that deserve special attention.

There is, first of all, the story in verse that comes to us from the folk, anonymous, the
heritage of the people. Some of these are tragic stories, some romantic, some humorous. The
best of them have a wonderful combination of the naive, the crude, and the extremely subtle.

One of the most admired of these old folk stories is "Edward":

"Why dois your brand[1] sae drap wi bluid,
                Edward, Edward?
Why dois your brand sae drap wi bluid,
  And why sae sad gang[2] yee O?"
"O I hae killed my hauke sae guid,
                Mither, mither,
O I hae killed my hauke sae guid,
  And I had nae mair bot[3] hee O."

"Your haukis bluid was nevir sae reid,[4]
                Edward, Edward,
Your haukis bluid was never sae reid,   11
  My deir son I tell thee O."
O I hae killed my reid-roan steid,
                Mither, mither,
O I hae killed my reid-roan steid,
  That erst was sae fair and frie O."

"Your steid was auld, and ye hae gat mair,
                Edward, Edward,

Your steid was auld, and ye hae gat mair;
  Sum other dule ye drie[5] O."   20
"O I hae killed my fadir deir,
                Mither, mither,
O I hae killed my fadir deir,
  Alas, and wae is mee O!"

"And whatten penance wul ye drie for that,
                Edward, Edward?
And whatten penance wul ye drie, for that?
  My deir son, now tell me O."
"Ile set my feit in yonder boat,
                Mither, mither,
Ile set my feit in yonder boat,   31
  And Ile fare ovir the sea O."

"And what wul ye doe wi your towirs and your
  ha,
                Edward, Edward?
And what wul ye doe wi your towirs and your ha,
  That were sae fair to see O?"
"Ile let thame stand tul they doun fa,
                Mither, mither,
Ile let thame stand tul they doun fa,

---

[24]An untameable hawk.
[25]Strings by which the hawk was held.
[26]Dandies.
[27]The horns of the deceived husband.
[28]Are born.

[1]Sword.
[2]Go.

---

[3]Had no more but he.
[4]Red.
[5]Sorrow you suffer.

For here nevir mair maun I bee[6] O."   40

For thame nevir mair wul I see O."   48

"And what wul ye leive[7] to your bairns[8] and your wife,

Edward, Edward?

And what wul ye leive to your bairns and your wife,
  Whan ye gang ovir the sea O?"
"The warldis[9] room, late them beg thrae life,
                    Mither, mither,
The warldis room, late them beg thrae life,

"And what wul ye leive to your ain mither deir,
                    Edward, Edward?
And what wul ye leive to your ain mither deir?
  My deir son, now tell me O."
"The curse of hell frae me sall ye beir,
                    Mither, mither,
The curse of hell frae me sall ye beir,
  Sic[10] counseils ye gave to me O."

We call such a narrative poem a *ballad,* and when, as in this instance, it comes from the folk, a *folk ballad.*

The word *ballad* means "dance-song." Originally these poems were danced to, and the marks of the dance-origin are still upon many of them. The repetitions and refrains—such as *Edward, Edward, Mither, mither,* and *O* in every stanza of this ballad—are possibly survivals of the turns of the dance. And for many of them we still have the old melodies —some of them hauntingly beautiful. But as poetry these folk ballads hold their own. How powerfully the picture is evoked for us in "Edward": the venomous mother, eager for the terrible news; the soul-sick son, trying to evade the fatal announcement of the deed.

No doubt many of the folk ballads were composed spontaneously to celebrate some actual event. Others weave legends of the fancy—notably a series of racy ballads about the deeds of Robin Hood. And those which are humorous are full of the salty, boisterous fun peculiar to folk humor. We do not know whether any given ballad was composed by an individual, and now anonymous, author, or cooperatively in the way Negro spirituals are made in the South—scholars have argued both theories. But however the ballads were composed, they belong to the people, and were handed on orally from generation to generation. This method of transmission explains the several versions which we have for the same ballad. The folk ballad in English represents our medieval literature at its most engaging.

They have indeed been so much admired that later poets have written in imitation of them. Coleridge's "The Rime of the Ancient Mariner" and Keats's "La Belle Dame Sans Merci" are well-known examples. Osbert Sitwell's (1892–1969) "The Ballad of Sister Anne" is an interesting ballad by a contemporary poet:

"Sister Anne, Sister Anne,
  You who have always been faithful to me,
Why do you stand there?

"Tell me, run to the window!
  What is it that I hear?
My bed is far from the window and I am restless,
  What is it that I hear?
I do not like to appear too curious
But I *must* know what it is I hear!

"Sister Anne, Sister Anne, I entreat you   10
  To tell me what it is I hear (I hear).
A new footstep sings to me from the asphalt pavement,
A new shape patterns old dust.

You don't hear it, Sister Anne? You must,
                    you must!

"Sister Anne, Sister Anne,
  Run to the window!
    What is it that I hear?
A footstep drawing near and nearer, surely toward
The Grange. Is it the stranger—tall, thin stranger—
  You told me you saw approaching   20
    Last night in the cards?"

"Miss Wetherby, Miss Wetherby, my love,
  It's only the new butcher's boy at the corner,
    Red as a rose,
Wearing his blue and white striped coat and apron,
Bearing a basket of raw legs and shoulders

[6]For here nevermore may I be.
[7]Leave.
[8]Children.
[9]World's.

[10]Such.

To give old people young strength.
 It's only the new butcher's boy at the corner,
  Whistling as he goes."

"Sister Anne, Sister Anne,
 Why do I tremble,   30
What is it that I hear?
Perhaps it's Mrs. Shrubfield in her carriage,
Driving down to the Marine Parade and the Pier;
Are her horses sleek still, do the dogs still follow,
 Does she still hold in her eye a tear?"

"Miss Wetherby, my love, you grow uneasy,
 What is there for you to fear
If it were only Mrs. Shrubfield passing near?
 But no,
  It's the grocer's van,
  Varnished, spick and span, 40
Bringing brown demerara[1] and candy and lump
   sugar
 And white sifted sugar, sifted fine,
And coffee, roasted and ground daily
 For your convenience and mine."

"Sister Anne, Sister Anne,
 I don't think I'm quite myself today.
Fetch me a thermometer and some sal volatile
 And the medicine-glass with a spout.
 What is it I hear, a sound of singing
—How can it be the alarm-clock ringing
At this hour, on Frances's day out?" 50

"Miss Wetherby, my love, it is a sound consoling,
 That of a great bell rolling
As it will toll one day for me—and you."

"Sister Anne, Sister Anne!
 Why do I hear the sound of wheels?
 Is it a hearse?
Is it old Miss Vanbrugh at number four
 Who called in Doctor Diggle, the new doc-
  tor,
  Did she grow worse?"

"Miss Wetherby, Miss Wetherby, my love, 60
 Do not yourself distress.

It's only the rumble of Madame Cockburn's van
 Delivering a new dress.
She told me all about it, a dress for Hallows Hall,
A white gown, she said, to be worn at a ball;
 A white cloud—
  Like a shroud."

" 'Like a shroud!' Today you use such odd ex-
   pressions,
 Sister Anne, Sister Anne,
I think I have a touch of fever, my teeth chat-
 ter—   70
  Is anything the matter,
  Sister Anne?"

"Miss Wetherby, Miss Wetherby,
 I've stretched my neck through the trees from
   the window
And can tell the truth now."

"Yes, Sister Anne, tell me; tell me
 That it's only once again
The grocer's van,
  The new butcher's boy,
  The dressmaker's man."   80

"You would like to hear the truth, Madam
   mine—
 We can do as we like. No one will interrupt us.
There's not a soul in sight, not a sign,
  Not a sign!"

"Sister Anne, Sister Anne!
 What is it gleams in your hand?
Is it the thermometer-case flashing, as you stand
There—but I've never been able to bear people to
   come near me;
  Don't draw so near!"

"Miss Wetherby, Miss Wetherby, my love, 90
 It's time to wake you from your dream.
 Now I'll tell you what you heard.
 The thin stranger in the cards
 Was Death, drawing near and nearer:
  It is Death you feared—
  Try not to scream!"

The form of the ballad has operated brilliantly here to provide the steady approach, through anguish and fear, to the shock and horror of the end of the story. We call such a ballad, written by a later poet in deliberate imitation of the old popular ballads, an *art ballad*.

Among the folk of many nations there is to be found a longer kind of narrative poem, an extensive poem celebrating the deeds of a hero of the race. One of the earliest poems in our literature, for instance, is the long narrative poem of the Anglo-Saxons, *Beowulf*. This interesting mixture of the pagan and the Christian, the faintly historical and the legendary,

[1]A kind of raw cane sugar imported from British Guiana.

recounts three major heroic enterprises of a Teutonic warrior-prince.

The first of these exploits has to do with the monster Grendel, who has been harassing the warriors of Hrothgar, lord of the Danes, in the latter's home, Heorot Hall. From Sweden, across the sea, comes the hero, Beowulf, with his fellow-warriors to visit Hrothgar. Observing the havoc wrought among the Danes by the Fen-Dragon, Grendel, Beowulf undertakes to rid Heorot of the monster without employing any weapons. Grendel appears, and Beowulf attacks the demon single-handed. He succeeds in ripping one of Grendel's arms from its socket. The monster, mortally wounded, escapes across the moors to the Fens, and dives into the waters down to the cave of his mother. In Heorot Hall there is rejoicing and feasting over the victory.

The second exploit of Beowulf has to do with Grendel's mother. That horror on the next night, while all are asleep, enters Heorot Hall and carries off Hrothgar's counsellor. Beowulf and his men immediately start out in pursuit of her, but she escapes to her hiding-place beneath the waters. At the water's edge, Beowulf accepts the warrior Unferth's sword, Hrunting:

After these words the Weder-Jute lord[1]
Sprang to his task, nor staid for an answer.
Swiftly he sank 'neath the swirling flood;
'Twas an hour's time ere he touched the bottom.
Soon the sea-hag,[2] savage and wild,   1280
Who had roamed through her watery realms at will,
For winters a hundred, was 'ware from below,
An earthling had entered her ocean domain.
Quickly she reached and caught the hero;
Grappled him grimly with gruesome claws.
Yet he got no scratch, his skin was whole;
His battle-sark shielded his body from harm.
In vain she tried, with her crooked fingers,
To tear the links of his close-locked mail.   1290
Away to her den the wolf-slut dragged
Beowulf the bold, o'er the bottom ooze.
Though eager to smite her, his arm was helpless.
Swimming monsters swarmed about him,
Dented his mail with dreadful tusks.
Sudden the warrior was 'ware they had come
To a sea-hall strange and seeming hostile,
Where water was not nor waves oppressed,
For the caverned rock all round kept back
The swallowing sea. He saw a light,   1300
A flicker of flame that flashed and shone.
Now first he discerned the sea-hag monstrous,
The water-wife wolfish. His weapon he raised,
And struck with his sword a swinging blow.
Sang on her head the hard-forged blade
Its war-song wild. But the warrior found
That his battle-flasher refused to bite,
Or maim the foe. It failed its master
In the hour of need, though oft it had cloven
Helmets, and carved the casques of the doomed
In combats fierce. For the first time now   1311

That treasure failed him, fallen from honor.
But Hygelac's earl[3] took heart of courage;
In mood defiant he fronted his foe.
The angry hero hurled to the ground,
In high disdain, the hilt of the sword,
The gaudy and jewelled; rejoiced in the strength
Of his arm unaided. So all should do
Who glory would find and fame abiding,
In the crash of conflict, nor care for their lives.
The Lord of the Battle-Jutes braved the encounter;   1321
The murderous hag by the hair he caught;
Down he dragged the dam of Grendel
In his swelling rage, till she sprawled on the floor.
Quick to repay in kind what she got,
On her foe she fastened her fearful clutches;
Enfolded the warrior weary with fighting;
The sure-footed hero stumbled and fell.
As helpless he lay, she leapt on him fiercely;
Unsheathed her hip-knife, shining and broad, 1330
Her son to avenge, her offspring sole.
But the close-linked corslet covered his breast,
Foiled the stroke and saved his life.
All had been over with Ecgtheow's son,
Under the depths of the ocean vast,
Had not his harness availed to help him,
His battle-net stiff, and the strength of God.
The Ruler of battles aright decided it;
The Wielder all-wise awarded the victory:
Lightly the hero leaped to his feet.   1340

He spied 'mongst the arms a sword surpassing,
Huge and ancient, a hard-forged slayer,
Weapon matchless and warriors' delight,
Save that its weight was more than another
Might bear into battle or brandish in war;
Giants had forged that finest of blades.

[1] Beowulf.
[2] Grendel's mother.

[3] Beowulf.

Then seized its chain-hilt the chief of the Scyld-
     ings;
His wrath was aroused, reckless his mood,
As he brandished the sword for a savage blow.
Bit the blade in the back of her neck,   1350
Cut the neck-bone, and cleft its way
Clean through her flesh; to the floor she sank;

The sword was gory; glad was the hero.
A light flashed out from the inmost den,
Like heaven's candle, when clear it shines
From cloudless skies. He scanned the cave,
Walked by the wall, his weapon upraised;
Grim in his hand the hilt he gripped.
Well that sword had served him in battle.*

A long narrative poem celebrating the exploits of a hero of the race is known as a *folk epic*.[†] *Beowulf* has all the characteristics of the true folk epic, affording us as it does a lively insight into the temperament, tastes, customs, and ethics of the race during a primitive time. It is our folk epic, an interesting one, and one of our earliest literary monuments.

Just as later poets have been inspired by the folk ballads to write their own ballads, so later poets have undertaken the epic too. In English the two outstanding epic poets have been Spenser and Milton. We are discussing the epic at some length because it is the form in which some of the world's greatest literature has been written. From the standpoint of nobility of undertaking, only poetic drama can rival the epic. This is the opening of *The Faerie Queene* by Edmund Spenser (d. 1599):

I

Lo! I, the man whose Muse whylome[1] did maske,
As time her taught, in lowly Shephards weeds,[2]
Am now enforst, a farre unfitter taske,
For trumpets sterne to chaunge mine Oaten
     reeds,[3]
And sing of Knights and Ladies gentle deeds;
Whose praises having slept in silence long,
Me, all too meane, the sacred Muse[4] areeds[5]
To blazon broade emongst her learned throng:
Fierce warres and faithfull loves shall moralize my
     song.

II

Helpe then, O holy virgin! chiefe of nyne,[6]   10
Thy weaker Novice to performe thy will;
Lay forth out of thine everlasting scryne[7]
The antique rolles, which there lye hidden still,
Of Faerie knights, and fayrest Tanaquill,[8]

Whom that most noble Briton Prince[9] so long
Sought through the world, and suffered so much
     ill,
That I must rue his undeserved wrong:
O, helpe thou my weake wit, and sharpen my dull
     tong!

III

And thou most dreaded impe[10] of highest Jove,
Faire Venus sonne, that with thy cruel dart   20
At that good knight so cunningly didst rove,
That glorious fire it kindled in his hart;
Lay now thy deadly Heben[11] bowe apart,
And with thy mother mylde come to mine ayde;
Come, both; and with you bring triumphant
     Mart,[12]
In loves and gentle jollities arraid,
After his murdrous spoyles and bloudie rage al-
     layd.

*Translated by J. Duncan Spaeth. In his fine translation Spaeth erroneously believed the Geats, a Swedish tribe, to be the Jutes.

†There is one mystery about *Beowulf.* The hero is not, as he ought to be, an Angle, a Saxon, or a Jute; he is a Geat from Sweden. His exploits, moreover, take place neither in England nor in the continental homeland of the Anglo-Saxons, but in Denmark and Sweden. Scholars, naturally, have their theories about all this.

[1]Formerly.

[2]A reference to *The Shepherd's Calendar,* which Spenser had already published.

[3]Trumpets are connected with the epic, reeds with the pastoral.

[4]Clio, muse of History.

[5]Designates.

[6]Clio.

[7]Desk.

[8]Daughter of Oberon, King of the Fairies; here the reference is to Elizabeth I.

[9]Arthur.

[10]Child,—i.e., Cupid.

[11]Ebony.

[12]Mars.

IV

And with them eke, O Goddesse[13] heavenly
  bright!
Mirrour of grace and Majestie divine,
Great Ladie of the greatest Isle, whose light   30
Like Phoebus lampe[14] throughout the world doth
  shine,
Shed thy faire beames into my feeble eyne,
And raise my thoughts, too humble and too vile,
To thinke of that true glorious type of thine,
The argument of mine afflicted stile:[15]
The which to heare vouchsafe, O dearest dread,
  a-while!

CANTO I

The Patrone of true Holinesse
Foule Errour doth defeate:
Hypocrisie, him to entrappe,
Doth to his home entreate.

I

A gentle Knight was pricking[1] on the plaine,
Ycladd in mightie armes and silver shielde,
Wherein old dints of deepe woundes did remaine,
The cruell markes of many a bloody fielde;
Yet armes till that time did he never wield.
His angry steede did chide his foming bitt,
As much disdayning to the curbe to yield:
Full jolly[2] knight he seemd, and faire did sitt,
As one for knightly giusts[3] and fierce encounters
  fitt.

II

And on his brest a bloodie Crosse he bore,   10
The deare remembrance of his dying Lord,
For whose sweete sake that glorious badge he
  wore,
And dead, as living, ever him ador'd:
Upon his shield the like was also scor'd,
For soveraine hope which in his helpe he had;
Right faithfull true he was in deede and word,
But of his cheere[4] did seeme too solemne sad,
Yet nothing did he dread, but ever was ydrad.[5]

[13]Elizabeth I.
[14]The sun.
[15]Modest pen.

[1]Spurring.
[2]Handsome.
[3]Jousts.
[4]Face.
[5]Feared.

III

Upon a great adventure he was bond,
That greatest Gloriana[6] to him gave,   20
(That greatest Glorious Queene of Faery lond)
To winne him worshippe, and her grace to have,
Which of all earthly thinges he most did crave:
And ever as he rode his hart did earne[7]
To prove his puissance in battell brave
Upon his foe, and his new force to learne,
Upon his foe, a Dragon[8] horrible and stearne.

IV

A lovely Ladie[9] rode him faire beside,
Upon a lowly Asse more white then snow,
Yet she much whiter; but the same did hide   30
Under a vele, that wimpled[10] was full low;
And over all a blacke stole shee did throw:
As one that inly mournd, so was she sad,
And heavie sate upon her palfrey slow;
Seemed in heart some hidden care she had,
And by her, in a line, a milkewhite lambe she
  lad.[11]

V

So pure and innocent, as that same lambe,
She was in life and every vertuous lore;
And by descent from Royall lynage came
Of ancient Kinges and Queenes, that had of yore
Their scepters stretcht from East to Westerne
  shore,   41
And all the world in their subjection held;
Till that infernall feend with foull uprore
Forwasted all their land, and them expeld;
Whom to avenge she had this Knight from far
  compeld.

VI

Behind her farre away a Dwarfe[12] did lag,
That lasie seemd, in being ever last,
Or wearied with bearing of her bag
Of needments at his backe. Thus as they past,
The day with cloudes was suddeine overcast,   50
And angry Jove an hideous storme of raine
Did poure into his Lemans lap[13] so fast,
That everie wight to shrowd[14] it did constrain;
And this faire couple eke to shroud themselves
  were fain.

[6]Elizabeth I.   [12]Prudence.
[7]Yearn.   [13]Lover's lap (i.e., the Earth).
[8]Sin.   [14]Find shelter.
[9]Una (Truth).
[10]Folded.
[11]Led.

VII

Enforst to seeke some covert nigh at hand,
A shadie grove not farr away they spide,
That promist ayde the tempest to withstand;
Whose loftie trees, yclad with sommers pride,
Did spred so broad, that heavens light did hide,
Not perceable with power of any starr:　60
And all within were pathes and alleies wide,
With footing worne, and leading inward farr.
Faire harbour that them seems, so in they entred
　ar.

VIII

And foorth they passe, with pleasure forward led,
Joying to heare the birdes sweete harmony,
Which, therein shrouded from the tempest dred,
Seemd in their song to scorne the cruell sky.
Much can they praise the trees so straight and hy,
The sayling Pine; the Cedar proud and tall;
The vine-propp Elme; the Poplar never dry;
The builder Oake, sole king of forrests all;
The Aspine good for staves; the Cypresse funer-
　all;

IX

The Laurell, meed[15] of mightie Conquerours
And Poets sage; the Firre that weepeth still:
The Willow, worne of forlorne Paramours;
The Eugh,[16] obedient to the benders will;
The Birch for shaftes; the Sallow[17] for the mill;
The Mirrhe sweete-bleeding in the bitter wound;
The warlike Beech; the Ash for nothing ill;
The fruitfull Olive; and the Platane[18] round;　80
The carver Holme;[19] the Maple seeldom inward
　sound.

X

Led with delight, they thus beguile the way,
Until the blustring storme is overblowne;
When, weening[20] to returne whence they did
　stray,
They cannot finde that path, which first was
　showne,
But wander too and fro in waies unknowne,
Furthest from end then, when they neerest
　weene,

[15]Reward.
[16]Yew.
[17]A kind of willow.
[18]Plane-tree.
[19]A kind of oak.
[20]Supposing.

That makes them doubt,[21] their wits be not their
　owne:
So many pathes, so many turnings seene,
That which of them to take, in diverse doubt they
　been.　90

XI

At last resolving forward still to fare,
Till that some end they finde, or in or out,
That path they take, that beaten seemd most
　bare,
And like to lead the labyrinth about;
Which when by tract they hunted had through-
　out,
At length it brought them to a hollowe cave,
Amid the thickest woods. The champion stout
Eftsoones dismounted from his courser brave,
And to the dwarfe a while his needless spere he
　gave.

XII

"Be well aware," quoth then that ladie milde,　100
"Least suddaine mischiefe ye too rash provoke:
The danger hid, the place unknowne and wilde,
Breedes dreadfull doubts: oft fire is without
　smoke,
And perill without show: therefore your stroke,
Sir knight, with-hold, till further tryall made."
"Ah, ladie," sayd he, "shame were to revoke
The forward footing for an hidden shade:
Vertue gives her selfe light, through darkenesse
　for to wade."

XIII

"Yea, but," quoth she, "the perill of this place
I better wot then you; though nowe too late　110
To wish you backe returne with foule disgrace,
Yet wisedome warnes, whilest foot is in the gate,
To stay the steppe, ere forcèd to retrate.
This is the wandring wood, this Errours den,
A monster vile, whom God and man does hate:
Therefore I read[22] beware." "Fly, fly!" quoth
　then
The fearefull dwarfe: "this is no place for living
　men."

XIV

But full of fire and greedy hardiment,
The youthfull knight could not for ought be
　staide,
But forth unto the darksom hole he went,　120
And lookèd in: his glistring armor made

[21]Fear.
[22]Advise.

A little glooming light, much like a shade,
By which he saw the ugly monster plaine,
Halfe like a serpent horribly displaide,
But th' other halfe did womans shape retaine,
Most lothsome, filthie, foule, and full of vile dis-
      daine.

XV

And as she lay upon the durtie ground,
Her huge long taile her den all overspred,
Yet was in knots and many boughtes[23] upwound,
Pointed with mortall sting. Of her there bred 130
A thousand yong ones, which she dayly fed,
Sucking upon her poisnous dugs, each one
Of sundrie shapes, yet all ill favorèd:
Soone as that uncouth light upon them shone,
Into her mouth they crept, and suddain all were
      gone.

XVI

Their dam upstart, out of her den effraide,[24]
And rushèd forth, hurling her hideous taile
About her cursèd head, whose folds displaid
Were stretcht now forth at length without en-
      traile.[25]
She lookt about, and seeing one in mayle   140
Armed to point, sought backe to turne againe;
For light she hated as the deadly bale,[26]
Ay wont[27] in desert darknes to remaine,
Where plain none might her see, nor she see any
      plaine.

XVII

Which when the valiant Elfe[28] perceiv'd, he lept
As Lyon fierce upon the flying pray,
And with his trenchand blade her boldly kept
From turning backe, and forced her to stay:
Therewith enrag'd she loudly gan to bray,
And turning fierce her speckled taile advaunst,
Threatning her angrie sting, him to dismay;   151
Who, nought aghast, his mightie hand en-
      haunst:[29]
The stroke down from her head unto her shoul-
      der glaunst.

[23]Coils.
[24]Frightened.
[25]Coiling.
[26]Destruction.
[27]Accustomed.
[28]The Red Cross knight was of elfin birth.
[29]Lifted up.

XVIII

Much daunted with that dint her sence was dazd;
Yet kindling rage her selfe she gathered round,
And all attonce her beastly bodie raizd
With doubled forces high above the ground:
Tho, wrapping up her wrethed sterne arownd,
Lept fierce upon his shield, and her huge traine
All suddenly about his body wound,   160
That hand or foot to stirr he strove in vaine.
God helpe the man so wrapt in Errours endlesse
      traine!

XIX

His Lady, sad to see his sore constraint,
Cride out, "Now, now, Sir knight, shew what ye
      bee:
Add faith unto your force, and be not faint;
Strangle her, els she sure will strangle thee."
That when he heard, in great perplexitie,
His gall did grate[30] for griefe[31] and high disdaine;
And, knitting all his force, got one hand free,
Wherewith he grypt her gorge[32] with so great
      paine,   170
That soone to loose her wicked bands did her
      constraine.

XX

Therewith she spewd out of her filthie maw[33]
A floud of poyson horrible and blacke,
Full of great lumps of flesh and gobbets[34] raw,
Which stunck so vildly, that it forst him slacke
His grasping hold, and from her turne him backe.
Her vomit full of bookes and papers[35] was,
With loathly frogs and toades, which eyes did
      lacke,   178
And creeping sought way in the weedy gras:
Her filthie parbreake[36] all the place defiled has.

XXI

As when old father Nilus gins to swell
With timely pride above the Aegyptian vale,
His fattie waves doe fertile slime outwell,
And overflow each plaine and lowly dale:
But, when his later spring gins to avale,[37]

[30]Stir.
[31]Anger.
[32]Throat.
[33]Stomach.
[34]Pieces.
[35]Attacks on the English church and state.
[36]Vomit.
[37]Subside.

Huge heapes of mudd he leaves, wherein there
    breed
Ten thousand kindes of creatures, partly male
And partly femall, of his fruitful seed;
Such ugly monstrous shapes elsewher may no
    man reed.[38]

XXII

The same so sore annoyed has the knight,   190
That, welnigh choked with the deadly stinke,
His forces faile, ne can no lenger fight:
Whose corage when the feend perceived to
    shrinke,
She poured forth out of her hellish sinke
Her fruitful cursed spawne of serpents small,
Deformed monsters, fowle, and black as inke,
Which swarming all about his legs did crall,
And him encombred sore, but could not hurt at
    all.

XXIII

As gentle shepheard in sweete eventide,
When ruddy Phebus gins to welke[39] in west,   200
High on an hill, his flocke to vewen wide,
Markes which doe byte their hasty supper best;
A cloud of cumbrous gnattes doe him molest,
All striving to infixe their feeble stinges,
That from their noyance he no where can rest;
But with his clownish hands their tender wings
He brusheth oft, and oft doth mar their murmur-
    ings.

XXIV

Thus ill bestedd, and fearefull more of shame
Then of the certeine perill he stood in,
Halfe furious unto his foe he came,   210
Resolvd in minde all suddenly to win,
Or soone to lose, before he once would lin;[40]
And stroke at her with more then manly force,
That from her body, full of filthie sin,
He raft[41] her hatefull heade without remorse:
A streame of cole black blood forth gushèd from
    her corse.

XXV

Her scattred brood, soone as their parent deare
They saw so rudely falling to the ground,
Groning full deadly, all with troublous feare,
Gathred themselves about her body round,   220
Weening their wonted entrance to have found
At her wide mouth: but being there withstood,
They flockèd all about her bleeding wound,
And suckèd up their dying mothers bloud,
Making her death their life, and eke her hurt their
    good.

XXVI

That detestable sight him much amazde,
To see th' unkindly[42] impes, of heaven accurst,
Devoure their dam; on whom while so he gazd,
Having all satisfide their bloudy thurst,
Their bellies swolne he saw with fulnesse burst,
And bowels gushing forth; well worthy end   231
Of such as drunke her life, the which them nurst!
Now needeth him no lenger labour spend;
His foes have slaine themselves, with whom he
    should contend.

XXVII

His lady, seeing all that chaunst, from farre,
Approcht in hast to greet his victorie.
And saide, "Faire knight, borne under happie
    starre,
Who see your vanquisht foes before you lye,
Well worthie be you of that armory,
Wherein ye have great glory wonne this day,   240
And proov'd your strength on a strong enimie,
Your first adventure: many such I pray,
And henceforth ever wish that like succeed it
    may."

XXVIII

Then mounted he upon his steede againe,
And with the lady backward sought to wend;
That path he kept which beaten was most plaine,
Ne ever would to any by way bend,
But still did follow one unto the end,
The which at last out of the wood them brought.
So forward on his way (with God to frend[43])   250
He passèd forth, and new adventure sought:
Long way he traveilèd, before he heard of ought.

To distinguish it from the folk epic we call such a poem an *art epic*. Beyond the fact
that the art epic also is a long poem recounting heroic deeds, it bears little similarity to the
folk epic. The art epic goes back for its traditions to Homer. The *Iliad* begins (the translation
is by Lang, Leaf and Myers):

[38]See.
[39]Wane.
[40]Stop.
[41]Took away.

[42]Unnatural.
[43]As friend.

> Sing, goddess, the wrath of Achilles Peleus' son, the ruinous wrath that brought on the Achaians[1] woes innumerable, and hurled down into Hades many strong souls of heroes, and gave their bodies to be prey to dogs and all winged fowls; and so the counsel of Zeus wrought out its accomplishment from the day when first strife parted Atreides,[2] king of men, and noble Achilles.
>
> Who then among the gods set the twain at strife and variance? Even the son of Leto and of Zeus;[3] for he in anger at the king sent a sore plague upon the host, that the folk began to perish, because Atreides had done dishonor to Chryses the priest.[4]

Here Homer begins by
1. appealing to the Muse ("Sing, goddess") to inspire him,
2. announcing the subject of his poem ("the wrath of Achilles"), and
3. plunging into the middle of his story.

Virgil, the great Roman poet, writing his epic under the spell of Homer, began the *Aeneid* in like fashion (the translation is by B.G.):

> I sing of arms and that hero whom Fate first drove from the shores of Troy to Italy and her Lavinian coast; a man who suffered much on land and sea from the unforgetting hate of cruel Juno—suffering much too in war while he strove to build his city and establish for his gods a place in Latium.[1] From him the Latins are descended and the Alban fathers, as well as the towering walls of Rome.
>
> O Muse, relate to me the causes—for what crimes against the goddess or what grief she knew—that the Queen of Heaven[2] should have driven a man of such piety to experience so many misfortunes and to endure so many hardships! Can heavenly spirits nurture—and for so long—such resentment?
>
> In olden times there stood a city facing from far away the river Tiber's mouth, its citizens colonists from Tyre, and Carthage was its name.

Ever since Virgil imitated Homer by beginning with an appeal to the muse, announcing the subject of his poem, and plunging into the middle of his story, these have been conventions for the art epic. Thus Ariosto, the great Italian poet, begins his *Orlando Furioso* (the translation is by William S. Rose):

> Of loves and ladies, knights and arms, I sing,
> And courtesies, and many a daring feat.

And Tasso, his compatriot, begins his *Jerusalem Delivered* (the translation is by J. H. Wiffin):

> I sing the pious arms and Chief, who freed
> The sepulchre of Christ from thrall profane.
> O thou, the Muse, that not with fading palms
> Circlest thy brows on Pindus, but among
> The Angels warbling their celestial psalms,
> Hast for thy coronal a golden throng
> Of everlasting stars! make thou my song
> Lucid and pure; breathe thou the flame divine
> Into my bosom.

And Spenser, in the opening passage to his *The Faerie Queene,* tells us that he is about to

> sing of Knights and Ladies gentle deeds ...
> Fierce warres and faithful loves shall moralize my song.

---

[1]The Greeks.

[2]Agamemnon, son of Atreus.

[3]Apollo.

[4]Of the Trojans.

[1]Italy.

[2]Juno.

In the second stanza, he appeals to the muse:

> Helpe then, O holy virgin! chiefe of nyne,
> Thy weaker Novice to performe thy will.

And he begins Canto I in the middle of the story.

Later, Milton in his *Paradise Lost* will open the greatest nondramatic poem in our language with the same conventions:

Of Man's first disobedience, and the fruit
Of that forbidden tree, whose mortal taste
Brought death into the world, and all our woe,
With loss of Eden, till one greater Man[1]
Restore us, and regain the blissful seat,
Sing, heavenly Muse, that on the secret top
Of Oreb, or of Sinai,[2] did'st inspire
That shepherd[3] who first taught the chosen seed,
In the beginning[4] how the heavens and earth
Rose out of chaos: or, if Sion[5] hill   10
Delight thee more, and Siloa's[6] brook that flowed
Fast by the oracle of God, I thence
Invoke thy aid to my adventurous song,
That with no middle flight intends to soar
Above the Aonian[7] mount, while it pursues
Things unattempted yet in prose or rime.
And chiefly thou, O Spirit, that dost prefer
Before all temples the upright heart and pure,
Instruct me, for thou know'st; thou from the first
Wast present, and, with mighty wings outspread,
Dove-like, sat'st brooding on the vast abyss,   21
And mad'st it pregnant: what in me is dark,
Illumine; what is low, raise and support;
That to the height of this great argument
I may assert eternal Providence,
And justify the ways of God to men.
    Say first—for heaven hides nothing from thy
      view,
Nor the deep tract of hell—say first, what cause
Moved our grand Parents, in that happy state,
Favored of Heaven so highly, to fall off   30
From their Creator, and transgress his will,
For[8] one restraint, lords of the world besides.
Who first seduced them to that foul revolt?
    The infernal Serpent; he it was, whose guile,
Stirred up with envy and revenge, deceived
The mother of mankind; what time his pride

Had cast him out from heaven, with all his host
Of rebel angels; by whose aid, aspiring
To set himself in glory above his peers,
He trusted to have equaled the Most High,   40
If he opposed; and, with ambitious aim
Against the throne and monarchy of God,
Raised impious war in heaven, and battle proud,
With vain attempt. Him the Almighty Power
Hurled headlong flaming from the ethereal sky,
With hideous ruin and combustion, down
To bottomless perdition; there to dwell
In adamantine chains and penal fire,
Who durst defy the Omnipotent to arms.
    Nine times the space that measures day and
      night   50
To mortal men, he with his horrid crew
Lay vanquished, rolling in the fiery gulf,
Confounded, though immortal. But his doom
Reserved him to more wrath; for now the thought
Both of lost happiness and lasting pain
Torments him; round he throws his baleful eyes,
That witnessed huge affliction and dismay,
Mixed with obdurate pride, and steadfast hate.
At once, as far as angels' ken, he views
The dismal situation waste and wild.   60
A dungeon horrible, on all sides round,
As one great furnace, flamed; yet from those
      flames
No light; but rather darkness visible
Served only to discover sights of woe,
Regions of sorrow, doleful shades, where peace
And rest can never dwell; hope never comes
That comes to all; but torture without end
Still urges, and a fiery deluge, fed
With ever-burning sulphur unconsumed.
Such place eternal justice had prepared   70
For those rebellious; here their prison ordained

---

[1]Christ.

[2]Mt. Horeb and Mt. Sinai, where God spoke to Moses.

[3]Moses.

[4]The opening words of Genesis, the authorship of which was traditionally ascribed to Moses.

[5]Mt. Zion, the site of Jerusalem.

[6]A stream near Jerusalem.

[7]Mt. Helicon in Greece, sacred to the Muses. Milton is saying that his subject is loftier than the subjects of the ancient classical epics.

[8]Except for.

In utter darkness, and their portion set
As far removed from God and light of heaven,
As from the center[9] thrice to the utmost pole.[10]
O, how unlike the place from whence they fell!
There the companions of his fall, o'erwhelmed

With floods and whirlwinds of tempestuous fire,
He soon discerns; and weltering by his side
One next himself in power, and next in crime,
Long after known in Palestine,[11] and named 80
Beëlzebub.

Here again we see the poet beginning his epic with the announcement of his subject (lines 1–5) and an appeal to the Muse for inspiration, though in this case no pagan divinity (lines 6–26). Milton, too, begins in the middle of his story.

There are other conventions epic poets employ, following Homer's practice: long dramatic dialogue, extended descriptive passages, elaborate similes, enumeration of the hosts of warriors. But one has only to compare our passages from Spenser and Milton to see that these established traditions in no way hinder a poet's genius. Though (in common with many great English poets) Milton owes much to Spenser, and both write in the art-epic tradition, they are more unlike than similar as epic poets. Nothing could be further from Spenser's sweet and delicate music or the effect of the remarkable stanza he invented for his poem, than the powerful orchestration of Milton's blank verse; nothing could be further from Spenser's easy-flowing lines with their addiction to antique words already obsolete in his time, than Milton's highly compressed, massively rolling lines with their inversions, intellectual diction, and highly original way with normal English structure. Our greatest poets have found it possible to be entirely original while keeping their roots soundly planted in tradition.

The art epic differs, too, from the folk epic in that its author does not necessarily choose his hero from his own country or race. Ariosto concerns himself with the knights of Charlemagne; Tasso with Godfrey of Bouillon, leader of the Crusades, and his followers; Milton with the father of mankind, Adam.

It might be asked, in passing, why a writer should deliberately choose to adopt conventions like those of an art epic. Again, why should the author of "The Ballad of Sister Anne," writing in the twentieth century, elect to imitate a medieval form? The truth is that nothing is more valuable or more delightful in the arts than the sense of the continuity of tradition in what is new, which works of art at their best are likely to communicate. An artist approaching his work is like the bride; he needs "something old, something new."

Everything about to be created is bound to have its roots in what has been created. That is part of its strength. And for us, the audience, that is also a constant and refreshing reminder of the continuity of human experience. It is a delight to recognize what came from Haydn in the music of Beethoven, what came from Bach in the music of Schumann, what came from Schumann in the music of Brahms. Originality is always striking; but it is never more satisfying than when it exercises itself in giving new life to the familiar. No subject can ever be stale while there lives an author who sees new possibilities in it. The stories in the Bible and in Greek mythology, because they are illustrative of eternally basic human experiences, are capable of an almost infinite series of variations, each one an original work in the best sense of the term. The Electra story, for instance, challenged the highest talents of all three leading dramatists in ancient Athens, Aeschylus, Sophocles, and Euripides, and of many playwrights after them; in the twentieth century alone it has been the subject of a brilliant play by von Hofmannsthal (*Elektra*) and another by Sartre (*The Flies*).

So, too, with literary forms, conventions and techniques. It is not characteristic of an important writer that he sees himself totally self-begotten, like a solitary tree in a vast tract of desert sand. Rather does he think of himself as a worthy part of a grove where literature flourishes. The author whose roots are in certain traditions reminds us of the great company he keeps.

[9]The Earth.

[10]The furthest of the ten concentric spheres circling the Earth according to the old astronomy.

[11]Milton accounts for the alter pagan gods as being the angels who fell with Lucifer.

We have devoted much consideration to one of the most ancient of literary categories, storytelling—and we have ahead of us still two full chapters on the subject, Drama and Prose Fiction—for its appeal is wide and its dominions vast.

STRUCTURE IN REFLECTIVE PROSE AND POETRY

Literary analysts have recognized a second category, of which this thoughtful little essay by Eric Hoffer (1902—) provides a useful example:

The capacity to resist coercion stems partly from the individual's identification with a group. The people who stood up best in the Nazi concentration camps were those who felt themselves members of a compact party (the Communists), of a church (priests and ministers), or of a close-knit national group. The individualists, whatever their nationality, caved in. The Western European Jew proved to be the most defenseless. Spurned by the Gentiles (even those within the concentration camps), and without vital ties with a Jewish community, he faced his tormentors alone—forsaken by the whole of humanity. One realizes now that the ghetto of the Middle Ages was for the Jews more a fortress than a prison. Without the sense of utmost unity and distinctness which the ghetto imposed upon them, they could not have endured with unbroken spirit the violence and abuse of those dark centuries. When the Middle Ages returned for a brief decade in our day, they caught the Jew without his ancient defenses and crushed him.

The unavoidable conclusion seems to be that when the individual faces torture or annihilation, he cannot rely on the resources of his own individuality. His only source of strength is in not being himself but part of something mighty, glorious and indestructible. Faith here is primarily a process of identification; the process by which the individual ceases to be himself and becomes part of something eternal. Faith in humanity, in posterity, in the destiny of one's religion, nation, race, party or family—what is it but the visualization of that eternal something to which we attach the self that is about to be annihilated?

It is somewhat terrifying to realize that the totalitarian leaders of our day, in recognizing this source of desperate courage, made use of it not only to steel the spirit of their followers but also to break the spirit of their opponents. In his purges of the old Bolshevik leaders, Stalin succeeded in turning proud and brave men into cringing cowards by depriving them of any possibility of identification with the party they had served all their lives and with the Russian masses.

These old Bolsheviks had long ago cut themselves off from humanity outside Russia. They had an unbounded contempt for the past and for history which could still be made by capitalistic humanity. They had renounced God. There was for them neither past nor future, neither memory nor glory outside the confines of holy Russia and the Communist party—and both these were now wholly and irrevocably in Stalin's hands. They felt themselves, in the words of Bukharin, "isolated from every thing that constitutes the essence of life." So they confessed. By humbling themselves before the congregation of the faithful they broke out of their isolation. They renewed their communion with the eternal whole by reviling the self, accusing it of monstrous and spectacular crimes, and sloughing it off in public.

The same Russians who cringe and crawl before Stalin's secret police displayed unsurpassed courage when facing—singly or in a group—the invading Nazis. The reason for this contrasting behavior is not that Stalin's police are more ruthless than Hitler's armies, but that when facing Stalin's police the Russian feels a mere individual while, when facing the Germans, he saw himself a member of a mighty race, possessed of a glorious past and an even more glorious future.

Similarly, in the case of the Jews, their behavior in Palestine could not have been predicted from their behavior in Europe. The British colonial officials in Palestine followed a policy sound in logic but lacking in insight. They reasoned that since Hitler had managed to exterminate six million Jews without meeting serious resistance, it should not be too difficult to handle the 600,000 Jews in Palestine. Yet they found that the Jews in Palestine, however recently arrived, were a formidable enemy: reckless, stubborn and resourceful. The Jew in Europe faced his enemies alone, an isolated individual, a speck of life floating in an eternity of nothingness. In Palestine he felt himself not a human atom, but a member of an eternal race, with an immemorable past behind it and a breathtaking future ahead.

The heart of this piece of writing is meditation or reflection. Such a work we call *reflective.* In prose the essay is the most usual form employed for reflective writing.

The structure of this little essay is clear. The author's subject is The Individual and the Group; his theme is: in times of stress the strength of the individual depends upon his identification with the group. The paragraphs, the units of structure, follow the order of logical presentation of the argument:

1. The individual's ability to resist oppression stems from his identification with the group.

2. In the face of torture the individual's strength stems from the faith afforded by identification with the group.

3. Realizing these truths, totalitarian leaders have isolated their opponents from their opponents' group in order to break their spirit.

4 and 5. The objects of oppression, whose spirits have been broken, can nevertheless be converted, given a renewed opportunity for faith in a group, from cringing victims to brave and heroic fighters. An essay whose thoughts follow this objective and logical procedure is known as a formal *essay,* and its structure is conditioned by the logical divisions of the ideas presented.

Here is another essay, "A Piece of Chalk," written by Gilbert Keith Chesterton (1874–1936):

I remember one splendid morning, all blue and silver, in the summer holidays, when I reluctantly tore myself away from the task of doing nothing in particular, and put on a hat of some sort and picked up a walking stick, and put six very bright-colored chalks in my pocket. I then went into the kitchen (which, along with the rest of the house, belonged to a very square and sensible old woman in a Sussex village) and asked the owner and occupant of the kitchen if she had any brown paper. She had a great deal; in fact, she had too much; and she mistook the purpose and the rationale of the existence of brown paper. She seemed to have an idea that if a person wanted brown paper he must be wanting to tie up parcels; which was the last thing I wanted to do; indeed, it is a thing which I have found to be beyond my mental capacity. Hence she dwelt very much on the varying qualities of toughness and endurance in the material. I explained to her that I only wanted to draw pictures on it, and that I did not want them to endure in the least; and that from my point of view, therefore, it was a question, not of tough consistency, but of responsive surface, a thing comparatively irrelevant in a parcel. When she understood that I wanted to draw, she offered to overwhelm me with note paper, apparently supposing that I did my notes and correspondence on old brown paper wrappers from motives of economy.

I then tried to explain the rather delicate logical shade, that I not only liked brown paper, but liked the quality of brownness in paper, just as I liked the quality of brownness in October woods, or in the peat streams of the North. Brown paper represents the primal twilight of the first toil of creation, and with a bright-colored chalk or two you can pick out points of fire in it, sparks of gold, and blood-red, and sea-green, like the first fierce stars that sprang out of divine darkness. All this I said (in an offhand way) to the old woman; and I put the brown paper in my pocket along with the chalks, and possibly other things. I suppose everyone must have reflected how primeval and how poetical are the things that one carries in one's pocket: the pocketknife, for instance, the type of all human tools, the infant of the sword. Once I planned to write a book of poems entirely about the things in my pockets. But I found it would be too long; and the age of the great epics is past.

With my stick and my knife, my chalks and my brown paper, I went out on the great downs. I crawled across those colossal contours that express the best quality of England, because they are at the same time soft and strong. The smoothness of them has the same meaning as the smoothness of great cart horses, or the smoothness of the beech tree; it declares in the teeth of our timid and cruel theories that the mighty are merciful. As my eye swept the landscape, the landscape was as kindly as any of its cottages, but for power it was like an earthquake. The villages in the immense valley were safe, one could see, for centuries; yet the lifting of the whole land was like the lifting of one enormous wave to wash them all away.

I crossed one swell of living turf after another, looking for a place to sit down and draw. Do not, for heaven's sake, imagine I was going to sketch from nature. I was going to draw devils and seraphim, and blind old gods that men worshiped before the dawn of right, and saints in robes of angry crimson, and seas of strange green, and all the sacred or monstrous symbols that look so well in bright colors on brown paper. They are much better worth drawing than nature; also they are much easier to draw. When a cow came slouching by in the field next to me, a mere artist might have drawn it; but I always get wrong in the hind legs of quadrupeds. So I drew the soul of the cow; which I saw there plainly walking before me in the sunlight; and the soul was all purple and silver, and had seven horns and the mystery that belongs to all the beasts. But though I could not with a crayon get the best out of the landscape, it does not follow that the landscape was not getting the best out of me. And this, I think, is the mistake that people make about the old poets who lived before Wordsworth, and were supposed not to care very much about nature because they did not describe it much.

They preferred writing about great men to writing about great hills; but they sat on the great hills to write it. They gave out much less about nature, but they drank in, perhaps, much more. They painted the white robes of their holy virgins with the blinding snow, at which they had stared all day. They blazoned the shields of their paladins with the purple and gold of many heraldic sunsets. The greenness of a thousand green leaves clustered into the live green figure of Robin Hood. The blueness of a score of forgotten skies became the blue robes of the Virgin. The inspiration went in like sunbeams and came out like Apollo.[1]

But as I sat scrawling these silly figures on the brown paper, it began to dawn on me, to my great disgust, that I had left one chalk, and that a most exquisite and essential chalk, behind. I searched all my pockets, but I could not find any white chalk. Now, those who are acquainted with all the philosophy (nay, religion) which is typified in the art of drawing on brown paper, know that white is positive and essential. I cannot avoid remarking here upon a moral significance. One of the wise and awful truths which this brown-paper art reveals is this, that white is a color. It is not a mere absence of color; it is a shining and affirmative thing, as fierce as red, as definite as black. When, so to speak, your pencil grows red-hot, it draws roses; when it grows white-hot, it draws stars. And one of the two or three defiant verities

of the best religious morality, of real Christianity, for example, is exactly this same thing; the chief assertion of religious morality is that white is a color. Virtue is not the absence of vices or the avoidance of moral dangers; virtue is a vivid and separate thing, like pain or a particular smell. Mercy does not mean not being cruel or sparing people revenge or punishment; it means a plain and positive thing like the sun, which one has either seen or not seen.

Chastity does not mean abstention from sexual wrong; it means something flaming, like Joan of Arc. In a word, God paints in many colors; but He never paints so gorgeously, I had almost said so gaudily, as when He paints in white. In a sense our age has realized this fact, and expressed it in our sullen costume. For if it were really true that white was a blank and colorless thing, negative and noncommittal, then white would be used instead of black and gray for the funeral dress of this pessimistic period. We should see city gentlemen in frock coats of spotless silver linen, with top hats as white as wonderful arum lilies. Which is not the case.

Meanwhile, I could not find any chalk.

I sat on the hill in a sort of despair. There was no town nearer than Chichester at which it was even remotely probable that there would be such a thing as an artist's colorman. And yet, without white, my absurd little pictures would be as pointless as the world would be if there were no good people in it. I stared stupidly round, racking my brain for expedients. Then I suddenly stood up and roared with laughter, again and again, so that the cows stared at me and called a committee. Imagine a man in the Sahara regretting that he had no sand for his hourglass. Imagine a gentleman in midocean wishing that he had brought some salt water with him for his chemical experiments. I was sitting on an immense warehouse of white chalk. The landscape was made entirely out of white chalk. White chalk was piled more miles until it met the sky. I stooped and broke a piece off the rock I sat on: it did not mark so well as the shop chalks do; but it gave the effect. And I stood there in a trance of pleasure, realizing that this southern England is not only a grand peninsula, and a tradition and a civilization; it is something even more admirable. It is a piece of chalk.

In this delightful and moving essay there is, of course, some narrative and also strong, even personal, feeling. But the incident as recounted and the feelings as revealed both seem subsidiary to the author's reflection. This piece of reflective writing, however, is written according to a different principle from that governing Hoffer's.

[1]The god of light.

First of all, it would be difficult to identify the subject. It would be begging the question to quote the title in this instance as the subject, for the piece of chalk is only an excuse for the author's reflections on a variety of topics: the quality of brownness in brown paper, the ideal subjects for a man to draw, the older writers' appreciation of nature, white as a color, the meaning of virtue, the white chalk of southern England. Among all these one is tempted to single out Virtue as the true subject of the essay; if it is, then the theme is: Virtue is a positive, not a negative, force.

Again, characteristically of the reflective, the structure follows the procession of the ideas presented. Since the progress of the ideas is charmingly wayward in "A Piece of Chalk," the structure is too. The principle upon which the ideas present themselves is not that of logical order, but rather that of association of ideas. The request for brown paper to draw upon brings up thoughts on the brownness of brown paper; the landscape traversed by the writer brings up thoughts on the ideal subjects for a man to draw, and these in turn invite a discussion of the older writers' appreciation of nature; the absence of white chalk among his crayons leads to reflections on white as a color, and these in turn lead to a consideration of the meaning of virtue; finally, the need for white chalk evokes the tribute to southern England as "a piece of chalk."

An essay whose thoughts follow this subjective and associational presentation of ideas is known as an *informal essay,* and its structure is conditioned by the more or less wayward movement from idea to idea.

A great deal of poetry belongs to the category of the reflective. Here is an example by William Butler Yeats (1865–1939), "An Irish Airman Foresees His Death":

> I know that I shall meet my fate
> Somewhere among the clouds above;
> Those that I fight I do not hate,
> Those that I guard I do not love;
> My country is Kiltartan Cross,
> My countrymen Kiltartan's poor,
> No likely end could bring them loss
> Or leave them happier than before.
> Nor law, nor duty bade me fight,
> Nor public men, nor cheering crowds,
> A lonely impulse of delight
> Drove to this tumult in the clouds;
> I balanced all, brought all to mind,
> The years to come seemed waste of breath,
> A waste of breath the years behind
> In balance with this life, this death.

10

Here again, as in the essays, the structure of the work is conditioned by the procession of ideas presented, as analysis of the poem will reveal. This is true as well of "To My Shadow" by the American poet John Banister Tabb (1845–1909):

> Friend forever in the light
>   Cleaving to my side,
> Harbinger of endless night,
>   That must soon betide;
>
> "Hither," seemest thou to say,
>   "From the twilight now;
> In the darkness when I stay,
>   Never thence wilt thou."

LYRICAL COMPOSITION AND ITS STRUCTURE

There is a third category of writings with its own characteristic structure. Let us consider one of the great romantic poems of the nineteenth century, John Keats's (1794–1821) "Ode to a Nightingale":

I

My heart aches, and a drowsy numbness pains
  My sense, as though of hemlock I had drunk,
Or emptied some dull opiate to the drains
  One minute past, and Lethe[1]-wards had sunk:
'Tis not through envy of thy happy lot,
  But being too happy in thine happiness,—
    That thou, light-winged Dryad[2] of the trees,
      In some melodious plot
Of beechen green, and shadows numberless,
      Singest of summer in full-throated 10

II

O, for a draught of vintage! that hath been
  Cool'd a long age in the deep-delved earth,
Tasting of Flora[3] and the country green,
  Dance, and Provençal song,[4] and sunburnt mirth!
O for a beaker full of the warm South,
  Full of the true, the blushful Hippocrene,[5]
    With beaded bubbles winking at the brim,
      And purple-stained mouth;
    That I might drink, and leave the world unseen,
    And with thee fade away into the forest dim. 20

III

Fade far away, dissolve, and quite forget
  What thou among the leaves hast never known,
The weariness, the fever, and the fret
  Here, where men sit and hear each other groan;
Where palsy shakes a few, sad, last grey hairs,
  Where youth grows pale, and spectre-thin, and dies;

Where but to think is to be full of sorrow
  And leaden-ey'd despairs,
Where Beauty cannot keep her lustrous eyes,
  Or new Love pine at them beyond tomorrow. 30

IV

Away! away! for I will fly to thee,
  Not charioted by Bacchus and his pards,[6]
But on the viewless wings of Poesy,
  Though the dull brain perplexes and retards:
Already with thee! tender is the night,
  And haply the Queen-Moon is on her throne,
    Cluster'd around by all her starry Fays;
      But here there is no light,
Save what from heaven is with the breezes blown
    Through verdurous glooms and winding mossy ways. 40

V

I cannot see what flowers are at my feet,
  Nor what soft incense hangs upon the boughs,
But, in embalmed darkness, guess each sweet
  Wherewith the seasonable month endows
The grass, the thicket, and the fruit-tree wild;
  White hawthorn, and the pastoral eglantine;
    Fast fading violets cover'd up in leaves;
      And mid-May's eldest child,
The coming musk-rose, full of dewy wine,
    The murmurous haunt of flies on summer eves. 50

VI

Darkling[7] I listen; and, for many a time
  I have been half in love with easeful Death,
Call'd him soft names in many a mused rhyme,
  To take into the air my quiet breath;
Now more than ever seems it rich to die,
  To cease upon the midnight with no pain,

[1]The river of forgetfulness, in ancient mythology.

[2]Tree-nymph.

[3]Roman goddess of the flowers.

[4]Provence, in the south of France, was the birthplace of medieval love poetry, as sung by the troubadours there.

[5]Keats mistakenly thought this the name of an ancient wine. Actually it was a fountain on Mt. Helicon, and was sacred to the Muses.

[6]Leopards. They drew the car of Bacchus, god of wine.

[7]As it darkens.

While thou art pouring forth thy soul
    abroad
    In such an ecstasy!
Still wouldst thou sing, and I have ears in
    vain—
    To thy high requiem become a sod.   60

VII

Thou wast nor born for death, immortal Bird!
    No hungry generations tread thee down;
The voice I hear this passing night was heard
    In ancient days by emperor and clown:
Perhaps the self-same song that found a path
    Through the sad heart of Ruth[8] When, sick
    for home,
    She stood in tears amid the alien corn;

    The same that oft-times hath
Charm'd magic casements, opening on the
    foam
    Of perilous seas, in faery lands forlorn. 70

VIII

Forlorn! the very word is like a bell
    To toll me back from thee to my sole self!
Adieu! the fancy cannot cheat so well
    As she is famed to do, deceiving elf.
Adieu! adieu! thy plaintive anthem fades
    Past the near meadows, over the still stream,
    Up the hill-side; and now 'tis buried deep
    In the next valley-glades:
Was it a vision, or a waking dream?   79
    Fled is that music:—Do I wake or sleep?

The poem, as is often the case with Keats, recounts an all-consuming emotional experience. From the very first words we are caught up in powerful feelings. The song of the nightingale brings to the poet sensations so acute that his heart pains and he feels himself at the point of swooning. This preoccupation with his emotional excitation continues throughout the ode—as he calls for wine of the South (stanza 2); as in imagination he makes ready to leave the world of men to join the bird (stanza 3); as he glories in the moonlit sky and in the fragrance of the night (stanzas 4 and 5), in his fancy by the side of the nightingale; as anew he listens to the ecstasy of the bird's song, wishing for death as most welcome when accompanied by such beauty (stanza 6); and as finally, as the bird's song fades in the night, he feels deserted and alone again (stanza 8).

When experience is presented to us as feelings of enthusiasm, despair, rapture, pain, exaltation, and the like, expressed in strongly emotional language, we call the writing *lyrical.*

Originally the word had a quite different connotation, and applied to anything adaptable to the lyre, and hence, in literature, signified a piece of writing suggestive of singing. A later, more limited meaning of *lyrical poetry* is thus precisely defined by the *Century Dictionary:* "that class of poetry which has reference to and delineates the poet's own thoughts and feelings, as opposed to *epic* or *dramatic poetry,* which details external circumstances and events." However, since the lyrical is found, though less frequently, sometimes in prose too, it is now unsatisfactory to equate the lyrical merely with the subjective in poetry; current usage tends to identify the word *lyrical* with such writing (prose or poetry) as has at its heart strong emotional expression.

In a lyrical composition it is the strong emotions which give the work its structure. The principle on which Keats's ode is constructed is the succession of emotional state by emotional state; thus the poem comes to us in waves of emotion. The "drowsy numbness" provoked by the bird's song (stanza 1) leads to the wish for a draught of heady wine that would help the poet fade away into the dim forest with the bird (stanza 2); to be in the forest with the bird would mean quitting "the fever and the fret" of man's world, where everything beautiful lives but a day (stanza 3); lacking the wine, he will fly to the bird on the wings of poetry; with one leap of the imagination he is with the bird in the moonlight (stanza 4) and is becoming intoxicated with all the varied fragrance of the forest (stanza 5); the bird's song, now his sole concentration, through its unalloyed beauty causes him to feel like

[8]A reference to the beautiful story of Ruth, as told in the book of that name in the Old Testament. After the death of her husband, Ruth left her native Moab to accompany her mother-in-law back to the latter's own country, Judah. There, to gather food for them both, she went into the fields to glean ears of corn overlooked by the reapers (Ruth 1:1–4:13).

swooning to death from sheer pleasure (stanza 6); but the nightingale itself, who can prompt this yearning for "easeful Death," is deathless, and has poured forth this same beauty to enraptured ears in all ages (stanza 7); and now the song fades and the poet is brought back, as from a dream, to the world of reality (stanza 8).

The strong emotions dictating the structure are further emphasized by the repetitions: "fade away" (line 20), "Fade far away" (line 21), "Away! away!" (line 31), "thy plaintive anthem fades" (line 75); "thy happy lot" (line 5), "too happy in thine happiness" (line 6); "Where palsy shakes" (line 25), "Where youth grows" (line 26), "Where but to think" (line 27), "Where Beauty cannot keep" (line 29); "faery lands forlorn" (line 70), "Forlorn!" (line 71); "Adieu!" (line 73), "Adieu! adieu!" (line 75). Also, the musical attributes of rhythm, rhyme and alliteration (see Chapter 4) enhance the emotional power as only musical attributes can.

LYRICAL PROSE

Though some critics feel that the proper sphere for lyricism is verse, it is a fact that many much-admired writings in prose are certainly lyrical. One of the most gifted of twentieth-century novelists, the American Thomas Wolfe (1900–1938), habitually abandons his narrative to compose highly lyrical passages, in the manner of this excerpt from "From Death to Morning":

> Were they not lost? Were they not lost, as all of us have been who have known youth and hunger in this land, and who have waited lean and mad and lonely in the night, and who have found no goal, no wall, no dwelling, and no door?
> The years flow by like water, and one day it is spring again. Shall we ever ride out of the gates of the East again, as we did once at morning, and seek again, as we did then, new lands, the promise of the war, and glory, joy, and triumph, and a shining city?
> O youth, still wounded, living, feeling with a woe unutterable, still grieving with a grief intolerable, still thirsting with a thirst unquenchable—where are we to seek? For the wild tempest breaks above us, the wild fury beats about us, the wild hunger feeds upon us—and we are houseless, doorless, unassuaged, and driven on forever; and our brains are mad, our hearts are wild and wordless, and we cannot speak.

The strong feelings characteristic of the lyrical permeate these paragraphs; and though cast in prose, their sharply marked rhythms evoke a sense of song (implicit in the original idea of the lyrical). Note, too, the repetitions, the product of strong emotion: "Were they not lost?" "Were they not lost"; "who have known," "who have waited," "who have found"; "no goal," "no wall," "no dwelling," "no door."

KINDS OF LYRICAL POETRY

In poetry, by nature a more emotional mode of expression than prose, the realm of the lyrical is large. The lyrical has particularly flourished in English poetry. We have, for instance, many poems which seem more than anything else a musical outpouring of strong feelings, such as this sunny one by Thomas Dekker (d. 1632), called "Content":

> Art thou poor, yet hast thou golden slumbers?
>   O sweet content!
> Art thou rich, yet is thy mind perplexed?
>   O punishment!
> Dost thou laugh to see how fools are vexed
> To add to golden numbers golden numbers?[1]

---

[1] I.e., money.

O sweet content, O sweet, O sweet content!
Work apace! apace! apace! apace!
Honest labor bears a lovely face.
Then hey noney, noney; hey noney, noney!   10
Canst drink the waters of the crispèd[2] spring?
                                    O sweet content!
Swim'st thou in wealth, yet sink'st in thine own tears?
                                    O punishment!
Then he that patiently want's burden bears[3]
No burden bears, but is a king, a king.
O sweet content, O sweet, O sweet content!

Work apace! apace! apace! apace!
Honest labor bears a lovely face.
Then hey noney, noney; hey noney, noney!   20

We call such a poetic composition a *song. A song is a short composition in meter, usually rhymed, that seems suitable for singing.* Possibly because of the rich beauty of the language, English has innumerable lovely songs.

It is true, of course, that there is no absence of idea in this song of Dekker's. Its concept of the meaning of contentment and the honest pleasure work can bring is thoroughly engaging, and possibly quite important. But the emphasis in the mode of its composition is on the fullness of heart of the author which makes him seem to be singing to us. This it is which makes the piece a song. Some songs are rich in ideas, some make no pretense to saying anything of importance. It is the singing which makes the song.

Keats's "Ode to a Nightingale" is clearly, on the grounds of length alone, a more ambitious kind of composition than a song. *An ode is a lyrical poem of exalted or elevated emotion.*

Sometimes the strong emotional tones of lyrical poetry are used in grief over the death of someone dearly loved or respected, as in this section from Alfred, Lord Tennyson's (1809–1892) *In Memoriam* (7), a work written in commemoration of his closest friend, Arthur Henry Hallam:

Dark house,[1] by which once more I stand
        Here in the long unlovely street,
        Doors, where my heart was used to beat
So quickly, waiting for a hand,

A hand that can be clasped no more—
        Behold me, for I cannot sleep,
        And like a guilty thing I creep
At earliest morning to the door.

He is not here; but far away
        The noise of life begins again,   10
        And ghastly thro' the drizzling rain
On the bald street breaks the blank day.

We call such a composition an *elegy. An elegy is a poem of lament for someone dead.*

Certain kinds of lyrical expression are more or less connected with particular verse techniques and forms, such as the *sonnet,* the *rondeau,* the *ballade,* and the *triolet.* These are defined in the Glossary. Of these forms the sonnet, though not always lyrical, is one of the most important.

It will suffice our present purposes to say of a sonnet that it *is written in fourteen lines of five stresses each,* with a certain arrangement of rhymes. Some poets, like Anne Marx,

[2]Rippling.   [1]The house in London where Hallam had lived.
[3]He who patiently bears the burdens of poverty.

occasionally write a group of sonnets in sequence—that is, connected in thought. (So have done Spenser, Shakespeare, Dante Gabriel Rossetti, Christina Rossetti and many others.) Such a sequence is known as a *sonnet sequence.*

The following three sonnets, "Their Critical Summer: Three Views of a Woodpile," are by the American poet Anne Marx (1913—):

1. *The Husband*

This woodpile saw me through my moodiest year
of early marriage, when I fought the pace
of life itself and learned up here to face
the rebels lurking in my blood. When fear
of failure throbbed beneath the frail veneer
of calm, I stormed this hill, this hiding-place
at dusk, to purge myself without disgrace,
my outbursts safe from any human ear.

Our baby slept. My wife, uniquely blessed
with confidence, sure to be warmed come winter
by wood her man had cut, wood meant to burn—
welcomed me back at night, and never guessed
the need behind my anguished axe to splinter
huge piles of doubt before I could return.

2. *The Daughter*

"You can't remember. You were much too young!"
my parents claim. Yet no one ever told
me of this pile of wood where I behold
a vision of my father, tall among
his fellow men, to whom my mother clung
as to a mighty tree. Made from one mold;
plain as his tools; he kept us safe from cold,
toiling undaunted, all his deeds unsung.

Today I wonder if my parents found
old love on fire sometimes, still to be shared
along those years, so settled and mature . . .
Back in my childhood bed, I hugged the sound
of father's steady axe, grateful he cared
above all else to keep my sleep secure.

3. *The Wife*

In search of solitude from family
and evening walls, he never understood
I knew what drove him here attacking wood
with vehemence—a common enemy
defying both of us. By the degree
of sound from his explosive axe, I could
measure the heavy pile of adulthood
that weighed him down, his struggle to come free.
Free for one hour, unhampered, as he hurled
all strength against a tree, the mind in flight
from grinding stress within; only that span
between late day and dusk to right his world.
Retimbered then, he came to fill my night
with greater tenderness than any man.

Each of the three sonnets which form the sequence of "Their Critical Summer," it will be noted, is made up of two parts; the division occurs at the end of the eighth line. A sonnet so constructed is called an *Italian* or *Petrarchan* sonnet. *An Italian sonnet is written in two units, one of eight lines, and one of six.*

There is another possible structure for the sonnet, as exhibited in this one, "Sonnet XVIII" by Shakespeare:

> Shall I compare thee to a summer's day?
> Thou art more lovely and more temperate:
> Rough winds do shake the darling buds of May,
> And summer's lease hath all too short a date;
> Sometime too hot the eye of heaven shines,
> And often is his gold complexion dimm'd;
> And every fair[1] from fair[2] sometime declines,
> By chance or nature's changing course untrimm'd;
> But thy eternal summer shall not fade,
> Nor lose possession of that fair thou owest,[3]   10
> Nor shall Death brag thou wander'st in his shade,
> When in eternal lines to time thou grow'st:
>   So long as men can breathe, or eyes can see,
>   So long lives this,[4] and this gives life to thee.

In this sonnet, it will be noted, the division occurs at the end of the twelfth line. A sonnet so constructed is called an *English sonnet. An English sonnet is written in two units, one of twelve lines and a concluding one of two.*

The effects produced by the Italian and the English sonnet are quite different. The concluding two lines of the English sonnet (which are always in rhyme) give a pithiness and a pointedness to that form which make it the more dramatic of the two. The Italian sonnet is perhaps the more elegant. A poet will choose one form or the other according to the effect he requires. Madeline Mason, as we shall later see, has in our own time introduced a new kind of sonnet, the so-called Mason Sonnet.

It is not, as we have said, always easy to decide whether a work is lyrical, narrative or reflective. Many of the works we have quoted partake of all three modes. The matter can be settled only by discovering whether the author was above all pouring out strong emotion, or having a story to tell, or presenting his readers with a significant piece of reflection.

A WORD ON SATIRE

Some critics would add the satirical to the divisions of literature which we have set forth. However, satire seems to us to be strictly a tone rather than a type; for satirical works, unlike lyrical, narrative or reflective works, have no characteristic structure. A satire, rather, will belong to one of our three divisions, depending on whether the author was above all pouring out strong emotion, or having a story to tell, or presenting his readers with a significant piece of reflection. In each case, we ought to be aware of what he was doing.

While he was a student at Oxford, Tom Brown (1663–1704) wrote:

> I do not love thee, Doctor Fell,
> The reason why I cannot tell;
> But this alone I know full well,
> I do not love thee, Doctor Fell.

This is plainly a venting of feelings. When Matthew Prior (1664–1721) wrote "Quit":

> To John I ow'd great obligation;
> But John unhappily thought fit

---

[1]Beautiful thing or being.   [3]Ownest.
[2]Beauty.   [4]I.e., this sonnet.

> To publish it to all the nation:
> Sure John and I are more than quit.

he was telling us a brief story. When Alexander Pope wrote his epigram, "The Balance of Europe":

> Now Europe's balanced, neither side prevails,
> For nothing's left in either of the scales.

he was giving us his reflection on a current political condition. Yet all three of these epigrams are satirical. The first we should call lyrical, the second narrative, the third reflective.

DIFFERENCES BETWEEN PROSE AND POETRY

Thus far we have made little distinction between poetry and prose. We have illustrated most of what we have had to say with quotations in both. We shall, indeed, hereafter, observe some traits peculiar to the former. Meter and rhyme, for instance, we shall remark as being suitable to poetry and not at all to prose. We shall also see that rhythms are more marked in poetry, and that devices like alliteration and assonance are of more importance there. On the other hand, we shall nowhere imply that a work possessing meter, rhyme, assonance, and/or alliteration* becomes thereby a poem.

What, then, is the essential difference, if any, between prose and poetry?

In Molière's hilarious comedy, *The Shopkeeper Become Gentleman,* a Doctor of Philosophy has something to say on the subject (II/IV, translation by Bernard Grebanier):

MR. JOURDAIN. I want you to help me write her [a lady of quality] something in a little letter that I'd like to let drop at her feet.

DOCTOR OF PHILOSOPHY. Certainly.

MR. J. That would be quite dashing, don't you think?

DOCT. OF PHIL. No doubt. Is it poetry that you want to write her?

MR. J. No, no! No poetry!

DOCT. OF PHIL. You want only prose, then?

MR. J. No! I don't want prose or poetry!

DOCT. OF PHIL. It's got to be one or the other.

MR. J. Why?

DOCT. OF PHIL. For the simple reason, sir, that for the purposes of expression there *is* noth-

ing but prose or poetry.

MR. J. There *is* nothing but prose or poetry?

DOCT. OF PHIL. There isn't. Everything that's not prose is poetry, and everything that's not poetry is prose.

MR. J. Well, now—when you're sort of talking—what do you call that?

DOCT. OF PHIL. Prose.

MR. J. Not really! You mean to say that when I say, "Nicole, bring me my slippers, and fetch me my nightcap"—*that's* prose?

DOCT. OF PHIL. Yes, sir.

MR. J. You don't say! Here I've been talking prose for more than forty years without knowing it! I'm much obliged to you for telling me.

It would be very convenient for the purposes of discussion if matters were that simple. The Doctor of Philosophy seems to be using the term *prose* in its original Latin meaning, "straightforward discourse." In this sense the efficient, nonliterary piece which we have quoted from *Barron's* in our first chapter, on page 4, is undeniably prose. Suppose we split that passage up into lines, does it become poetry?

> Any day now
> The dredges and tugs of the Great Lakes Dredge and Dock Co.
> Of Chicago,
> And the Arundel Corp.
> Of Baltimore,
> Will chug out into Boston Harbor,
> And start scooping out the bottom
> For an extension to the President Roads anchorage ...

*Meter, rhyme, assonance, alliteration, etc. are fully discussed in the chapters on Musical Attributes and Verse Techniques.

and so on to the thrilling end:

> As the
> Budget Bureau clamped down
> On non-defense
> Government spending
> In the wake of the
> Sputniks.

In some unenlightened quarters, it would erroneously pass as satisfactory "free verse." Could we transform the passage, which is still no more poetic than the original quotation, to poetry by introducing meter? Let's try pentameters (i.e., lines with five stresses in each line):

> Ány dáy now, yés, on ány dáy,
> The drédges ánd the túgs of twó fine fírms,
> The Gréat Lakes Drédge and Dóck (Chicágo-básed)
> And Árundél (of Báltimóre) will chúg
> Into old Bóston Hárbor, thére begín
> To scóop the bóttom tó exténd yet móre
> The ánchoráge now námed the Président Róads ...

and so on to the conclusion:

> For thén the Búdget Búreau clámped down hárd
> Upón all Góvernment spénding for nón-defénse
> That fóllowed ín the fáteful wáke of spútniks.

No, despite some alliterative (*d*ay, *d*redges; *f*ine *f*irms, etc.) and assonantal (Gr*ea*t, L*a*kes, b*a*sed, etc.) effects which we have added, this can hardly claim status as poetry. To enforce the point, shall we subscribe to the illiterate notion that all that is needed in poetry is rhyme? Let us try an ode:

> Any dáy now the drédge and the túg
>   From maríne-bounded Máryland
>   And Íllinois' fáiryland
> Into óld Boston Hárbor will chúg
>   (Rejoice Gréat Lakes and Dóck's
>   —Also Árundel's—stócks!)
> And scóop out the óoze
> From the tóo-shallow béd of the Président Róads
>   So that stéamers which crúise
> Soon may ánchor at éase and dispóse of their lóads ...

Before it is too late—we shudder as we approach the possibilities of rhyme in "sputniks" —let us halt the music. It is clear that an ode *was not* in order. Despite the good Doctor, all which is not prose is demonstrably not necessarily poetry. Perhaps muddle-headed Mr. Jourdain comes unintentionally nearer the truth when he later is trying to instruct his good wife in all that he presumably has learned from the Doctor (III/iii):

> MR. J. I ask you—what I'm talking to you, what all this while I've been speaking to you—what is it?
> MRS. J. Rubbish.
> MR. J. No, no, not that! What we've both been talking—the language we're speaking now?
> MRS. J. What about it?
> MR. J. What do they call it?
> MRS. J. Let them call it whatever they like.
> MR. J. Ignoramus! It's *prose!*
> MRS. J. Prose?
> MR. J. Yes, prose. Everything that is prose isn't poetry.

A perfectly safe conclusion! Everything that is prose is certainly not poetry. And that is why our three attempts to transform the passage from *Barron's* are not poetry.

What is it, then, which we did to the passage in the three rewritings? We *versified* it —just that, and nothing more. The word *verse* comes from the Latin, meaning in that language "a line or row." Strictly speaking, therefore, the difference between prose and verse is merely a matter of the way words are arranged on a page. Prose is, thus, discourse arranged in an unbroken succession—excepting for paragraph divisions—and verse is discourse broken up into lines. When printed, prose and verse on the surface show merely a typographical difference. For the important fact is that *all that is verse is not necessarily poetry.* We shall soon see what musical attributes like rhythm, rhyme and assonance contribute to a poem. But our three versifications on the Great Lakes Dredge and Dock Company, despite our use of such effects, remain essentially prosaic.

Without reference to literature as such, i.e., in the sense in which we defined it in our first chapter, it would be proper, therefore, to say that everything which is not verse is prose.

Nothing could make literature of the piece from *Barron's* because its point of view has nothing to do with the quintessences of life and human experiences. And, as we have several times agreed, those quintessences are basic to literature. The enlarging of Boston Harbor is a subject which might so much widen a writer's field of vision that it might conceivably inspire him with ideas which would admit of literary, of even poetic treatment. He might find himself in so exalted a state over the possibilities that he might even be moved to write a fine ode. But our author was interested exclusively, as befits a writer for a business weekly, in the financial aspects of a mechanical operation—not in any human values that might be involved. There are no materials for literature when your point of view is the financial aspects of a mechanical operation—although the financial aspects of an operation can make excellent *motivation for a subject and theme* concerned with human quintessences, as witness the bond which Antonio signs for Shylock in *The Merchant of Venice.* It is not that the world of business is exiled from literature—that is merely a piece of Bohemian snobbery. Shakespeare himself does not disdain to draw some powerful images from the language of commerce and trade:

> ROMEO. I am no pilot; yet wert thou as far
> As that vast shore wash'd with the farthest sea,
> I should venture for such merchandise.
> > —*Romeo and Juliet,* II/ii/82–84

> JULIET. O, I have bought the mansion of a love,
> But not possess'd it.
> > —*Romeo and Juliet,* III/ii/25–26

> DUKE.   Nature never lends
> The smallest scruple of her excellence,
> But like a thrifty goddess she determines
> Herself the glory of a creditor,
> Both thanks and use.[1]
> > —*Measure for Measure,* I/i/37 seq.

But, as can be seen, if he deals with the world of business, it is only to throw light on human relationships.

Prose, then, is a term which is used in and out of literature; so too with verse. Nobody will claim that

> Thirty days hath September,
> April, June and November . . .

though verse, is poetry.

Within the province of literature, the difference is between poetry and prose. The difference is, as our many quotations from both prove, not so much in subject matter as in

---

[1] I.e., interest on the principal.

means of expression. Prose remains, even in literature, essentially a form of discourse which is straightforward. Poetry makes no such attempt.

There may be plenty of imagination, contagious emotion, and lyricism in a piece of good prose, such as this excerpt from *Lavengro* by George Borrow (1803–1881):

In less than two hours I had made the circuit of the Devil's Mountain, and was returning along the road, bathed with perspiration, but screaming with delight; the cob laughing in his equine way, scattering foam and pebbles to the right and left, and trotting at the rate of sixteen miles an hour.

Oh, that ride! that first ride!—most truly it was an epoch in my existence; and I still look back to it with feelings of longing and regret. People may talk of first love—it is a very agreeable event, I dare say—but give me the flush, and triumph, and glorious sweat of a first ride, like mine on the mighty cob! My whole frame was shaken, it is true; and during one long week I could hardly move foot or hand; but what of that? By that one trial I had become free, as I may say, of the whole equine species. No more fatigue, no more stiffness of joints, after that first ride round the Devil's Hill on the cob. Oh, that cob; that Irish cob!—may the sod lie lightly over the bones of the strongest, speediest, and most gallant of its kind! Oh! the days when, issuing from the barrack-gate of Templemore, we commenced our hurry-skurry just as inclination led—now across the fields—direct over stone walls and running brooks—mere pastime for the cob!—sometimes along the road to Thurles and Holy Cross, even to distant Cahir!—what was distance to the cob?

It was thus that the passion for the equine race was first awakened within me—a passion which, up to the present time, has been rather on the increase than diminishing. It is no blind passion; the horse being a noble and generous creature, intended by the All-Wise to be the helper and friend of man, to whom he stands next in the order of creation. On many occasions of my life I have been much indebted to the horse, and have found in him a friend and coadjutor, when human help and sympathy were not to be obtained. It is therefore natural enough that I should love the horse; but the love which I entertain for him has always been blended with respect; for I soon perceived that, though disposed to be the friend and helper of man, he is by no means inclined to be his slave; in which respect he differs from the dog, who will crouch when beaten; whereas the horse spurns, for he is aware of his own worth, and that he carries death within the horn of his heel. If, therefore, I found it easy to love the horse, I found it equally natural to respect him.

There may be less of emotion and lyricism in fine poetry than in prose. Compare this little song of Emily Dickinson (1830–1886) with the passage from *Lavengro:*

It dropped so low—in my Regard—
I heard it hit the Ground—
And go to pieces on the Stones
At bottom of my Mind—

Yet blamed the Fate that fractured—less
Than I reviled Myself
For entertaining Plated Wares
Upon my Silver Shelf—

Nonetheless there is no mistaking that these lines are poetry; they are radically different in their means of expression from the prose passage.

In prose, no matter how fraught with emotion and excitement, the means employed involves a chain of some sort of ordered sequence. We note in the passage from *Lavengro,* for instance, despite the enthusiasm suffusing it, that the author proceeds in a certain order from one paragraph to the next. As we read him, we move with intellectual ease from idea to idea because they are linked to one another. In Poetry, however, the chain of connection from idea to idea is not important to the poet, for he is working in an intenser medium. It is for the reader to supply the links. In her little poem, Emily Dickinson, as is the way with poets, simply projects before us a series of pictures; she does not tell us what they mean in rational terms; it is for us to make the connections that bind the pictures into one idea.

Poetry thus is a more condensed, more vivid, more intense medium of expression than prose. Prose cannot entirely dispense with the language of ideas, which is abstract, no matter how rich in imagery any given passage may be. Strictly speaking, in prose images are, as we have already said, less generic than in poetry. "With most poets," we have remarked, "imagery has been the lifeblood of their poetry. ... While in prose the image is often the riveter of our attention or the welcome oasis in the desert—in poetry the image becomes the tissue itself of the poet's thought." We said this so long ago, that we are in hopes it will in this place have fresh meaning. Vice versa, abstractions are not generic to poetry, though a poet may introduce a philosophic idea nakedly:

> Beauty is truth, truth beauty
> —"Ode on a Grecian Urn" by KEATS

A poem is not necessarily better for the intrusion of such an abstraction, and some poets would certainly insist on conveying such an idea through imagery rather than permit themselves to state it so baldly. At any rate, if the rest of Keats's ode were written in that kind of language, it would not be a poem at all. The "Ode on a Grecian Urn" contains, except for its conclusion, a series of magnificent images; the poet, therefore, may be permitted his moment of prose, which is affixed as a sort of motto at the conclusion.

It is the fact that poetry lives by the image that distinguishes it from prose. And that is its advantage. That is what enables a poet to say far more in a few lines than prose could say in a page, and yet leave still more implied. In prose, a pessimistic philosopher might say:

> Life has no meaning. Regarded superficially, it gives the illusion of significance.
> We exert ourselves, we become involved in all sorts of plans, activities, hopes,
> ambitions. But when the totality of these endeavors is examined, we can
> discern in them no recognizable design, no goal achieved, no purpose uniting
> the whole. All our anguish, despair, joy, ecstasy, rebellion are without import.

He might multiply his words many times over, but he could never manage to say more in this strain than Macbeth does in a few words (V/v/27 seq.):

> It is a tale
> Told by an idiot, full of sound and fury,
> Signifying nothing.

One brilliant image of a poem says more than a paragraph of prose.

This intensity of meaning conveyed by the language of imagery, since imagery is fundamental to poetry, is the chief distinguishing trait of poetry. But there are other differences from prose.

Words when spoken make sound, and there are therefore inevitably certain musical attributes which attach to language. Writing in prose or verse, the author has available to him a variety of these musical attributes, which become part of his meaning too. In poetry these musical attributes are relatively more formal and at the same time more basic than in prose. Rhythm, for instance, is based on firmer patterns in poetry than in prose. Rhyme, which can be a source of much power and beauty in poetry, has almost no place in prose at all. Musical attributes, then, are by the differences in their uses in poetry and prose a further cause of differences between the two media.

It is to the musical resources at the disposal of the writer that we now turn.

MUSICAL ATTRIBUTES

ᏧᏫ 4 ᏧᏫ

From harmony, from heavenly harmony,
This universal frame began:
When Nature underneath a heap
Of jarring atoms lay,
And could not heave her head,
The tuneful voice was heard from high:
"Arise, ye more than dead."*

THUS the poet John Dryden (1631–1700) makes the beginning of the Creation not the word but the word and the music. Speaking of literary creation, we need not challenge him. In literature the music is a matter of the words: it emanates from the way, singly and in combination, words sound.

MUSIC IN LITERATURE

Poetry from the outset was closely allied to its sister art, music. Many centuries before men came to write literature down, it was sung by the poets; the very notion of the "bard" implies quite as much the singer as the poet. And poetry has never escaped its lineage: even though read on a printed page, it appeals more to the ear than to the eye, and the reader must train himself to *hear* what he reads. (If necessary, no matter what the neighbors think, he can practise reading it aloud.) Poets, like Browning, who seem "difficult" when read only with the eye, often become quite easy to follow when *heard,* just because they were addressing the ear and not at all the eye.

It is still common for poets to speak of poetry as "song," and many of them would insist that in the frenzy of composition they are often more led by the music of the lines than by anything else. William Blake in the "Introduction" to his volume *Songs of Innocence* makes this revelation as to his method of composition:

Piping down the valleys wild,
    Piping songs of pleasant glee,
On a cloud I saw a child,
    And he laughing said to me:

"Pipe a song about a Lamb!"
    So I piped with merry cheer.
"Piper, pipe that song again;"
    So I piped: he wept to hear.

---

*From "A Song for St. Cecilia's Day."

117

"Drop thy pipe, thy happy pipe;
    Sing thy songs of happy cheer!"   10
So I sung the same again,
    While he wept with joy to hear.

"Piper, sit thee down and write
    In a book that all may read.
So he vanished from my sight;
    And I plucked a hollow reed,

And I made a rural pen,
    And I stained the water clear,
And I wrote my happy songs
    Every child may joy to hear.   20

Notice what Blake tells us. When directed by his inspiration to compose his song, he is first required to pipe it. He does this. Then he is asked to play the song over again on his instrument. After the second performance of the melody, he is then directed to sing his song. It is only after he has twice played it and also sung it that he is at last ready to write it down "that all may read." Blake is, in short, not only telling us that the music of his words was highly essential to him, but he is also revealing that the music was quintessential to his meaning.

The rhythm and sound of the words make the music of a poem; hearing that music is essential in understanding the total meaning of the poem.

SIMILARITIES AND DISSIMILARITIES AMONG THE ARTS

Of course, literature is not music, any more than it is painting or sculpture. To derive the maximum pleasure from each of the arts it is perhaps necessary to be quite aware of how much they have in common and how utterly dissimilar they are too. They are fundamentally at one in their concern with the quintessences of life and experience, but they are unlike in the kinds of quintessences they can represent. The burning of Moscow before Napoleon's army, for instance, would make for hideous sculpture (even though many a city is defaced with public works attempting such a subject) and dreadful music (even though Tschaikovsky in an unhappy moment decided to write the *1812 Overture*); yet Napoleon's engagements are fairly adaptable to the purposes of painting (Delacroix could have done wonders with them) and are perfect for literary treatment (Hugo's *Les Misérables,* Thackeray's *Vanity Fair,* and Tolstoi's *War and Peace* did nobly with them). A sunset is impossible to sculpture, possible to poetry, and perfect for painting (Turner made a career out of sunsets); in music you could show not the sunset itself but the mood evoked by it. As for sculpture, it is unique in its power to do three-dimensional justice to the body.

Further, all the arts have in common certain fundamental attributes—rhythm, for instance. But rhythm manifests itself very differently in the various arts; it is one thing in music, another in painting, another in sculpture, and still another in literature. In painting it has something to do with color but also, as in sculpture, something to do with geometric forms and with lines. In music and in literature rhythm reveals itself as a matter of sound; there is therefore a certain affinity between musical rhythm and literary rhythm.

What we mean, then, when we speak of the musical attributes of literature is not a confusion with a sister art, but an affinity to it. (In other connections it would be fair to hint at literature's alliances with sculpture as, for example, when we speak of chiseled lines, or with painting, when we speak of design and color.) What are these affinities with music? Since we have spoken of rhythm, let us begin with it. Of all aspects of music, it may very well be the basic one. Among primitive peoples barely aware of melody and not at all aware of harmony, a strong impulse for rhythm will be found in their native music. In the poem that follows the rhythm is the very life of the expression.

THE NATURE OF RHYTHM IN PROSE AND POETRY

In this wonderfully vivid poem, "The Centaurs," the Irish poet-novelist James Stephens (1882–1950) gives reality to the half-men-half-horse creations of myth:

> Playing upon the hill three centaurs were!
> They lifted each a hoof! They stared at me!
> And stamped the dust!
>
> They stamped the dust! They snuffed upon the air!
> And all their movements had the fierce glee
> Of power, and pride, and lust!
>
> Of power and pride and lust! Then, with a shout,
> They tossed their heads, and wheeled, and galloped round,
> In furious brotherhood!
>
> In furious brotherhood! Around, about,
> They charged, they swerved, they leaped! Then, bound on bound,
> They raced into the wood!

10

Read the poem aloud, pausing as you would naturally pause at the end of sentences, also (in this instance) after the commas. You will find marvelously depicted the leaping movements of the creatures, their speed, their restless equine prancings. In case you are tempted to believe that these effects are achieved only through the meanings of the words, see what happens when one paraphrases these lines in prose, employing much of the original vocabulary.

> Three centaurs, playing upon the hill, lifted each a foot and stared at me. They stamped the dust and snuffed upon the air, all their movements having the fierce glee of power, pride and lust. Then, shouting, they tossed their heads, wheeled, and galloped around in furious brotherhood; they charged, swerved and leaped. Then in bounds they raced into the wood.

The magic of the original is all gone.

How did Stephens achieve the wonderful effects in his poem? Through pauses and repetitions. The pauses are so cunningly placed that they give the illusion of the sudden starts and halts of the centaurs. And there are speed and leaps in the clever repetition of the last line of each stanza as the beginning of the next:

> And stamped the dust!
>
> They stamped the dust! They snuffed upon the air!

This recurrent repetition of the last line of each stanza establishes a design, part of the rhythmic pattern of the poem. *Repetition and recurrence of an arrangement of words makes for rhythm* in prose too:

> It was the best of times, it was the worst of times, it was the age of wisdom, it was the age of foolishness, it was the epoch of belief, it was the epoch of incredulity, it was the season of Light, it was the season of Darkness, it was the spring of hope, it was the winter of despair, we had everything before us, we had nothing before us, we were all going direct to Heaven, we were all going direct the other way.

This, the opening of Charles Dickens' (1812–1870) historical novel on the French Revolution, *A Tale of Two Cities,* is a passage of very marked and strong rhythms based on various kinds of repetitions, recurrences and pauses. Ten clauses in succession begin with *it was the,* and each of these clauses concludes the same way: a noun followed by *of* followed by another noun. Both factors establish, to begin with, an insistent rhythmic pattern. But these ten clauses are further divided into five groups of antitheses:

> It was the best of times, it was the worst of times; it was the age of wisdom,
> it was the age of foolishness; [etc.]

and this pattern is continued to the end:

> we had everything before us, we had nothing before us; we were all going direct
> to Heaven, we were all going direct the other way.

These antitheses themselves constitute a recurrence—a recurrence of opposites—and are in themselves another basis of rhythmic pattern.

Notice too:

1. that each first half of these antitheses constitutes roughly as much of a mouthful when you speak it as the second half which follows it. This *approximate equality in time-length* of each clause in the pair *makes a rhythmic pattern:*

> It was the best of times, it was the worst of times.

2. that there are two kinds of pauses here: a short pause after the first of the pair, and a longer pause at the end of the antithesis:

> It was the best of times, (short pause)
> it was the worst of times, (longer pause)
> it was the age of wisdom, (short pause)
> it was the age of foolishness, (longer pause).

This constitutes a double rhythm: one rhythm for each part of the antithesis, and another rhythm in which the unit is the whole antithesis (i.e., both clauses) and the effect is achieved from the procession of antitheses:

> It was the best . . . worst of times,
> it was the age of wisdom . . . age of foolishness . . .

The elaborately incisive rhythms of this paragraph, which remind one of a polyphonic passage in music, are, of course, not particularly common to prose; when they are found at all, it is more usually in oratory. And indeed the paragraph does have the ring of a speech. But one has not far to seek in deciding why Dickens should have opened a novel on the French Revolution this way. The very rhythms of the balances and antitheses give one a very powerful impression of the marshaling of opposing forces, as well as a sense of the violent confusion attendant on the clash of hostile ideas.

Let us see rhythm at work in great oratory:

> But, in a larger sense, we cannot dedicate—we cannot consecrate—we cannot hallow—this ground. The brave men, living and dead, who struggled here, have consecrated it far above our poor power to add or detract. The world will little note nor long remember what we say here, but it can never forget what they did here. It is for us, the living, rather, to be dedicated here to the unfinished work which they who fought here, have thus far so nobly advanced. It is rather for us to be here dedicated to the great task remaining before us—that from these honored dead we take increased devotion to that cause for which they gave the last full measure of devotion; that we here highly resolve that these dead shall not have died in vain; that this nation, under God, shall have a new birth of freedom; and that government of the people, by the people, for the people, shall not perish from the earth.

Everyone admires the eloquent simplicity of the language in Lincoln's "Gettysburg Address"; but not the least of its power comes from the strong rhythms employed. Note the recurrence, as in the Dickens paragraph, of a pattern of expression:

> *we cannot* dedicate, *we cannot* consecrate, *we cannot* hallow;
> we cannot *consecrate*—we cannot hallow—this ground. The brave men, living
> and dead, who struggled here, have *consecrated* it;
> It is for us, the living, *rather, to be dedicated here.* . . . It is *rather* for us *to
> be here dedicated;*
> *that* from these honored dead *we* take increased devotion . . . ; *that we* here
> highly resolve that these dead shall not have died in vain; *that* this
> nation, under God, shall have a new birth of freedom; and *that* govern-
> ment of the people, by the people, for the people, shall not perish from
> the earth;
> that from these honored dead we take increased *devotion* to that cause for
> which they gave the last full measure of *devotion;*
> government of *the people,* by *the people,* for *the people.*

Note too the antitheses:

> *living* and *dead*
> *to add* or *detract*
> *The world will little note* nor *long remember what we say here,* but *it can never
> forget what they did here.*

Of such rhythms within rhythms was Dickens' and Lincoln's eloquence compounded.

In nonoratorical prose, rhythms are less obviously to be perceived. But all good prose
has some sort of rhythmic rightness. In a novelette, "Neighbor Rosicky," the American
novelist Willa Cather (1876–1947) thus described a snowstorm falling quietly in the open
country:

> On his cap and shoulders, on the horses' backs and manes, light, delicate,
> mysterious it fell; and with it a dry cool fragrance was released into the air.
> It meant rest for vegetation and men and beasts, for the ground itself; a season
> of long nights for sleep, leisurely breakfasts, peace by the fire. This and much
> more went through Rosicky's mind, but he merely told himself that winter was
> coming, clucked to his horses, and drove on.

The rhythms here are more subtle—softer, as is befitting the subject. The first two sentences
echo the feeling of the steady, gentle fall of snow by the perfect spacing of the pauses. Here
too there are delicate recurrences which make for gentle rhythmic patterns:

> on his cap and shoulders, on the horses' backs and manes,
> light, delicate, mysterious;
> vegetation, and men, and beasts;
> for vegetation and men and beasts, for the ground itself;
> long nights for sleep, leisurely breakfasts, peace by the fire;
> winter was coming, clucked to his horses, and drove on.

Not all writers have been gifted with an ear. Some, with other talents, have been lacking
in the musical gift. George Eliot (1819–1880), for instance, whatever her powers as a novelist
in characterization, truth to life, and compassion, was curiously unable to impart the lustre
of beauty to her prose style. This passage, for example, from her *Silas Marner,* is nothing
like the one we have just cited:

In the days when the spinning-wheels hummed busily in the farmhouses—and even great ladies, clothed in silk and thread-lace, had their toy spinning-wheels of polished oak—there might be seen in districts far away among the lanes, or deep in the bosom of the hills, certain pallid undersized men, who, by the side of the brawny country-folk, looked like the remnants of a disinherited race. The shepherd's dog barked fiercely when one of these alien-looking men appeared on the upland, dark against the early winter sunset; for what dog likes a figure bent under a heavy bag?—and these pale men rarely steered abroad without that mysterious burden. The shepherd himself, though he had good reason to believe that the bag held nothing but flaxen thread, or else the long rolls of strong linen spun from that thread, was not quite sure that this trade of weaving, indispensable though it was, could be carried on entirely without the help of the Evil One. In that far-off time superstition clung easily round every person or thing that was at all unwonted, or even intermittent and occasional merely, like the visits of the pedlar or the knife-grinder. No one knew where wandering men had their homes or their origin; and how was a man to be explained unless you at least knew somebody who knew his father and mother? To the peasants of old times, the world outside their own direct experience was a region of vagueness and mystery; to their untravelled thought a state of wandering was a conception as dim as the winter life of the swallows that came back with the spring; and even a settler, if he came from distant parts, hardly ever ceased to be viewed with a remnant of distrust, which would have prevented any surprise if a long course of inoffensive conduct on his part had ended in the commission of a crime; especially if he had any reputation for knowledge, or showed any skill in handicraft. All cleverness, whether in the rapid use of that difficult instrument the tongue, or in some other art unfamiliar to villagers, was in itself suspicious; honest folk, born and bred in a visible manner, were mostly not over-wise or clever—at least, not beyond such a matter as knowing the signs of the weather; and the process by which rapidity and dexterity of any kind were acquired was so wholly hidden that they partook of the nature of conjuring. In this way it came to pass that those scattered linen-weavers—emigrants from the town into the country—were to the last regarded as aliens by their rustic neighbours, and usually contracted the eccentric habits which belong to a state of loneliness.

Here is a prose that possesses honesty, conscientiousness (which can be a rather depressing virtue in the arts!) and thoroughness, but it lacks all grace, charm or excitement. And this is because, above everything else, its movement is cumbersome and heavy, and communicates nothing of the feeling of loneliness which is, presumably, the keynote of the paragraph. You will note the absence of significant recurrences and the presence of pauses without rhythmic significance—as though there were no patterns present at all. (E.g., the long sentence beginning "To the peasants of old times.")

Let us now consider the nature of rhythm as manifested in poetry, where the affinities with music are much closer. In verse that is metrical (verse with a pattern of recurring stresses) the basis for rhythm is much firmer than in prose, that is to say, much tighter and more confining. Repetition and recurrence, as ever, are at the heart of rhythm here too.

In the art of music, rhythms are based upon the regular recurrence of stresses, what is called *time* in that art. Thus, if in any given composition every quarter note is allotted one count and every third count is stressed (ONE, two, three, ONE, two, three) we have what is called three-quarter time—the pattern in which waltzes, minuets, and mazurkas (among other dances) have been written. If every fourth count is stressed (ONE, two, three, four, ONE, two, three, four) we have what is called four-quarter time—the pattern in which marches have been written. And so on. In all poetry, with the exception of what is called "free verse," the equivalent of this basic pattern is known as *meter.*

METRICAL PATTERNS

Let us discover what is meant by meter.
Pronounce these words:

Was this?

There is no feeling of rhythm here, because there is no pattern, no recurrence of stress.
But now pronounce:

Was this the face?

Something like rhythm begins to emerge. If you have read the words normally you have naturally read *the* as weak and *face* as stressed:

the FACE.

And because there is an emphasis implied in *this* you have also tended to read the four words as:

Was THIS the FACE?

And having read them this way, you are beginning to get a pattern: a procession of alternating weak and STRESSED syllables. Now, if you read this celebrated line of Marlowe in its entirety:

Was this the face that launched a thousand ships?

(addressed to an image of Helen of Troy), and if you have read it normally it went like this:

Was THIS the FACE that LAUNCHED a THOUsand SHIPS?

Launched is naturally stronger than *that; thousand* can be accented in only one way; and at the end of the procession of weak-STRESSED-weak-STRESSED, *ships* falls naturally into a stressed position. The pattern is clear, and from it emerges clearly a rhythm.

Now let us try this line from Longfellow:

This is the forest primeval. The murmuring pines and the hemlocks.

Read naturally, it will come out:

THIS is the FORest priMEval. The MURmuring PINES and the HEMlocks,

—a pattern of recurring stresses each (except the last) followed by two weak syllables.

How, you may ask, does it happen that the line must be read this way? The answer is, surprisingly, fairly simple. Every word of more than one syllable in English has a normal, correct stress on one of the syllables (the accent as indicated in the dictionary). It would be a violation of our language to pronounce the words as *forEST, PRImeval* or *primeVAL, murMURing* or *murmurING,* or *hemLOCKS.* Precision in stressing the correct syllable of a word is so important in English as to become a mark of social differentiation. We brand as illiterate those who say *comPARable* instead of *COMparable,* and as affected those Americans who insist on saying *laBOratory* instead of *LABoratory.*

The line from Longfellow, then, gives you no choice in pronouncing *FORest, priMEval, MURmuring,* and *HEMlocks.*

As for the words of one syllable, of which there are a vast number in English, you are compelled neither to stress them nor to leave them weak, for monosyllables are neither stressed nor unstressed by nature. But they are subject to a certain logic. It is simply common sense that unimportant words like *a, the, and, of, in,* etc. ought not be made prominent by stressing them. From a literary point of view it is utterly absurd that we cry out to our sweet land of liberty:

OF thee i SING,

when the meaning clearly is

of THEE i SING.

From such considerations, we must in Longfellow's line say:

the FORest priMEval. The MURmuring—

and since *pines* is an important word, and since it falls into the already established pattern when we stress it, we are moved to continue:

the FORest priMEval. The MURmuring PINES and the HEMlocks.

And since *this* is an emphatic monosyllable, we naturally stress it; that places it perfectly into the pattern of the rest of the line:

> THIS is the FORest priMEval. The MURmuring PINES and the HEMlocks.

The important thing, then, at the basis of rhythm in English poetry is the correct placing of stress—because of the importance of stress in the pronunciation of our language. This correct placing of stress is fairly simple to manage if you read the lines naturally, stressing the correct syllable in polysyllabic words and stressing monosyllables when the meaning calls for it. (There are occasional exceptions to this principle which need not detain us here.) Of course many poets have exercised considerable ingenuity in employing variety in rhythms; but if the reader will follow our recommendation to read the lines normally, the lines will bring him close to the poet's intentions. Generally speaking, if you place your stresses correctly in a line and allow the weak (unstressed) syllables to cluster around the stresses, you are sure to hear the rhythm intended. In the days of our earliest poetry this was precisely the manner in which poets composed their verses. Thus, in *Beowulf* (c. 750), one of our oldest poems, the basis of the line is simply that it have four stresses. This is a sample, as rendered into modern English by Spaeth:

> In the DARKness DWELT a DEmon-SPRITE
> Whose HEART was FILLED with FUry and HATE,
> When he HEARD each NIGHT the NOISE of REVel
> LOUD in the HALL, LAUGHter and SONG.
> To the SOUND of the HARP the SINGer CHANTed
> LAYS he had LEARNED, of LONG aGO.

Read that passage with the stresses evenly spaced, and despite the varying number of weak syllables, the effect is one of perfect regularity.

Running weak syllables together is a practice that has by no means ended with Anglo-Saxon times, though not done as consistently now as then. Poets still slip in an extra weak syllable here and there in their lines to vary the rhythm a little. Did you notice in the first line of Blake's quatrain on page 59 the extra weak syllable?

> To SEE the WORLD in a GRAIN of SAND

Obviously the pattern of the line is one of alternating weak and stressed syllables. But between WORLD and GRAIN Blake has two weak syllables. This was easy and natural to do because in normal speech we do run *in* and *a* together so that they take no more time to utter than might a single weak syllable.

We do not in this chapter propose going into the technicalities of meter and verse forms. Our intention is simply to make you aware that these exist. If you desire to investigate them further, you will find that Chapter 7 concerns itself exclusively with verse techniques. For our present purposes it is quite enough that you hear the rhythmic patterns as set by the stresses.

In setting the rhythm for the whole poem, the *number* of stresses in a line is important.

Some poems retain the same number of stresses in each line, as in this song from *Alice's Adventures in Wonderland:*

> TWINkle, TWINkle, LITtle BAT!
> HOW i WONder WHAT you're AT!
> UP aBOVE the WORLD you FLY,
> LIKE a TEA-tray IN the SKY.

And some poems vary the number of stresses per line, as in this piece from Lewis Carroll's *Sylvie and Bruno:*

He THOUGHT he SAW an ALbaTROSS*
That FLUTtered ROUND the LAMP:
He LOOKED aGAIN, and FOUND it WAS
a PENny POSTage STAMP.
"You'd BEST be GETting HOME," he SAID:
"The NIGHTS are VEry DAMP."

These lines alternate in a pattern of four and three stresses. A poet may retain the same number of stresses in each line in a given poem—indeed, some verse techniques, such as blank verse and the sonnet, call for that; or he may vary the number of stresses in the procession of lines. The decision is imposed upon him by what he is trying to say. It works the other way too: the metrical pattern, like all formal elements of a poem, determining what a poet can say.

We have already indicated that the basic rhythm of a line can be varied by the addition or omission of weak syllables. There is another subtle way in which the basic rhythm of a line is subject to constant variations.

TIME VALUES

Although the fundamental rhythmic fact about English words is the correct placing of accents, there is another aspect of syllables which has its importance too. Irrespective of the matter of stress, is the factor of length and shortness of syllables. Certain syllables are obviously short, as for example the words *a, the, of, in,* because they are to be uttered in a brief instant of time; others are plainly long, as for example the words *sword, strength, fire, moon, straight,* because they take more time to utter. Thus, in our line:

THIS is the FORest priMEval. The MURmuring PINES and the HEMlocks,

is, the, and are short but *est, pri, mur,* and *locks,* though weak, are longer. (*Val* is not particularly long.) When read correctly, it will be heard that the line achieves a further variety from the difference in time values between the short and long syllables. A long vowel (e.g., *pri*) or a combination of succeeding consonants (e.g., *locks*) generally makes a syllable long. Note too that among the accented syllables, *this* and *hem* are shorter than *me, mur* and *pines.*

Poets sometimes get remarkable effects by cunning use of the time value of syllables. In "L'Allegro" Milton achieves a wonderful feeling of lightness in lines like:

Come, and trip it, as you go,
On the light fantastic toe

—where nearly all the syllables are short (*come, and, trip, it, as, on, the, fan, tas, tic*). Their being short is unaffected by the fact that they may be stressed (or weak). It would certainly be impossible to argue that the lightness of "L'Allegro" is attributable to its being written in four-stress lines. For in a companion poem, "Il Penseroso," the same poet achieves exactly the opposite effect in lines which also have four stresses:

Sweet bird, that shunn'st the noise of folly,
Most musical, most melancholy!
Thee, chauntress, oft the woods among
I woo, to hear thy even-song. . . .

*Notice the fact that this word is given two stresses. We are required to accent the first syllable, AL. Now, in a given word of three or more syllables there is always a primary accent and often one or more secondary accents, as indicated in most dictionaries. (In priMEval there is only one accent; in ALbaTROSS there are two accents—AL bearing the primary and TROSS the secondary accent.) A poet is free to use or not to use the secondary accent as a stress in the metrical pattern of his line; e.g., *undeniable* could have one stress or three stresses: undeNIable or UNdeNIaBLE. As for our line, *since the pattern is of alternating weak and stressed syllables,* the poet naturally gave the word two stresses, ALbaTROSS.

The many long syllables (*sweet, bird, shunn'st, noise, most, mu, most, chol, thee, chaunt, ress, oft, mong, I, woo, hear, thy, e, song*), stressed and unstressed, lend an air of gravity and thoughtfulness to the lines.

BASIC AND ACTUAL RHYTHM

It will have been noticed that we have thus far been careful to speak of the *basic* rhythm —a term we have preferred in this chapter. What we have called "basic rhythm" is, usually, technically called *meter*. As we have observed, the meter is made up of:

1. the number of stresses in a line (4 in the two passages from Milton; 4 in the passage from *Beowulf*; 5 in the line by Marlowe; 6 in the line by Longfellow);

2. the fundamental arrangement of stressed and weak syllables in a line (stressed-weak in "L'Allegro" and the song from *Alice's Adventures in Wonderland*; weak-stressed in "Il Penseroso," the song from *Sylvie and Bruno*, and the line by Marlowe; stressed-weak-weak in the line by Longfellow). When each stress is most frequently preceded by a weak syllable (or weak syllables) the line is said to have a *rising* rhythm; when each stress is followed by a weak syllable (or weak syllables) the line is said to have a *falling* rhythm. The lines from "L'Allegro" have a falling rhythm; those from "Il Penseroso" a rising rhythm;

3. uniformity or variation in the number of stresses in each line (uniformity in the passages by Milton, from *Beowulf*, from *Alice in Wonderland*; and variation in the passage from *Sylvie and Bruno*—an alternation of four- and three-stress lines).

But we have seen that poets by no means conform in every line to the fundamental arrangement of stressed and weak syllables (2, above). Thus, at the end of the line by Longfellow there was a weak syllable *missing*; in the middle of Blake's there was an *extra* weak syllable. There were, moreover, modifying effects upon the basic rhythm as a product of the use of *long* and *short* syllables, irrespective of the stresses. We must therefore conclude that:

1. Sometimes the poet *conforms precisely* to the *basic rhythm* of a line and sometimes he *departs* from it. When he departs from it, it is either by

a. omitting a weak syllable or

b. adding a weak syllable.

From the allotted *number of stresses* in a line he *rarely varies.* To increase or diminish the number of stresses is almost always to annihilate the rhythm. (E.g., let us assassinate

> Come, and trip it, as you go,
> On the light fantastic toe ...

by adding an extra stress to the second line:

> Come and trip it, as you go,
> On the light fantastic pointed toe.

You hear how the whole effect is ruined!) When a poet varies the allotted number of stresses it is probably through error.

2. The poet endlessly varies the basic rhythm through his choice of short and long syllables. In this he must be directed by the thought in every line, and the effect he wishes to achieve.

The *fluctuation from conformance to variation of the basic rhythm gives us the actual rhythm* in metrical poetry. Perhaps an analogy will elucidate the difference between *basic* and *actual* rhythm. When a pianist plays a Chopin waltz, the accompaniment (usually in his left hand) beats out fairly consistently the basic rhythm, that is, the ONE-two-three of waltz time. But the melody (usually in his right hand) sometimes coincides with this ONE-two-three but sometimes departs from that basic pattern—by an interpolation between these beats of more rapid notes on some occasions, or on other occasions by the omission on the beat of any new note at all. For example, these are the opening measures of Chopin's C# minor Waltz:

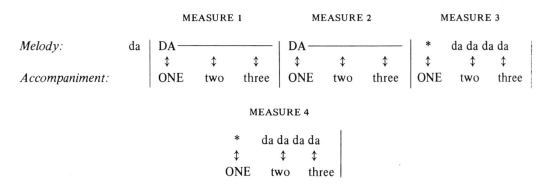

In Measures 1 and 2 the stress in the melody coincides with the stress in the accompaniment. In Measures 3 and 4 there is no such coinciding because of the rest in the melody on the stressed beat; moreover, extra notes are interpolated in the melody between beats. This *coinciding-and-failure-to-coincide* of the melody's rhythm with the accompaniment's rhythm *gives the actual rhythm of the waltz.*

Just so, *the coinciding-and-failure-to-coincide of the line's rhythm with the established basic rhythm* in poetry *gives the actual rhythm thus:*

The line:	To	SEE	the	WORLD	in	a	GRAIN	of	SAND
	↕	↕	↕	↕	↕		↕	↕	↕
Basic rhythm:	weak	STRESS	weak	STRESS	weak		STRESS	weak	STRESS

Before the third stress in the line an extra weak syllable has been interpolated; here we have a failure-to-coincide as part of the rhythm.

Again in:

> A casement high and triple-arched there was,
> All garlanded with carven imag'ries
> Of fruits, and flowers, and bunches of knot-grass . . .

the rhythm may be thus analyzed:

The line:	a	CASE	-ment	HIGH	and	TRI	-ple	ARCHED	there	WAS
	↕	↕	↕	↕	↕	↕	↕	↕	↕	↕
Basic rhythm:	weak	STRESS	weak	STRESS	weak	STRESS	weak	STRESS	weak	STRESS

The line:	all	GAR	-land	-ED	with	CARV	-en	IM	-ag'	-RIES
	↕	↕	↕	↕	↕	↕	↕	↕	↕	↕
Basic rhythm:	weak	STRESS	weak	STRESS	weak	STRESS	weak	STRESS	weak	STRESS

The line:	of	FRUITS	and	FLOWERS	and	BUNCH	-es	of	KNOT	*	-GRASS
	↕	↕	↕	↕	↕	↕	↕		↕	↕	↕
Basic rhythm:	weak	STRESS	weak	STRESS	weak	STRESS	weak		STRESS	weak	STRESS

In the third line there are two examples of a failure-to-coincide as part of the actual rhythm:
1. There is an extra weak syllable before the fourth stress (KNOT).

*Here in the melody there is a rest, "a note of silence."

2. There is a weak syllable missing (*) before the fifth stress (GRASS).

Before leaving our discussion of rhythm in verse it would be well to make a cautionary observation. In Tennyson's "Tears, Idle Tears," a song from *The Princess,* these are the opening lines:

> Tears, idle tears, I know not what they mean,
> Tears from the depth of some divine despair
> Rise in the heart, and gather to the eyes,
> In looking on the happy Autumn-fields,
> And thinking of the days that are no more.

One might easily be tempted to read the first line this way:

> TEARS, Idle TEARS, i KNOW NOT WHAT they MEAN—

i.e., with seven stresses—or perhaps this way:

> TEARS, Idle TEARS, i KNOW not WHAT they MEAN—

—i.e., with six stresses. But it is clear from the lines which follow that there are only five stresses in each line. Indeed, the entire song is written in five-stress lines. Sometimes, in short, we cannot tell from the first line or lines of a poem how many stresses are to be allotted. The rest of the poem, however, will make the design clear. From the rest of Tennyson's song we realize that this is the correct meter:

> Tears, ídle téars, I knów not whát they méan,
> Téars from the dépth of sóme divíne despáir
> Ríse in the héart, and gáther tó the éyes,
> In lóoking ón the háppy Aútumn-fíelds,
> And thínking óf the dáys that áre no móre.
>
> Frésh, as the fírst beam glíttering ón a sáil,
> That bríngs our fríends úp from the únderwórld,
> Sád as the lást which réddens óver óne
> That sínks with áll we lóve belów the vérge;
> So sád, so frésh, the dáys that áre no móre.

From the second line on it is clear that there are five stresses in each line. The basic rhythmic pattern is set in lines 4, 5, 9, and 10: weak-stressed-weak-stressed-weak-stressed-weak-stressed-weak-stressed. In line 1 the first word is *long but not stressed* (*I, not,* and *they* are similarly long but unstressed.) Lines 2, 3, 6, and 8 vary a little from the basic rhythmic pattern by omitting the first weak syllable and by employing *the* as an extra weak syllable.

Again, in e. e. cummings' poem (see page 21) "when faces called flowers float out of the ground," one might be tempted to read the opening line in a number of ways. But the rest of the poem makes it plain that it must be read:

> when fáces called flówers float óut of the gróund
> and bréathing is wíshing and wíshing is háving—
> but kéeping is dównward and dóubting and néver.

Before deciding on the rhythm of the opening passage of a poem, therefore, one is wise to study the rhythmic design of the succeeding lines.

RHYTHMIC DESIGN IN PROSE

Prose, of course, is not subject to the discipline of meter. The rhythms of prose are therefore more or less free. Nevertheless, literary prose will be seen to have its own patterns.

---

*This corresponds to "a note of silence" in music.

Consider the opening paragraph of Oliver Goldsmith's (1730?–1774) "Beau Tibbs":

> I am apt to fancy I have contracted a new acquaintance whom it will be no easy matter to shake off. My little Beau yesterday overtook me again in one of the public walks, and slapping me on the shoulder, saluted me with an air of the most perfect familiarity. His dress was the same as usual, except that he had more powder in his hair, wore a dirtier shirt, a pair of temple spectacles, and his hat under his arm.

Taking cognizance of the normal stresses and pauses, we may break up the passage as follows:

(a) I am ápt to fáncy (short pause)
(b) I have contrácted a néw acquáintance (short pause)
(c) whom it will be no éasy mátter to sháke off. (long pause)
(d) My líttle Béau yésterday (short pause)
(e) overtóok me agáin (short pause)
(f) in one of the públic wálks, (medium pause)
(g) and slápping me on the shóulder, (short pause)
(h) salúted me with an air of the most pérfect familiárity. (long pause)
(i) His dréss was the same as úsual, (medium pause)
(j) except that he had more pówder in his háir, (medium pause)
(k) wore a dírtier shírt, (medium pause)
(l) a pair of témple spéctacles, (medium pause)
(m) and his hát under his árm. (long pause)

It will be noted that:

1. Most of the groups contain two stresses (a, e, f, g, i, j, k, l, and m); these are varied with groups of three stresses (b, c, d, and h).
2. The first two sentences terminate in a group of three stresses (c and h).

Let us look at the next paragraph:

> As I knew him to be a harmless, amusing little thing, I could not return his smiles with any degree of severity; so we walked forward on terms of the utmost intimacy, and in a few minutes discussed all the usual topics preliminary to particular conversation.

This may be broken up as follows:

(n) As I knew him to be a hármless, amúsing little thíng, (short pause)
(o) I cóuld not retúrn his smíles (short pause)
(p) with any degrée of sevérity; (long pause)
(q) so we wálked fórward (short pause)
(r) on terms of the útmost íntimacy, (medium pause)
(s) and in a féw mínutes (short pause)
(t) discussed all the úsual tópics (short pause)
(u) prelíminary to partícular conversátion. (long pause)

In this second paragraph:

1. Most of the groups contain two stresses (p, q, r, s, t); these too are varied with groups of three stresses (n, o, u).
2. The sentence again terminates in a group of three stresses. It is clear, then, that Goldsmith's piece of prose has a free but perceptible basic rhythmic design. It is the presence of this basic design which lends grace to the passage.

Here is a piece of contemporary prose, Mary McCarthy's (1912—) rather savage criticism of Tennessee Williams' *A Streetcar Named Desire* from her *Sights and Spectacles.* This is the opening paragraph:

> You are an ordinary guy and your wife's sister comes to stay with you. Whenever you want to go to the toilet, there she is in the bathroom, primping or having a bath or giving herself a shampoo and taking her time about it. You go and hammer on the door ("For Christ's sake, aren't you through yet?"), and your wife shushes you frowningly: Blanche is very sensitive and you must be careful of her feelings. You get sore at your wife; your kidneys are sensitive too. My God, you yell, loud enough so that Blanche can hear you, can't a man pee in his own house, when is she getting out of here? You are pretty sick too of feeling her criticize your table-manners, and does she have to turn on the radio when you have a poker game going, who does she think she is? Finally you and your wife have a fight (you knew all along that She was turning the little woman against you), you decide to put your foot down, Blanche will have to go. Your wife reluctantly gives in—anything for peace, don't think it's been a treat for *her* ("But let me handle it, Stanley; after all, she's my own *sister!*"). One way or another (God knows what your wife told her) Blanche gets the idea. You buy her a ticket home. But then right at the end, when you're carrying her bags downstairs for her, you feel sort of funny; maybe you were too hard; but that's the way the world is, and, Boy, isn't it great to be alone?

The passage may be broken up as follows:

  (a) You are an órdinary gúy (medium pause)
  (b) and your wífe's síster cómes to stáy with you. (long pause)
  (c) Whenéver you want to gó to the tóilet, (short pause)
  (d) there she ís in the báthroom, (medium pause)
  (e) prímping or háving a báth (medium pause)
  (f) or gíving hersélf a shampóo (medium pause)
  (g) and táking her tíme about it. (long pause)
  (h) You gó and hámmer ón the dóor (short pause)
  (i) "For Chríst's sáke, áren't you thróugh yet?" (medium pause)
  (j) and your wífe shúshes you frówningly: (medium pause)
  (k) Blánche is véry sénsitive (short pause)
  (l) and you múst be cáreful of her féelings. (long pause)
  (m) You get sóre at your wífe; (medium pause)
  (n) your kídneys are sénsitive tóo. (long pause)
  (o) My Gód, you yéll, (short pause)
  (p) lóud enough so that Blánche can héar you, (medium pause)
  (q) can't a man pée in his ówn hóuse, (medium pause)
  (r) whén is she getting óut of hére? (long pause)
  (s) You are prétty síck tóo (short pause)
  (t) of féeling her críticize your táble-mánners, (medium pause)
  (u) and does she háve to túrn on the rádio (short pause)
  (v) when you have a póker game góing, (medium pause)
  (w) whó does she thínk she ís? (long pause)
  (x) Fínally yóu and your wífe have a fight (medium pause)
  (y) (you knéw all alóng (short pause)
  (z) that Shé was túrning the líttle wóman agáinst you), (medium pause)
  (aa) you decíde to pút your fóot down, (short pause)
  (bb) Blánche will háve to gó. (long pause)
  (cc) Your wífe relúctantly gives ín— (short pause)
  (dd) ánything for péace, (medium pause)

(ee) Don't thínk it's been a tréat for *hér* (short pause)

(ff) ("But lét mé hándle it, Stánley; (short pause)

(gg) after áll, she's my ówn *síster!*"). (long pause)

(hh) Óne wáy or anóther (short pause)

(ii) (Gód knóws what your wífe tóld her) (short pause)

(jj) Blanche géts the idéa. (long pause)

(kk) You búy her a tícket hóme. (medium pause)

(ll) But thén ríght at the énd, (short pause)

(mm) when you're cárrying her bágs dównstairs fór her, (short pause)

(nn) you féel sort of fúnny; (medium pause)

(oo) máybe you were tóo hárd; (medium pause)

(pp) but thát's the wáy the wórld ís, (medium pause)

(qq) and, Bóy, (short pause)

(rr) ísn't it gréat to bé alóne? (long pause)

In this paragraph:

1. Most of the groups contain three stresses (c, e, f, j, k, l, n, p, q, r, s, u, w, aa, bb, cc, ee, gg, hh, kk, ll, oo); these are varied nearly evenly with groups of two stresses (a, d, g, m, o, v, y, dd, jj, nn) and groups of four stresses (b, h, i, t, x, ff, ii, mm, pp, rr).

2. At emphatic places there is a group with one stress (qq) and a group with five stresses (z).

3. Most of the sentences terminate in a group of three stresses (l, n, r, w, bb, gg); the others terminate in groups of four (b and rr) or two (g and jj).

Here again we observe a perceptible basic rhythmic design.

Concerning the rhythms of these two pieces of prose, we might point out various niceties, but we shall be satisfied to note that they both have something of a larger design than that of the stresses. In the Goldsmith passages it is to be noted that the second, third, and fifth long pauses (h, m, and u) come after five groups each; the other two long pauses (c and p) come after three groups each. This makes for a larger rhythmic pattern, of which the groups are the elements. In the McCarthy paragraph, of the ten long pauses, five of them come after five groups each (g, l, w, bb, and gg); the others after two, three, four, and eight. The last long pause comes after an extended group of eight, and thus has the intended effect of a climactic conclusion.

Earlier in this chapter we quoted a paragraph from George Eliot (see page 121) and said of it that "it lacks all grace, charm, or movement," and that it "communicates nothing of the feeling of loneliness which is, presumably, the keynote" of the passage. We are now in a better position to analyze the stylistic shortcomings of the paragraph. Let us examine its groupings:

(a) In the dáys when the spínning-wheels hummed búsily in the fármhouses— (short pause)

(b) and éven gréat ládies, clothed in sílk and thréad-láce, (short pause)

(c) had their tóy spínning-whéels of pólished óak— (medium pause)

(d) there míght be séen (short pause)

(e) in dístricts far awáy amóng the lánes, (short pause)

(f) or déep in the bósom of the hílls, (short pause)

(g) cértain pállid úndersized mén, (short pause)

(h) whó, (short pause)

(i) by the síde of the bráwny cóuntry-folk, (short pause)

(j) lóoked like the rémnants of a disinhérited ráce. (long pause)

(k) The shépherd's dóg barked fíercely (short pause)

(l) when óne of these álien-looking mén appéared on the úpland, (short pause)

(m) dárk against the éarly wínter súnset; (medium pause)

(n) for whát dóg líkes a fígure bént under a héavy bág?— (medium pause)

(o) and thése pále mén rárely stéered abróad (short pause)

(p) withóut that mystérious búrden. (long pause)

(q) The shépherd himsélf, (short pause)

(r) though he had góod réason to belíeve that the bág held nóthing but fláxen thréad, (short pause)

(s) or élse the long rólls of stróng línen spún from that thréad, (short pause)

(t) was nót quíte súre (short pause)

(u) that thís tráde of wéaving, (short pause)

(v) indispénsable though it wás, (short pause)

(w) could be cárried ón entírely without the hélp of the Évil One. (long pause)

(x) In thát fár-off tíme (short pause)

(y) superstítion clung éasily (short pause)

(z) round évery pérson or thíng that was at áll unwónted, (short pause)

(aa) or éven intermíttent and occásional mérely, (short pause)

(bb) like the vísits of the pédlar or the knífe grínder. (long pause)

(cc) Nó one knéw where wándering mén had their hómes or their órigin; (medium pause)

(dd) and hów was a mán to bé expláined (short pause)

(ee) unléss you at least knéw sómebody who knéw his fáther and móther? (long pause)

(ff) To the péasants of óld tímes, (short pause)

(gg) the wórld outsíde their ówn diréct expérience (short pause)

(hh) was a région of vágueness and mýstery; (long pause)

(ii) to théir untrávelled thóught (short pause)

(jj) a státe of wándering (short pause)

(kk) was a concéption as dím as the wínter lífe of the swállows (short pause)

(ll) that came báck with the spríng; (long pause)

(mm) and éven a séttler, (short pause)

(nn) if he cáme from dístant párts, (short pause)

(oo) hardly éver céased to be víewed with a rémnant of distrúst, (short pause)

(pp) which would have prevénted ány surpríse (short pause)

(qq) if a lóng cóurse of inoffénsive cónduct on hís párt (short pause)

(rr) had énded in the commíssion of a críme; (short pause)

(ss) espécially if he had ány reputátion for knówledge, (short pause)

(tt) or showed ány skíll in hándicraft. (long pause)

(uu) Áll cléverness, (short pause)

(vv) whether in the rápid úse of that dífficult ínstrument the tóngue, (short pause)

(ww) or in some óther árt unfamíliar to víllagers, (short pause)

(xx) was in itsélf suspícious; (long pause)

(yy) hónest fólk, (short pause)

(zz) bórn and bréd in a vísible mánner, (short pause)

(aaa) were mostly nót over-wíse or cléver— (short pause)

(bbb) at léast, not beyónd such a mátter as knówing the sígns of the wéather; (medium pause)

(ccc) and the prócess by which rapídity and dextérity of ány kínd were acquíred (short pause)

(ddd) was so whólly hídden (short pause)

(eee) that they partóok of the náture of cónjuring. (long pause)

(fff) In this wáy it cáme to páss (short pause)

(ggg) that thóse scáttered línen-wéavers— (short pause)
(hhh) émigrants from the tówn into the cóuntry— (short pause)
(iii) were to the lást regárded as áliens by their rústic néighbours, (short pause)
(jjj) and úsually contrácted the eccéntric hábits (short pause)
(kkk) which belóng to a státe of lóneliness. (long pause)

It will be seen that there is no basic rhythmic grouping here: there is a group of one stress (h), and groupings of two, three, four, five, six and seven stresses. There are eleven groupings of two stresses (d, q, v, y, jj, ll, mm, uu, xx, yy, and ddd), nineteen of three stresses (f, i, k, p, t, u, x, ff, hh, ii, nn, pp, rr, tt, aaa, eee, fff, hhh, and kkk), thirteen of four stresses (a, e, g, j, m, aa, bb, dd, ss, ww, zz, ggg, and jjj), nine of five stresses (c, l, w, z, gg, kk, oo, vv, and iii), eight of six stresses (b, o, s, cc, ee, qq, bbb, and ccc), and two of seven stresses (n and r). There is, in short, no characteristic tendency in this long paragraph. Moreover, the recurrence of the same groupings is haphazard; for example, there is not another two-stress group between d and q, but two of them follow in ll and mm, and two in xx and yy; again, four of the three-stress groupings occur in the last few lines. Even allowing for possible differences of interpretation in the scansion, we should not be able to discover any pattern in the stress groupings.

But more revealing of the lack of grace in the paragraph is the fact that in the eleven long pauses of the paragraph there emerges no rhythmic design at all; these pauses occur at

> j, after ten groupings;
> p, after six groupings;
> w, after seven groupings;
> bb, after five groupings;
> ee, after three groupings;
> hh, after three groupings;
> ll, after four groupings;
> tt, after eight groupings;
> xx, after four groupings;
> eee, after seven groupings;
> kkk, after six groupings.

The author of this passage was assuredly writing without an ear for rhythmic design. Goldsmith and Mary McCarthy, we may be sure, did not work out their rhythms mechanically, but were guided by their dependable ears.

RHYME, ASSONANCE AND ALLITERATION

We come now to certain musical attributes which are peculiar to the art of literature: rhyme, assonance and alliteration.

Rhyme is, of course, though one of the delights of literature, by no means essential to it. In prose it has no place at all—unless for comic purposes. Unintended rhyme in prose can have even a disastrous effect upon serious writing:

> In the tense hush I saw him blush.

And poetry itself is written with or without rhyme. Our earliest poetry had none; one of the most important of verse techniques, blank verse (5-stress lines unrhymed in which the usual arrangement of syllables is weak-stress) excludes rhyme. But in a vast portion of our great poetry, rhyme is a part of the meaning and the beauty of the lines.

Let us cite in this context the limerick quoted in our discussion of Tone, the anonymous sally on "Relativity":

> There was a young woman named Bright
> Who traveled much faster than light.
>   She started one day
>   In a relative way,
> And returned on the previous night.

Suppose we remove the rhyme:

> There was a young woman named Jones
> Who traveled much faster than light.
>   She started one morn
>   In a relative way,
> And returned on the previous eve.

What has happened to the genial satire once the rhyme is absent? Obviously, in this case —no rhyme, no satire.

To the poets rhyming may be in itself a joy. As witness this exuberance from the pen of Eleanor Dowson:

> I felt in such fine fettle,
> I really could not settle,
> It put me on my mettle;
> I firmly grasped the nettle,
> Climbed Popocatepetl
> And boiled my copper kettle.

Here the writer, plainly intoxicated with the heady pleasures of rhyme, has let herself go. It is equally clear that for her (as for most poets) rhyming is not a device that hampers creativity.

What, in English, constitutes a rhyme? It will be no revelation to the reader that *bright, light,* and *night* rhyme with one another; and that *fettle, settle, mettle, nettle, Popocatepetl,* and *kettle* do likewise. In the first group the rhyme involves only one syllable: IGHT. In the second group the rhyme involves two syllables: ETtle.

Rhyme, then, as found in English may be defined as the *coinciding in the final stressed vowel sounds* of two words or arrangements of words, *and in all the sounds following that vowel sound, the preceding consonant sound* (if any) *being different.* Thus:

1. *Bright* and *deLIGHT* are rhymes.
2. *Light* and *deLIGHT* are not true rhymes because the IGHT is preceded by the same consonant, L.
3. *Sigh* and *deCRY* are rhymes; *eye* would be admitted as a rhyme to both, even though it has *no* consonant preceding the vowel.
4. But *deCRY* and *cry* are not true rhymes because the vowel is preceded by the same consonant, the K sound.
5. *FETtle* and *KETtle* are rhymes; but *disPEL* does not rhyme with them because the *el* sound in *fettle* and *kettle* contains no stressed vowel, whereas the *el* sound in *dispel* does contain a stressed vowel; *disPEL* would rhyme with *beFELL* or *shell.* There would not be a true rhyme in *disPEL* and *comPEL* because the preceding consonant is the same, P.
6. These are rhymes:
   > *dreamed, unredeemed.*
   > *full, insurmountable, wool.*
   > *appearing, endearing, volunteering.*
7. These are not rhymes:
   > *bring, endearing.*
   > *mistress, distress.*

8. These are not true rhymes:
> *full, beautiful.*
> *distress, stress.*

In defining rhyme, we have spoken of the possibility that the coinciding of the final stressed vowel may involve "two words or arrangements of words." *Bright* and *light* is a rhyme involving two words. But consider the rhymes in the following song from W. S. Gilbert's *The Mikado:*

> Young man, despair,
> > Likewise go to,
> Yum-Yum the fair
> > You must not woo.
> It will not do:
> I'm sorry for you,
> You very imperfect ablutioner!

> This very day
> > From school Yum-Yum
> Will wend her way,   10
> And homeward come,
> With beat of drum
> And a rum-tum-tum,
> To wed the Lord High Executioner! . . .

> It's a hopeless case,
> > As you may see,
> And in your place
> > Away I'd flee;
> But don't blame me—
> I'm sorry to be   20
> Of your pleasure a diminutioner.

> They'll vow their pact
> > Extremely soon,
> In point of fact
> > This afternoon.
> Her honeymoon
> With that buffoon
> At seven commences, so *you* shun her!

The rhyming of *ablutioner, Executioner, diminutioner,* and *you shun her,* in the last instance involves an arrangement of words. When we accent *you* as the author's italics require us to do, all the sounds following the stressed vowel are the same in *ablutioner, Executioner, diminutioner,* and *you shun her.* It is also to be noted that in this case the rhyme involves *three* syllables, Utioner. A rhyme involving three syllables usually has, as here, a comic effect. Byron was fond of this device, and W. S. Gilbert was past master in the use of it.

Besides rhyme, we also find in poetry (and sometimes in prose) another kind of correspondence in sound, *assonance.* We meet one kind of assonance in the following passage from Wilfred Owen's (1893–1918) "Strange Meeting":

> It seemed that out of battle I escaped,
> Down some profound dull tunnel, long since scooped
> Through granites which titanic wars had groined.
> Yet also there encumbered sleepers groaned,
> Too fast in thought or death to be bestirred.
> Then, as I probed them, one sprang up and stared

> With pitiless recognition in fixed eyes,
> Lifting distressful hands as if to bless.
> And by his smile, I knew that sullen hall,
> By his dead smile I knew we stood in Hell.   10

At the end of each pair of lines the final stressed vowel is different but the consonants coincide. This device we call *consonantal assonance* (it is sometimes called *consonance*): *escaped* and *scooped; groined* and *groaned; bestirred* and *stared; hall* and *Hell*. (The correspondence between *eyes* and *bless* is less complete—but no less agreeable—because the final *s* in the former has a different sound from the double *s* in the latter.) *Consonantal assonance* may be defined as a *coinciding of the consonants in the final stressed syllable, the stressed vowel itself differing.*

Closely allied to consonantal assonance is a charming effect known as *imperfect rhyme* (or, alternately, as half-rhyme or slant rhyme). These stanzas are from Elinor Wylie's (1886–1928) "Address to My Soul":

> My soul, be not disturbed
> By planetary war;
> Remain securely orbed
> In this contracted star.
>
> Fear not, pathetic flame;
> Your sustenance is doubt:
> Glassed in translucent dream
> They cannot snuff you out.

Disturbed and *orbed; war* and *star; flame* and *dream* are almost normal rhymes (note that *doubt* and *out* are), but the vowel values in the stressed syllable, though close, are slightly different. These are *imperfect rhymes,* which can be used with delightful results as a departure from normal rhymes. *Imperfect rhyme* may be defined as a *variation of the same or similar stressed vowel, and the coinciding of all the sounds following that vowel, the preceding consonant* (if any) *being different.*

There is another kind of assonance known as *vocalic assonance.* (It is sometimes called simply *assonance.*) Consider these excerpts from Emily Dickinson's "The Final Inch":

> As if a Goblin with a Gauge—
> Kept measuring the Hours—
> Until you felt your Second weigh,
> Helpless, in his Paws—
>
> As if your Sentence stood—pronounced—
> And you were frozen led
> From Dungeon's luxury of Doubt
> To Gibbets, and the Dead—

The vowels in *Gauge* and *weigh,* and in *pronounced* and *Doubt* are the same but the sounds following them are different. *Vocalic assonance* may be defined as the *coinciding of the final stressed vowel, with the sounds following that vowel differing.*

Rhyme and the various kinds of assonance may be established during the course of a poem in a regular pattern so as to give the poem a consistent rhyme or assonance pattern. For instance, the first two stanzas of the song from *The Mikado* which we have quoted show a regular design:

despair	(a)
to	(b)
fair	(a)
woo	(b)
do	(b)

you	(b)
ablutioner	(c)
day	(d)
Yum	(e)
way	(d)
come	(e)
drum	(e)
tum	(e)
Executioner	(c)

We have designated the matching rhymes, as in common practice, by the same letter of the alphabet. It will be observed that the pattern set up in the first stanza is followed in the succeeding stanzas: lines 1 and 3 rhyme; lines 2, 4, 5, and 6 rhyme; and the last lines of each stanza rhyme with one another (c). Such consistency of pattern through the stanzas gives firm shape to a poem and is part of its structure. The device of having the last lines of each stanza in rhyme helps give unity to the entire poem.

Certain poetic techniques (see Chapter 7) require a set scheme of rhymes. For example, the little piece on "Relativity" shows the established form for the limerick:

Bright	(a)
light	(a)
day	(b)
way	(b)
night	(a)

Such is the regular rhyme scheme for the limerick: *a, a, b, b, a.*

Regular designs may also be found in the use of assonance. For instance, in "Strange Meeting" we have:

escaped	(a)
scooped	(a)
groined	(b)
groaned	(b)
bestirred	(c)
stared	(c)

Here the consonantal assonance is in pairs of lines.

Rhyme and assonance are sometimes used with telling effect not only at the ends of lines but within the line as well. In Percy Bysshe Shelley's (1792–1822) "The Cloud":

> That orbèd maiden with white fire laden,
> Whom mortals call the moon,
> Glides glimmering o'er my fleece-like floor,
> By the midnight breezes strewn;
> And wherever the beat of her unseen feet,
> Which only the angels hear,
> May have broken the woof of my tent's thin roof,
> The stars peep behind her and peer;
> And I laugh to see them whirl and flee,
> Like a swarm of golden bees,   10
> When I widen the rent in my wind-built tent,
> Till the calm rivers, lakes, and seas,
> Like strips of the sky fallen through me on high,
> Are each paved with the moon and these.

Here we have not only the rhymes of *moon* and *strewn; hear* and *peer; bees, seas,* and *these;* but also within each of the unrhyming lines what we call *internal rhyme: maiden* and *laden;*

o'er and *floor; beat* and *feet; woof* and *roof; see* and *flee, rent* and *tent; sky* and *high.*

It might be asked why Shelley, instead of using these internal rhymes, did not make two lines of each line where they occur; thus:

> That orbèd maiden
> With white fire laden,
> Whom mortals call the moon,
> Glides glimmering o'er
> My fleece-like floor,
> By the midnight breezes strewn.

Had he done this, his poem would have been composed of a series of two two-stress lines followed by a three-stress line—the effect of which would have been too staccato for his subject, the life history of a cloud. Shelley wished to impart a sense of aerial suspension to the lines, as the cloud speaks to us of its experiences, and for that his poetic sensibilities unerringly directed him to a stanza in which a four-stress line alternates with a three-stress line. The internal rhymes lend a wonderful buoyancy to the longer lines; and the longer line was needed to vary with the three-stress line for the appropriate feeling of movement-and-rest, which is true of a cloud:

> with wings FOLDed i REST, on mine AIRy NEST,
> as STILL as a BROODing DOVE.

(Read the quoted stanza aloud, and you can hardly fail to hear Shelley's marvelous technical accomplishment in this poem.)

Assonance too can be used internally with a resulting enrichment of the music of a line. There are many magical effects in Coleridge's "Kubla Khan":

> In Xanadu did Kubla Khan
> A stately pleasure-dome decree;
> Where Alph, the sacred river, ran
> Through caverns measureless to man
> Down to a sunless sea.

In the first line *in* and *did, Xan* and *Khan* are vocalic assonances. *Du* and *Ku* have the same vowel. Assonance appears again in the succeeding lines: *Alph, ran, cav* (of *caverns*), and *man; state* (of *stately*) and *sa* (of *sacred*).

In the above brief quotation from "Kubla Khan" another musical device may have been noted: *K*ubla *K*han; *d*ome *d*ecree; *r*iver *r*an; *m*easureless *m*an; *s*unless *s*ea. The device is known as *alliteration, the use in proximity of words beginning with the same consonantal sound or of words beginning with vowels.* (*All* initial vowels are considered as being in alliteration with one another.)

Alliteration in our language is as old as our poetry, for in Anglo-Saxon times it was one of the very bases of verse; every line contained alliteration. Professor Spaeth has faithfully maintained this characteristic of Anglo-Saxon poetry in his translation of *Beowulf:*

> He vented his *j*ealousy. The *j*ourney of Beowulf,
> His *s*ea-adventure, *s*orely displeased him.
> It filled him with *e*nvy that *a*ny other*
> Should *w*in among men more *w*ar-like glory,
> More fame under *h*eaven than *h*e *h*imself.

Some poets have been very fond of alliteration; Algernon Charles Swinburne (1837–1909) has been charged with being too much addicted to it. Here is a stanza from his "Itylus":

---

*This line exhibits the fact that all vowels beginning a word are in alliteration with one another.

> O *s*wallow, *s*ister, O *f*air *s*wift *s*wallow,
> *W*hy *w*ilt *th*ou *f*ly after *s*pring to *the s*outh,
> *The s*oft *s*outh *w*hither *th*ine heart is *s*et?
> Shall not *the* grief of *the* old time follow?
> Shall not *the s*ong *th*ereof cleave to *th*y mouth?
> Hast *th*ou *f*orgotten *e*re *I f*orget?

Not content with the rhyme and this abundance of alliteration, Swinburne has repeated some of these same alliterative sounds (*s, w, th, f*) within various of the words: sou*th,* whi*th*er, mou*th*; si*s*ter, i*s*. There is also assonance in si*s*ter, sw*i*ft, w*i*lt, spr*i*ng, wh*i*ther; th*ou*, s*ou*th; *O, o*ld; n*o*t, f*o*llow, there*o*f, forg*o*tten; s*o*ft, s*o*ng; and elsewhere. For some tastes all this adds up to a music that is excessively rich, though in the opinion of others Swinburne has never been surpassed as a master-musician in verse.

Rhyme, we have remarked, has little or no place in prose. What of the other devices which are of such advantage to poetry?

Here is a tribute to Queen Elizabeth by John Lyly (d. 1606), from his *Euphues and His England:*

> This is that good *p*elican,[1] that to feed her *p*eople spareth not to rend her own *p*erson. This is that mighty eagle, that hath thrown *d*ust into the eyes of the hart that went about to work *d*estruction to her subjects, into whose wings although the *b*lind *b*eetle would have crept, and so being carried into her nest, *d*estroyed her young ones, yet hath she with the virtue of her *f*eathers, consumed that *f*ly in his own *f*raud. She hath exiled the *s*wallow that *s*ought to *s*poil the gra*ss*hopper, and given bitter almonds to the ravenous wolves that en*d*eavored to *d*evour the *s*illy[2] lambs, *b*urning even with the *b*reath of her mouth like the princely *s*tag, the *s*erpents that were engendered by the breath of the huge elephant, so that now all her enemies are as whist[3] as the bird Attagen, who never singeth any *t*une after she is *t*aken, nor they being so over-*t*aken.

We have italicized some of the alliterations. Because of Lyly's influence, alliteration became popular in the discourse of courtly circles. Today it strikes us as only silly, an unsuccessful straining at elegance. Shakespeare thought so too, for he ridiculed the fashion of alliterating in prose in a celebrated passage in *Henry IV, Part One* (II/iv/456 seq.):

> For, Harry, now I do not speak to thee in drink but in tears, not in *p*leasure but in *p*assion, not in *w*ords only but in *w*oes also.

However, for special effects prose may avail itself of alliteration and even rhyme and assonance. Consider these vivacious opening pages of Dylan Thomas' (1914–1953) "A Visit to America":

Across the United States of America, from New York to California and back, glazed, again, for many months of the year, there streams and sings for its heady supper a dazed and prejudiced procession of European lecturers, scholars, sociologists, economists, writers, authorities on this and that and even, in theory, on the United States of America. And breathlessly, between addresses and receptions, in planes and trains and boiling hotel bedroom ovens, many of these attempt to keep journals and diaries.

At first, confused and shocked by shameless profusion and almost shamed by generosity, unaccustomed to such importance as they are assumed, by their hosts, to possess, and up against the barrier of a common language, they write in their notebooks like demons, generalizing away, on character and culture and the American political scene. But, towards the middle of their middle-aged whisk through middle-

---

[1] According to Pliny, the pelican was the kindest of all birds; she ripped open her bosom and fed her young on her own blood.

[2] Innocent.

[3] Silent.

western clubs and universities, the fury of the writing flags; their spirits are lowered by the spirit with which they are everywhere strongly greeted and which, in ever increasing doses, they themselves lower; and they begin to mistrust themselves, and their reputations—for they have found, too often, that an audience will receive a lantern-lecture on, say, Ceramics, with the same uninhibited enthusiasm that it accorded the very week before to a paper on the Modern Turkish Novel. And in their diaries, more and more do such entries appear as, "No way of escape!" or "Buffalo!" or "I am beaten," until at last they cannot write a word. And, twittering all over, old before their time, with eyes like rissoles[1] in the sand, they are helped up the gangway of the home-bound liner by kind bosom friends (of all kinds and bosoms) who boister them on the back, pick them up again, thrust bottles, sonnets, cigars, addresses, into their pockets, have a farewell party in their cabin, pick them up again, and, snickering and yelping, are gone: to wait at the dockside for another boat from Europe and another batch of fresh, green lecturers.

There they go, every spring, from New York to Los Angeles: exhibitionists, polemicists, histrionic publicists, theological rhetoricians, historical hoddy-doddies, balletomanes, ulterior decorators, windbags and bigwigs and humbugs, men in love with stamps, men in love with steaks, men after millionaires' widows, men with elephantiasis of the reputation (huge trunks and teeny minds), authorities on gas, bishops, bestsellers, editors looking for writers, writers look-

ing for publishers, publishers looking for dollars, existentialists,[2] serious physicists with nuclear missions, men from the BBC[3] who speak as though they had the Elgin marbles[4] in their mouths, potboiling philosophers, professional Irishmen (very lepri-corny),[5] and, I am afraid, fat poets with slim volumes.

And see, too, in that linguacious[6] stream, the tall monocled men, smelling of saddle soap and club armchairs, their breath a nice blending of whisky and fox's blood, with big protruding upper-class tusks and county mustaches, presumably invented in England and sent abroad to advertise *Punch*,[7] who lecture to women's clubs on such unlikely subjects as "The History of Etching in the Shetland Islands"; and the brassy-bossy men-women, with corrugated-iron perms,[8] and hippo hides, who come, self-announced, as "ordinary British housewives," to talk to rich mink chunks of American matronhood about the iniquity of the Health Services, the criminal sloth of the miners, the *visible* tail and horns of Mr. Aneurin Bevan,[9] and the fear of everyone in England to go out alone at night because of the organized legions of coshboys[10] against whom the police are powerless owing to the refusal of those in power to equip them with revolvers and to flog to ribbons every adolescent offender on any charge at all.

And there shiver and teeter also, meek and driven, those British authors unfortunate enough to have written, after years of unadventurous forgotten work, one bad novel which became enormously popular on both sides of the Atlantic.

This is prose which is both lyrical and satirical. For the intensification of both tones, the author employs musical devices not commonly employed in prose. To cite just a few examples:

1. Rhymes: *glazed . . . dazed*   (paragraph one)
    planes . . . trains   ("   ")
2. Near-rhymes: *hoddy-doddies*   (paragraph three)
    bigwigs   ("   ")

[1] A small fried cake of minced meat or fish and bread crumbs.

[2] Representatives of a new literary and philosophic movement originating in France in the 1940's under the leadership of Jean-Paul Sartre.

[3] The offical headquarters for broadcasting in England.

[4] The major part of the friezes surviving from the Parthenon in Athens were carried off to England by Lord Elgin in 1801–1803.

[5] A pun on *leprechaun* and the slang *corny.*

[6] Talkative.

[7] The famous English comic weekly magazine.

[8] Permanent waves (ladies' hairdressing).

[9] Prominent radical, a leader of the Labor Party.

[10] Juvenile delinquents.

3. Alliteration: *s*treams . . . *s*ings . . . *s*upper   (paragraph one)
   *p*rejudiced *p*rocession   ("   "   )
   *b*oiling . . . *b*edroom   ("   "   )
   *c*haracter . . . *c*ulture   (paragraph two)
   *f*ury . . . *f*lags   ("   "   )
   *B*uffalo . . . *b*eaten   ("   "   )
   *s*melling . . . *s*addle *s*oap   (paragraph four)
   *b*rassy-*b*ossy   ("   "   )
   *h*ippo *h*ides   ("   "   )
   *m*ink . . . *m*atronhood   ("   "   )
4. Assonance: *glazed, again*   (paragraph one)
   pot-boiling *philosophers*   (paragraph three)
   brassy-bossy   (paragraph four)
   rich mink chunks   ("   "   )

Dylan Thomas is being deliberately preposterous, for the fun of it, and these devices, normally found only in poetry, help him in being so. But it cannot be pretended that such a style is typical of the overwhelming majority of prose writings.

SOUND AND MEANING

There remains one more musical aspect of literature, which is fairly impossible to analyze, the superiority of some words over others for their euphony. Before writing these lines we asked of several people whose taste we respect, "Name some words which you find particularly beautiful to the ear, irrespective of their meaning." This is the result of our gathering: *box, entwining, eternity, amaryllis, tributary, turpentine, carminative, eloquent.* No doubt the charm of any word's sound would depend upon the quality of the voice uttering it and the cultivation with which each was pronounced. Beyond that, we must be content to say that it is in *combination* only that vowels and consonants achieve beauty. No single vowel or consonant is beautiful or ugly in itself, any more than any single note played upon a piano could be thought to qualify for an esthetic evaluation. Which combinations make for beauty and which fail to do so is a matter that must be left to the judgment of each poet. As readers we can only judge by our own ears, whose reliability will be in proportion to their sensitiveness and awareness.

But unlike the sounds produced by music, the sounds produced in literature are all connected with intellectual meanings. And every word, no matter what its sound, is limited by what it means when it stands alone. Hence, however agreeable the combination of vowels and consonants makes *carminative* and *turpentine,* their meanings would probably make them exiles from the sphere of beauty. Words, on the other hand, like *eternity, entwining,* and *amaryllis* have the advantage of associations which are in themselves either stirring or lovely, and are therefore difficult to appraise as pure sound.

In English we have a great many words in which the sound is remarkably suggestive of the sense. This is but a handful of such: *clang, roar, boom, hubbub, blare, toot, honk, rattle, crash, crack, click, toll, hum, buzz, purr, rustle, tinkle, jangle.* When the hero of Coleridge's *Ancient Mariner* says:

> And every soul, it passed me by
> Like the whizz of my cross-bow!

he charges the atmosphere with terror through the use of that one powerful word *whizz.* When, as here, the sound represents the meaning, we have the device known as *onomatopoeia.*

English is the richest of European languages, possessing as it does by far the largest vocabulary in any modern language. It has therefore the greatest resources of any modern language for varied music, and it is not surprising that England's particular contribution to Western culture has been her poetry. There are some poets of standing, of course, who have preferred not to avail themselves of the musical treasures in our language. Wordsworth very often chooses to be plain, as in "We Are Seven":

> I met a little cottage girl:
> She was eight years old, she said.

In the interest of energy, Donne almost disdains music in "The Canonization":

> For God's sake hold your tongue, and let me love;
> Or chide my palsy, or my gout;
> My five gray hairs, or ruined fortune flout.

Browning knows the value of discordant sound when he needs it, as in "Rabbi Ben Ezra":

> Irks care the crop-full bird? Frets doubt the maw-crammed beast?

But lovely sound can be found everywhere in English poetry, the euphony supporting and making richer the meaning. Browning was master of a sweet music when he needed it, as in these lines from "Saul":

> the cool silver shock
> Of the plunge in a pool's living water, the hunt of the bear,
> And the sultriness showing the lion is couched in his lair.
> And the meal, the rich dates yellowed over with gold dust divine,
> And the locust-flesh steeped in the pitcher, the full draft of wine,
> And the sleep in the dried river-channel where the bulrushes tell
> That the water was wont to go warbling so softly and well.

Shakespeare's words would be music even if they conveyed nothing of their intellectual import in "Sonnet CXVI":

> Love's not Time's fool, though rosy lips and cheeks
> Within his bending sickle's compass come.

No one had a more delicate ear than Spenser; this is from the "Prothalamion":

> With that I saw two swannes of goodly hewe
> Come softly swimming downe along the lee;
> Two fairer birds I yet did never see:
> The snow which doth the top of Pindus strew
> Did never whiter shew,
> Nor Jove himselfe, when he a swan would be
> For love of Leda, whiter did appear:
> Yet Leda was, they say, as white as he,
> Yet not so white as these, nor nothing neare:
> So purely white they were,
> That even the gentle streame, the which them bare,
> Seem'd foule to them, and bad his billowes spare
> To wet their silken feathers, least they might
> Soyle their fayre plumes with water not so fayre,
> And marre their beauties bright,
> That shone as heavens light,
> Against their brydale day, which was not long:
> Sweete Themmes, runne softly, till I end my song.

10

You hardly need to know the meanings of the words to gather Shelley's meaning in such lines as these, from "Ode to the West Wind":

> Thou who didst waken from his summer dreams
> The blue Mediterranean, where he lay,
> Lulled by the coil of his crystalline streams,
> Beside a pumice isle in Baiae's bay,
> And saw in sleep old palaces and towers
> Quivering within the wave's intenser day,
> All overgrown with azure moss and flowers.

Tennyson can charm you into drowsiness with the lost souls of "The Lotos-Eaters":

> And like a downward smoke, the slender stream
> Along the cliff to fall and pause and fall did seem.

Keats can almost start your salivary glands operating with the euphony of "The Eve of St. Agnes":

> . . . candied apple, quince, and plum, and gourd;
> With jellies soother than the creamy curd,
> And lucent syrops, tinct with cinnamon;
> Manna and dates.

With the aid of the music Pope can make his sylphs indeed of airy substance in "The Rape of the Lock":

> The lucid squadrons round the sails repair: . . .
> Some to the sun their insect-wings unfold,
> Waft on the breeze, or sink in clouds of gold;
> Transparent forms, too fine for mortal sight,
> Their fluid bodies half dissolved in light.

And, of course, that arch-magician with sound, John Milton, can do anything he wishes with his music, from the dewy loveliness of these lines in "Lycidas":

> He must not float upon his watery bier
> Unwept, and welter to the parching wind,
> Without the meed of some melodious tear.

to the glorious radiance of other lines in the same poem:

> So sinks the day-star in the ocean-bed,
> And yet anon repairs his beams, and with new-spangled ore
> Flames in the forehead of the morning sky.

—or from the solemn organ tones of "On the Late Massacre in Piedmont":

> . . . in thy book record their groans
> Who were they sheep, and in their ancient fold
> Slain by the bloody Piedmontese, that rolled
> Mother with infant down the rocks. Their moans
> The vales redoubled to the hills, and they
> To heaven. . . .

to the tenderness of such passages as these in *Paradise Lost:*

> . . . But now lead on;
> In me is no delay; with thee to go
> Is to stay here; without thee here to stay,
> Is to go hence unwillingly; thou to me
> Art all things under Heaven, all places thou.

With the rich English language his instrument, each of our poets has created such music as was within his scope to make. In this chapter we have attempted to analyze the aspects of music as found in our literature. The result of such an analysis may possibly be to make them seem too much like "devices." Beginners probably always find devices helpful, but it would be impossible to discover to what extent (if any) an accomplished author *consciously uses* them, and if he does so, in which instances. It would also be of little value to make such discoveries, so far as the reader's understanding is concerned. All that can be of importance is what is to be heard in the finished work itself, and it is to aid the reader's hearing that we have analyzed what in many cases must certainly have been an unconscious artistry. Some creators assure us that literary inspiration is to them a roaring furnace; others have urbanely insisted that literary inspiration is essentially the practice of tirelessly applying the file. A poet may labor hard, revising and revising, to make a lyric sound spontaneous. What matter to us whether the music came to the poet sought or unsought—so long as it is there in the poem for us to hear?

PROSE
FICTION

5

About the year 1620, a Large Swarm of Dissenters fled thither from the Severities of their Stepmother, the Church. These Saints conceiving the same Aversion to the Copper Complexion of the Natives, with that of the First Adventurers to Virginia, would, on no Terms, contract Alliances with them, afraid perhaps, like the Jews of Old, lest they might be drawn into Idolatry by those Strange Women.

Whatever disgusted them I cant say, but this false delicacy creating in the Indians a Jealousy[1] that the English were ill affected towards them, was the Cause that many of them were cut off, and the rest Exposed to various Distresses.

This Reinforcement was landed not far from Cape Codd, where, for their greater Security they built a Fort, and near it a Small Town, which in Honour of the Proprietors, was call'd New Plymouth. But they Still had many discouragements to Struggle with, tho' by being well Supported from Home, they by Degrees Triumph't over them all.

Their Bretheren, after this, flockt over so fast, that in a few Years they extended the Settlement one hundred Miles along the Coast, including Rhode Island and Martha's Vineyard.

Thus the Colony throve apace, and was throng'd with large Detachments of Independents and Presbyterians, who thought themselves persecuted at home.

Tho' these People may be ridiculd for some Pharisaical Particularitys in their Worship and Behaviour, yet they were very useful Subjects, as being Frugal and Industrious, giving no Scandal or bad Example, at least by any Open and Public Vices. By which excellent Qualities they had much the Advantage of the Southern Colony, who thought their being Members of the Establish't Church sufficient to Sanctifie very loose and Profligate Morals. For this Reason New England improved much faster than Virginia, and in Seven or Eight Years New Plimouth, like Switzerland, seemd too Narrow a Territory for its Inhabitants.

—from *The History of the Dividing Line*
by WILLIAM BYRD (1674–1744)

THIS IS a characteristic passage from a work of one of our first historians, a distinguished son of Virginia. In the broadest sense of the word it is a *story,* since it *provides an account of a "series of connected events"* (*Webster's New World Dictionary*). Its prime purpose, clearly, is to inform.

NONFICTION AND FICTION

The province of this passage, however, is outside belles-lettres. Not that we fail to be interested in what it has to say, for naturally Americans will listen attentively to any authoritative account of our beginnings. We are certainly likely to be interested in learning about early experiences of the Puritans with the Indians. But the criterion of literature is,

[1]Suspicion.

145

Are the *values* of human experience involved in the narration? It is not the events through which people move that make for literature, but the values involved. The presentation of such values requires the presence in a story of individuals whom we can see and come to know, not the human race in aggregates or mass. Insofar as historians do not deal with what in journalism is termed "human interest"—the values of human relationships—history is largely outside the domain of literature.

Of course there are important exceptions to this tendency. There have been historians whose brilliant style and grasp of human values enroll them among men of letters (like Edward Gibbon), and biographers who create the illusion of the reality of life itself as powerfully as the best of novels (like the prince of them all, James Boswell).

There are stories the prime purpose of which is not to inform but to move or delight us. Such stories are works of *fiction* (from the Latin *fictus,* "made, fashioned, molded"), and it is as fiction that we find the bulk of literary prose narratives. History, as such, undertakes to report the facts and to interpret them, not to exhibit fashioning or molding by the historian's own imagination or observation. An historian who permitted himself flights of creative fancy in the narration of historical events would be a pariah in his profession. The narration of events involving the values of human experience, on the other hand, calls upon the writer's imagination or creative observation. It does not at all mean that the writer of fiction is debarred from employing historical fact for his material. A literary man might, for instance, seize on Byrd's statement that the Dissenters would on no account contract alliances with the Indians, "afraid perhaps, like the Jews of old, lest they might be drawn into idolatry by these strange women," and by weaving a story about a particular Puritan's temptation and self-disciplining in the case of a particular Indian girl, create a work of fiction. Historical novels (like Thackeray's *Henry Esmond,* or Pater's *Marius the Epicurean*) sometimes call on a considerable body of fact; but these facts are simply ingredients subject to the fashioning of the novelist's creative imagination.

A piece of fiction, then, may use as material either fact or imagined events. It is the fashioning of them so that they exhibit the values of human experience which distinguishes the world of literature. Let us turn now to that world.

KINDS OF FICTION

Not many years ago there lived in the south of Scotland a somewhat eccentric clergyman, who had been preaching most vigorously on the impropriety of profane swearing, and denouncing the rather common habit of using one of Satan's names in ordinary conversation. On the Monday he set out to visit a few of his people. Just as he was entering a neighboring village, he overtook an old woman, who was carrying home a young pig which she meant to rear. The old woman's strength and patience both became exhausted, and waxing very wroth, she exclaimed, "The deevil choke ye, beast!"

The minister was passing at the moment, but he simply looked, heaved a sigh, and went on his way. On reaching the further end of the village, however, he found another old woman assiduously attempting to induce a flock of ducklings to enter in at a stable door. The old dame was completely baffled; and as she stood wiping her face with her apron, the minister heard her give vent to her spleen in these words: "Deevil tak ye, beasts, will ye no gang[1] in?"

He evidently thought this was a great deal too much, and stepping forward, he thus accosted her: "Ay, ay, just thole[2] a wee, my woman; the deevil's busy at the ither end o' the toon[3] chokin' a sow; but he'll be your way in a whilie, I'le warrant ye—just thole a wee."

—*The Book of Scottish Anecdote,*
collected by ALEXANDER HISLOP (1874)

[1]Go.
[2]Wait.   [3]Town.

The narration of such an incident is called an anecdote. *An anecdote is the relation of an interesting or amusing incident,* generally illustrative of biography or private life, *and is always reported as being true.* Whether factually true or not, it comes to us after being fashioned in the telling and retelling by many men; in the process it moves out of history into fiction. We do not know any more that such a Scottish minister did live and did have the experience recounted, nor do we care. We are willing to think he did, and that is all fiction demands of us. In anecdotes we are asked to believe that the incident related probably did occur.

Anecdotes are either of the folk or of more or less celebrated persons. For example, here is one concerning a member of the United States House of Representatives:

> During the heat of a Congressional debate, a member of the House, representing Indiana, so much lost his temper as to call a Representative from Illinois a jackass. Immediately, of course, someone in the House rose to protest a breach of Congressional manners. The gentleman from Indiana at once withdrew his statement, but added, "Mr. Speaker, I must still insist that the gentleman from Illinois is out of order."
> "How am I out of order?" demanded the attacked Congressman.
> The other's reply was safely enough within parliamentary phrasing this time to remain on the record: "Probably a veterinary surgeon could tell you."

We do not remember the name of the representative from Indiana who so nimbly played with the words "out of order," nor does it really matter any more. For we listen to the anecdote not in search of biographical materials of the witty legislator concerned, but simply for pleasure. For this reason anecdotes tend to have varied careers. We have told the latter one as we remember its being told to us, though we must unconsciously have added variations because of the use of our own phraseology. One of our readers, hereafter, liking it well enough, but forgetting the original setting, may in retelling it attribute it to a senator. As it goes the rounds, it may be taken out of Congress altogether—may even be eventually attributed to Confucius! But, despite changes in locale, the anecdote will probably remain essentially unchanged.

The anecdote of the Scottish minister, however, has elements in it close to the folk. Given time, such an anecdote might have worked its way among the Scottish farmers until, spun out and added to, it could have emerged as a story in which, possibly, the deevil himself might have figured as a character. That process has, unfortunately, been halted by the spread of literacy; the treasures of folklore come to us from times when reading and writing were still major mysteries to the people. At any rate we have here one of the ways in which fiction comes into being.

In the *Hitopadesha,* a Sanskrit compilation of narratives dating, in some instances, many centuries before the Christian Era, we find many like the following (the translation is by Sir Edwin Arnold):

> There was a trader in Vikrama-poora, who had a very beautiful wife, and her name was Jewel-bright. The lady was as unfaithful as she was fair, and had chosen for her last lover one of the household servants. Ah! womankind! . . .
> Now it befell one day that as Jewel-bright was bestowing a kiss on the mouth of the servant, she was surprised by her husband; and seeing him she ran up hastily and said, "My lord! Here is an impudent varlet! He eats the camphor[1] which I procured for you. I was actually smelling it on his lips as you entered."
> The servant catching her meaning, affected offence. "How can a man stay in a house where the mistress is always smelling one's breath for a little camphor?" he said.
> And thereat he was for going off, and was only constrained by the good man to stay, after much entreaty.

[1] Valued in the East for its cooling aromatic taste.

Here we have anecdote crossing the line into something else, a realm where there is no pretence of relating fact.

We have used the word *story* in the very broad sense of "a series of connected events." But within the province of literature, *story* is used in a narrower sense, as *distinguished from anecdote: a story* may be true or fictitious, but it *is never told with the intention of its being accepted as fact.* The anecdote of the unabashed wife seems to cross the line into story. It lacks one of the traits of story, however, since *a story is* usually *made up of a series of incidents* (arranged, of course, so as to be moving or entertaining).

For the rest of our discussion, we shall be using the word *story* in its narrower, literary sense (i.e., not in the first, broad sense in which it might be applied to history).

One of the earliest collections of stories in modern English was William Painter's *The Palace of Pleasure* (1566). Here is an amusing one from that work, "A Doctor of the Laws":

In the city of Bologna in Italy, there was a worshipful doctor of the laws, called Master Florien, which in other things saving his profession was but a sloven, and of so ill behavior as none of his faculty[1] the like: who by saving of many crusts, had laid up so good a store of crowns, as he caused to be made a very great and costly cup of silver, for payment of which cup he went to the goldsmith's house, and having paid for the silver, the gilt, and for the fashion,[2] being without his clerk to carry it home, he prayed the goldsmith to lend him his man.

By chance there were newly come to the city, two young men that were Romans, which ranged up and down the streets with ears upright, to view and mark everything done in the same, bearing about them counterfeit jewels and lingots,[3] gilt of Saint Martin's touch,[4] to deceive him that would play the fool to buy them. One of them was called Liello and the other Dietiquo. These two merchants being at good leisure to wander the streets, beholding the passengers[5] to and fro, by fortune espied the goldsmith's man, who (to set forth the workmanship and making of the cup) carried the same open.

These gallants bearing a spite to the cup, more for the silver than for other malice, purposed to invent some slight to get the cup, and afar off with sly pace, followed the goldsmith's man, of whom they craftily enquired of the owner of the cup, and where he had left Master Florien. When they had concluded upon their enterprise, Liello (the finest boy of them both) went straight to buy a lamprey[6] of great price, and hiding the same under his cloak, repaired directly to Master Doctor's house, where finding his wife of semblable

wit and behaviour that her husband was, with unshamefast face and like grace, said unto her: "Mistress, Master Florien your husband hath sent you a fish, and prayeth you to dress it and to make dinner ready, because he bringeth a company of other doctors with him: in the mean time he requireth you, to return unto him the cup again, which he sent you this morning by the goldsmith's man, because he had forgotten to stamp his arms upon it." The woman receiving the fish, frankly delivered him the cup, and went about to prepare dinner.

Liello which hunted after gain but better caught his prey hied him apace and conveyed himself with speed to the house of one of his countrymen, and there rejoiced with his companion, attending for the coming of the roister[7] Dietiquo, who tarried in the town, waiting and viewing what pursuit was made after his fellow. Soon after Master Florien returned to his house and finding his dinner more delicate than it was wont to be, marvelled, and asked his wife who was at all that cost. His wife very scornfully answered: "Why sir, have you forgotten that you sent me word this morning that you would bring home with you divers gentlemen to dinner?" "What" (quoth the doctor) "I think you be a fool." "I am not" (said she) "and for better witness you sent me this fish, that I would you had been better advised before you had bestowed such cost." "I assure thee:" quoth he, "I sent thee no fish, but belike it was some foolish knave that had forgotten his errand and mistaken the house: but howsoever it was, wife, we at this time will be content to fare well, at other men's charge." "Why sir" [said his wife] "call yourself to better remem-

---

[1] Profession.
[2] Making of it (or, possibly, the design of it).
[3] Cast gold.
[4] I.e., sham gold.

[5] Passersby.
[6] A pseudofish resembling an eel.
[7] Riotous fellow.

brance, for he that brought the lamprey, came to me for your cup, by this token that you would have your arms engraven upon the same."

At those words the poor doctor, after he had discharged three or four cannons laden with hail shot of scolding words went out into the street, running hither and thither demanding of all them he met, if they saw none carry a lamprey home to his house. And you would have said if you had seen the doctor with his hood hanging at one side, that he had been out of his wits.

Dietiquo stood still in a corner, and beheld the doctor's frantic order and albeit that he was sure the stealing of the cup by Liello his companion was impossible to be known, yet being sorry that the lamprey cost so much, determined also to play his part, and seeing the doctor stayed from making further complaints and pursuit, he went home to the doctor's house, where smiling with a good grace and bold countenance said unto his wife: "Mistress Doctor, good news, the cup is found, one whom you know caused the same to be done in sport to bring your husband Master Florien in a choler, who now is amongst divers of his friends jesting at the pleasant deceit, and hath sent me hither to fetch their dinner, wherein they pray you to remember the lamprey, and to come yourself to take part of the same, because they purpose to be merry."

The woman joyful of those news began somewhat to complain of the grief which she had taken for loss of the cup, and delivered to Dietiquo the roasted lamprey with the sauce, between two platters who incontinently[8] hid the same under his cloak, and with so much speed as he could, went to seek out his companion Liello, and their countrymen, which all that while had tarried for him: and God knoweth whether those good fellows did laugh and mock the poor doctor, and his wife or not, and when she had made herself gay and trim to go eat part of the lamprey, as she was going out she met Master Florien looking loweringly upon the matter, to whom she said (smiling like a frumenty[9] pot) "How now, sir, come they hither to dinner? I have sent you that lamprey ready dressed."

Then Master Doctor after fair talk, began to discharge his double cannons, calling his wife whore, bitch, and beast, and understanding that he was twice beguiled and could not tell by whom, for spite and despair he tore off his beard and the hair of his head, which bruited and known in the city, the jesters and pleasant fellows bent themselves to laugh, and devise pastime[10] at the[11] poor beguiled doctor and his wife.

Painter drew some of his stories from ancient Greek and Roman writers, but most of them come from the Italian and French. The French word for this kind of story is *conte,* the Italian *novella.* There is no accepted word for it in English, and many scholars identify it by the Italian. Though not a precise equivalent, our word *tale* is, in a sense, the nearest equivalent. We shall in this chapter use the word *tale* as the English for *novella.* The best known collection of *novelle* is, of course, Boccaccio's *Decameron,* a book adolescents are eager to read for the wrong reasons. We are glad, whatever the reasons, to be able to assume that most of our readers have dipped into that compendium, for we may then also assume that they are acquainted with a number of tales demonstrating traits quite characteristic of the *novella,* or tale.

We have thus far defined *story* as the relation of a "series of connected events." The distinguished novelist E. M. Forster puts his finger on the essence of story when he observes that on the elementary level interest in a story depends on the audience's wondering, "What happens next?" He imagines a primitive audience of "shock-heads" listening with gaping mouths after a hard day's hunt to the tribal storyteller. "As soon as the audience guessed what happened next, they either fell asleep or killed him."* The whole task of storytelling, from this standard, is to maintain the audience's interest at all costs. The simplest way of doing that is to multiply incidents. This was the wily Shahrazad's method of saving her own scalp and ending the mayhem being visited upon the more comely of her sex.

[8]Swiftly.

[9]A dish made of wheat boiled in milk, and seasoned with cinnamon and sugar.

[10]Sport

[11](Expense of the).

*E. M. Forster, *Aspects of the Novel* (New York, 1927), p. 46.

For King Shahryar, having witnessed the perfidy of his wife and having put her to death and also all his concubines, swore an oath that he would take a new bride every night and put her to death the next morning.

> On this wise he continued for the space of three years; marrying a maiden every night and killing her the next morning, till folk raised an outcry against him and cursed him.*

Now the king's chief wazir had a daughter Shahrazad who had

> collected a thousand books of histories relating to antique races and departed rulers. She had perused the works of the poets and knew them by heart; she had studied philosophy and the sciences, arts and accomplishments; and she was pleasant and polite, wise and witty, well read and well bred.

It was with this formidable equipment that Shahrazad proposed to rescue her sex. She urged her father to allow her to be a ransom for the virgins of the Moslems. When her father could in no way dissuade her, and found her adamant, he sorrowfully agreed to marry her to the king. On their wedding night, Shahrazad looked unhappy and the king asked,

> "What aileth thee?" She replied, "O King of the age, I have a younger sister and lief would I take leave of her this night before I see the dawn."

So he sent for the younger sister, and she was allowed to sit near the foot of the royal couch. At midnight, Shahrazad signaled to her sister, who by prearrangement said,

> "O my sister, recite to us some new story, delightsome and delectable, wherewith to while away the waking hours of our latter night." "With joy and goodly gree,"[1] answered Shahrazad, "if this pious and auspicious king permit me." "Tell on," quoth the king . . .

And King Shahryar walked right into the trap, and Shahrazad

> thus, on the first night of the Thousand Nights and a Night, . . . began the "Tale of the Trader and the Jinni,"

which she was careful to have contain stories within stories, so that it could not be completed in one night. The eager king was anxious to spare her life so that she might continue:

> "By Allah, I will not slay her until I hear the rest of her tale, for truly it is wondrous."

By beginning a new tale as soon as she had completed the current one, and by managing never to finish any tale at the dawn, Shahrazad kept the king so enchanted that, understandably, he could hardly wait each night for the sequel. During the thousand and one nights, she had borne the king three sons; on the last night, she formally asked release from the doom of death:

> "An[2] thou kill me, they will be motherless." . . . When the king heard this, he wept and straining the boys to his bosom, said, "By Allah, O Shahrazad, I pardoned thee before the coming of these children, for that I found thee chaste, pure, ingenuous and pious!"

*The Book of the Thousand Nights and a Night, translated by Sir Richard F. Burton.
[1]Goodwill.
[2]If.

Shahrazad thus became the savior of her sex by intriguing the king's interest with a long series of tales. A *tale,* as illustrated in our example from Painter, *is a story made up of a number of incidents strung together in a manner lively enough to be entertaining.* The focus of interest in a tale is, "What happens next?" There is no great attempt made in such a work to present characters in any dimension or to deal with events in a way to make them psychologically credible. The characters, indeed, remain little more than names throughout. It is so in Shahrazad's long collection of tales. In the *Decameron* there is no single convincing portrait of a man or a woman—unless one wishes to state the excessively patient Griselda as an exception.

The whole effort of the author of a tale is to keep us amused, as was King Shahryar, by a rapid succession of events, which need have no important logical connection with one another. A tale, in short, is a story without a plot.*

It is interesting to note that a great many tales deal with roguish deeds. This is the case with our tale from Painter. The earliest attempts at novel-writing were also of this kind; they were indeed little more than a *long* string of incidents dealing with the tricks and escapades of the hero-rogue. (E.g., Defoe's *Moll Flanders;* Fielding's *Tom Jones.*) Apparently mankind has always been diverted by the story of a clever rascal outwitting the sober-minded.

Beyond a liveliness in the telling, no great art was demanded of the author of the old tales, provided his material was entertaining. In modern times a more carefully wrought form of the shorter prose work of fiction, the short story, has developed into one of the most important of literary types.

Here is a fine example, by one of the earliest of American realists, Mary E. Wilkins Freeman (1862–1930), "The Revolt of 'Mother' ":

"Father!"

"What is it?"

"What are them men diggin' over there in the field for?"

There was a sudden dropping and enlarging of the lower part of the old man's face, as if some heavy weight had settled therein; he shut his mouth tight, and went on harnessing the great bay mare. He hustled the collar on to her neck with a jerk.

"Father!"

The old man slapped the saddle upon the mare's back.

"Look here, father, I want to know what them men are diggin' over in the field for, an' I'm goin' to know."

"I wish you'd go into the house, mother, an' 'tend to your own affairs," the old man said then. He ran his words together, and his speech was almost as inarticulate as a growl.

But the woman understood; it was her most native tongue. "I ain't goin' into the house till you tell me what them men are doin' over there in the field," said she.

Then she stood waiting. She was a small woman, short and straight-waisted like a child in her brown cotton gown. Her forehead was mild and benevolent between the smooth curves of gray hair; there were meek downward lines about her nose and mouth; but her eyes, fixed upon the old man, looked as if the meekness had been the result of her own will, never of the will of another.

They were in the barn, standing before the wide open doors. The spring air, full of the smell of growing grass and unseen blossoms, came in their faces. The deep yard in front was littered with farm wagons and piles of wood; on the edges, close to the fence and the house, the grass was a vivid green, and there were some dandelions.

The old man glanced doggedly at his wife as he tightened the last buckles on the harness. She looked as immovable to him as one of the rocks in his pasture-land, bound to the earth with generations of blackberry vines. He slapped the reins over the horse, and started forth from the barn.

"*Father!*" said she.

The old man pulled up. "What is it?"

"I want to know what them men are diggin' over there in that field for."

"They're diggin' a cellar, I s'pose, if you've got to know."

---

*We have been using the word *tale* as a term of technical differentiation. It is, of course, often used in a general sense to mean, simply, a piece of fiction. This is the sense in the titles of Dickens' *A Tale of Two Cities* and Conrad's *Tales of Unrest.*

"A cellar for what?"

"A barn."

"A barn? You ain't goin' to build a barn over there where we was goin' to have a house, father?"

The old man said not another word. He hurried the horse into the farm wagon, and clattered out of the yard, jouncing as sturdily on his seat as a boy.

The woman stood a moment looking after him, then she went out of the barn across a corner of the yard to the house. The house, standing at right angles with the great barn and a long reach of sheds and out-buildings, was infinitesimal compared with them. It was scarcely as commodious for people as the little boxes under the barn eaves were for doves.

A pretty girl's face, pink and delicate as a flower, was looking out of one of the house windows. She was watching three men who were digging over in the field which bounded the yard near the road line. She turned quietly when the woman entered.

"What are they digging for, mother?" said she. "Did he tell you?"

"They're diggin' for—a cellar for a new barn."

"Oh, mother, he ain't going to build another barn?"

"That's what he says."

A boy stood before the kitchen glass combing his hair. He combed slowly and painstakingly, arranging his brown hair in a smooth hillock over his forehead. He did not seem to pay any attention to the conversation.

"Sammy, did you know father was going to build a new barn?" asked the girl.

The boy combed assiduously.

"Sammy!"

He turned, and showed a face like his father's under his smooth crest of hair. "Yes, I s'pose I did," he said reluctantly.

"How long have you known it?" asked his mother.

"'Bout three months, I guess."

"Why didn't you tell of it?"

"Didn't think 'twould do no good."

"I don't see what father wants another barn for," said the girl, in her sweet, slow voice. She turned again to the window, and stared out at the digging men in the field. Her tender, sweet face was full of gentle distress. Her forehead was as bald and innocent as a baby's, with the light hair strained back from it in a row of curl-papers. She was quite large, but her soft curves did not look as if they covered muscles.

Her mother looked sternly at the boy. "Is he goin' to buy more cows?" said she.

The boy did not reply; he was tying his shoes.

"Sammy, I want you to tell me if he's goin' to buy more cows."

"I s'pose he is."

"How many?"

"Four, I guess."

His mother said nothing more. She went into the pantry, and there was a clatter of dishes. The boy got his cap from a nail behind the door, took an old arithmetic from the shelf, and started for school. He was lightly built, but clumsy. He went out of the yard with a curious spring in the hips, that made his loose home-made jacket tilt up in the rear.

The girl went to the sink, and began to wash the dishes that were piled up there. Her mother came promptly out of the pantry, and shoved her aside. "You wipe 'em," said she; "I'll wash. There's a good many this mornin'."

The mother plunged her hands vigorously into the water, the girl wiped the plates slowly and dreamily. "Mother," said she, "don't you think it's too bad father's going to build that new barn, much as we need a decent house to live in?"

Her mother scrubbed a dish fiercely. "You ain't found out yet we're women-folks, Nanny Penn," said she. "You ain't seen enough of men-folks yet to. One of these days you'll find it out, an' then you'll know that we know only what men-folks think we do, so far as any use of it goes, an' how we'd ought to reckon men-folks in with Providence, an' not complain of what they do any more than we do of the weather."

"I don't care; I don't believe George is anything like that, anyhow," said Nanny. Her delicate face flushed pink, her lips pouted softly, as if she were going to cry.

"You wait an' see. I guess George Eastman ain't no better than other men. You hadn't ought to judge father, though. He can't help it, 'cause he don't look at things jest the way we do. An' we've been pretty comfortable here, after all. The roof don't leak—ain't never but once—that's one thing. Father's kept it shingled right up."

"I do wish we had a parlor."

"I guess it won't hurt George Eastman any to come to see you in a nice clean kitchen. I guess a good many girls don't have as good a place as this. Nobody's ever heard me complain."

"I ain't complained either, mother."

"Well, I don't think you'd better, a good father an' a good home as you've got. S'pose your father made you go out an' work for your livin'? Lots o girls have to that ain't no stronger an' better able to than you be."

Sarah Penn washed the frying-pan with a conclusive air. She scrubbed the outside of it as faithfully as the inside. She was a masterly keeper of her box of a house. Her one living-room never seemed to have in it any of the dust which the friction of life with inanimate matter produces. She swept, and there seemed to be no dirt to go before the broom; she cleaned, and one could see no difference. She was like an artist so perfect that he has apparently no art. Today she got out a mixing bowl and a board, and rolled some pies, and there was no more flour upon her than upon her daughter who was doing finer work. Nanny was to be married in the fall, and she was sewing on some white cambric and embroidery. She sewed industriously while her mother cooked; her soft milk-white hands and wrists showed whiter than her delicate work.

"We must have the stove moved out in the shed before long," said Mrs. Penn. "Talk about not havin' things, it's been a real blessin' to be able to put a stove up in that shed in hot weather. Father did one good thing when he fixed that stove-pipe out there."

Sarah Penn's face as she rolled her pies had that expression of meek vigor which might have characterized one of the New Testament saints. She was making mince-pies. Her husband, Adoniram Penn, liked them better than any other kind. She baked twice a week. Adoniram often liked a piece of pie between meals. She hurried this morning. It had been later than usual when she began, and she wanted to have a pie baked for dinner. However deep a resentment she might be forced to hold against her husband, she would never fail in sedulous attention to his wants.

Nobility of character manifests itself at loopholes when it is not provided with large doors. Sarah Penn's showed itself today in flaky dishes of pastry. So she made the pies faithfully, while across the table she could see, when she glanced up from her work, the sight that rankled in her patient and steadfast soul—the digging of the cellar of the new barn in the place where Adoniram forty years ago had promised her their new house should stand.

The pies were done for dinner. Adoniram and Sammy were home a few minutes after twelve o'clock. The dinner was eaten with serious haste. There was never much conversation at the table in the Penn family. Adoniram asked a blessing, and they ate promptly, then rose up and went about their work.

Sammy went back to school, taking soft sly lopes out of the yard like a rabbit. He wanted a game of marbles before school, and feared his father would give him some chores to do. Adoniram hastened to the door and called after him, but he was out of sight.

"I don't see what you let him go for, mother," said he. "I wanted him to help me unload that wood."

Adoniram went to work out in the yard unloading wood from the wagon. Sarah put away the dinner dishes, while Nanny took down her curl-papers and changed her dress. She was going down to the store to buy some more embroidery and thread.

When Nanny was gone, Mrs. Penn went to the door. "Father!" she called.

"Well, what is it?"

"I want to see you jest a minute, father."

"I can't leave this wood nohow. I've got to git it unloaded an' go for a load of gravel afore two o'clock. Sammy had ought to helped me. You hadn't ought to let him go to school so early."

"I want to see you jest a minute."

"I tell ye I can't, nohow, mother."

"Father, you come here." Sarah Penn stood in the door like a queen; she held her head as if it bore a crown; there was that patience which makes authority royal in her voice. Adoniram went.

Mrs. Penn led the way into the kitchen, and pointed to a chair. "Sit down, father," said she; "I've got somethin' I want to say to you."

He sat down heavily; his face was quite stolid, but he looked at her with restive eyes. "Well, what is it, mother?"

"I want to know what you're buildin' that new barn for, father?"

"I ain't got nothin' to say about it."

"It can't be you think you need another barn?"

"I tell ye I ain't got nothin' to say about it, mother; an' I ain't goin' to say nothin'."

"Be you goin' to buy more cows?"

Adoniram did not reply; he shut his mouth tight.

"I know you be, as well as I want to. Now, father, look here"—Sarah Penn had not sat down; she stood before her husband in the humble fashion of a Scripture woman—"I'm goin' to talk real plain to you; I never have sence I married you, but I'm goin' to now. I ain't never complained, an' I ain't goin' to complain now, but I'm goin' to talk plain. You see this room here, father; you look at it well. You see there ain't no carpet on the floor, an' you see the paper is all dirty, an' droppin' off the walls. We ain't had no new paper on it for ten year, an' then I put it on myself, an' it didn't cost but ninepence a roll. You see this room, father; it's all the one I've had to work in an' eat in an' sit in sence we was married. There ain't another woman in the whole town whose husband ain't got half the means you have but what's got better. It's all the room Nanny's got to have her company in; an' there ain't one of her mates but what's got better, an' their fathers not so able as hers is. It's all the room she'll have to be married in. What would you have thought, father, if we had had our weddin' in a room no better than this? I was married in my mother's parlor, with a carpet on the floor, an' stuffed furniture, an' a mahogany card-table. An' this is all the room my daughter will have to be married in. Look here, father!"

Sarah Penn went across the room as though it were a tragic stage. She flung open a door and disclosed a tiny bedroom, only large enough for a bed and bureau, with a path between. "There, father," said she—"there's all the room I've had to sleep in forty year. All my children were born there—the two that died, an' the two that's livin'. I was sick with a fever there."

She stepped to another door and opened it. It led into the small, ill-lighted pantry. "Here," said she, "is all the buttery I've got—every place I've got for my dishes, to set away my victuals in, an' to keep my milk-pans in. Father, I've been takin' care of the milk of six cows in this place, an' now you're goin' to build a new barn, an' keep more cows, an' give me more to do in it."

She threw open another door. A narrow crooked flight of stairs wound upward from it. "There, father," said she, "I want you to look at the stairs that go up to them two unfinished chambers that are all the places our son an' daughter have had to sleep in all their lives. There ain't a prettier girl in town nor a more ladylike one than Nanny, an' that's the place she has to sleep in. It ain't so good as your horse's stall; it ain't so warm an' tight."

Sarah Penn went back and stood before her husband. "Now, father," said she, "I want to know if you think you're doin' right an' accordin' to what you profess. Here, when we was married, forty year ago, you promised me faithful that we should have a new house built in that lot over in the field before the year was out. You said you had money enough, an' you wouldn't ask me to live in no such place as this. It is forty year now, an' you've been makin' more money, an' I've been savin' of it for you ever sence, an' you ain't built

no house yet. You've built sheds an' cow-houses an' one new barn an' now you're goin' to build another. Father, I want to know if you think it's right. You're lodgin' your dumb beasts better than you are your own flesh an' blood. I want to know if you think it's right."

"I ain't got nothin' to say."

"You can't say nothin' without ownin' it ain't right, father. An' there's another thing—I ain't complained; I've got along forty year, an' I s'pose I should forty more, if it wa'n't for that—if we don't have another house. Nanny she can't live with us after she's married. She'll have to go somewheres else to live away from us, an' it don't seem as if I could have it so, noways, father. She wa'n't ever strong. She's got considerable color, but there wa'n't never any backbone to her. I've always took the heft of everything off her, an' she ain't fit to keep house an' do everything herself. She'll be all worn out inside of a year. Think of her doin' all the washin' an' ironin' an' bakin' with them soft white hands an' arms, an' sweep-in'! I can't have it so, noways, father."

Mrs. Penn's face was burning; her mild eyes gleamed. She had pleaded her little cause like a Webster; she had ranged from severity to pathos; but her opponent employed that obstinate silence which makes eloquence futile with mocking echoes. Adoniram arose clumsily.

"Father, ain't you got nothin' to say?" said Mrs. Penn.

"I've got to go off after that load of gravel. I can't stan' here talkin' all day."

"Father, won't you think it over, an' have a house built there instead of a barn?"

"I ain't got nothin' to say."

Adoniram shuffled out. Mrs. Penn went into her bedroom. When she came out, her eyes were red. She had a roll of unbleached cotton cloth. She spread it out on the kitchen table, and began cutting out some shirts for her husband. The men over in the field had a team to help them this afternoon; she could hear their halloos. She had a scanty pattern for the shirts; she had to plan and piece the sleeves.

Nanny came home with her embroidery, and sat down with her needlework. She had taken down her curl-papers and there was a soft roll of fair hair like an aureole over her forehead; her face was as delicately fine and clear as porcelain. Suddenly she looked up, and the tender red flamed all over her face and neck "Mother," said she.

"What say?"

"I've been thinking—I don't see how we're

goin' to have any—wedding in this room. I'd be ashamed to have his folks come if we didn't have anybody else."

"Mebbe we can have some new paper before then; I can put it on. I guess you won't have no call to be ashamed of your belongin's."

"We might have the wedding in the new barn," said Nanny, with gentle pettishness. "Why, mother, what makes you look so?"

Mrs. Penn had started, and was staring at her with a curious expression. She turned again to her work, and spread out a pattern carefully on the cloth. "Nothin'," said she.

Presently Adoniram clattered out of the yard in his two-wheeled dump cart, standing as proudly upright as a Roman charioteer. Mrs. Penn opened the door and stood there a minute looking out; the halloos of the men sounded louder.

It seemed to her all through the spring months that she heard nothing but the halloos and the noises of saws and hammers. The new barn grew fast. It was a fine edifice for this little village. Men came on pleasant Sundays, in their meeting suits and clean shirt bosoms, and stood around it admiringly. Mrs. Penn did not speak of it, and Adoniram did not mention it to her, although sometimes, upon a return from inspecting it, he bore himself with injured dignity.

"It's a strange thing how your mother feels about the new barn," he said, confidentially, to Sammy one day.

Sammy only grunted after an odd fashion for a boy; he had learned it from his father.

The barn was all completed ready for use by the third week in July. Adoniram had planned to move his stock in on Wednesday; on Tuesday he received a letter which changed his plans. He came in with it early in the morning. "Sammy's been to the post-office," said he, "an' I've got a letter from Hiram." Hiram was Mrs. Penn's brother, who lived in Vermont.

"Well," said Mrs. Penn, "what does he say about the folks?"

"I guess they're all right. He says he thinks if I come up country right off there's a chance to buy jest the kind of a horse I want." He stared reflectively out of the window at the new barn.

Mrs. Penn was making pies. She went on clapping the rolling-pin into the crust, although she was very pale, and her heart beat loudly.

"I dun' know but what I'd better go," said Adoniram. "I hate to go off just now, right in the midst of hayin', but the ten-acre lot's cut, an' I guess Rufus an' the others can git along without me three or four days. I can't get a horse round here to suit me, nohow, an' I've got to have another for all that wood-haulin' in the fall. I told Hiram to watch out, an' if he got wind of a good horse to let me know. I guess I'd better go."

"I'll get out your clean shirt an' collar," said Mrs. Penn calmly.

She laid out Adoniram's Sunday suit and his clean clothes on the bed in the little bedroom. She got his shaving-water and razor ready. At last she buttoned on his collar and fastened his black cravat.

Adoniram never wore his collar and cravat except on extra occasions. He held his head high, with a rasped dignity. When he was all ready, with his coat and hat brushed, and a lunch of pie and cheese in a paper bag, he hesitated on the threshold of the door. He looked at his wife, and his manner was defiantly apologetic. "If them cows come today, Sammy can drive 'em into the new barn," said he; "an' when they bring the hay up, they can pitch it in there."

"Well," replied Mrs. Penn.

Adoniram set his shaven face ahead and started. When he had cleared the door-step, he turned and looked back with a kind of nervous solemnity. "I shall be back by Saturday if nothin' happens," said he.

"Do be careful, father," replied his wife.

She stood in the door with Nanny at her elbow and watched him out of sight. Her eyes had a strange, doubtful expression in them; her peaceful forehead was contracted. She went in, and about her baking again. Nanny sat sewing. Her wedding-day was drawing nearer, and she was getting pale and thin with her steady sewing. Her mother kept glancing at her.

"Have you got that pain in your side this mornin'?" she asked.

"A little."

Mrs. Penn's face, as she worked, changed, her perplexed forehead smoothed, her eyes were steady, her lips firmly set. She formed a maxim for herself, although incoherently with her unlettered thoughts. "Unsolicited opportunities are the guideposts of the Lord to the new roads of life," she repeated in effect, and she made up her mind to her course of action.

"S'posin' I *had* wrote to Hiram," she muttered once, when she was in the pantry—"s'posin' I had wrote, an' asked him if he knew of any horse? But I didn't an' father's goin' wa'n't none of my doin'. It looks like a providence." Her voice rang out quite loud at the last.

"What you talkin' about, mother?" called Nanny.

"Nothin'."

Mrs. Penn hurried her baking; at eleven o'clock it was all done. The load of hay from the west field came slowly down the cart track, and drew up at the new barn. Mrs. Penn ran out. "Stop!" she screamed—"stop!"

The men stopped and looked; Sammy upreared from the top of the load, and stared at his mother.

"Stop!" she cried out again. "Don't you put the hay in that barn; put it in the old one."

"Why, he said to put it in here," returned one of the hay-makers, wonderingly. He was a young man, a neighbor's son, whom Adoniram hired by the year to help on the farm.

"Don't you put the hay in the new barn; there's room enough in the old one, ain't there?" said Mrs. Penn.

"Room enough," returned the hired man, in his thick, rustic tones. "Didn't need the new barn, nohow, far as room's concerned. Well, I s'pose he changed his mind." He took hold of the horses' bridles.

Mrs. Penn went back to the house. Soon the kitchen windows were darkened, and a fragrance like warm honey came into the room.

Nanny laid down her work. "I thought father wanted them to put the hay into the new barn?" she said wonderingly.

"It's all right," replied her mother.

Sammy slid down from the load of hay, and came in to see if dinner was ready.

"I ain't goin' to get a regular dinner today, as long as father's gone," said his mother. "I've let the fire go out. You can have some bread an' milk an' pie. I thought we could get along." She set out some bowls of milk, some bread, and a pie on the kitchen table. "You'd better eat your dinner now," said she. "You might jest as well get through with it. I want you to help me afterward."

Nanny and Sammy stared at each other. There was something strange in their mother's manner. Mrs. Penn did not eat anything herself. She went into the pantry, and they heard her moving dishes while they ate. Presently she came out with a pile of plates. She got the clothes-basket out of the shed, and packed them in it. Nanny and Sammy watched. She brought out cups and saucers, and put them in with the plates.

"What you goin' to do, mother?" inquired Nanny, in a timid voice. A sense of something unusual made her tremble, as if it were a ghost. Sammy rolled his eyes over his pie.

"You'll see what I'm goin' to do," replied Mrs. Penn. "If you're through, Nanny, I want you to go upstairs an' pack up your things; an' I want you, Sammy, to help me take down the bed in the bedroom."

"Oh, mother, what for?" gasped Nanny.

"You'll see."

During the next few hours a feat was performed by the simple, pious New England mother which was equal in its way to Wolfe's[1] storming of the Heights of Abraham. It took no more genius and audacity of bravery for Wolfe to cheer his wondering soldiers up those steep precipices, under the sleeping eyes of the enemy, than for Sarah Penn, at the head of her children, to move all their little household goods into the new barn while her husband was away.

Nanny and Sammy followed their mother's instructions without a murmur; indeed, they were overawed. There is a certain uncanny and superhuman quality about all such purely original undertakings as their mother's was to them. Nanny went back and forth with her light loads, and Sammy tugged with sober energy.

At five o'clock in the afternoon the little house in which the Penns had lived for forty years had emptied itself into the new barn.

Every builder builds somewhat for unknown purposes, and is in a measure a prophet. The architect of Adoniram Penn's barn, while he designed it for the comfort of four-footed animals, had planned better than he knew for the comfort of humans. Sarah Penn saw at a glance its possibilities. Those great box-stalls, with quilts hung before them, would make better bedrooms than the one she had occupied for forty years, and there was a tight carriage-room. The harness-room, with its chimney and shelves, would make a kitchen of her dreams. The great middle space would make a parlor, by-and-by, fit for a palace. Upstairs there was as much room as down. With partitions and windows, what a house would there be! Sarah looked at the row of stanchions before the allotted space for cows, and reflected that she would have her front entry there.

At six o'clock the stove was up in the harness-room, the kettle was boiling, and the table was set for tea. It looked almost as home-like as the abandoned house across the yard had ever done. The young hired man milked, and Sarah directed him calmly to bring the milk to the new barn. He came gaping, dropping little blots of foam from the brimming pails on the grass. Before the next morning he had spread the story of Adoniram Penn's wife moving into the new barn all over the

[1]English general who defeated the French at Quebec.

little village. Men assembled in the store and talked it over, women with shawls over their heads scuttled into each other's houses before their work was done. Any deviation from the ordinary course of life in this quiet town was enough to stop all progress in it. Everybody paused to look at the staid, independent figure on the side track. There was a difference of opinion with regard to her. Some held her to be insane; some, of a lawless and rebellious spirit.

Friday the minister went to see her. It was in the forenoon, and she was at the barn door shelling peas for dinner. She looked up and returned his salutation with dignity, then she went on with her work. She did not invite him in. The saintly expression of her face remained fixed, but there was an angry flush over it.

The minister stood awkwardly before her, and talked. She handled the peas as if they were bullets. At last she looked up, and her eyes showed the spirit that her meek front had covered for a lifetime.

"There ain't no use talkin', Mr. Hersey," said she, "I've thought it all over an' over an' I believe I'm doin' what's right. I've made it the subject of prayer, an' it's betwixt me an' the Lord an' Adoniram. There ain't no call for nobody else to worry about it."

"Well, of course, if you have brought it to the Lord in prayer, and feel satisfied that you are doing right, Mrs. Penn," said the minister, helplessly. His thin gray-bearded face was pathetic. He was a sickly man; his youthful confidence had cooled; he had to scourge himself up to some of his pastoral duties as relentlessly as a Catholic ascetic, and then he was prostrated by the smart.

"I think it's right jest as much as I think it was right for our forefathers to come over from the old country 'cause they didn't have what belonged to 'em," said Mrs. Penn. She arose. The barn threshold might have been Plymouth Rock[1] from her bearing. "I don't doubt you mean well, Mr. Hersey," said she, "but there are things people hadn't ought to interfere with. I've been a member of the church for over forty years. I've got my own mind an' my own feet, an' I'm goin' to think my own thoughts an' go my own ways, an' nobody but the Lord is goin' to dictate to me unless I've a mind to have him. Won't you come in an' set down? How is Mis' Hersey?"

"She is well, I thank you," replied the minister. He added some more perplexed apologetic remarks; then he retreated.

He could expound the intricacies of every character study in the Scriptures, he was competent to grasp the Pilgrim Fathers and all historical innovators, but Sarah Penn was beyond him. He could deal with primal cases, but parallel ones worsted him. But, after all, although it was aside from his province, he wondered more how Adoniram Penn would deal with his wife than how the Lord would. Everybody shared the wonder. When Adoniram's four new cows arrived, Sarah ordered three to be put in the old barn, the other in the house shed where the cooking-stove had stood. That added to the excitement. It was whispered that all four cows were domiciled in the house.

Towards sunset on Saturday, when Adoniram was expected home, there was a knot of men in the road near the new barn. The hired man had milked, but he still hung around the premises. Sarah Penn had supper all ready. There were brown-bread and baked beans and a custard pie; it was the supper that Adoniram loved on a Saturday night. She had on a clean calico, and she bore herself imperturbably. Nanny and Sammy kept close at her heels. Their eyes were large, and Nanny was full of nervous tremors. Still there was to them more pleasant excitement than anything else. An inborn confidence in their mother over their father asserted itself.

Sammy looked out of the harness-room window. "There he is," he announced, in an awed whisper. He and Nanny peeped around the casing. Mrs. Penn kept on about her work. The children watched Adoniram leave the new horse standing in the drive while he went to the house door. It was fastened. Then he went around to the shed. That door was seldom locked, even when the family was away. The thought how her father would be confronted by the cow flashed upon Nanny. There was a hysterical sob in her throat. Adoniram emerged from the shed and stood looking about in a dazed fashion. His lips moved. He was saying something, but they could not hear what it was. The hired man was peeping around a corner of the old barn, but nobody saw him.

Adoniram took the new horse by the bridle and led him across the yard to the new barn. Nanny and Sammy slunk close to their mother. The barn doors rolled back, and there stood Adoniram, with the long mild face of the great Canadian farm horse looking over his shoulder.

Nanny kept behind her mother, but Sammy stepped suddenly forward, and stood in front of her.

Adoniram stared at the group. "What on airth you all down here for?" said he. "What's the matter over to the house?"

[1]Where the Pilgrim Fathers are said first to have landed.

"We've come here to live, father," said Sammy. His shrill voice quavered out bravely.

"What"—Adoniram sniffed—"what is it smells like cookin'?" said he. He stepped forward and looked in the open door of the harness-room. Then he turned to his wife. His old bristling face was pale and frightened. "What on airth does this mean, mother?" he gasped.

"You come in here, father," said Sarah. She led the way into the harness-room and shut the door. "Now, father," said she, "you needn't be scared. I ain't crazy. There ain't nothin' to be upset over. But we've come here to live, an' we're goin' to live here. We've got jest as good a right here as new horses an' cows. The house wa'n't fit for us to live in any longer, an' I made up my mind I wa'n't goin' to stay there. I've done my duty by you forty year, an' I'm goin' to do it now; but I'm goin' to live here. You've got to put in some windows and partitions; an' you'll have to buy some furniture."

"Why, mother!" the old man gasped.

"You'd better take your coat off an' get washed —there's the wash-basin—and then we'll have supper."

"Why, mother!"

Sammy went past the window, leading the new horse to the old barn. The old man saw him, and shook his head speechlessly. He tried to take off his coat, but his arms seemed to lack the power. His wife helped him. She poured some water into the tin basin, and put in a piece of soap. She got the comb and brush, and smoothed his thin gray hair after he had washed. Then she put the beans, hot bread, and tea on the table. Sammy came in, and the family drew up. Adoniram sat looking dazedly at his plate, and they waited.

"Ain't you goin' to ask a blessin', father?" said Sarah. And the old man bent his head and mumbled.

All through the meal he stopped eating at intervals, and stared furtively at his wife, but he ate well. The home food tasted good to him, and his old frame was too sturdily healthy to be affected by his mind. But after supper he went out, and sat down on the step of the smaller door at the right of the barn, through which he had meant his Jerseys to pass in stately file, but which Sarah designed for her front house door, and he leaned his head on his hands.

After the supper dishes were cleared away and the milk-pans washed, Sarah went out to him. The twilight was deepening. There was a clear green glow in the sky. Before them stretched the smooth level of field; in the distance was a cluster of hay-stacks like the huts of a village; the air was very cool and calm and sweet. The landscape might have been an ideal one of peace.

Sarah bent over and touched her husband on one of his thin, sinewy shoulders. "Father!"

The old man's shoulder heaved; he was weeping.

"Why, don't do so, father," said Sarah.

"I'll—put up the—partitions, an'—everything you—want, mother."

Sarah put her apron up to her face; she was overcome by her own triumph.

Adoniram was like a fortress whose walls had no active resistance, and went down the instant the right besieging tools were used. "Why, mother," he said, hoarsely, "I hadn't no idee you were so set on't as all this comes to."

"The Revolt of 'Mother'" is many times the length of our tale, "The Doctor of Laws." It is plain, therefore, that the adjective "short" as employed in the type-description of *short story* is used only relatively. Ordinarily, a short story is shorter than the average novel. But there are short novels, which we therefore call *novelettes,* some of which are briefer than some short stories. The term *short story* is best thought of as a technical signification, identifying a certain literary form.

POE ON THE SHORT STORY

It will have been perceived that, despite its being longer, Mrs. Freeman's story possesses a feeling of compactness and unity entirely absent from Painter's tale. Edgar Allan Poe laid down the following strictures for the short story:

1. It ought to be of a length to permit one to read it at one sitting, so that it may derive "the immense force" which comes "from *totality.*" (The time element, it should be noted however, is in itself relative. How long is one sitting? Poe is specific: from a half hour to two hours. But his stipulation is fairly untenable. Any one of us is willing to sit for hours with

an absorbing story, and yet will chafe with restlessness and finally give up at the reading of a dull one, no matter how brief.)

2. It must achieve a single effect; if the "very initial sentence tends not to the outbringing of this effect, then it has failed in its first step."

3. It must be written with suitable sparseness and compression. Every moment of the story must push the action towards its conclusion and contribute towards the author's intended effect. In the writing "there should be no word written of which the tendency, direct or indirect, is not to the one pre-established design."

4. There is but one correct arrangement for the details of a story. Many people imagine that all a short story requires is "complexity of incident." In a true plot "no component atom can be removed" without ruining the whole.

5. An "originality" of attack must distinguish a good short story. This quality is displayed "in novelty of *tone* as in novelty of manner." Originality is a matter of subject, arrangement of material, and in the "atmosphere" created by the whole. (This requirement is as true of any other kind of writing as of the short story.) Actually all but the last of these laws have to do with the principle of unity.

Let us examine "A Doctor of Laws" and "The Revolt of 'Mother' " in terms of these five strictures:

1. Both can easily be read at a single sitting, though certainly the latter with more inner compulsion to continue reading. The tale does not particularly give us a sense of totality. It would have been possible to take away one of the episodes or to add several others without greatly altering the effect.

2. The effect of the tale is not single, that of the short story is. A modern writer would have ended the first sentence of the tale with the phrase, *of his faculty the like.* If we take that to end the first sentence, the information conveyed up to that point contains much that is irrelevant to the narrative, though the victim-to-be is identified. It is amusing to be told that Master Florien was the greatest sloven and the most unattractive lawyer in Bologna, but the comic effect does not absolutely depend upon our knowing that. On the other hand, "The Revolt of 'Mother' " plunges at once into the heart of the matter, the building of the new barn:

> "Father!"
> "What is it?"
> "What are them men diggin' over there in the field for?"

3. Brief as it is, the tale is rather less compressed and certainly less sparse in its detail than is the short story. Everything in the latter is relevant.

4. There is some kind of meaningful arrangement in both tale and short story. But in the tale we could remove one of the two important incidents (not to speak of many a "component atom") without seriously damaging the effect of the whole. In "The Revolt of 'Mother' " no detail could be omitted without injuring the effect.

5. Our tale, far from being "original," is in tone exactly like hundreds of other tales of rascality. Mrs. Freeman's originality is displayed in the selection of her deeply human material, original despite its simplicity; in her austere arrangement of material; and no less in her perfect creation of atmosphere—the tone of the story is as strong and tender as the New England landscape of which it is a part. It creates a perfect illusion of life itself.

PLOT

The center of unity in such a story as "The Revolt of 'Mother' " is the plot. A *plot* is distinguished from a series of incidents, as Aristotle in his *Poetics* pointed out long ago, in that it *has a beginning, a middle, and an end; the roots of the middle are in the beginning;*

the roots of the end are in the middle; the end must make complete what was begun in the beginning.

If I tell a series of incidents connected with the same person I do not necessarily have a plot. Perhaps the reader remembers the story of Epam'nondas, of which children have always been fond:

Epam'nondas was a little boy who was always getting into trouble.

One day, when he went to visit his grandmother, she gave him some eggs to bring home to his mother. On the way home, however, he just couldn't resist taking a jump now and a skip then. And the eggs fell one by one out of his little hands, until they were all broken. When he got home, his mother said, "Epam'nondas, what you got dere?"

"Nothin' but a lot of smashed egg-shells. Grandma done give me some eggs for you, but dey fell out of my hands one by one and dey is all broke, sure 'nough."

"You stupid chile!" his mother said. "Next time your grandma give you somethin' like dat, carry 'em home in your hat, an' dey'll be safe."

The next time Epam'nondas went to his grandmother's she gave him a pound of butter to bring home to his mother. Epam'nondas put the butter in his hat, and his hat on his head. But the sun was shining brightly, and the butter melted little by little, and ran down all over his face and clothes. When he got home, his mother said, "Epam'nondas, what you got dere?"

"A pound of butter. I done put it in my hat the way you said, but it done got all melted, and spoiled my clothes."

"You stupid chile!" his mother said. "Next time your grandma give you somethin' like dat, take it to the stream first to cool it off on the way

home. Den it come here in one piece."

The next time Epam'nondas went to his grandmother's she gave him a little puppy to bring home to his mother. Epam'nondas stopped at the stream half way home to cool the puppy. But he kept the puppy under water so long that it drowned. When he got home, his mother said, "Epam'nondas, what you got dere?"

"A dead puppy. I done took it to the stream to cool it off like you said, but it done got drowned."

"You stupid chile!" his mother said. "Next time your grandma give you somethin' like dat, tie a rope around its neck and lead it home along the road."

The next time Epam'nondas went to his grandmother's she gave him a fresh loaf of bread to bring home to his mother. Epam'nondas tied a rope around it, and dragged it home along the road. When he got home, his mother said, "Epam'nondas, what you got dere?"

"A dirty ole loaf of bread. I done tied a rope around it the way you said, and brought it home along the road. And jes' look at it!"

"You stupid chile!" his mother said. "I ain't goin' to let you go alone to your grandma's no more. Now I jes' got through bakin' some nice pies, and dey's coolin' on the back porch. Be careful how you steps in dem, you silly chile!"

And Epam'nondas stepped into each and every one of them very carefully.

This is a story which has no plot. It is merely a series of incidents supplying the answer to "And what happened next?" There is a beginning, though not much of one, and certainly no end. There is no reason why Epom'nondas should not continue his amiable idiocies indefinitely. The story stops only because the storyteller has had enough of the boy's adventures.

We have given the Aristotelian concept of plot. E. M. Forster makes the point another way:

> "The King died and the Queen died" is a story. "The King died, and then the Queen died of grief" is a plot.*

In other words, in a tale we simply want to know, "What next?" In a plot we want to know, "Why?"

It is interesting to consider that in *The Arabian Nights*—to use the more familiar title —though the tales themselves do not have a proper plot, there is a rudimentary plot in the *framework* of the stories:

*Forster, p. 130.

The beginning: Shahrazad, the chief wazir's daughter, knowing of the king's habit of killing his bride of the night before each morning, determines, despite her father's pleas, to put an end to the terror.

The middle: Having worn down her father's objections, she presents herself as the new bride to the king.

To be settled by the end: Will she succeed in causing the king to end his daily murders by preserving her own life?

This is a plot. The roots of the middle are in the beginning; the roots of the end are in the middle. The end terminates what was begun by Shahrazad's decision to break the king's lethal habit. To be sure, this plot is not the business of *The Arabian Nights;* and the beginning and the middle are introduced in the first pages of Volume I, and nothing more is said of the question to be settled until it is at last taken up again at the conclusion of the tales in Volume X.* But it is easy to see that had the storyteller been interested in writing either a short story or a novel, he could have managed to wind up this plot without abandoning it (as he has done) until after a thousand and one nights of tales had passed. The short story and the novel, however, are fairly modern forms of storytelling—though here and there we can find an old story possessing a true plot among more ancient pieces of literature, as for example the Book of Ruth in the Old Testament. To the author of *The Arabian Nights* the rudimentary plot was only a device for the presentation of his tales; for that very reason it served his purposes to keep it dangling for nine and one-half volumes.

But in "The Revolt of 'Mother' " we find a strong, simple plot holding the story together by its own inherent logic:

The beginning: "Mother," who feels desperately the need of a larger, better house to live in, is unable to convince "Father" that he ought to be building a new house instead of a new barn.

The middle: When "Father" goes off in search of a horse to purchase, "Mother" sees, in the completion of the new barn, an opportunity to have the house they need.

To be settled by the end: Will she succeed in compelling "Father" to give the family the house it needs?"

Here we find a beginning leading logically into the middle, and the middle leading logically to the end, which leaves nothing unanswered. Poe in his discussion of the short story as a literary form insists that the conclusion of a short story must provide a sense of finality; it must give the reader the satisfying sense that nothing of consequence has been left unrevealed. "The Revolt of 'Mother' " certainly meets this criterion.

Poe also stipulates that a short story must create the illusion of reality; that illusion of reality, he states, is indeed to a very great degree the aim of the writer. Of course, this requirement is no more applicable to the short story than it is to the drama and the novel. It is interesting to note, on the other hand, that neither "A Doctor of Laws" nor any of the tales in *The Arabian Nights*—nor, for that matter, the story of Epam'nondas—makes any pretensions to involve our complete credulity. "The Revolt of 'Mother,' " as we have said, creates a perfect illusion of life as it is lived.

It will be noted that in our analysis of plot, we have put the end in the form of a question:

Will Shahrazad succeed in causing the king to stop his daily murders by preserving her own life? and

Will "Mother" succeed in compelling "Father" to give the family the house it needs?

We so stated each end because all plots of any worth must keep the reader in some sort of suspense. Not suspense in the mystery-story way, we mean, but suspense as to how the reader's wonder about the characters and their acts will be answered. It is this wonder which

---

*In the Burton Edition, which is a complete translation.

involves the reader in the story. There is always some question to be settled by the resolution of the plot. The internal logic of a plot raises the question; the end provides the answer.

It is probable that in the construction of his plot nothing is of more importance to the writer than determining what shall be the climax of his story. For the climax fixes the line by which the story is to reach its conclusion. It is therefore fundamental to the architecture of the work. Certainly, it is less crucial that the reader *recognize the climax as such while he is reading;* indeed it is hard to see how he could recognize it for what it is until later in the story, perhaps not until the end. But it is always interesting to identify the climax while analyzing the plot; in some instances, it may clarify the author's purposes; in others, the absence of a satisfactory climax may explain the failure of the story as a whole to convince us as a work of art.

There is, unhappily, a great deal of vagueness in the usage of the word. The climax is popularly thought of as "the most exciting moment" of the action, or "the point of greatest emotional intensity," and it is surprising how much of critical discussion is invalidated when based on this view. After all, if that were what is involved in climax, what would be the value of mentioning it? Every reader naturally will know what has been the most exciting moment in what he has read, and nothing more need be said about it.

We desire, rather, to consider *climax* as part of the plot-structure. As such we therefore define the word in a limited, technical sense. It *is the moment during which the central character does something which determines the course of the remaining action.** It is the turning point, the point of no return. In "The Revolt of 'Mother' " it occurs in the paragraph in which we are told that "Sarah Penn, at the head of her children," moved "all their little household goods into the new barn."

That paragraph is certainly not as *exciting* as a number of other passages in the story —as, for example, when "Mother" forces her husband to listen to her bill of complaints, or when his return from his trip is recounted. But that paragraph does fix the course of the rest of the story. Also, without our being aware of it at the time, it is preparing the answer to the question raised by the plot, "Will she succeed in compelling 'Father' to give the family the house it needs?" It, indeed, exemplifies a thoroughly good climax:

1. It relates an act of the central character.
2. This act is the product of the personal traits of the central character.
3. This act determines the course of the rest of the action.

Concerning climax we have more to say in our next chapter; in drama climax is of crucial significance.

We have been speaking of the "central character." Every plot must have one and only one *central character.* He *is the doer of the action* which forms the beginning, middle and end of the plot. (Note that in analyzing the two plots, we have had to speak in each step of Shahrazad or of "Mother.") Without one central character there can be no focus to the plot, no internal logic, no center of interest. The presence of one central character makes it possible for the reader to take up his own position with respect to all the persons of the story, and identify himself as for or against everyone concerned. (Characteristically, having no plot our excerpt from *The History of the Dividing Line* has no central character; neither has "A Doctor of Laws.") Many stories which fail to impress us will reveal, upon analysis, a fatal shift in focus. This sort of thing is typical:

1. Harry, in love with the wife of his best friend, Rudolph, leaves town to avoid being entangled in a clandestine affair.
2. Rudolph, unaware of Harry's passion, suddenly must go to Mexico on business. In midair the airplane carrying him explodes, killing all seventy-two aboard.

*Some critics call this moment the *crisis.*

3. Clarissa, Rudolph's wife, long nurturing a love for Harry, calls Harry back to town, declares her love and marries him.

In pursuit of a happy ending, Hollywood has often perpetrated such travesties of plot, leaving us confused and unsatisfied. They neither move nor delight because they lack all internal logic. At the beginning of this story Harry seems to be the central character. But in the middle the central character becomes Rudolph—or, rather, the airplane. At the end, Clarissa leaves the background, where she has been lurking, to take over everything.

Obviously, the requirements of plot imply a literary form far more highly wrought than that of the tale. Traditionally plot has been of basic importance to the drama, the novel, and the short story. For Aristotle, indeed, plot was the cardinal consideration in drama; he went so far as to say that the author's conception of his characters must be molded by the requirements of the plot.

RECENT CONCEPTIONS OF SHORT-STORY PLOT

With the growth of naturalism* during most of the twentieth century, however, writers whose prime objective has been to re-create the actualities of everyday living have tended to minimize the importance of plot. Except in the case of death, they argue, life itself does not provide endings to situations, and even death is not an ending for the persons connected with the one who dies; events blend into one another; life is a continuous flow, and to draw the line that marks an end is to defy the facts of living. There are some novels of the twentieth century which have as a beginning the birth of the hero and as their end his death; in between the birth and death are recorded the comings and goings of other people into his life, with no attempt to establish the classic idea of plot in their relationships. (Romain Rolland's epochal *Jean Christophe* was the prototype of such books.) Among short-story writers the naturalists (some of them resent that name, and prefer to be known as a variety of realist) have developed a species of story in which there are a beginning and a middle but—in the sense which Aristotle and Poe meant—no end.

A story published in 1958 by R. Prawer Jhabvala provides not only a good example of this newer conception but also in many ways an interesting study of contrasts with Mrs. Freeman's story. It is called "Better than Dead":

What made me first care for my husband was that he was so kind to me. It was a very difficult time for me; I think it is a difficult time for every girl when she is first married and taken away from her own home to go and live with her husband's family. I had been happy and excited when my parents arranged my marriage for me, because, like every girl, I was eager to be a bride. But when the marriage festivities were over, and it was time for me to be sent away with the stranger who was now my husband, then I was very much frightened. I was thirteen years old at the time, and I had never been out of the village where my father had his land. But now I had to go all the way to Delhi and live with my husband's family in a house in the middle of the city. Everything there was so different from my own home, and I longed for my mother and my younger sisters and our courtyard, where we sat together doing our household work. I had not known before how happy I had been at home. Outside the house where we lived, there was a big old tree, to which one of my brothers had tied a swing for us; we sat on this swing and swung up high among the leaves of the tree, and we laughed, and sometimes we sang songs. I think we were laughing and singing most of the time. In my husband's house, there was also a lot of laughing, but it was different. Everybody there was so big. There were my husband's brothers— five of them—and they were all taller than anyone I had ever seen before, and their shoulders were broader and their chests wider and their voices louder. Their wives also were big and with loud voices, and so were my mother-in-law and my sisters-in-law. All were tall and big, and all ate a lot and shouted; sometimes their shouting was in fun and sometimes it was in anger, but to me it

*A product of scientific determinism. Such writings, less selective than realism, use the eye as a camera, the ear as a dictaphone.

always sounded the same, and it always frightened me. I was frightened most of the time. I sat in a corner and hoped nobody would see me or speak to me. They were never unkind to me, but, all the same, I was frightened. I felt so small and weak that I thought if they wanted to they could crush me and I would be dead.

My husband was not as big as the others. His hands—even though he is a carpenter and works with them all the time—are like a woman's, and so are his feet; his voice is low and gentle. But at that time—seven years ago, when we were first married—I was frightened of him, too. Perhaps I was even more afraid of him than of the others, because he was my husband and therefore my master, and could do with me what he liked. I had always been told that a woman's husband is her god, and that she must worship him and obey him in everything. I knew that some husbands were very bad to their wives, so I was afraid of what he might do to me. When he spoke to me, I trembled and my heart beat loudly and I could never answer him. "What is it?" he would say. "What is the matter? Please tell me." But I could never speak. And what to tell him? How could I tell him, "I am frightened and unhappy; please send me home again"? He might be angry with me; they might all be angry with me, and then what would I do? So I sat quiet and said nothing, though he said, over and over again, "Please tell me what is the matter." His voice was sweet and gentle as he spoke to me, and so was his face as he looked at me, but I never realized this, because I was so frightened that I could hear only the beating of my heart and a rushing in my ears.

Once he really was angry—not with me but with the others. "What are you all doing to her," he said, "to make her sit day and night like this in a corner?" Then they all shouted with their loud voices—my mother-in-law and my sisters-in-law. "What do we do?" they shouted. "All day we beg her to come and sit with us, come and eat with us, but never can we get her out of her corner!" It was true; they did try to make me come to them, but I felt safe only by myself, as far away from them as possible.

"You are frightening her!" my husband shouted. It was the first time I had heard him shout, for he was usually very quiet.

"Son," cried my mother-in-law, "I swear to you"—and she beat her fist against her heart so hard I thought surely she must have hurt herself—"swear to you we try to be kind to her!" My sisters-in-law, too, shouted, and then my brothers-in-law joined in—all of them standing

there facing one another and roaring like lions. I thought at any moment they would turn and tear me to pieces, and I was so frightened that I began to scream. I hid my face behind my hands and I screamed. I couldn't help myself. My husband lifted me up and carried me and laid me on a bed. Then I was so tired I went to sleep; I think he stayed sitting on the bed, looking at me, but I can't be sure. Anyway, when I woke up next morning he was no longer sitting there.

It was a few days after this that he came home one evening from his work and said to me, "Pack up your things." I got up and I wrapped my things into a bundle, and we left the house together. I thought he was taking me home to my parents' house, and though that was what I had wanted most ever since my marriage, now I felt hurt and ashamed. I knew it was the greatest shame a woman can endure to be sent back to her parents' house. But soon I noticed that he was not taking me to the railway station. I knew the station was near the house, but now we seemed to be walking a much longer way. We walked through many narrow roads, all crowded with shops and people, and there were bullock carts and cycle rickshaws going down the middle of the road, and sometimes also cars came, hooting loudly, so that I had to walk close to the wall. My husband went in front of me, clearing a path for me through the crowd; I kept my eyes fixed on his back, for I was afraid of losing him. What would happen to me if I lost him or if he decided to abandon me now in the street? I would never be able to find my way back to the house, and I would be quite alone and forsaken in Delhi, where I knew no one except my husband and his family. So I kept as close behind him as I could; he was like a friend to me in all that crowd of strangers. Once he stopped at a sweetmeat shop and bought a few sweetmeats for me. I ate them as I walked behind him.

At last, he went into a doorway beside a tailor's shop, and I followed him up a very dark and narrow staircase. Once I stumbled, and he put out his hand to me; I held it, and then it was easier for me to climb the stairs. We stopped at one door, and he took out a key and opened the door, and we walked into a room. There were two beds in the room, and in one corner there was a place to make a fire for cooking, and a few cooking utensils, which were shining and new. My husband said, "This is where we shall live. Only you and I." He saw that I did not understand him, so he made me sit down and he talked to me for a long time. He talked about how he believed that husband and wife should be alone, away from their families, and how they should make their own life and be free and happy. But though I did not understand most of what he was saying, I noticed he was talking in a gentle, kind way, so I was not at all afraid of him. And I began to think that perhaps he would be good to me and that it might be possible for me to be happy living with him.

He went to his work every morning and came home at night, and I cooked for him and cleaned our room. At first, it was very strange for me to be alone, without a family; in my own home there had always been so many of us—my grandmother and my parents and uncles and brothers and sisters—and in my husband's house there had been his brothers and their families. But after a time I became used to being alone with my husband, and I even began to like it. My husband gave me money for our food, and I went out and bought a little store of rice and flour and lentils; and sometimes I went to buy vegetables at the bazaar, where I bargained with the shopkeepers and kept a sharp lookout to make sure that they gave me only fresh things and weighed them right. And I swept out our room and rolled up our bedding neatly in a corner and made everything sweet and nice.

There was a water tap in the courtyard, where all the women in the house came to get water. Often they quarrelled about who would fill her bucket first. I always let everyone else go before me, so that they could not quarrel with me, for I was rather afraid of all the shouting and abuse. But when I was alone, cooking my husband's food or cleaning out our room, then I sang the way I had sung in my father's house. Only it was different from my father's house, because all the time I was waiting, impatient and waiting, for night to come; and when I heard his step on the stairs, my heart beat loudly, but now it was no longer beating in fear.

I remember the time I was expecting my first child. Though it was such a happy time for me, when I think back on it now I begin to cry. I cry most of the time now; my children look at me, and I know it hurts them that I am crying, but I can't help it—my tears won't stop flowing. But at that time, during my first pregnancy, I was always happy and laughing. And, looking at me, my husband, though he was usually quiet and serious, would also begin to laugh, and we were like two children together. Yes, at that time I could still make him laugh, and call him away

from his serious thoughts and his books. Even then, he was often reading and thinking. He had learned to read in a school in the city, and I had never known anyone to sit so much with a book as he did. He wanted me to learn to read and write, too, and even tried to teach me. But when he was being my teacher and sitting close to me, my thoughts always turned away from the lesson, and I would begin to stroke the back of his hand or touch his cheek gently with my fingertip. At first, he would frown and say, "No, you must learn," but soon he would not be able to resist my caresses and he would love me.

When my baby was to be born, he took me home to my parents; and when he was first shown our baby, and held it, I could see that there were tears in his eyes. Afterward, he sat by my bed and talked to me for a long time. He said many things, most of which I did not understand. But I was used to his talking strange things; he often made me sit and listen while he talked about— I don't know what. About God and the world and people, and being happy and not being happy—all things like that, which I think he must have read about in his books. But when he talked that way after the baby came, I could hear my sisters talking and laughing outside, and I was impatient for him to finish so that I could call to them and join in their talk and laugh with them. In the end, I could not bear it any more; I had to call to them, "Why don't you come in?" Then they came running, still laughing, and they stood round my bed, and we all talked together and were so merry. Only my husband was quiet, and after a time he got up and went away.

Eleven months later, I had another child, and the year after that I was pregnant once again. But that time my husband did not take me to my home, because my mother had died in the meantime and my sisters had all been married and my brothers had brought in their new wives, so it wasn't home for me any more. I did not like to go to my husband's family, for though I was no longer so much afraid of them, I always felt shy and could never love them. So I stayed at home in our own room and had the child there. But something went wrong and the child died, and I nearly died, too. But the next year I had another child, and that one lived. I had become weak after the third child, and after the fourth I felt so bad that I could hardly stand. But I could never rest, because there was so much work to do—looking after the children and cooking and washing and cleaning and carrying the water up the stairs. My husband was also working very hard, to bring money home for us. We always had enough food, and in the winter I could make warm clothes for the children, and if they were sick, I had money to pay for medicine. Often, too, he brought little toys and sweetmeats, and, for me, colored glass bangles. He played with our children and told them stories, so that they loved him very much and waited at night for him to come home. I was always glad when he was home, though I was usually too tired to speak much with him. It had been a long time since he tried to teach me to read and write, but he still liked to sit and talk to me about what he read in his books and the thoughts that were in his head. He would talk and I would try to listen, but I was always so tired and I could not really understand what he was saying. There were many other things I had to think about, such as why our store of rice was finishing too quickly this month—was it because the grocer had not given me the right weight, or had someone come and stolen some out of the stone jar in which I stored it? And then I thought about whether I would be able to buy a piece of cloth to make a shirt for my eldest child, or would it not be better to make one for my husband instead, because his was getting very frayed. But most of all, I thought about the water tap in the courtyard. My thoughts were always very bitter about this, because the older women pushed us younger ones out of the way and quarrelled with one another about who would take the water first, so that there was shouting and abuse almost every day. Once or twice I tried to tell my husband. But he would not listen to me. All he said was "Why quarrel with people? Why fight?" and then he went on talking the way he liked to talk. I think he must have noticed that I was not really listening to him. Once he became quite impatient, and he said, "You never even try to understand." When he spoke like that, I began to cry, and then he was sorry and was gentle with me again. But he spoke with me less after that; instead, he would read his books or only sit silent, with his cheek on his hand.

But we would have been happy together again. Perhaps one day there would have been less work, and then I need not have been so tired, and we would have laughed together again and been happy, the way we were when we first came to live in this house. It could have happened like that. But now Fatima has come, and my husband is different and everything is different. Fatima came six months ago. She rented a room downstairs and came to live there with her two broth-ers. She has no husband; at first I thought that perhaps she was a widow, but later I found out that she had been divorced. Fatima is a Moslem, and it is very easy for Moslems to get a divorce; they only have to go to their priest and say three times that they want a divorce, and then it is all finished. So now Fatima lived with her two broth-ers, and cooked for them and washed their clothes. We saw her when she came down into the courtyard to get water, but she never talked to any of us. She was very different from the other women living in the house. Of course, she was a Moslem and we were all Hindus, but it was not only that. She was different in every way—the way she moved and looked. She seemed so proud, somehow. She wore a burka, as all Moslem women do to hide their faces and bodies. But she always had the front of the burka open, so that her face could be seen. How fair her face seemed, looking out from the black burka! But her eyes were very dark and long, and they always seemed to be moving, as if she wanted to see everything; and really it was as if she saw everything and knew everything. But she never spoke to us—not because she was shy, of that we were sure, but perhaps because she was too proud. We did not like her at all, but no one ever quarrelled with her —not even about the water—for there was some-thing about her that made one a little afraid of her. And though we did not like her, we could not help seeing that she was beautiful. She never showed herself in anything except her black burka, which covered her from head to foot, with only her face looking out. But when she moved there was a jingling sound, as of earrings and many bracelets, so that one had to think that under her burka she wore the costliest ornaments of gold, and perhaps also thin, fine silken clothes. We could not help thinking that, even though we knew she was poor like the rest of us. Her broth-ers were tailors who did not even have their own shop.

One day my youngest child was sick with fever, and I was very worried. I did not like to leave him alone, even for a moment, but I had to go down quickly to get the water. It seemed I was lucky, for most of the women had already taken their water and there remained only a few of us wait-ing. When I thought it was my turn, I placed my bucket under the tap, but suddenly it was kicked aside, and someone pushed my shoulder and said, "Get out, you! It's my turn!" I looked and saw it was the old woman who lived in the room on the top floor; she lived there with her four sons, none of whom ever did any decent work, so that she was always scolding them. The whole house could hear how she screamed at them, and sometimes we could hear her beating them, too. She was a terrible old woman. Any other time, I would have picked up my bucket quietly and waited for her to fill hers, but that day I was so worried about my child's fever that I said, "Please let me. My child—the littlest one—he is sick." Then she screamed again, "Get out!," so I knew I would have to wait. But just as I was stooping to pick up my bucket, Fatima said, "Let her go first." She spoke in a low voice, but everyone heard her at once. The old woman was very much surprised, and for a moment she said nothing. Fatima took my bucket and placed it under the tap again and stood by it while it was filling. She never moved at all—not even when the old woman began to shout abuses at her. When my bucket was full, she said to me, "Go," and she moved aside to let me pick it up. I hurried away with it as fast as I could. I don't know what happened between Fatima and the old woman after I had gone.

My child's fever went higher in the evening, and I sat by him with my hand on his forehead. I was very worried, yet I also kept thinking about what had happened at the tap. I wondered why Fatima should have done this thing for me. I was glad and grateful for what she had done, but I wished also that she had been friendly to me. She had never even looked at me, and when she said "Go," her voice, even though it was such a sweet voice, had not sounded friendly. I felt that she had done this thing for me not as she would have done it for a friend or a person for whom she had regard but as for anyone who was weaker than she was, even for a dog or a cat. I felt that I was no more to her than a dog or a cat, and I was hurt.

When my husband came home, he also sat down by the sick child, and he rubbed his hair and softly sang to him. The other children came in from playing, and I gave them their food. I would have liked to tell my husband about what had happened at the tap, but I was afraid that he would think I had quarrelled, so I said nothing. We were sitting like that, my husband quietly singing to the sick child and I feeding the two other children, when Fatima came into the room. She was not at all shy or embarrassed, the way other people are when they come for the first time to a strange home. She looked round the room, her large black eyes moving quickly, the way they always did, so that I knew she was seeing everything: the tin trunk in which we kept our valuables; our two string beds, one of which had lost

a leg and was supported on an old kerosene tin; the piece of carpet on which the two elder children slept, and which I had washed so often that the edges had frayed and the color had faded; the little statues of Vishnu and Ganesa, made out of plaster of Paris; and the gilded picture of Siva and Parvati, in front of which we said our prayers and did all our ceremonies. I knew she saw all that, and more—she saw and knew us all and everything about us. I lowered my eyes and felt shy and even a little ashamed. But Fatima took no notice of me. She said to my husband "Your child is sick?" and, without waiting for an answer, went straight to the bed. My husband moved aside without a word. We all watched her in silence while she looked at the child. She laid her hand first on his forehead and then on his chest, and then she pulled up the lids of his eyes. After a while, she said, "I will give you medicine. He will be well in a day or two." None of us spoke; we only stood and looked at her. It was so strange to see her in our room, in her black burka, with her beautiful, fair face looking out of it, and to hear the gentle rustling and jingling sound she made every time she moved.

Suddenly she laughed. How her eyes and teeth sparkled when she laughed! "Why are you surprised?" she said to my husband, and her voice sounded sweeter than ever, for though it was mocking, it was also tender. She smiled and looked at him closely, so that he had to smile, too, though I could see he was shy. "Why are you surprised?" she said again, and she moved nearer to him and looked into his eyes. He looked back at her, and at that moment I knew what was going to happen between them, and my heart began to pound in fear. "You think I am a witch?" she said to him, and laughed. "No," she went on. "I have only taught myself a little homeopathy, that is all. I will make up some powders, and you may come and fetch them."

"You are kind," my husband said.

"Yes, I am very kind," she said, and she looked at him, and her eyes were bright with laughter. Later, he went down to her room to fetch the powders. I could not think of anything to say that would stop him. When he came back, he never said a word to me. He gave the child the medicine, and then he lay down on his bed. But I knew he did not go to sleep, for I, too, lay awake for a long time, and I could hear him moving.

From that day on, Fatima often came to our room in the evenings. My husband began to come home earlier, but he no longer sat with his books, as he used to do, nor did he play with the children or try to teach them. He was impatient and waiting, and it was strange for me to see him like that, for he had always been gentle and calm and full of rest. But now he could not stay still, and his hands touched everything but took up nothing; if the children asked him to play with them, he answered them impatiently. When she came, his face changed and all his impatience left him. She came in, jingling and rustling, her eyes bright, her mouth smiling. She would clap her hands at the children and cry "Who will have the most today?" and then she would throw a handful of little sweets onto the floor, scattering them all over, so that the children, shouting and laughing, had to look for them. Sometimes she would help to pick them up, and she would say "Just see, I am quicker than any of you!" and really she was —she was quick, like a bird. And she would also make my husband get down on the floor to play, and they would all be laughing, she and the children, and my husband too, while he looked and looked into her face, and I stood and looked into his. When she was tired of playing, she would say, "Now, enough," and she would sit down by the little low window that looked out over the street. Suddenly she was very still and calm, sitting there on the floor by the window. Even the children knew that when she said "Now, enough" like that, the game really was finished. My husband sat beside her, and both had their backs half turned to the room as they looked out of the window. There was nothing very much to see from that window—only horse tongas and cycle rickshaws passing up and down, a man with a little wooden barrow who sold slices of watermelon, and, just opposite our house, a row of open stalls occupied, from one end to the other, by a vender of gold-embroidered slippers, a man who sold sweetmeats freshly prepared in pure ghee, and a doctor who pulled teeth at one rupee each. My husband and Fatima sat and looked out, and he talked to her in a very low voice. He went on and on, talking the way he had once talked to me, and sometimes she answered him, also in a low voice, or questioned him. They talked about all those strange things that I had never understood. Fatima always seemed to be listening with great interest. Only sometimes she was in a mood where she would not listen. Then she would laugh at everything he said, and tease him, and finally she would jump up and call to the children again, "Who is playing with me?" How gay she would be as she played, her bangles jingling like music! The children loved her; they

followed her like slaves, like dogs, and I knew that she had no more feeling for them than she would have had for slaves or dogs—that she had no more feeling for them than she had for me. My husband would remain sitting on the floor, and his eyes were very sad as they followed her round the room. I felt sorry for him and would have liked to go to him and to lay my hand on his cheek, the way I had always done when he was sad. But Fatima never even looked at him, she was so busy laughing and playing with the children, though sometimes she passed very close to him.

I did not like to see all this, but where could I go? If it had been summer, it would have been easier, for in the summer we lived mostly in the courtyard or on the roof of the house. But in the winter we had to stay in our room, and I had to be close to them and see everything. There was nothing I could do or say. Once, though, I did stay close by the door, just as she was going out, and I said to her, "Why do you come into my house?" But I said it in such a low voice that it was easy for her to pretend she had not heard. I could not speak to my husband, either. What was there I could say to him? And I could see he did not wish me to speak to him. When we were alone together, he kept his head lowered and avoided my eyes and sat in silence, and as soon as he could, he would lie down on the bed and pretend to be sleeping. It was as if he were afraid I would speak to him.

On two days a week, I began to notice, my husband did not come home till late in the night. I soon discovered that on those two days Fatima's brothers worked late, and so he could spend that time in her room. Our room seemed very quiet on those nights. The children, after waiting for their father and Fatima, fell asleep disappointed. And I sat alone, waiting and thinking. But it was even worse than when they were there in front of me, for it was so still that I felt I would be alone forever and ever while they were together down in her room. I thought about what they were doing there, and I cried, quietly, so as not to disturb the children. At last, when I heard my husband's step on the stairs, I would run quickly to my bed and pretend to be sleeping. But one night I could bear it no longer, and I crept down the stairs, softly in the dark, till I stood before Fatima's door. I looked through the crack and I saw them. The pain was so great for me that I sank to my knees and leaned my head against the door. Suddenly a voice screamed, "Yes, look at them! Look at them! See what they are doing—

your husband and your friend!" I started to my feet and saw the old woman from upstairs. "Have you seen?" she screamed into my face. I whispered, "Please be quiet," and even tried to put my hand over her mouth, but she struck it aside and laughed and screamed. Other doors opened, and people came and looked at us. Only Fatima's door remained shut. I ran stumbling up the stairs, putting my hands over my ears, so as not to have to hear the old woman shouting and laughing. I woke up the children and dressed them. I was crying all the time; the children looked at me, but they never said a word, and did whatever I told them. I carried the youngest child, and we ran through the dark streets a long way, till we came to the house where my husband's mother and his brothers lived. I knew of nowhere else to go.

It was very late when we got there, and everybody was asleep. My mother-in-law always slept alone in the place they used for cooking, so I crept quietly round to her and touched her on the shoulder. I was still sobbing. She started up and cried, "Who is it?" I told her, and when she saw me there with the children and heard me sobbing, she suddenly cried, "My son is dead!" The words were like a knife to me; I caught her hand and whispered, "No. Oh, no!" She was sitting up on her bed, with her hand clutched to her heart, and she was breathing heavily in fright. I, too, was very frightened, and I kept whispering, "No no." My mother-in-law called in a weak voice to my eldest sister-in-law, who woke up at once and came to see what was the matter. "Oh, my God," my mother-in-law moaned. "God, my God."

"No," I said. "No, he is not dead." I could hardly speak the word "dead," it frightened me so.

My sister-in-law lit a kerosene lamp, and said, "First put the children to sleep." We laid them to sleep, and then I told the women why I had come. It was difficult for me to tell, for I had never yet told anyone one word of it all, though it was many weeks now since my husband first saw Fatima. My mother-in-law only said, "Thank God." She was still trembling at the thought that something had happened to him. My sister-in-law began to laugh. "And is it only the first time?" she asked. She sat cross-legged on the bed, her head thrown back on her big neck, and laughed. I was afraid that she would wake the others with her laughter, and that they would all get up and she would shout out to them what I had told her. I could see them all standing round me—the men and the women, all of them big and strong, like giants—shaking with loud laughter. I crept qui-

etly into the corner where my children were sleeping, and I lay down beside them. I kept hearing the way my mother-in-law had cried, "My son is dead!" I thought of him dead, and it was worse than thinking of him with Fatima.

I left early in the morning. I awakened my children and dressed them very quietly, so as not to wake the others, and walked home. The streets through which I had to pass were crowded with men pushing barrows piled with vegetables, and others sitting by the roadside selling eggs out of baskets, and milkmen cycling back to their villages with empty cans. There were also people who had come out early to buy the day's provisions—women like myself with babies on their hips and their money tied into the end of their saris, and old men sent out to the bazaar by their daughters-in-law, and little girls carefully carrying earthenware pots full of curds, and the servants of the rich come out to buy meat and fish and fruits. I carried my youngest child and made the two elder ones hold tight to my sari on each side of me, for there was much pushing and jostling, and every few moments someone would shout "Mind yourself!" from behind us, and we would have to move aside to let a piled-up barrow pass, or a coolie carrying firewood in a basket on his head. I thought of the first time I had come from my mother-in-law's house to my own home, and how my husband had walked in front of me, clearing a way, so that it was easy and safe for me to walk. Now there was no one to walk before me, and I had to look after myself and my children. But he was not dead; I would see him again. I would still every day see him move, and hear him speak with his gentle voice, and in the night listen to him breathing on the bed next to me. What cause was there for me to be unhappy? If he had been dead, there would have been cause, but he was not dead.

When I got home, I at once began to work very hard. I swept out our room and washed the floor with water; I cleaned the window, the door, and our two beds; I scrubbed our pots till they shone. Then I began to cook; I cooked rice and a curry made of curds, which was my husband's favorite dish. Afterward, I went down to the tap and carried up more water, and I gave all three children a bath. Then I bathed myself, and combed out my hair and put oil on it. I opened our big tin trunk and took from it the new sari with the red border that my husband had given me seven months before, which I had never yet worn. I sent the eldest child to go out and buy a fresh flower garland to hang round the picture of Siva and

Parvati, and then I made the children sit in front of this picture, and I said a prayer. I was calm now and almost happy, waiting for him to come home.

When he came, I gave him the food I had cooked for him, but I don't think he noticed that it was his favorite dish. I wondered if he was angry that I had gone away in the night, but he did not look angry; he looked only impatient and waiting, the way he did every night when she had not yet come. The children asked him to play with them, but he said, "Later, later," as if he were thinking of something else. It became quite late, and still she had not come. The children, too, were waiting for her, and my husband began to walk up and down the room. I sat still in a corner, content that he was there with me in the room and not dead. Suddenly he stopped walking and he cried, "But why are you staring at me like that? What harm have I done you?" I looked at him, and the tears came welling out of my eyes, for I saw that he was looking at me the way one looks at someone one does not like. "Always tears!" he said, and his voice was not like his at all, but shrill and loud, like that of an angry stranger. "Wherever I go, there are your tears!" he said. I covered my face so that he would not see them. There was a step on the stairs, and then a jingling and rustling, and the children cried, "At last she has come!"

Though India is separated by its customs from New England by more than oceans, the common denominator of fundamental human emotion dispels any extreme strangeness which might have attached to such a picture. We are soon as much at one with the wife of "Better than Dead" as with "Mother" in Mrs. Freeman's story. Still, how different have been the lot, the expectations, and the philosophy of the American from that of the Indian woman!

The differences between the two authors' notions of what makes a good story, however, has less to do with nationalities than with the period in which each wrote, realists though both of them are. Poe would have been pleased with the sense of finality with which "The Revolt of 'Mother'" concludes; he would probably have declared that "Better than Dead" has no end at all. We can imagine Poe arguing: "At the end of her story we know that 'Mother' will have her new house. What do we know about the future relationship of the Indian wife, her husband, and his mistress? The author may be implying that the wife is resigned to acceptance of her rival. But how is she to bear a life in which her husband feels dislike for her and only impatience with her misery—a life in which even her children prefer her rival? We are given no clue as to how she is ever to resolve her problem. We are therefore left at the end with a disturbing uncertainty."

But a contemporary realist might answer: "Life does not usually present solutions. Such a woman, having nowhere to go, would continue her life of wretchedness, alternating between relief that she still has her husband, and despair at his distance—without ever finding a way out. To pretend otherwise would be contrary to the facts. Only art pretends to find answers to riddles like these."

And Poe might answer: "Exactly—only art! For art does not pretend to be life or to provide a carbon copy of it. Why should a story, therefore, not leave the mind satisfied with a sense of completeness admittedly absent from life itself, while, at the same time, extracting the quintessences of experience for the reader's contemplation?"*

*"Better than Dead" has certainly the beginning of a plot:
  1. The woman falls in love with the man to whom she has been given in marriage;
and a middle:
  2. Because her energy fails after the birth of children, and because she is not interested in the things which interest him, she loses him to another woman, and knows this the moment it happens.
This middle also raises a question for the end to answer:
  3. Will she win back his love?
From a traditional point of view, it may be felt that the question is not completely answered, even though the answer is implied.

The story also clearly has a climax: she looks into the room where her husband and the other woman are together, while the rest of the house hounds her with its knowledge of what she is seeing.

It is only in the conclusion, therefore, that such a story as this has not the traditional conception of an ending.

We do not mean to give Poe the last word, for a great many storytellers today prefer the inconclusive conclusion which leaves us with the feeling that man is trapped either by circumstances or his own character. Such was the case with Virginia Woolf's short story, "The New Dress" (see page 68); it left us with less knowledge concerning the future of its central character than does the ending of "Better than Dead."

How do such authors achieve unity in their work, if they do not choose to tie up the ends of their plot? Through mood and characterization. On both these scores the authors of "The New Dress" and of "Better than Dead" must be admitted to have been eminently successful. There is a flawless consistency in all the characters and in their motivations, which manages to give each story its own kind of unity.

CHARACTERIZATION

In the tale of "A Doctor of Laws" since the author's intent was to amuse us with a couple of racy incidents, it was not to his purpose to depict as living persons the characters in the story. There is only a feeble attempt to make us see the lawyer himself; the wife we guess to be simpleminded; and the rogues are rogues and no more. We feel with none of them. In "The Revolt of 'Mother' " we know much about the man, the wife and their children. In "Better than Dead" we know a great deal about the wife, the husband, the mistress, and more than a little about the members of his parents' family. In "The New Dress" we penetrate deeply into the makeup of the central character.

Of course, it would be too much to say that these three authors have given us full-length portraits of any of these people. The comparative brevity of the short story makes it unnecessary and inadvisable for the writer to give us more about his characters than we need know for the theme of the story. Indeed, all three are as admirable for their exclusion of superfluous information about their characters as for their communicating to us what is essential. In "The New Dress" no one but the central character is revealed in any dimension as a person; in no case are we given more than the theme requires us to know.

In the novel, of course, there is ample room for elaborate portraiture, not only of the major figures but even of secondary characters. The author may enrich his novel by stepping in, in his own person, to describe them for us. But in a short story there is not time for such extensive and powerful character-discussion of minor figures such as this of the Duke of Marlborough in Thackeray's novel *Henry Esmond:*

And now, having seen a great military march through a friendly country, the pomps and festivities of more than one German court, the severe struggle of a hotly contested battle, and the triumph of victory, Mr. Esmond beheld another part of military duty: our troops entering the enemy's territory, and putting all around them to fire and sword; burning farms, wasted fields, shrieking women, slaughtered sons and fathers, and drunken soldiery, cursing and carousing in the midst of tears, terror, and murder. Why does the stately Muse of History, that delights in describing the valour of heroes and the grandeur of conquest, leave out these scenes, so brutal, mean, and degrading, that yet form by far the greater part of the drama of war? You, gentlemen of England, who live at home at ease, and compliment yourselves in the songs of triumph with which our heroes are bepraised—you pretty maidens, that come tumbling down the stairs when the fife and drum call you, and huzzah for the British Grenadiers—do you take into account that these items go to make up the amount of the triumph you admire, and form part of the duties of the heroes you fondle? Our chief, whom England and all Europe, saving only the Frenchmen, worshipped almost, had this of the godlike in him, that he was impassible before victory, before danger, before defeat. Before the greatest obstacle or the most trivial ceremony; before a hundred thousand men drawn in battalia, or a peasant slaughtered at the door of his burning hovel; before a carouse of drunken German lords, or a monarch's court or a cottage table, where his plans were laid, or an enemy's battery, vomiting flame and death, and strewing corpses round about him;—he was always cold, calm, resolute, like fate. He performed a treason or a court-bow, he told a falsehood as black as Styx, as easily as he paid a compliment or spoke about the weather. He took a mistress, and left her; he betrayed his benefactor, and supported him, or would have murdered him, with the same calmness always, and having no more remorse than Clotho when she weaves the thread, or Lachesis[1] when she cuts it. In the hour of battle I have heard the Prince of Savoy's officers say, the Prince became possessed with a sort of warlike fury; his eyes lighted up; he rushed hither and thither, raging; he shrieked curses and encouragement, yelling and harking his bloody wardogs on, and himself always at the first of the hunt. Our Duke was as calm at the mouth of the cannon as at the door of a drawing-room. Perhaps he could not have been the great man he was, had he had a heart either for love or hatred, or pity or fear, or regret or remorse. He achieved the highest deed of daring, or deepest calculation of thought, as he performed the very meanest action of which a man is capable; told a lie, or cheated a fond woman, or robbed a poor beggar of a halfpenny, with a like awful serenity and equal capacity of the highest and lowest acts of our nature.

His qualities were pretty well known in the army, where there were parties of all politics, and plenty of shrewdness and wit; but there existed such a perfect confidence in him, as the first captain of the world, and such a faith and admiration in his prodigious genius and fortune, that the very men whom he notoriously cheated of their pay, the chiefs whom he used and injured—(for he used all men, great and small, that came near him, as his instruments alike, and took something of theirs, either some quality or some property— the blood of a soldier, it might be, or a jewelled hat, or a hundred thousand crowns from a king, or a portion out of a starved sentinel's three-farthings or [when he was young] a kiss from a woman, and the gold chain off her neck, taking all he could from man or woman, and having, as I have said, this of the godlike in him, that he could see a hero perish or a sparrow fall, with the same amount of sympathy for either. Not that he had no tears; he could always order up this reserve at the proper moment to battle; he could draw upon tears or smiles alike, and whenever need was for using this cheap coin. He would cringe to a shoeblack, as he would flatter a minister or a monarch; be haughty, be humble, threaten, repent, weep, grasp your hand, or stab you whenever he saw occasion).—But yet those of the army, who knew him best and had suffered most from him, admired him most of all; and as he rode along the lines to battle or galloped up in the nick of time to a battalion reeling from before the enemy's charge or shot, the fainting men and officers got new courage as they saw the splendid calm of his face, and felt that his will made them irresistible.

Few short stories devote that much attention to an analysis of even the principal characters. Usually the author is content to sketch in the salient points in a few telling strokes.

In "The Revolt of 'Mother' " we are told of the central character that she "was a small woman, short and straight-waisted like a child in her brown cotton gown. Her forehead was mild and benevolent beneath the smooth curves of gray hair; there were meek downward lines about her nose and mouth; but her eyes . . . looked as if the meekness had been the result of her own will." Elsewhere we have a glimpse of her as appearing to her husband "as immovable as one of the rocks in his pasture-land."

We see "Father" reacting with "a sudden dropping and enlarging" of his jaw "as if some heavy weight had settled" in it. When he speaks he runs "his words together, and his speech was almost as inarticulate as a growl."

There is, it must be admitted, a touch of the Victorian in the depiction of the daughter as "pink and delicate as a flower" with her "tender, sweet face." But she is real enough before our eyes: "Her forehead was as bald and as innocent as a baby's, with the light hair strained back from it in a row of curl-papers. She was quite large, but her soft curves did not look as if they covered muscles."

The son is very much the farm boy. "He was lightly built, but clumsy. He went out of the yard with a curious spring in the hips, that made his loose home-made jacket tilt up in the rear." When he goes back to school, he takes "sly lopes out of the yard like a rabbit. He wanted a game of marbles before school, and feared his father would give him some chores to do."

[1]Clotho and Lachesis, two of the three Fates.

These touches do much to bring the characters before us.

In "Better than Dead" the author does not delineate the wife directly. But the husband and his family are graphically described in various phrases of the first two paragraphs, and by contrast we know what she is like. We are impressed with the bigness and loudness of her husband's relatives; we know thereby how small and timid she is. The husband, with his hands "like a woman's," is gentler than the others. But it is for the enchantress, Fatima, that the fullest description is reserved. We are aware at once of her arrogance; we see the open burka revealing her long dark eyes; we hear the jingling of her jewelry, and later her laughter. But in this story too the analyses of character are brief.

There are other methods of delineating character. One of the most engaging is through expressive dialogue, which, at its best, also carries the story forward. Here fiction is close to drama, where dialogue is the chief medium for furthering plot and revealing character and motive.

DIALOGUE

While amusing dialogue may be in itself diverting, it always is, in the hands of a master, at the service of story and characterization. A good example of dialogue brilliantly employed is the following passage from Jane Austen's novel *Pride and Prejudice*. It is so masterfully managed that it becomes almost superfluous to tell the reader, even though we set him down at the nineteenth chapter, about the characters involved:

Mr. Collins, a clergyman who is a distant relative of the Bennets, is in some hopes of inheriting Mr. Bennet's property, since the latter has no sons. Upon the advice of his patroness, Mr. Collins decides to propose marriage to Elizabeth Bennet, who on her own part would never marry unless for love. Mrs. Bennet has made her life occupation trying to marry off all her daughters:

The next day opened a new scene at Longbourn. Mr. Collins made his declaration in form. Having resolved to do it without loss of time, as his leave of absence extended only to the following Saturday, and having no feelings of diffidence to make it distressing to himself even at the moment, he set about it in a very orderly manner, with all the observances, which he supposed a regular part of the business. On finding Mrs. Bennet, Elizabeth, and one of the younger girls together, soon after breakfast, he addressed the mother in these words: "May I hope, madam, for your interest with your fair daughter Elizabeth, when I solicit for the honour of a private audience with her in the course of this morning?"

Before Elizabeth had time for anything but a blush of surprise, Mrs. Bennet instantly answered, "Oh dear!—yes—certainly. I am sure Lizzy will be very happy—I am sure she can have no objection. Come, Kitty, I want you upstairs." And, gathering her work together, she was hastening away, when Elizabeth called out:

"Dear madam, do not go. I beg you will not go. Mr. Collins must excuse me. He can have nothing to say to me that anybody need not hear. I am going away myself."

"No, no, nonsense, Lizzy. I desire you will stay where you are." And upon Elizabeth's seeming really, with vexed and embarrassed looks, about to escape, she added: "Lizzy, I *insist* upon you staying and hearing Mr. Collins."

Elizabeth would not oppose such an injunction —and a moment's consideration making her also sensible that it would be wisest to get it over as soon and as quietly as possible, she sat down again, and tried to conceal, by incessant employment, the feelings which were divided between distress and diversion. Mrs. Bennet and Kitty walked off, and as soon as they were gone Mr. Collins began.

"Believe me, my dear Miss Elizabeth, that your modesty, so far from doing you any disservice, rather adds to your other perfections. You would have been less amiable in my eyes had there *not* been this little unwillingness; but allow me to assure you, that I have your respected mother's permission for this address. You can hardly doubt the purport of my discourse, however your natural delicacy may lead you to dissemble; my attentions have been too marked to be mistaken. Almost as soon as I entered the house, I singled you out as the companion of my future life. But before I am run away with my feelings on this subject, perhaps it would be advisable for me to state my reasons for marrying—and, moreover, for coming into Hertfordshire with the design of selecting a wife, as I certainly did."

The idea of Mr. Collins, with all his solemn

composure, being run away with by his feelings, made Elizabeth so near laughing, that she could not use the short pause he allowed in any attempt to stop him farther, and he continued:

"My reasons for marrying are, first, that I think it a right thing for every clergyman in easy circumstances (like myself) to set the example of matrimony in his parish; secondly, that I am convinced it will add very greatly to my happiness; and thirdly—which perhaps I ought to have mentioned earlier, that it is the particular advice and recommendation of the very noble lady whom I have the honour of calling patroness. Twice has she condescended to give me her opinion (unasked too!) on this subject; and it was but the very Saturday night before I left Hunsford—between our pools at quadrille,[1] while Mrs. Jenkinson was arranging Miss de Bourgh's footstool, that she said, 'Mr. Collins, you must marry. A clergyman like you must marry. Choose properly, choose a gentlewoman for *my* sake; and for your *own,* let her be an active, useful sort of person, not brought up high, but able to make a small income go a good way. This is my advice. Find such a woman as soon as you can, bring her to Hunsford, and I will visit her.' Allow me, by the way, to observe, my fair cousin, that I do not reckon the notice and kindness of Lady Catherine de Bourgh[2] as among the least of the advantages in my power to offer. You will find her manners beyond anything I can describe; and your wit and vivacity, I think, must be acceptable to her, especially when tempered with the silence and respect which her rank will inevitably excite. Thus much for my general intention in favour of matrimony; it remains to be told why my views were directed to Longbourn instead of my own neighbourhood, where I assure you there are many amiable young women. But the fact is, that being, as I am, to inherit this estate after the death of your honoured father (who, however, may live many years longer), I could not satisfy myself without resolving to choose a wife from among his daughters, that the loss to them might be as little as possible, when the melancholy event takes place—which, however, as I have already said, may not be for several years. This has been my motive, my fair cousin, and I flatter myself it will not sink me in your esteem. And now nothing remains for me but to assure you in the most animated language of the violence of my affection. To fortune I am perfectly indifferent, and shall make no demand of that nature on your father, since I am well aware that it could not be complied with; and that

one thousand pounds in the four per cents, which will not be yours till after your mother's decease, is all that you may ever be entitled to. On that head, therefore, I shall be uniformly silent; and you may assure yourself that no ungenerous reproach shall ever pass my lips when we are married."

It was absolutely necessary to interrupt him now.

"You are too hasty, sir," she cried. "You forget that I have made no answer. Let me do it without further loss of time. Accept my thanks for the compliment you are paying me. I am very sensible of the honour of your proposals, but it is impossible for me to do otherwise than decline them."

"I am not now to learn," replied Mr. Collins, with a formal wave of the hand, "that it is usual with young ladies to reject the addresses of the man whom they secretly mean to accept, when he first applies for their favour; and that sometimes the refusal is repeated a second or even a third time. I am therefore by no means discouraged by what you have just said, and shall hope to lead you to the altar ere long."

"Upon my word, sir," cried Elizabeth, "your hope is rather an extraordinary one after my declaration. I do assure you that I am not one of those young ladies (if such young ladies there are) who are so daring as to risk their happiness on the chance of being asked a second time. I am perfectly serious in my refusal. You could not make *me* happy, and I am convinced that I am the last woman in the world who would make you so. Nay, were your friend Lady Catherine to know me, I am persuaded she would find me in every respect ill qualified for the situation."

"Were it certain that Lady Catherine would think so," said Mr. Collins very gravely—"but I cannot imagine that her ladyship would at all disapprove of you. And you may be certain that when I have the honour of seeing her again, I shall speak in the highest terms of your modesty, economy, and other amiable qualifications."

"Indeed, Mr. Collins, all praise of me will be unnecessary. You must give me leave to judge for myself, and pay me the compliment of believing what I say. I wish you very happy and very rich, and by refusing your hand, do all in my power to prevent your being otherwise. In making me the offer, you must have satisfied the delicacy of your feelings with regard to my family, and may take possession of Longbourn estate whenever it falls, without any self-reproach. This matter may be

---

[1] An eighteenth-century card game.

[2] Mr. Collins's noble patroness.

considered, therefore, as finally settled." And rising as she thus spoke, she would have quitted the room, had not Mr. Collins thus addressed her:

"When I do myself the honour of speaking to you next on the subject, I shall hope to receive a more favourable answer than you have now given me; though I am far from accusing you of cruelty at present, because I know it to be the established custom of your sex to reject a man on the first application, and perhaps you have even now said as much to encourage my suit as would be consistent with the true delicacy of the female character."

"Really, Mr. Collins," cried Elizabeth with some warmth, "you puzzle me exceedingly. If what I have hitherto said can appear to you in the form of encouragement, I know not how to express my refusal in such a way as may convince you of its being one."

"You must give me leave to flatter myself, my dear cousin, that your refusal of my addresses is merely words of course. My reasons for believing it are briefly these: It does not appear to me that my hand is unworthy of your acceptance, or that the establishment I can offer would be any other than highly desirable. My situation in life, my connections with the family of de Bourgh, and my relationship to your own, are circumstances highly in my favour; and you should take it into further consideration, that in spite of your manifold attractions, it is by no means certain that another offer of marriage may ever be made you. Your portion is unhappily so small that it will in all likelihood undo the effects of your loveliness and amiable qualifications. As I must therefore conclude that you are not serious in your rejection of me, I shall choose to attribute it to your wish of increasing my love by suspense, according to the usual practice of elegant females."

"I do assure you, sir, that I have no pretensions whatever to that kind of elegance which consists in tormenting a respectable man. I would rather be paid the compliment of being believed sincere. I thank you again and again for the honour you have done me in your proposals, but to accept them is absolutely impossible. My feelings in every respect forbid it. Can I speak plainer? Do not consider me now as an elegant female, intending to plague you, but as a rational creature, speaking the truth from her heart."

"You are uniformly charming!" cried he, with an air of awkward gallantry; "and I am persuaded that when sanctioned by the express authority of both your excellent parents, my proposals will not fail of being acceptable."

To such perseverance in wilful self-deception Elizabeth would make no reply, and immediately and in silence withdrew; determined, that if he persisted in considering her repeated refusals as flattering encouragement, to apply to her father, whose negative might be uttered in such a manner as must be decisive, and whose behaviour at least could not be mistaken for the affectation and coquetry of an elegant female.

Mr. Collins was not left long to the silent contemplation of his successful love; for Mrs. Bennet, having dawdled about in the vestibule to watch for the end of the conference, no sooner saw Elizabeth open the door and with quick step pass her towards the staircase, than she entered the breakfast-room, and congratulated both him and herself in warm terms on the happy prospect of their nearer connection. Mr. Collins received and returned these felicitations with equal pleasure, and then proceeded to relate the particulars of their interview, with the result of which he trusted he had every reason to be satisfied, since the refusal which his cousin had steadfastly given him would naturally flow from her bashful modesty and the genuine delicacy of her character.

This information, however, startled Mrs. Bennet; she would have been glad to be equally satisfied that her daughter had meant to encourage him by protesting against his proposals, but she dared not believe it, and could not help saying so.

"But, depend upon it, Mr. Collins," she added, "that Lizzy shall be brought to reason. I will speak to her about it myself directly. She is a very headstrong, foolish girl, and does not know her own interest; but I will *make* her know it."

"Pardon me for interrupting you, madam," cried Mr. Collins; "but if she is really headstrong and foolish, I know not whether she would altogether be a very desirable wife to a man in my situation, who naturally looks for happiness in the marriage state. If therefore she actually persists in rejecting my suit, perhaps it were better not to force her into accepting me, because if liable to such defects of temper, she could not contribute much to my felicity."

"Sir, you quite misunderstand me," said Mrs. Bennet, alarmed. "Lizzy is only headstrong in such matters as these. In everything else she is as good-natured a girl as ever lived. I will go directly to Mr. Bennet, and we shall very soon settle it with her, I am sure."

She would not give him time to reply, but hurrying instantly to her husband, called out as she entered the library, "Oh! Mr. Bennet, you are wanted immediately; we are all in an uproar. You must come and make Lizzy marry Mr. Collins, for she vows she will not have him, and if you do not make haste he will change his mind and not have *her.*"

Mr. Bennet raised his eyes from his book as she entered, and fixed them on her face with a calm unconcern which was not in the least altered by her communication.

"I have not the pleasure of understanding you," said he, when she had finished her speech. "Of what are you talking?"

"Of Mr. Collins and Lizzy. Lizzy declares she will not have Mr. Collins, and Mr. Collins begins to say that he will not have Lizzy."

"And what am I to do on the occasion? It seems an hopeless business."

"Speak to Lizzy about it yourself. Tell her that you insist upon her marrying him."

"Let her be called down. She shall hear my opinion."

Mrs. Bennet rang the bell, and Miss Elizabeth was summoned to the library.

"Come here, child," cried her father as she appeared. "I have sent for you on an affair of importance. I understand that Mr. Collins has made you an offer of marriage. Is it true?" Elizabeth replied that it was. "Very well—and this offer of marriage you have refused?"

"I have, sir."

"Very well. We now come to the point. Your mother insists upon your accepting it. Is it not so, Mrs. Bennet?"

"Yes, or I will never see her again."

"An unhappy alternative is before you, Elizabeth. From this day you must be a stranger to one of your parents. Your mother will never see you again if you do *not* marry Mr. Collins, and I will never see you again if you *do.*"

Nothing could be more delightful than this series of conversations; yet, besides amusing us, the novelist gives us insight into all the speakers and their motives, and at the same time winds up one of the threads of her story—Mr. Collins' attentions to Elizabeth.

Again, in a short story there is obviously not enough time to indulge in passages of such length of dialogue, unless they occur at crucial moments of the narrative. Usually what we find is a snatch of dialogue here and there, giving the effect of a strong light suddenly illuminating this or that moment of the story. "The Revolt of 'Mother' " opens with such a passage, penetrating at once into the heart of the matter; throughout its following pages there are significant pieces of conversation; the longest stretch is "Mother's" impressive monologue beginning: "Now, father, look here . . . I'm goin' to talk real plain to you."—which, at first, would seem her last stand for her rights. But as her plan comes into being, a series of short conversations helps heighten the tension. It was a stroke of fine artistry, and entirely in character, that "Father" should emit no more than a gasped, "Why, mother!" when he comes home to find the revolution which has taken place. And, when at last he can speak, his final hoarse words are far more moving and revealing than any oration could possibly be.

In "Better than Dead" we again find conversation chiefly in snatches; the husband's attempt to find out the cause of his wife's unhappiness in his mother's house; his brief announcements of their going away and again of where they are to live; the scene at the water tap and so forth. When Fatima enters the story, there is a little more dialogue. But at no point is it extensive, though where it occurs it does much to make the progress of events more vivid.

In short stories dialogue usually is selective and illustrative rather than complete. (Hemingway sometimes narrates exclusively by dialogue.)

ACTION

Of course, no method of revealing character is more satisfactory than through the action itself, if only because the very idea of story implies action (i.e., movement) of some sort.

Following is a dramatic scene from Thackeray's novel *Vanity Fair.* The beautiful adventuress Becky Sharp has married good-natured, simple-minded, ineffectual Colonel Rawdon Crawley, who is madly in love with her. She has accepted him only because he had every expectation of coming into a large inheritance from his aunt; but it turned out that the old lady cut him off without a farthing just because of his marriage to Becky. In London

Becky and the colonel have rented a large house where they live on a grandiose scale through Becky's skill in managing on "nothing a year." Her ambition knows no bounds. Soon she contrives to catch the amorous interest of a rich, depraved old nobleman, Lord Steyne, who, cynic though he is, is fascinated by Becky's charms and manipulations. The colonel has such confidence in his wife and her cleverness that he never asks himself how they can possibly be living so luxuriously on the scant pickings he occasionally wins at card games. With the backing of Lord Steyne Becky's star has risen higher and higher; at length she is even presented at Court. All society is gossiping about her and Lord Steyne; only Rawdon is ignorant of what is going on. The colonel's debts have accumulated so long that one of his creditors has brought suit, and he is carted off to Mr. Moss's "spunging-house."[1] Rawdon writes to his wife:

DEAR BECKY, *I hope you slept well.* Don't be *frightened* if I don't bring you in your *coffy.* Last night as I was coming home smoking, I met with an *accadent.*[2] I was *nabbed* by Moss of Cursitor Street—from whose *gilt and splendid parler* I write this—the same that had me this time two years. Miss Moss brought in my tea—she is grown very *fat,* and as usual, had *her stockens down at heal.*

It's Nathan's business—a hundred-and-fifty—with costs, hundred-and-seventy. Please send me my desk[3] and some *cloths*[4] —I'm in pumps and a white tye (something like Miss M.'s stockings) —I've seventy in it. And as soon as you get this, Drive to Nathan's—offer him seventy-five down, and ask *him to renew*—say I'll take wine—we may as well have some dinner sherry; but not *picturs,* they're too dear.

If he won't stand it. Take my ticker[5] and such of your things as you can *spare,* and send them to Balls—we must, of coarse, have the sum to-night. It won't do to let it stand over, as to-morrow's Sunday; the beds here are not very *clean,* and there may be other things[6] out against me—I'm glad it an't Rawdon's Saturday for coming home.[7] God bless you.
                                   Yours in haste, R.C.
PS.—Make haste and come.

This letter, sealed with a wafer, was dispatched by one of the messengers who are always hanging about Mr. Moss's establishment; and Rawdon, having seen him depart, went out in the court-yard, and smoked his cigar with a tolerably easy mind—in spite of the bars overhead; for Mr. Moss's courtyard is railed in like a cage, lest the gentlemen who are boarding with him should take a fancy to escape from his hospitality.

Three hours, he calculated, would be the utmost time required, before Becky should arrive and open his prison doors: and he passed these pretty cheerfully in smoking, in reading the paper, and in the coffee-room with an acquaintance, Captain Walker, who happened to be there, and with whom he cut for sixpences for some hours, with pretty equal luck on either side.

But the day passed away and no messenger returned,—no Becky. Mr. Moss's tably-de-hoty was served at the appointed hour of half-past five, when such of the gentlemen lodging in the house as could afford to pay for the banquet, came and partook of it in the splendid front parlour before described, and with which Mr. Crawley's temporary lodging communicated, when Miss M. (Miss Hem, as her papa called her) appeared without the curl-papers of the morning, and Mrs. Hem did the honours of a prime boiled leg of mutton and turnips, of which the colonel ate with a very faint appetite. Asked whether he would "stand" a bottle of champagne for the company, he consented, and the ladies drank to his 'ealth, and Mr. Moss, in the most polite manner "looked towards him."

In the midst of this repast, however, the door-bell was heard,—young Moss of the ruddy hair, rose up with the keys and answered the sum-

---

[1]A tavern where persons arrested for debt were kept by a bailiff before being lodged in prison, so that their friends might have the opportunity to settle their debts for them.

[2]Rawdon, it will be noted, though a gentleman, is only half educated.

[3]I.e., a portable writing-desk.

[4](He means *clothes.*)

[5]I.e., watch.

[6]I.e., other debts.

[7]From where he is boarding.

mons, and coming back, told the colonel that the messenger had returned with a bag, a desk and a letter, which he gave him. "No ceremony, colonel, I beg," said Mrs. Moss, with a wave of her hand, and he opened the letter rather tremulously.—It was a beautiful letter, highly scented, on a pink paper, and with a light green seal.

MON PAUVRE CHER PETIT[8] (Mrs. Crawley wrote), I could not sleep *one wink* for thinking of what had become of *my odious old monstre:*[9] and only got to rest in the morning after sending for Mr. Blench (for I was in a fever), who gave me a composing draught and left orders with Finette that I should be disturbed *on no account.* So that my poor old man's messenger, who had *bien mauvaise mine,*[10] Finette says, and *sentait le genièvre,*[11] remained in the hall for some hours waiting my bell. You may fancy my state when I read your poor dear old ill-spelt letter.

Ill as I was, I instantly called for the carriage, and as soon as I was dressed (though I couldn't drink a drop of chocolate—I assure you I couldn't without my *monstre* to bring it to me), I drove *ventre à terre*[12] to Nathan's. I saw him— I wept—I cried—I fell at his odious knees. Nothing would mollify the horrid man. He would have all the money, he said, or keep my poor *monstre* in prison. I drove home with the intention of paying that *triste visite chez mon oncle*[13] (when every trinket I have should be at your disposal though they would not fetch a hundred pounds, for some, you know, are with *ce cher oncle*[14] already), and found Milor there with the Bulgarian old sheep-faced monster, who had come to compliment me upon last night's performances. Paddington came in, too, drawling and lisping and twiddling his hair; so did Champignac, and his chef—everybody with *foison*[15] of compliments and pretty speeches—plaguing poor me, who longed to be rid of them, and was thinking *every moment of the time of mon pauvre prisonnier.*[16]

When they were gone, I went down on my knees to Milor; told him we were going to pawn everything, and begged and prayed him to give me two hundred pounds. He pish'd and psha'd in a fury—told me not to be such a fool as to pawn

—and said he would see whether he could lend me the money. At last he went away, promising that he would send it me in the morning: when I will bring it to my poor old monster with a kiss from his affectionate

BECKY.

I am writing in bed. Oh, I have such a headache and such a heartache!

When Rawdon read over this letter, he turned so red and looked so savage that the company at the table d'hôte easily perceived that bad news had reached him. All his suspicions, which he had been trying to banish, returned upon him. She could not even go out and sell her trinkets to free him. She could laugh and talk about compliments paid to her, whilst he was in prison. Who had put him there? Wenham had walked with him. Was there . . . He could hardly bear to think of what he suspected. Leaving the room hurriedly, he ran into his own—opened his desk, wrote two hurried lines, which he directed to Sir Pitt[17] or Lady Crawley, and bade the messenger carry them at once to Gaunt Street, bidding him to take a cab, and promising him a guinea if he was back in an hour.

In the note he besought his dear brother and sister, for the sake of God; for the sake of his dear child and his honour; to come to him and relieve him from his difficulty. He was in prison: he wanted a hundred pounds to set him free—he entreated them to come to him.

He went back to the dining-room after dispatching his messenger, and called for more wine. He laughed and talked with a strange boisterousness, as the people thought. Sometimes he laughed madly at his own fears, and went on drinking for an hour; listening all the while for the carriage which was to bring his fate back.

At the expiration of that time, wheels were heard whirling up to the gate—the young janitor went out with his gate-keys. It was a lady whom he let in at the bailiff's door.

"Colonel Crawley," she said, trembling very much. He with a knowing look, locked the outer door upon her—then unlocked and opened the inner one, and calling out, "Colonel, you're

[8]My poor little dear. (Becky affectedly peppers her letters with French.)
[9]Monster.
[10]A wicked enough face.
[11]Smelled of gin.
[12]In a mad rush.

[13]Sad visit to my uncle's. (*Uncle* is still a euphemism for *pawnbroker.*)
[14]That dear uncle.
[15]Plenty.
[16]My poor prisoner.
[17]Rawdon's elder brother.

wanted," led her into the back parlour, which he occupied.

Rawdon came in from the dining-parlour where all those people were carousing, into his back-room; a flare of coarse light following him into the apartment where the lady stood, still very nervous.

"It is I, Rawdon," she said, in a timid voice, which she strove to render cheerful. "It is Jane." Rawdon was quite overcome by that kind voice and presence. He ran up to her—caught her in his arms—gasped out some inarticulate words of thanks, and fairly sobbed on her shoulder. She did not know the cause of his emotion.

The bills of Mr. Moss were quickly settled, perhaps to the disappointment of that gentleman, who had counted on having the colonel as his guest over Sunday at least; and Jane, with beaming smiles and happiness in her eyes, carried away Rawdon from the bailiff's house, and they went homewards in the cab in which she had hastened to his release. "Pitt was gone to a Parliamentary dinner," she said, "when Rawdon's note came, and so, dear Rawdon, I—I came myself," and she put her kind hand in his. Perhaps it was well for Rawdon Crawley that Pitt was away at that dinner. Rawdon thanked his sister a hundred times, and with an ardour of gratitude which touched and almost alarmed that soft-hearted woman. "Oh," said he, in his rude, artless way, "you— you don't know how I'm changed since I've known you, and—and little Rawdy. I—I'd like to change somehow. You see I want—I want—to be ——."—He did not finish the sentence, but she could interpret it. And that night after he left her, and as she sat by her own little boy's bed, she prayed humbly for that poor wayworn sinner.

Rawdon left her and walked home rapidly. It was nine o'clock at night. He ran across the streets, and the great squares of Vanity Fair, and at length came up breathless opposite his own house. He started back and fell against the railings, trembling as he looked up. The drawing-room windows were blazing with light. She had said that she was in bed and ill. He stood there for some time, the light from the rooms on his pale face.

He took out his door-key and let himself into the house. He could hear laughter in the upper rooms. He was in the ball-dress in which he had been captured the night before. He went silently up the stairs; leaning against the banisters at the stair-head.—Nobody was stirring in the house besides—all the servants had been sent away. Rawdon heard laughter within—laughter and singing. Becky was singing a snatch of the song of the night before; a hoarse voice shouted, "Brava! Brava!"—it was Lord Steyne's.

Rawdon opened the door and went in. A little table with a dinner was laid out—and wine and plate. Steyne was hanging over the sofa on which Becky sat. The wretched woman was in a brilliant full toilette, her arms and all her fingers sparkling with bracelets and rings; and the brilliants on her breast which Steyne had given her. He had her hand in his, and was bowing over it to kiss it, when Becky started up with a faint scream as she caught sight of Rawdon's white face. At the next instant she tried a smile, a horrid smile, as if to welcome her husband: and Steyne rose up, grinding his teeth, pale, and with fury in his looks.

He, too, attempted a laugh—and came forward holding out his hand. "What, come back! How d'ye do, Crawley?" he said, the nerves of his mouth twitching as he tried to grin at the intruder.

There was that in Rawdon's face which caused Becky to fling herself before him. "I am innocent, Rawdon," she said; "before God I am innocent." She clung hold of his coat, of his hands; her own were all covered with serpents, and rings, and baubles. "I am innocent.—Say I am innocent," she said to Lord Steyne.

He thought a trap had been laid for him, and was as furious with the wife as with the husband. "You innocent! Damn you," he screamed out. "You innocent! Why, every trinket you have on your body is paid for by me. I have given you thousands of pounds which this fellow has spent, and for which he has sold you. Innocent, by——! You're as innocent as your mother, the ballet-girl,[18] and your husband the bully. Don't think to frighten me as you have done others. Make way, sir, and let me pass," and Lord Steyne seized up his hat, and, with flame in his eyes, and looking his enemy fiercely in the face, marched upon him, never for a moment doubting that the other would give way.

But Rawdon Crawley springing out, seized him by the neckcloth, until Steyne, almost strangled, writhed, and bent under his arm. "You lie, you dog!" said Rawdon. "You lie, you coward and villain!" And he struck the peer twice over the face with his open hand, and flung him bleeding to the ground. It was all done before Rebecca

---

[18]Becky's mother, a Frenchwoman, had been a ballet dancer.

could interpose. She stood there trembling before him. She admired her husband, strong, brave, and victorious.

"Come here," he said.—She came up at once.

"Take off those things."—She began, trembling, pulling the jewels from her arms, and the rings from her shaking fingers, and held them all in a heap, quivering and looking up at him. "Throw them down," he said, and she dropped them. He tore the diamond ornament out of her breast, and flung it at Lord Steyne. It cut him on his bald forehead. Steyne wore the scar to his dying day.

"Come upstairs," Rawdon said to his wife. "Don't kill me, Rawdon," she said. He laughed savagely.—"I want to see if that man lies about the money as he has about me. Has he given you any?"

"No," said Rebecca, "that is——"

"Give me your keys," Rawdon answered, and they went out together.

Rebecca gave him all the keys but one: and she was in hopes that he would not have remarked the absence of that. It belonged to the little desk which Amelia had given her in early days, and which she kept in a secret place. But Rawdon flung open boxes and wardrobes, throwing the multifarious trumpery of their contents here and there, and at last he found the desk. The woman was forced to open it. It contained papers, love-letters many years old—all sorts of small trinkets and woman's memoranda. And it contained a pocketbook with bank-notes. Some of these were dated ten years back, too, and one was quite a fresh one—a note for a thousand pounds which Lord Steyne had given her.

"Did he give you this?" Rawdon said.

"Yes," Rebecca answered.

"I'll send it to him to-day," Rawdon said (for day had dawned again, and many hours had passed in this search), "and I will pay Briggs, who was kind to the boy, and some of the debts. You will let me know where I shall send the rest to you. You might have spared me a hundred pounds, Becky, out of all this—I have always shared with you."

"I am innocent," said Becky. And he left her without another word.

In this climactic chapter from *Vanity Fair*—climactic because after this chapter begins Becky's decline, step by step, from bright glory—we see three of the principals revealing themselves by what they do. To take their actions in the order in which they occur: Rawdon, so doting on Becky that he will not disturb her night's rest, waiting till morning to write for help; apologizing for not being home to bring her morning coffee; still optimistic, making light of his difficulties; standing treat, despite his debts, for a bottle of champagne "for the company." Becky being her hypocritical self in her affected letter with its unseasonable gaiety, egocentricity, and patronizing kindness. Rawdon, after reading the letter, becoming rash, wildly boisterous, calling for more wine. Steyne summoning urbanity on Rawdon's unexpected appearance. Becky swiftly reading her husband's thoughts and at once trying to save herself. Steyne cynically interpreting the situation now as a trap, turning furiously on Becky with an account of his gifts to her. Rawdon reacting in the only way he knows, with his open hand; violently returning Steyne's gifts and ransacking Becky's effects; insisting for honor's sake on sending Steyne his money back, yet taking another portion of Becky's ill-gotten money to settle his debts; sentimentally recriminating Becky before he leaves. This chapter even when read by itself tells the reader volumes about these three as they act and react.

In our two short stories we find character also revealed in action. "Father" avoiding his wife's questions about the digging, refusing to justify the building of the new barn; "Mother" recovering from her anger with her dishwashing, defending "Father" to their daughter, conscientiously making her mince pies, passionately pointing out the bare floor and dirty wallpaper to "Father," flinging open the doors to their tiny bedroom and cramped pantry for him to inspect. "Father" still refusing to respond; stubbornly priding himself on the new barn as it is a-building. "Mother" unwilling to commit herself to seeing the cows and the hay placed in the barn, stopping the men from pitching the hay in the barn, emptying the house of its furnishings into the barn, standing up to the minister and routing him, ordering the new cows put in the old barn. "Father" looking around dismayed on finding the house locked on his return. "Mother" helping him wash up before dinner in their new quarters. "Father" weeping, as he at last understands. "Mother" putting up her apron to her face, "overcome by her own triumph."

In the other story: The husband's relatives eating and shouting. The wife sitting timidly in the corner. The husband becoming angry with the others, bringing his wife to their new home. The wife tending contentedly to her household tasks, finding happiness in her first pregnancy, delighted at being in her parents' house for a visit. The husband giving his family his best attention, trying to teach his wife to read and to interest her in his thoughts. Fatima arriving at the house; keeping her distance from them at first; speaking up for the wife at the water tap, coming to help their sick child, mocking the husband's interest in her. The husband coming home earlier now; waiting for Fatima to appear. Fatima playing with the children; including the husband in their games, sitting beside him looking out the window, listening to his talk. The wife miserably trying to obliterate herself in their presence, spying through a crack in Fatima's door at her husband's unfaithfulness, bearing the brunt of the neighbors' knowledge of the affair, running off with her children to her mother-in-law's house, finding no sympathy there, returning in sorrow to her own home, pathetically attempting to please her husband with his favorite food and a fresh garland. All of them waiting, at the end, for Fatima to reappear.

Whatever stand we take upon plot (i.e., for a complete or incomplete ending), this much is clear: action is the soul of storytelling; and in the best fiction character reveals itself in the action of the story. It is, indeed, the best way in which character can be revealed in fiction or drama. Character description has been proved in the modern novel to be largely superfluous. Dialogue, too, as the chapters from *Pride and Prejudice* demonstrate, must further the action of the story while it helps depict character. This emphasis on the action everywhere in the novel was a cardinal principle with the great American novelist and short story writer Henry James. "Don't state . . .—render! Don't tell us what is happening, let it happen."*

DESCRIPTION

It will also have been noticed that in both short stories and in each of the excerpts from novels there are passages of description.

Description as such is like the little girl with the curl right in the middle of her forehead: when it is good, it can be very very good, and when it is bad it is horrid.

We are all familiar with descriptive writing such as this, from a report in a daily paper:

> Escorted by her father, the bride wore a gown of white peau de soie, fashioned with a fitted bodice with a square neckline and long sleeves, and a full skirt terminating in a chapel-length train. Her veil of heirloom lace was arranged in mantilla fashion, and she carried a prayer book with calla lilies.†

Here description is an end in itself. With the exception of the touch of the prayer book, which may or may not indicate the piety of the bride, no other purpose is served in the account than to itemize the things the bride wore. The effect would be the same if a dressmaker's dummy had been inside of them. We know no more about the bride or her marriage when we have read the paragraph, than if it had never been written. This kind of empty, purposeless description is writing at its worst.

But description can also exhibit writing at its best. Very often the most unforgettable moments of a novel or story may be those in which the author has by powerful description

---

*"So I would translate Henry James," says Allen Tate, "Techniques of Fiction," from *On the Limits of Poetry* (New York, 1948), p. 140.

†From *The New York Times,* June 8, 1958.

brought the scene before our senses. Such is the superb passage we quote from George Meredith's novel *The Ordeal of Richard Feverel.*

Young Richard Feverel, whose father, Sir Austin Feverel, had raised the motherless boy according to his own very special system, blighted Sir Austin's hopes by secretly marrying Lucy, niece to a neighboring farmer. The father, more embittered by Richard's secrecy than by the love match itself, was too proud to attempt reconciliation with his son. On the Isle of Wight the newlyweds became acquainted with the corrupt Lord Mountfalcon and his sophisticated friends. Totally inexperienced, Richard asks Mountfalcon to keep guard over Lucy during his absence while he himself goes to London to win back his father's favor. Mountfalcon, with his own designs on Lucy, bribes an adventuress in London to ensnare the guileless Richard in her wiles. Richard succumbs; while he is philandering in the metropolis, Mountfalcon is trying to seduce Lucy. When at length Sir Austin, yearning to see his son again, agrees to the meeting, he still refuses to accept Lucy as his daughter-in-law. Awakened to shame at his own inconstancy, Richard is cast down by remorse, and feels unfit to face his wife. (Unknown to him, she has been brought by a kind woman friend of theirs back to Kensington to live with her.) Richard, tortured in mind, goes to the Continent, wandering about aimlessly. It is there that he learns that Lucy, during his absence, has borne him a child.

The moon was surpassingly bright, the summer air heavy and still. He left the high road and pierced into the forest. His walk was rapid; the leaves on the trees brushed his cheeks, the dead leaves heaped in the dells noised to his feet. Something of a religious joy—a strange sacred pleasure —was in him. By degrees it wore; he remembered himself; and now he was possessed by a proportionate anguish. A father! he dared never see his child. And he had no longer his phantasies to fall upon. He was utterly bare to his sin. In his troubled mind it seemed to him that Clare[1] looked down upon him—Clare who saw him as he was —and that to her eyes it would be infamy for him to go and print his kiss upon his child. Then came stern efforts to command his misery and make the nerves of his face iron.

By the log of an ancient tree half buried in dead leaves of past summers, beside a brook, he halted as one who had reached his journey's end. There he discovered that he had a companion in Lady Judith's little dog. He gave the friendly animal a pat of recognition, and both were silent in the forest silence.

It was impossible for Richard to return; his heart was surcharged. He must advance, and on he footed, the little dog following.

An oppressive slumber hung about the forest-branches. In the dells and on the heights was the same dead heat. Here where the brook tinkled it was no cool-lipped sound, but metallic, and with-out the spirit of water. Yonder in a space of moonlight on lush grass, the beams were as white fire to sight and feeling. No haze spread around. The valleys were clear, defined to the shadow of their verges; the distances sharply distinct, and with the colours of day but slightly softened. Richard beheld a roe moving across a slope of sward far out of rifle mark. The breathless silence was significant, yet the moon shone in a broad blue heaven. Tongue out of mouth trotted the little dog after him; couched panting when he stopped an instant; rose wearily when he started afresh. Now and then a large white night-moth flitted through the dusk of the forest.

On a barren corner of the wooded highland looking inland stood grey topless ruins set in nettles and rank grass-blades. Richard mechanically sat down on the crumbling flints to rest, and listened to the panting of the dog. Sprinkled at his feet were emerald lights; hundreds of glow-worms studded the dark dry ground.

He sat and eyed them, thinking not at all. His energies were expended in action. He sat as a part of the ruins, and the moon turned his shadow Westward from the South. Overhead, as she declined, long ripples of silver cloud were imperceptibly stealing toward her. They were the van of a tempest. He did not observe them, or the leaves beginning to chatter. When he again pursued his course with his face to the Rhine, a huge mountain appeared to rise sheer over him, and he had

---

[1]Richard's cousin, who adored him, and once dreamed of being his bride. After he fell in love with Lucy, and Clare found herself forgotten, she married on older man, and soon died brokenhearted.

it in his mind to scale it. He got no nearer to the base of it for all his vigorous out-stepping. The ground began to dip; he lost sight of the sky. Then heavy thunder-drops struck his cheek, the leaves were singing, the earth breathed, it was black before him and behind. All at once the thunder spoke. The mountain he had marked was bursting over him.

Up started the whole forest in violet fire. He saw the country at the foot of the hills to the bounding Rhine gleam, quiver, extinguished. Then there were pauses; and the lightning seemed as the eye of heaven, and the thunder as the tongue of heaven, each alternately addressing him; filling him with awful rapture. Alone there —sole human creature among the grandeurs and mysteries of storm—he felt the representative of his kind, and his spirit rose, and marched, and exulted, let it be glory, let it be ruin! Lower down the lightened abysses of air rolled the wrathful crash; then white thrusts of light were darted from the sky, and great curving ferns, seen steadfast in pallor a second, were supernaturally agitated, and vanished. Then a shrill song roused in the leaves and the herbage. Prolonged and louder it sounded, as deeper and heavier the deluge pressed. A mighty force of water satisfied the desire of the earth. Even in this, drenched as he was by the first outpouring, Richard had a savage pleasure; keeping in motion he was scarcely conscious of the wet, and the grateful breath of the weeds was refreshing. Suddenly he stopped short, lifting a curious nostril. He fancied he smelt meadow sweet. He had never seen the flower in Rhineland—never thought of it; and it would hardly be met with in a forest. He was sure he smelt it fresh in dews. His little companion wagged a miserable wet tail some way in advance. He went on slowly, thinking indistinctly. After two or three steps he stopped and stretched out his hand to feel for the flower, having, he knew not why, a strong wish to verify its growth there. Groping about his hand encountered something warm that started at his touch, and he, with the instinct we have, seized it, and lifted it to look at it. The creature was very small, evidently quite young. Richard's eyes, now accustomed to the darkness, were able to discern it for what it was, a tiny leveret,[2] and he supposed that the dog had probably frightened its dam[3] just before he found it. He put the little thing on one hand in his breast, and stepped out rapidly as before.

The rain was now steady; from every tree a fountain poured. So cool and easy had his mind become that he was speculating on what kind of shelter the birds could find, and how the butterflies and moths saved their coloured wings from washing. Folded close they might hang under a leaf, he thought. Lovingly he looked into the dripping darkness of the coverts on each side, as one of their children. Then he was musing on a strange sensation he experienced. It ran up one arm with an indescribable thrill, but communicated nothing to his heart. It was purely physical, ceased for a time, and recommenced, till he had it all through his blood, wonderfully thrilling. He grew aware that the little thing he carried in his breast was licking his hand there. The small rough tongue going over and over the palm of his hand produced this strange sensation he felt. Now that he knew the cause, the marvel ended; but now that he knew the cause, his heart was touched, and made more of it. The gentle scraping continued without intermission as on he walked. What did it say to him? Human tongue could not have said so much just then.

A pale grey light on the skirts of the flying tempest displayed the dawn. Richard was walking hurriedly. The green drenched weeds lay all about in his path, bent thick, and the forest drooped glimmeringly. Impelled as a man who feels a revelation mounting obscurely to his brain, Richard was passing one of those little forest chapels, hung with votive wreaths, where the peasant halts to kneel and pray. Cold, still, in the twilight it stood, rain-drops pattering round it. He looked within, and saw the Virgin holding her Child. He moved by. But not many steps had he gone ere his strength went out of him, and he shuddered. What was it? He asked not. He was in other hands. Vivid as lightning the Spirit of Life illumined him. He felt in his heart the cry of his child, his darling's touch. With shut eyes he saw them both. They drew him from the depths; they led him, a blind and tottering man. And as they led him he had a sense of purification so sweet he shuddered again and again.

When he looked out from his trance on the breathing world, the small birds hopped and chirped; warm fresh sunlight was over all the hills. He was on the edge of the forest, entering a plain clothed with ripe corn under a spacious morning sky.

[2]Young hare.   [3]Mother.

Unlike the description of the bride's dress, writing which is purely static, here everything moves—in both senses of the word. Not only does the landscape alter with Richard's advance, but what he sees and hears, as he traverses it, also find an important echo in his tumultuous breast. As we proceed along his path, we participate in the great catharsis he is undergoing; for this landscape is more than a setting for his emotional strife, it is part of it. Such description serves important artistic ends: it furthers the progress of the story and entwines itself in the threads of a character's inner life. It is description of the kind which, even when found among notable pages, is likely to remain engraved upon our memories. Charged with meaning, the language is concrete throughout—now denotative, now connotative—with a rapid rush of brilliant imagery that overwhelms the senses as we read. We are, in short, *there* with Richard.

Significant bits of description are not wanting, either, in our two short stories. In one: the brief pictures of the New England farmyard, of the small house juxtaposed to the "long reach of sheds and out-buildings," of the neighbors admiring the new barn, of "Father" dressed in Sunday best for his trip, of his wife's face as she comes to her great decision. In the other: of the wife's childhood home, of her mother-in-law's household, of her new home, of dangerous Fatima, of the waiting for the husband's late return, of the early morning streets after the wife's retreat from her mother-in-law's. Not one of these was written for description's sake alone. Every one of them intensifies the story, its mood, and its meaning.

Its meaning? That, of course, is in all works of art impossible to analyze into all its component parts, if only because the meaning of a created work is involved in the synthesis of those parts. To the meaning of a story the theme, the action or plot, the characters, their motives—all contribute; the meaning itself emanates from these no more, however, than it does from the way these are presented. The shape of the work, just as it clearly does in sculpture, ultimately delivers the meaning of any piece of literature. Change the shape and you change the meaning; add or subtract a detail and you add to or subtract from the meaning; bungle a passage and you becloud the meaning. Descriptions which can move us powerfully, therefore, become an integral part of the meaning of a work, quite as much as any other component part of the whole.

THEME

We ought to say a word again about theme, the central or pervading idea (or ideas) of a work. When a writer selects his material, he does so because he feels it contains a theme with which he can illuminate or elucidate a vision of human experience; the theme must, as one of our gifted novelists reminds us, "respond in some way to that mysterious need of a judgment on life of which the most detached human intellect, provided it be a normal one, cannot, apparently, rid itself."* A story without that "judgment on life"—even though that judgment can be only part of the total meaning—is sure to be meaningless, to partake of Chaos itself. Even when we are forced to disagree with that judgment of the writer, we are enriched by the experience, for our own vision and our spiritual sympathies are enlarged. The judgment itself is his illumination or elucidation of human experience. It is why he writes his story and why we listen to him.

It is not to be inferred that this judgment necessarily involves his leaving us with a copybook moral—such as "And *that* goes to show that a stitch in time saves nine!" There are, however, stories that are written primarily, if not only, for the moral: the parable (a story from the simple incidents of which a moral truth is to be drawn) and the fable (a story from the simple incidents of which a useful truth is to be drawn). Such can be engrossing enough as story if there is a wonderful appropriateness in the incidents to the idea represented— as in Christ's parable of the laborers in the vineyard:

*Edith Wharton, *The Writing of Fiction* (London, 1925), p. 27.

For the kingdom of heaven is like unto a man that is a householder, which went out early in the morning to hire laborers into his vineyard. And when he had agreed with the laborers for a penny a day, he sent them into his vineyard.

And he went out about the third hour, and saw others standing idle in the marketplace, and said unto them: "Go ye also into the vineyard, and whatsoever is right I will give you." And they went their way.

Again he went out about the sixth and ninth hour, and did likewise. And about the eleventh hour he went out, and found others standing idle, and saith unto them, "Why stand ye here all the day idle?" They say unto him, "Because no man hath hired us." He saith unto them, "Go ye also unto the vineyard; and whatsoever is right, that shall ye receive."

So when even was come, the lord of the vineyard saith unto his steward, "Call the laborers, and give them their hire, beginning from the last unto the first." And when they came that were hired about the eleventh hour, they received every man a penny. But when the first came, they supposed that they should have received more; and they likewise received every man a penny. And when they had received it, they murmured against the goodman of the house, saying, "These last have wrought but one hour, and thou hast made them equal unto us, which have borne the burden and heat of the day."

But he answered one of them, and said, "Friend, I do thee no wrong: didst not thou agree with me for a penny? Take that thine is, and go thy way: I will give unto this last, even as unto thee. Is it not lawful for me to do what I will with mine own? Is thine eye evil, because I am good?"

So the last shall be first, and the first last: for many be called, but few chosen.*

Or, a story with an obvious moral can be diverting because it is composed with humor or wit—as in an amusing skit, "Fame and the Poet" by Lord Dunsany (1878–1957).

The Poet, having devoted his years to worshipping at the altar of Fame, at which he has offered all his creations without reward or recognition, has just completed his best work, a sonnet. But now he feels that his life has in fact been wasted in pursuit of illusion, for a Fame he shall never see. He decides to give up his career; and is just about to burn all his work, when suddenly Fame herself—in Greek dress, with a long golden trumpet in hand —stands before him. "Divine fair lady!" he exclaims in awe, "you have come!" Reverently he offers her his latest achievement, the sonnet:

POET. This is my sonnet. Is it well done?

[*Fame takes it, reads it in silence, while the Poet watches rapturously.*]

FAME. You're a bit of all right.

POET. What?

FAME. Some poet.

POET. I—I—scarcely . . . understand.

FAME. You're IT.

POET. But . . . it is not possible . . . are you she that knew Homer?

FAME. Homer? Lord, yes. Blind old bat, 'e couldn't see a yard.

[*Fame walks beautifully to the window. She opens it and puts her head out.*]

FAME [*in a voice with which a woman in an upper story would cry for help if the house was well alight*]. Hi! Hi! Boys! Hi! Say, folks! Hi!

[*The murmur of a gathering crowd is heard. Fame blows her trumpet.*]

FAME. Hi, he's a poet. [*Quickly, over her shoulder*] What's your name?

POET. De Reves.[1]

FAME. His name's de Reves.

POET. Harry de Reves.

FAME. His pals call him Harry.

THE CROWD. Hooray! Hooray! Hooray!

FAME. Say, what's your favorite color?

POET. I . . . I . . . I don't quite understand.

FAME. Well, which do you like best, green or blue?

POET. Oh—er—blue. [*She blows her trumpet out of the window.*] No—er—I think green.

FAME. Green is his favorite color.

THE CROWD. Hooray! Hooray! Hooray!

FAME. 'Ere, tell us something. They want to know all about yer.

POET. Wouldn't you perhaps . . . would they care to hear my sonnet, if you would—er . . .

FAME [*picking up quill*]. Here, what's this?

POET. Oh, that's my pen.

FAME [*after another blast on her trumpet*]. He writes with a quill.

[*Cheers from The Crowd*]

*Matthew 20:1–16.

[1]Literally, *of dreams* (French).

FAME [*going to a cupboard*]. Here, what have you got in here?

POET. Oh ... er ... those are my breakfast things.

FAME [*finding a dirty plate*]. What have yer had on this one?

POET [*mournfully*]. Oh, eggs and bacon.

FAME [*at the window*]. He has eggs and bacon for breakfast.

THE CROWD. Hip hip hip *hooray!* Hip hip hip *hooray!* Hip hip hip *hooray!*

FAME. Hi, and what's this?

POET [*miserably*]. Oh, a golf stick.

FAME. He's a man's man! He's a virile man! He's a manly man!

[*Wild cheers from The Crowd, this time only from women's voices*]

POET. Oh, this is terrible. This is terrible. This is terrible.

[*Fame gives another peal on her horn. She is about to speak.*]

POET [*solemnly and mournfully*]. One moment, one moment ...

FAME. Well, out with it.

POET. For ten years, divine lady, I have worshipped you, offering all my songs ... I find ... I find I am not worthy ...

FAME. Oh, you're all right.

POET. No, no, I am not worthy. It cannot be. It cannot possibly be. Others deserve you more. I must say it! *I cannot possibly love you.* Others are worthy. You will find others. But I, no, no, no. It cannot be. It cannot be. Oh, pardon me, but it *must* not.

[*Meanwhile Fame has been lighting one of his cigarettes. She sits in a comfortable chair, leans right back, and puts her feet right up on the table amongst the poet's papers.*]

POET. Oh, I fear I offend you. But—it cannot be.

FAME. Oh, that's all right, old bird; no offence. I ain't going to leave you.

POET. But—but—but—I do not understand.

FAME. I've come to stay, I have.

[*She blows a puff of smoke through her trumpet.*]

[*Curtain*]*

The drollery of this piece excuses the obviousness of its moral. But such works are exceptions, something in the nature of curiosities. Few works of literature point so transparently to a moral. Shakespeare did not write *King Lear* "to show that you should be kind to your father." Nor did Oscar Wilde, as one student's report had it, write *Salomé* "to show that people shouldn't go around beheading prophets." That is not the kind of "judgment on life" with which literature is concerned.

Nor is it to be inferred that making a judgment on life implies that stories are written to *illustrate* some concept in the mind of the author. E.g., Convinced that "crime doesn't pay," he invents a hero who, to help a widowed mother, robs a bank; the cashier sounds the alarm, the police arrive, our hero is killed in a gun battle. That procedure can only result in a work deadly mechanical and contrived; it is what makes propaganda fiction usually nauseating.

In determining what is the author's judgment on life in a given work, one is wiser first to isolate the theme or themes. A vast work like *King Lear* (like many less ambitious works of fiction and drama) has a number of themes; they will be found worked out in the various interrelationships of character: Goneril-Regan-Lear; Lear-Cordelia; Gloucester-Edgar; Kent-Lear; Goneril-Regan-Cornwall-Lear; Edmund-Edgar-Gloucester; Albany-Lear; Kent-the Fool-Lear. Some of the themes in *King Lear* are: despite great love and kindness of a parent, some children will respond only with barbarous cruelty and inhumanity (Goneril-Regan-Lear); despite unpardonable injustice of a parent, some children will respond only with loyalty and love (Lear-Cordelia, Gloucester-Edgar); true love will persist in the face of every deprivation and demand for self-sacrifice (Kent-the Fool-Lear); an ungovernable temper will cause a man to visit injustice on those whose love he has most reason to be sure of (Lear-Cordelia, Lear-Kent); alliances among the greedy and self-seeking are sure to be short-lived (Goneril-Regan-Edmund); to stand by silent while inhumanity is being meted out to a fellow-human being is to invite villainy on one's own head (Albany-Lear-Goneril). But

*From "Fame and the Poet," in the *Atlantic Monthly,* August, 1919.

King Lear pronounces no meaningless banalities such as: "Children are monsters"—for we remember Cordelia and Edgar; or "Virtue and loyalty are always rewarded"—for we remember the prices paid by Gloucester and Cordelia for their love and loyalty to Lear. No, Shakespeare has something vaster to say in his great tragedy. It is ourselves we view as he holds up the mirror of his art, and we become ashamed and also vastly proud of the human race as reflected in this great tragedy. We are ashamed of the depravity of which self-seekers are capable, of the inadequacy of even good people's efforts to repay love. And at the same time we are vastly proud of the capacity of those who love all to forgive all, to endure all, to remain loving and courageous despite direst personal hazard. Such were Shakespeare's judgments on life as revealed in this play.

In *Vanity Fair* Thackeray has studied that strange admixture of opposing qualities which are to be found in human nature: the stupidity and foolish injustice of which good people are capable; the arrant wickedness of which clever people who are aware of what they do can yet be guilty. In *The Ordeal of Richard Feverel* we witness the absurdity and fatality of trying to mold human nature according to any artificial system of education, no matter how high minded and well intentioned. The title of *Pride and Prejudice* indicates the subject on which Jane Austen was studying various themes as they operate in courtship and marriage relationships. The titles of "The Revolt of 'Mother' " and "Better than Dead" also point to the subject and theme, respectively, of those stories.

POINT OF VIEW

There remains an important matter to consider. It is a technical aspect of storytelling, of far more importance to the author than to the reader. To the former it is cardinal; the latter may be forced into an awareness of its exigencies only at times when the author falls short of them. The writer must carefully consider before he decides on the *point of view* from which (i.e., through whose eyes) the story is to be presented. Yet it is well that the reader too understand whose point of view is being advanced—particularly when that point of view is not the author's—else he may miss the meaning of what is being said. The author has five possible choices:

1. Telling the story in the third person. This enables the author to be omniscient, to be everywhere and anywhere he pleases, to interpret and explain. His characters can be unimpeded in time or place, for he can be at their side wherever they are. The chief limitation of this method is that it too easily tempts the author to step in between us and the characters to inform us about their inner life, when he should make that inner life reveal itself. This has been, in any case, the preferred method of most of the world's great novels and many of its best short stories. *Pride and Prejudice, Vanity Fair, Richard Feverel,* and "The Revolt of 'Mother' " are told in the third person.

At the opposite pole is

2. Telling the story in the first person. Here the fiction is that the principal character is telling his own story. This method has the great advantages of making the reader feel himself personally addressed, and of the resultant directness, immediacy and excitement involved in personal revelation. The chief limitation is that the narrator can tell us no more than he (as a character in the story) has seen, heard or experienced himself. He can be only at one place at a time; he cannot know what is going on behind the door while he is speaking to someone in the room with him. Also, despite its vividness, some readers profess to dislike this method for two reasons: they are repelled by the approach of being told personal intimacies in confidence and/or they think the method too "easy" a way out for the author. (The latter objection must be declared too easy a criterion. There is no "easy way" of writing well.) "Better than Dead" employs the first person narrator, as does a number of fine novels (e.g., Dickens' *David Copperfield*).

There are two possible combinations of these methods:

3. Telling the story through one of the minor characters, who acts as observer-reporter. The method has the advantage of allowing the narrator a certain freedom of movement in time and place as well as the opportunity to comment (method 1) and at the same time it has some directness and immediacy because of the narrator's use of the first person (method 2). Its limitations (as well as its advantages), though to a lesser degree, are those of both methods. Willa Cather's magnificent novelette *My Mortal Enemy* is told this way. So are many fine short stories (e.g., Poe's "The Fall of the House of Usher," Capote's "Children on Their Birthdays").

4. Telling the story as it was told to the narrator by someone else. This method enables the author to combine the first and second methods in another way. Although he cannot be personally present during the transactions of the story, he is free to comment on it and on the person who told him the story. The narrative itself can be told with all the advantages of the first person (since the author is presumably quoting the original teller), and yet kept in a certain perspective by being given to us once-removed. It was a favorite method of one of our greatest storytellers, Joseph Conrad; he makes us feel, as a critic has put it, as though we were in "a hall of mirrors." The method can be found in Conrad's fine novel *Lord Jim,* and in many of his short stories (e.g., "Youth").

The last method is a special modification of the first, and has been a favorite of certain modern authors:

5. Telling the story in the third person while the author refrains from being omniscient tells us nothing of what is happening inside the characters, and reports, as though he himself were an observer, only what physically happens and what actually is said. This method has the chief limitation of the first-person approach (method 2) but by being third person in the telling it can concentrate impartially on all the characters. Tending to an impersonal presentation of a succession of scenes, without a comment or an analysis from the author, the technique approaches the domain of drama. A good example is Crane's short story, "The Upturned Face."

One might, perhaps, identify a sixth method: in which the omniscient author, writing in the third person, rigidly adheres to the point of view of only one of the characters—telling the story, that is, only as it could have appeared to that character. This is a variation of the first method somewhat approaching the second. James's *The Beast in the Jungle* is a brilliant example of this technique, as is Aiken's "Silent Snow, Secret Snow."

It is also possible in a novel to vary the methods, using one technique here and another elsewhere in the same work. In Dickens' masterful *Bleak House,* for instance, the first person is used in some portions of the story, the third person in others.

Percy Lubbock, a distinguished British critic and novelist, argues* that the most important consideration for a novelist is to determine the best possible point of view from which to tell the story; for it is the point of view which in turn must determine the form of the story. It is via the point of view that what Allen Tate calls "the controlling intelligence"† behind the story must limit "the range and quality of the scene and the action."

DIFFERENCES BETWEEN THE SHORT STORY AND NOVEL

Thus far we have spoken of many matters common to short story and novel. We must now consider the differences between the two forms, differences upon which we have occasionally already touched. Considerations of space, unhappily, make it impossible to pursue here the procedure we have followed elsewhere in this book. We cannot print even one novel *in toto,* ask you to read it, and only then discuss its characteristics. Nor do we consider that

*In *The Craft of Fiction.*
†In "Techniques of Fiction" in *On the Limits of Poetry.*

the excerpts you have read can have given you more than (we trust) an appetite-whetting hint of what the entire novel is like. We are therefore going to append a brief but highly selected list culled from our own favorite English and American novels—we make no further claims than that they are among our favorites—in the hopes that if it is impossible to expect you to read a couple of them before you finish this chapter, you will hasten to do so afterwards.

A good writer probably feels that he has no choice, as he confronts his material, between a novel or a short story. The material itself perforce dictates one form or the other.

A theme which requires the gradual unfolding of character, its slow developing or deterioration from one state to another, obviously cannot be managed within the narrow confines of a short story, but demands the larger spaces and reaches of the novel. The same may be said of any theme in which it is important that the reader be aware of the steady passage of time. For the short story focuses on only one main event, and thereby achieves the chief source of its unity; a novel may contain a number of striking incidents, and these can be separated from one another by considerable lapses of time. The conversion of the new barn into a home is the central incident in "The Revolt of 'Mother' "; the wife's loss of her husband to Fatima is the chief event of "Better than Dead." In the larger setting of the novel, one such incident could have formed one of several striking incidents. On the other hand, it is hard to see how the chapter we have quoted from *Vanity Fair* could have been employed as the main incident in a short story; to give it meaning, we must have behind it Becky's long rise to social success and equally long deception, Rawdon's history of reckless irresponsibility and credulity, Lord Steyne's amused backing of Becky.

This concentration of the short story on one significant happening, not the actual number of pages required in composition, is the essential distinction between the two forms of fiction. Reduce the events of a good novel to an account of the bare essentials of the events which occur, and you have not a short story, only a dull synopsis—which is neither novel nor short story. Because the elaboration of one significant happening is the chief business of the short story it would be fair to say that the short story has the effect of being more concerned with situation and the novel has the effect of being more concerned with character. (The same distinction exists, as we shall see, between the one-act play and the full-length play.) We say "has the effect" because both forms must above all be concerned with action. If we are more aware of character in the novel than in the short story, the novelist has nonetheless the obligation of revealing character largely through action too. When one thinks of a character in a short story or a novel one has read it is almost impossible to do so without at the same time thinking of something that character has done.

Because the short story deals with one significant happening, it is also true that the short story more easily impresses us with a sense of its form than does the novel. Unity in the novel is a far more complicated matter, and depends upon a thousand aspects of consistency in tone, character development, subordination and elaboration of incidents. The unity of the novel is looser and larger.

There is, of course, no ideal length for a novel. Its success depends upon our not feeling at the end that it was too long. Far better that we should wish it had been longer! We choose our suggested readings, despite the differences in length, somewhat on such a criterion. *Vanity Fair,* for instance, seems to us not a page too long. Many short novels not on our list have seemed to us endless.

SUGGESTED READINGS IN THE ENGLISH AND AMERICAN NOVEL AND SHORT STORY

Jane Austen (1775–1817), *Emma; Pride and Prejudice; Sense and Sensibility*
Nathaniel Hawthorne (1804–1864), *The Scarlet Letter; The House of the Seven Gables;*
     "Rappaccini's Daughter"
William M. Thackeray (1811–1863), *Vanity Fair; Henry Esmond*

Charles Dickens (1812–1870), *Bleak House; Great Expectations; David Copperfield*
Emily Brontë (1818–1848), *Wuthering Heights*
Herman Melville (1819–1891), *Moby Dick*
George Meredith (1828–1909), *The Egoist; The Ordeal of Richard Feverel; Diana of the
    Crossways*
Walter Pater (1839–1894), *Marius the Epicurean*
Thomas Hardy (1840–1928), *Jude the Obscure; The Return of the Native*
Henry James (1843–1916), *The Turn of the Screw; Portrait of a Lady; Washington Square;
    The Spoils of Poynton; The Beast in the Jungle; The Lesson of the Master; The Real Thing*
Joseph Conrad (1857–1924), *Lord Jim; The Nigger of the Narcissus; Nostromo; Tales of
    Unrest; The Secret Sharer*
Edith Wharton (1862–1937), *Ethan Frome; The Age of Innocence; Mme. de Treymes*
Theodore Dreiser (1871–1945), *Sister Carrie*
Max Beerbohm (1872–1956), *Zuleika Dobson; Seven Men*
W. S. Maugham (1874–1965), *Of Human Bondage; The Moon and Sixpence*
Willa Cather (1876–1947), *A Lost Lady; My Mortal Enemy; Death Comes for the Archbishop;
    Youth and the Bright Medusa*
James Branch Cabell (1879–1958), *Jurgen; Figures of Earth*
E. M. Forster (1879–1970), *A Passage to India; Howard's End; Where Angels Fear to Tread;
    The Longest Journey*
Mary Webb (1881–1927), *Precious Bane*
Virginia Woolf (1882–1941), *Mrs. Dalloway; To the Lighthouse*
James Stephens (1882–1950), *The Crock of Gold; Deirdre; Demi-Gods*
James Joyce (1882–1941), *A Portrait of the Artist as a Young Man*
D. H. Lawrence (1885–1930), *Women in Love; Sons and Lovers*
Aldous Huxley (1894–1963), *Point Counter Point; Brave New World; Antic Hay; Those
    Barren Leaves*
Katherine Anne Porter (1894–), *Ship of Fools; Flowering Judas*
F. Scott Fitzgerald (1896–1940), *Tender Is the Night; The Great Gatsby*
Thornton Wilder (1897–), *The Bridge of San Luis Rey; The Eighth Day*
William Faulkner (1897–1962), *The Sound and the Fury; Light in August*
Ernest Hemingway (1899–1961), *A Farewell to Arms; The Old Man and the Sea*
Elizabeth Bowen (1899–1973), *The House in Paris*
Thomas Wolfe (1900–1938), *Look Homeward, Angel*
Evelyn Waugh (1903–1966), *A Handful of Dust; Brideshead Revisited; Decline and Fall*
Truman Capote (1924–), *Other Voices, Other Rooms; The Grass Harp*
Flannery O'Connor (1925–1964), *The Violent Bear It Away*

DRAMA

꩜ 6 ꩜

FAUST. *I have heard that great-bellied[1] women do long for some dainties or other: what is it, madam? tell me, and you shall have it.*

DUCHESS. *Thanks, good Master Doctor; and for[2] I see your courteous intent to please me, I will not hide from you the thing my heart desires; and were it now summer, as it is January and the dead time of winter, I would desire no better meat[3] than a dish of ripe grapes.*

FAUST. *Alas, madam, that's nothing! Mephistophilis, begone.*
[Exit Mephistophilis.]
Were it a greater thing than this, so it would content you, you should have it.
[Enter Mephistophilis with the grapes.]
Here they be, madam; wilt please you taste on them?

DUKE. *Believe me, Master Doctor, this makes me wonder above the rest,[4] that being the dead time of winter, and in the month of January, how you should come by these grapes.* *

THE VISUAL ELEMENT

TODAY, of course, if the Duchess had a yearning for grapes in January, she would need only to reach into her deep-freeze and take them out. But in Marlowe's time the miracle of grapes in January was so great as to require the assistance of the Devil. We can well imagine the delight and wonder of the Elizabethan audience at this moment of the play. To see grapes in January before one's very eyes! That told more of the Master Doctor's magic, for the power over which he had bartered away his immortal soul, than pages of speeches describing the marvels he could achieve. For one of the prime sources of energy in drama is in what drama permits us to *see.*

DRAMA IN THE THEATRE AND IN THE LIBRARY

A play worthy of the name is written to be presented in some sort of theatre with or without scenery, with or without lighting and sound effects, but always by actors who have come under the unifying control of a director, and always before an audience.[†] A great

---

[1]I.e., pregnant.

[2]Because.

[3]Food.

[4]I.e., of the wonders Faustus has performed for them.

*From *Doctor Faustus* by Christopher Marlowe.

[†]A certain number of poetical works have been cast into the semblance of drama—that is, in a succession of acts or scenes, the whole being arranged in speeches assigned to various characters—without any thought of their suitability to the stage (e.g., Shelley's *Prometheus Unbound,* Wordsworth's *The Borderers,* Byron's *Cain,* Browning's *Pippa Passes*). Such dramas, meant only to be read, and known therefore as *closet dramas,* are poems in dramatic form rather than true plays. It is no impeachment of their poetic worth to say this. There are few poems which can lay claim to the sublimities of Shelley's *Prometheus,* for instance. But for all that, mounting *Prometheus* would be an enterprise doomed to failure on the stage. Reading it is an important experience; in the theatre it would certainly be dull. It violates every fundamental law of drama, and there is nothing in it to maintain the interest of the eye (except in the undramatic way that a pageant does)—though it possesses everything for the eye of the imagination.

deal has been written and said in our time to remind us that a play is really not a play unless it is being seen in the theatre. To read a play, we are told, is as incomplete an experience as it would be to study a blueprint in lieu of looking at the building itself. We are reminded, too, that when a play is acted before us

1. The player can so modulate his voice as to give deeper and even special meaning to his lines;

2. The fact that we hear the lines spoken gives the illusion of perfect reality;

3. The coordinated movements and gestures of live people with the dialogue give new dimension to the lines, and sometimes afford diverting stage-pictures;

4. The stage setting, costumes and lighting may enhance the vividness of the drama and underscore its mood; and

5. Background music may intensify the emotional values of the work.

There is no denying that all this may be true under the ideal conditions of a perfect or near-perfect performance. But how often have we ourselves witnessed that kind of presentation? In a lifetime of assiduous theatregoing, about six. The fact is that the various elements that go into making a theatrical performance are so many and so complicated, the task of the conductor of a symphony orchestra is simple compared to that of the director of a play. Against the advantages abovementioned, it must in cold truth be counterstated:

1. The player is just as likely to miss the deeper meaning of a phrase and even give an utterly erroneous implication to a passage. For example, in the famous line in *Romeo and Juliet,* when Juliet speaks softly into the night:

> O Romeo, Romeo! wherefore art thou Romeo?

she means, "Why are you a Montague, the one family in Verona my family hates?" But the actress, possibly because she does not know that *wherefore* means *why,* often delivers the line:

> O Romeo, Romeo! wherefore ART thou, Romeo?

This means (particularly when, as usual, a comma is implied after *thou* by the speaker), "Why do you exist at all, Romeo?" Obviously Shakespeare's meaning requires that the line be read:

> O Romeo, Romeo! wherefore art thou ROMEO?

since the next line is:

> Deny thy father and refuse thy name!

and a little further Juliet murmurs:

> 'Tis but thy name that is my enemy.

This practice of rendering silly a serious line is but a passing example of what is always occurring, particularly in Shakespearean troupes, where the actors trouble themselves so little about the actual meaning of what they are saying, that they seem to be indulging in vocal exercises rather than giving a dramatic interpretation. In consequence the audience is either given a false impression of the author's intent or allowed to remain oblivious of any intent at all.

2. That we have in the threatre living people before us may have upon an audience the effect, not always fortunate, of forever identifying a character in a play with a particular actor. We ourselves find it necessary to exert our will to banish several Macbeths, Othellos, Iagos, Oedipuses, for instance—and many, many Hamlets—from our minds because they now intrude between us and the play.

3. The ineptness of a performance may render even the sublime ridiculous; under such conditions the author's meaning, instead of being enhanced, is murdered. Moreover, the misinterpretation of a skillful actor may forever distort the author's idea.*

4. Stage setting, costume, and lighting are indeed so powerful in their influence on the production that any one of them or all of them may dwarf the play itself.† Thus, many productions of Shakespeare degenerate into mere parades of period costumes, or a series of pretty or exciting stage pictures.

In Shakespeare's own theatre, the "effects" had to be communicated by the lines themselves. In the opening passage of Act Five of *The Merchant of Venice,* for instance, though the setting is presumed to be a moonlit garden in Belmont, the audience would actually have seen only a bare wooden stage lit by such light as a late London afternoon afforded (since the theatre, which was roofless, was unequipped with artificial lighting). In the modern theatre we could have a realistic moon painted on the backdrop, gigantic and romantic trees on the stage, a garden studded with flowers and laid out along charming paths, the cleverest of wind-machines gently rustling the leaves of the trees. As Lorenzo and Jessica enter, arm in arm, the most radiantly streaming moonbeams could be arranged to light upon Jessica's hair and rebound into Lorenzo's eyes. If necessary, someone (courtesy of Guerlain, Inc.) could with a spray-gun offstage be charging the air with perfume. Lacking any such mechanical effects, the Elizabethan dramatist had to create magic in the lines themselves. Let us listen to them:

> LORENZO. The moon shines bright: in such a night as this,
> When the sweet wind did gently kiss the trees
> And they did make no noise, in such a night
> Troilus methinks mounted the Troyan walls,
> And sighed his soul toward the Grecian tents,
> Where Cressid lay that night.
> JESSICA. In such a night
> Did Thisbe fearfully o'ertrip the dew,
> And saw the lion's shadow ere himself,
> And ran dismayed away. . . .
> LORENZO. How sweet the moonlight sleeps upon this bank!
> Here will we sit, and let the sounds of music
> Creep in our ears; soft stillness and the night
> Become the touches of sweet harmony.
> Sit, Jessica. Look how the floor of heaven
> Is thick inlaid with patines[1] of bright gold:
> There's not the smallest orb which thou behold'st
> But in his[2] motion like an angel sings,
> Still[3] quiring[4] to the young-eyed cherubins.   —V/i/1–9, 54–62

*If we may be permitted a brief sally into autobiography: When we were at high school we witnessed one of the celebrated *Hamlets* of our time. The brilliant actress who performed the role of Gertrude managed by a powerful interchange of looks with Claudius to communicate the idea that she had been a partner to her late husband's murder. Those looks remained so vividly engraved in our memory that it was another decade before we realized that in the play which Shakespeare wrote Gertrude was completely innocent of even the knowledge of the crime!

†A good example of this was a cinema version of *The Importance of Being Earnest* in which, despite an almost perfect cast of exceedingly gifted British actors, a heavily late-Victorian setting converted one of the most dazzling and timelessly sophisticated comedies in our language into a piece of faintly amusing "quaintness." In the desire to place the play in its period, the director overlooked the fact that the late Victorians were not quaint to themselves.

[1]Metal plates used to hold the bread in the Eucharist.

[2]Its.

[3]Always.

[4]Choiring.

It is hard to conceive how, when such lines are spoken on the stage, the most ingenious of mechanical resources can do other than render the imaginative appeal of their exquisite cadences quite pallid.

5. Background music on the stage is often insufficiently in the background. Actors find themselves shouting the lines in order to be heard over the music. If the music is poor, it injures the play. If it is good, a music-lover finds himself listening to the music instead of to the lines. (Music as background for a play is intolerable unless hardly audible.)

We have labored the point that witnessing a play is not necessarily more advantageous than reading it, only because there has been too much disparagement of the reading of plays. We agree, of course, that the test of any play is first of all its suitability to theatrical performance. On the other hand, in discussing the drama no one seems to have remembered that the test of any piece of literature as such is its effectiveness when read. It is a common occurrence that a play which ingeniously employs the mechanical resources of the modern theatre and which is therefore interesting to an audience in the theatre, becomes, as a piece of writing, beneath contempt when read in the leisure of the study. The reason in such cases is that the dramatic effects were often to be found written by the playwright in the stage directions and not in the lines themselves. A play, like any other literary form, is a piece of literature only if it can be *read* with pleasure.

The world's greatest plays, the history of drama demonstrates, are those which can be acted and also read with pleasure. And naturally, when we read such plays, we read them as if they were being acted before us. The visual and the auditory elements remain the most important ones as we read; we imagine the facial expressions of the speakers and of those spoken to, their significant movements and gestures; we hear the inflections and modulations of their voices. And having the time to linger over the printed page, we can arrange an ideal performance for ourselves.* These things we can do, of course, only in proportion to the play's suitability to the requirements of the theatre. A play without these requirements, no matter how literary, affords the imagination no materials with which to create a performance.

SEVERITY OF DRAMATIC FORM

Because plays are written for a theatre, they have perhaps more restrictions imposed upon them than any other form of literature. First of all, because plays are written to be enacted by live people they undertake to come closer to a sense of actual living than does any other form of writing. This fact results in a paradox. By cutting away a wall, the side of a ship, or the other side of the street, the theatre invites the audience to witness and overhear scenes of such intimacy and privacy as no outsider is ever privileged to see or hear; consequently, although plays are produced only because an audience is there to see and hear, drama usually pretends that no one other than the persons on the stage is present. We the audience are, at one and the same time, supposed to be there and not there. If we were there, moments of such intimacy and privacy could not take place; if we were not there, there would be no reason for a play.

Because plays are written for a theatre, they are subject to the tyranny of time. A so-called full-length play, unlike the novel or short story, must conform to certain well-established notions of length. A novel or a short story may be picked up and laid down at

*Charles Lamb went so far as to say that it is better to read *King Lear* than to see it acted. "The contemptible machinery by which they mimic the storm which he [Lear] goes out into, is not more inadequate," Lamb said, "to represent the horrors of the real elements than any actor can be to represent Lear; they might more easily propose to personate the Satan of Milton upon a stage, or one of Michelangelo's terrible figures." But this is less an indictment of the suitability of Shakespeare's tragedy to the boards than a reflection on the vast demands made by the play on the resources of actor, director and stage technician. On the contrary, we ourselves have been continually surprised at how magnificent that work can be in the theatre, often despite the best efforts of all those concerned in the production to destroy it.

the reader's pleasure; there is no limit placed upon the hours he may choose to spend reading it. But a play begins at a certain fixed hour and ends at a reasonable one (the curtain must not rise so early that the audience will have had to rush through their dinners, and the final curtain must not fall so late that the audience miss the last train for the suburbs!)—and this in itself is an extraordinary artifice. For in the theatre we pretend that a segment of life which is unfolded before us must not take more than some two and a half hours. A dramatist who ignored this requirement—unless he were either a classic or a celebrity—would soon find himself without audiences.

Because plays are written for a theatre, they must be so composed as to deliver their meaning, moment by moment, instantaneously. The novelist can, if he likes, manage his story with a certain amount of artistically conceived mystification: he can deliberately pretend to be casual about matters which later will turn out to have been of cardinal importance. For his reader is always free to turn back to an earlier page and reread what he is unsure of. The novelist can also spring with the suddenness of a cat, by some unforeseen revelation catching the reader off guard and sending him reeling. At such times the reader is free to allow the book to rest in his lap while he digests the import of what he has just read and reappraises what has gone before. In the theatre there can be no such turning back. Anything missed at any moment is forever lost. The audience cannot, during a performance, cry out: "Stop, please! Before the play proceeds would you mind doing the middle of the first act over again? We seem to have overlooked something." Nor can the dramatist afford to stun his audience quite to the degree that the novelist can, since he would not want them to be so dazed by the unexpected that they are unable to follow the next fifteen minutes of the play. Here again, the audience cannot demand: "A moment, if you don't mind! We'd like to consider for a while the meaning of what's just been said!"

For these reasons as well as for the two-and-a-half-hours limitation, drama has a tendency to be stripped of matters unessential to the plot. The audience's mind cannot be cluttered with irrelevancies, be they ever so charming. Nor can a play indulge in those stretches of philosophic abstraction which break out here and there in the pages of some German novelists like a rash (and make those works seem utterly profound to a certain type of reader). In the best plays everything counts: there is no place for tangential material or merely graceful adornments.

CHARACTERIZATION, DIALOGUE AND MOVEMENT

Oscar Wilde's (1856–1900) *The Importance of Being Earnest* has the following first act:

SCENE: *Morning-room in Algernon's flat in Half-Moon Street. The room is luxuriously and artistically furnished. The sound of a piano is heard in the adjoining room.*

Lane is arranging afternoon tea on the table, and after the music has ceased, Algernon enters.

ALGER. Did you hear what I was playing, Lane?

LANE. I didn't think it polite to listen, sir.

ALGER. I'm sorry for that, for your sake. I don't play accurately—anyone can play accurately—but I play with wonderful expression. As far as the piano is concerned, sentiment is my forte. I keep science for Life.

LANE. Yes, sir.

ALGER. And, speaking of the science of Life, have you got the cucumber sandwiches cut for Lady Bracknell?

LANE. Yes, sir. [*Hands them on a salver.*]

ALGER. [*inspects them, takes two, and sits down on the sofa*]. Oh! . . . by the way, Lane, I see from your book that on Thursday night, when Lord Shoreman and Mr. Worthing were dining with me, eight bottles of champagne are entered as having been consumed.

LANE. Yes, sir; eight bottles and a pint.

ALGER. Why is it that at a bachelor's establishment the servants invariably drink the champagne? I ask merely for information.

LANE. I attribute it to the superior quality of the wine, sir. I have often observed that in married households the champagne is rarely of a first-rate brand.

ALGER. Good heavens! Is marriage so demoralizing as that?

LANE. I believe it *is* a very pleasant state, sir. I have had very little experience of it myself up to the present. I have only been married once. That was in consequence of a misunderstanding between myself and a young person.

ALGER. [*languidly*]. I don't know that I am much interested in your family life, Lane.

LANE. No, sir; it is not a very interesting subject. I never think of it myself.

ALGER. Very natural, I am sure. That will do, Lane, thank you.

LANE. Thank you, sir. [*Lane goes out.*]

ALGER. Lane's views on marriage seem somewhat lax. Really, if the lower orders don't set us a good example, what on earth is the use of them? They seem, as a class, to have absolutely no sense of moral responsibility.

[*Enter Lane.*]

LANE. Mr. Ernest Worthing.

[*Enter Jack. Lane goes out.*]

ALGER. How are you, my dear Ernest? What brings you up to town?

JACK. Oh, pleasure, pleasure! What else should bring one anywhere? Eating as usual, I see, Algy!

ALGER. [*stiffly*]. I believe it is customary in good society to take some slight refreshment at five o'clock. Where have you been since last Thursday?

JACK. [*sitting down on the sofa*]. In the country.

ALGER. What on earth do you do there?

JACK. [*pulling off his gloves*]. When one is in town one amuses oneself. When one is in the country one amuses other people. It is excessively boring.

ALGER. And who are the people you amuse?

JACK [*airily*]. Oh, neighbors, neighbors.

ALGER. Got nice neighbors in your part of Shropshire?

JACK. Perfectly horrid! Never speak to one of them.

ALGER. How immensely you must amuse them! [*Goes over and takes sandwich.*] By the way, Shropshire is your county, is it not?

JACK. Eh? Shropshire? Yes, of course. Hallo! Why all these cups? Why cucumber sandwiches? Why such reckless extravagance in one so young? Who is coming to tea?

ALGER. Oh! merely Aunt Augusta and Gwendolen.

JACK. How perfectly delightful!

ALGER. Yes, that is all very well; but I am afraid Aunt Augusta won't quite approve of your being here.

JACK. May I ask why?

ALGER. My dear fellow, the way you flirt with Gwendolen is perfectly disgraceful. It is almost as bad as the way Gwendolen flirts with you.

JACK. I am in love with Gwendolen. I have come up to town expressly to propose to her.

ALGER. I thought you had come up for pleasure? . . . I call that business.

JACK. How utterly unromantic you are!

ALGER. I really don't see anything romantic in proposing. It is very romantic to be in love. But there is nothing romantic about a definite proposal. Why, one may be accepted. One usually is, I believe. Then the excitement is all over. The very essence of romance is uncertainty. If ever I get married, I'll certainly try to forget the fact.

JACK. I have no doubt about that, dear Algy. The Divorce Court was especially invented for people whose memories are so curiously constituted.

ALGER. Oh! there is no use speculating on that subject. Divorces are made in Heaven—[*Jack puts out his hand to take a sandwich. Algernon at once interferes.*] Please don't touch the cucumber sandwiches. They are ordered specially for Aunt Augusta. [*Takes one and eats it.*]

JACK. Well, you have been eating them all the time.

ALGER. That is quite a different matter. She is my aunt. [*Takes plate from below.*] Have some bread and butter. The bread and butter is for Gwendolen. Gwendolen is devoted to bread and butter.

JACK [*advancing to table and helping himself*]. And very good bread and butter it is, too.

ALGER. Well, my dear fellow, you need not eat as if you were going to eat it all. You behave as if you were married to her already. You are not married to her already, and I don't think you ever will be.

JACK. Why on earth do you say that?

ALGER. Well, in the first place girls never marry the men they flirt with. Girls don't think it right.

JACK. Oh, that is nonsense!

ALGER. It isn't. It is a great truth. It accounts for the extraordinary number of bachelors that one sees all over the place. In the second place, I don't give my consent.

JACK. Your consent!

ALGER. My dear fellow, Gwendolen is my first cousin. And before I allow you to marry her, you will have to clear up the whole question of Cecily. [*Rings bell.*]

JACK. Cecily! What on earth do you mean? What do you mean, Algy, by Cecily? I don't know anyone of the name of Cecily.

[*Enter Lane.*]

ALGER. Bring me that cigarette case Mr. Worthing left in the smoking-room the last time he dined here.

LANE. Yes, sir. [*Lane goes out.*]

JACK. Do you mean to say you have had my cigarette case all this time? I wish to goodness you had let me know. I have been writing frantic letters to Scotland Yard about it. I was very nearly offering a large reward.

ALGER. Well, I wish you would offer one. I happen to be more than usually hard up.

JACK. There is no good offering a large reward now that the thing is found.

[*Enter Lane with the cigarette case on a salver. Algernon takes it at once. Lane goes out.*]

ALGER. I think that is rather mean of you, Ernest, I must say. [*Opens case and examines it.*] However, it makes no matter, for, now that I look at the inscription, I find that the thing isn't yours after all.

JACK. Of course it's mine. [*Moving to him.*] You have seen me with it a hundred times, and you have no right whatsoever to read what is written inside. It is a very ungentlemanly thing to read a private cigarette case.

ALGER. Oh! it is absurd to have a hard-and-fast rule about what one should read and what one shouldn't. More than half of modern culture depends on what one shouldn't read.

JACK. I am quite aware of the fact, and I don't propose to discuss modern culture. It isn't the sort of thing one should talk of in private. I simply want my cigarette case back.

ALGER. Yes; but this isn't your cigarette case. This cigarette case is a present from someone of the name of Cecily, and you said you didn't know anyone by that name.

JACK. Well, if you want to know, Cecily happens to be my aunt.

ALGER. Your aunt!

JACK. Yes. Charming old lady she is, too. Lives at Tunbridge Wells. Just give it back to me, Algy.

ALGER. [*retreating to back of sofa*]. But why does she call herself little Cecily if she is your aunt and lives at Tunbridge Wells? [*Reading.*] "From little Cecily with her fondest love."

JACK [*moving to sofa and kneeling upon it*]. My dear fellow, what on earth is there in that? Some aunts are tall, some aunts are not tall. That is a matter that surely an aunt may be allowed to decide for herself. You seem to think that every aunt should be exactly like your aunt! That is absurd! For heaven's sake give me back my cigarette case. [*Follows Algy round the room.*]

ALGER. Yes. But why does your aunt call you her uncle? "From little Cecily, with her fondest love to her dear Uncle Jack." There is no objection, I admit, to an aunt being a small aunt, but why an aunt, no matter what her size may be,

should call her own nephew her uncle, I can't quite make out. Besides, your name isn't Jack at all; it is Ernest.

JACK. It isn't Ernest; it's Jack.

ALGER. You have always told me it was Ernest. I have introduced you to everyone as Ernest. You answer to the name of Ernest. You look as if your name was Ernest. You are the most earnest-looking person I ever saw in my life. It is perfectly absurd your saying that your name isn't Ernest. It's on your cards. Here is one of them. [*Taking it from case.*] "Mr. Ernest Worthing, B. 4, The Albany." I'll keep this as a proof your name is Ernest if ever you attempt to deny it to me, or to Gwendolen, or to anyone else. [*Puts the card in his pocket.*]

JACK. Well, my name is Ernest in town and Jack in the country, and the cigarette case was given to me in the country.

ALGER. Yes, but that does not account for the fact that your small Aunt Cecily, who lives at Tunbridge Wells, calls you her dear uncle. Come, old boy, you had much better have the thing out at once.

JACK. My dear Algy, you talk exactly as if you were a dentist. It is very vulgar to talk like a dentist when one isn't a dentist. It produces a false impression.

ALGER. Well, that is exactly what dentists always do. Now, go on! Tell me the whole thing. I may mention that I have always suspected you of being a confirmed and secret Bunburyist; and I am quite sure of it now.

JACK. Bunburyist? What on earth do you mean by a Bunburyist?

ALGER. I'll reveal to you the meaning of that incomparable expression as soon as you are kind enough to inform me why you are Ernest in town and Jack in the country.

JACK. Well, produce my cigarette case first.

ALGER. Here it is. [*Hands cigarette case.*] Now produce your explanation, and pray make it improbable. [*Sits on sofa.*]

JACK. My dear fellow, there is nothing improbable about my explanation at all. In fact it's perfectly ordinary. Old Mr. Thomas Cardew, who adopted me when I was a boy, made me in his will guardian to his grand-daughter, Miss Cecily Cardew. Cecily, who addresses me as her uncle from motives of respect that you could not possibly appreciate, lives at my place in the country under the charge of her admirable governess, Miss Prism.

ALGER. Where is that place in the country, by the way?

JACK. That is nothing to you, dear boy. You are not going to be invited. . . . I may tell you candidly that the place is not in Shropshire.

ALGER. I suspected that, my dear fellow! I have Bunburyed all over Shropshire on two separate occasions. Now, go on. Why are you Ernest in town and Jack in the country?

JACK. My dear Algy, I don't know whether you will be able to understand my real motives. You are hardly serious enough. When one is placed in the position of guardian, one has to adopt a very high moral tone on all subjects. It's one's duty to do so. And as a high moral tone can hardly be said to conduce very much to either one's health or one's happiness, in order to get up to town I have always pretended to have a younger brother of the name of Ernest, who lives in the Albany, and gets into the most dreadful scrapes. That, my dear Algy, is the whole truth pure and simple.

ALGER. The truth is rarely pure and never simple. Modern life would be very tedious if it were either, and modern literature a complete impossibility!

JACK. That wouldn't be at all a bad thing.

ALGER. Literary criticism is not your forte, my dear fellow. Don't try it. You should leave that to people who haven't been at a University. They do it so well in the daily papers. What you really are is a Bunburyist. I was quite right in saying you were a Bunburyist. You are one of the most advanced Bunburyists I know.

JACK. What on earth do you mean?

ALGER. You have invented a very useful young brother called Ernest, in order that you may be able to come up to town as often as you like. I have invented an invaluable permanent invalid called Bunbury, in order that I may be able to go down into the country whenever I choose. Bunbury is perfectly invaluable. If it wasn't for Bunbury's extraordinary bad health, for instance, I wouldn't be able to dine with you at Willis's tonight, for I have been really engaged to Aunt Augusta for more than a week.

JACK. I haven't asked you to dine with me anywhere tonight.

ALGER. I know. You are absurdly careless about sending out invitations. It is very foolish of you. Nothing annoys people so much as not receiving invitations.

JACK. You had much better dine with your Aunt Augusta.

ALGER. I haven't the smallest intention of doing anything of the kind. To begin with, I dined there on Monday, and once a week is quite enough to dine with one's own relations. In the second place, whenever I do dine there I am always treated as a member of the family, and sent down with either no woman at all, or two. In the

third place, I know perfectly well whom she will place me next to, tonight. She will place me next Mary Farquhar, who always flirts with her own husband across the dinner-table. That is not very pleasant. Indeed, it is not even decent . . . and that sort of thing is enormously on the increase. The amount of women in London who flirt with their own husbands is perfectly scandalous. It looks so bad. It is simply washing one's clean linen in public. Besides, now that I know you to be a confirmed Bunburyist, I naturally want to talk to you about Bunburying. I want to tell you the rules.

JACK. I'm not a Bunburyist at all. If Gwendolen accepts me, I am going to kill my brother, indeed I think I'll kill him in any case. Cecily is a little too much interested in him. It is rather a bore. So I am going to get rid of Ernest. And I strongly advise you to do the same with Mr. . . . with your invalid friend who has the absurd name.

ALGER. Nothing will induce me to part with Bunbury, and if you ever get married, which seems to me extremely problematic, you will be very glad to know Bunbury. A man who marries without knowing Bunbury has a very tedious time of it.

JACK. That is nonsense. If I marry a charming girl like Gwendolen, and she is the only girl I ever saw in my life that I would marry, I certainly won't want to know Bunbury.

ALGER. Then your wife will. You don't seem to realize, that in married life three is company and two is none.

JACK [*sententiously*]. That, my dear young friend, is the theory that the corrupt French Drama has been propounding for the last fifty years.

ALGER. Yes; and that the happy English home has proved in half the time.

JACK. For heaven's sake, don't try to be cynical. It's perfectly easy to be cynical.

ALGER. My dear fellow, it isn't easy to be anything now-a-days. There's such a lot of beastly competition about. [*The sound of an electric bell is heard.*] Ah! that must be Aunt Augusta. Only relatives, or creditors, ever ring in that Wagnerian manner. Now, if I get her out of the way for ten minutes, so that you can have an opportunity for proposing to Gwendolen, may I dine with you tonight at Willis's?

JACK. I suppose so, if you want to.

ALGER. Yes, but you must be serious about it. I hate people who are not serious about meals. It is so shallow of them.

[*Enter Lane.*]

LANE. Lady Bracknell and Miss Fairfax.

[*Algernon goes forward to meet them. Enter Lady Bracknell and Gwendolen.*]

LADY B. Good afternoon, dear Algernon, I hope you are behaving very well.

ALGER. I'm feeling very well, Aunt Augusta.

LADY B. That's not quite the same thing. In fact the two things rarely go together. [*Sees Jack and bows to him with icy coldness.*]

ALGER. [*to Gwendolen*]. Dear me, you are smart!

GWEND. I am always smart! Aren't I, Mr. Worthing?

JACK. You're quite perfect, Miss Fairfax.

GWEND. Oh! I hope I am not that. It would leave no room for developments and I intend to develop in *many directions.* [*Gwendolen and Jack sit down together in the corner.*]

LADY B. I'm sorry if we are a little late, Algernon, but I was obliged to call on dear Lady Harbury. I hadn't been there since her poor husband's death. I never saw a woman so altered; she looks quite twenty years younger. And now I'll have a cup of tea, and one of those nice cucumber sandwiches you promised me.

ALGER. Certainly, Aunt Augusta. [*Goes over to tea-table.*]

LADY B. Won't you come and sit here, Gwendolen?

GWEND. Thanks, mamma, I'm quite comfortable where I am.

ALGER. [*picking up empty plate in horror*]. Good heavens! Lane! Why are there no cucumber sandwiches? I ordered them specially.

LANE. [*gravely*]. There were no cucumbers in the market this morning, sir. I went down twice.

ALGER. No cucumbers!

LANE. No, sir. Not even for ready money.

ALGER. That will do, Lane, thank you.

LANE. Thank you, sir. [*Goes out.*]

ALGER. I am greatly distressed, Aunt Augusta, about there being no cucumbers, not even for ready money.

LADY B. It really makes no matter, Algernon. I had some crumpets with Lady Harbury, who seems to me to be living entirely for pleasure now.

ALGER. I hear her hair has turned quite gold from grief.

LADY B. It certainly has changed its color. From what cause I, of course, cannot say. [*Algernon crosses and hands tea.*] Thank you. I've quite a treat for you tonight, Algernon. I am going to send you down with Mary Farquhar. She is such a nice woman, and so attentive to her husband. It's delightful to watch them.

ALGER. I am afraid, Aunt Augusta, I shall have to give up the pleasure of dining with you tonight after all.

LADY B. [*frowning*]. I hope not, Algernon. It would put my table completely out. Your uncle would have to dine upstairs. Fortunately he is accustomed to that.

ALGER. It is a great bore, and, I need hardly say, a terrible disappointment to me, but the fact is I have just had a telegram to say that my poor friend Bunbury is very ill again. [*Exchanges glances with Jack.*] They seem to think I should be with him.

LADY B. It is very strange. This Mr. Bunbury seems to suffer from curiously bad health.

ALGER. Yes; poor Bunbury is a dreadful invalid.

LADY B. Well, I must say, Algernon, that I think it is high time that Mr. Bunbury made up his mind whether he was going to live or to die. This shilly-shallying with the question is absurd. Nor do I in any way approve of the modern sympathy with invalids. I consider it morbid. Illness of any kind is hardly a thing to be encouraged in others. Health is the primary duty of life. I am always telling that to your poor uncle, but he never seems to take much notice . . . as far as any improvement in his ailments goes. I should be obliged if you would ask Mr. Bunbury, from me, to be kind enough not to have a relapse on Saturday, for I rely on you to arrange my music for me. It is my last reception, and one wants something that will encourage conversation, particularly at the end of the season when everyone has practically said whatever they had to say, which, in most cases, was probably not much.

ALGER. I'll speak to Bunbury, Aunt Augusta, if he is still conscious, and I think I can promise you he'll be all right by Saturday. Of course, the music is a great difficulty. You see, if one plays good music, people don't listen, and if one plays bad music, people don't talk. But I'll run over the program I've drawn out, if you will kindly come into the next room for a moment.

LADY B. Thank you, Algernon. It is very thoughtful of you. [*Rising, and following Algernon.*] I'm sure the program will be delightful, after a few expurgations. French songs I cannot possibly allow. People always seem to think that they are improper, and either look shocked, which is vulgar, or laugh, which is worse. But German sounds a thoroughly respectable language, and indeed, I believe is so. Gwendolen, you will accompany me.

GWEND. Certainly, mamma. [*Lady Bracknell and Algernon go into the music-room, Gwendolen remains behind.*]

JACK. Charming day it has been, Miss Fairfax.

GWEND. Pray don't talk to me about the weather, Mr. Worthing. Whenever people talk to me about the weather, I always feel quite certain that they mean something else. And that makes me so nervous.

JACK. I do mean something else.

GWEND. I thought so. In fact, I am never wrong.

JACK. And I would like to be allowed to take advantage of Lady Bracknell's temporary absence. . . .

GWEND. I would certainly advise you to do so. Mamma has a way of coming back suddenly into a room that I have often had to speak to her about.

JACK. [*nervously*]. Miss Fairfax, ever since I met you I have admired you more than any girl . . . I have ever met since . . . I met you.

GWEND. Yes, I am quite aware of the fact. And I often wish that in public, at any rate, you had been more demonstrative. For me you have always had an irresistible fascination. Even before I met you I was far from indifferent to you. [*Jack looks at her in amazement.*] We live, as I hope you know, Mr. Worthing, in an age of ideals. The fact is constantly mentioned in the more expensive monthly magazines, and has reached the provincial pulpits I am told; and my ideal has always been to love someone of the name of Ernest. There is something in that name that inspires absolute confidence. The moment Algernon first mentioned to me that he had a friend called Ernest, I knew I was destined to love you.

JACK. You really love me, Gwendolen?

GWEND. Passionately!

JACK. Darling! You don't know how happy you've made me.

GWEND. My own Ernest!

JACK. But you don't really mean to say that you couldn't love me if my name wasn't Ernest?

GWEND. But your name is Ernest.

JACK. Yes, I know it is. But supposing it was something else? Do you mean to say you couldn't love me, then?

GWEND. [*glibly*]. Ah! that is clearly a metaphysical speculation, and like most metaphysical speculations has very little reference at all to the actual facts of real life, as we know them.

JACK. Personally, darling, to speak quite candidly, I don't much care about the name of Ernest. . . . I don't think the name suits me at all.

GWEND. It suits you perfectly. It is a divine name. It has a music of its own. It produces vibrations.

JACK. Well, really, Gwendolen, I must say that I think there are lots of other much nicer names. I think Jack, for instance, a charming name.

GWEND. Jack? . . . No, there is very little music in the name Jack, if any at all, indeed. It does not thrill. It produces absolutely no vibrations . . . I have known several Jacks, and they all, without exception, were more than usually plain. Besides, Jack is a notorious domesticity for John! And I pity any woman who is married to a man called John. She would probably never be allowed to know the entrancing pleasure of a single moment's solitude. The only really safe name is Ernest.

JACK. Gwendolen, I must get christened at once—I mean we must get married at once. There is no time to be lost.

GWEND. Married, Mr. Worthing?

JACK [*astounded*]. Well . . . surely. You know that I love you, and you led me to believe, Miss Fairfax, that you were not absolutely indifferent to me.

GWEND. I adore you. But you haven't proposed to me yet. Nothing has been said at all about marriage. The subject has not even been touched on.

JACK. Well . . . may I propose to you now?

GWEND. I think it would be an admirable opportunity. And to spare you any possible disappointment, Mr. Worthing, I think it only fair to tell you quite frankly beforehand that I am fully determined to accept you.

JACK. Gwendolen!

GWEND. Yes, Mr. Worthing, what have you got to say to me?

JACK. You know what I have got to say to you.

GWEND. Yes, but you don't say it.

JACK. Gwendolen, will you marry me? [*Goes down on his knees.*]

GWEND. Of course, I will, darling. How long you have been about it! I am afraid you have had very little experience in how to propose.

JACK. My own one, I have never loved anyone in the world but you.

GWEND. Yes, but men often propose for practice. I know my brother Gerald does. All my girl-friends tell me so. What wonderfully blue eyes you have, Ernest! They are quite, quite, blue. I hope you will always look at me just like that, especially when there are other people present.

[*Enter Lady Bracknell.*]

LADY B. Mr. Worthing! Rise, sir, from this semirecumbent posture. It is most indecorous.

GWEND. Mamma! [*He tries to rise; she restrains him.*] I must beg you to retire. This is no place for you. Besides, Mr. Worthing has not quite finished yet.

LADY B. Finished what, may I ask?

GWEND. I am engaged to Mr. Worthing, mamma. [*They rise together.*]

LADY B. Pardon me, you are not engaged to anyone. When you do become engaged to someone, I, or your father, should his health permit him, will inform you of the fact. An engagement should come on a young girl as a surprise; pleasant or unpleasant, as the case may be. It is hardly a matter that she could be allowed to arrange for herself. . . . And now I have a few questions to put to you, Mr. Worthing. While I am making these inquiries, you, Gwendolen, will wait for me below in the carriage.

GWEND. [*reproachfully*]. Mamma!

LADY B. In the carriage, Gwendolen! [*Gwendolen goes to the door. She and Jack blow kisses to each other behind Lady Bracknell's back. Lady Bracknell looks vaguely about as if she could not understand what the noise was. Finally turns round.*] Gwendolen, the carriage!

GWEND. Yes, mamma. [*Goes out, looking back at Jack.*]

LADY B. [*sitting down*]. You can take a seat, Mr. Worthing. [*Looks in her pocket for note-book and pencil.*]

JACK. Thank you, Lady Bracknell, I prefer standing.

LADY B. [*pencil and note-book in hand*]. I feel bound to tell you that you are not down on my list of eligible young men, although I have the same list as the dear Duchess of Bolton has. We work together, in fact. However, I am quite ready to enter your name, should your answers be what a really affectionate mother requires. Do you smoke?

JACK. Well, yes, I must admit I smoke.

LADY B. I am glad to hear it. A man should always have an occupation of some kind. There are far too many idle men in London as it is. How old are you?

JACK. Twenty-nine.

LADY B. A very good age to be married at. I have always been of opinion that a man who desires to be married should know either everything or nothing. Which do you know?

JACK [*after some hesitation*]. I know nothing, Lady Bracknell.

LADY B. I am pleased to hear it. I do not approve of anything that tampers with natural ignorance. Ignorance is like a delicate exotic fruit; touch it and the bloom is gone. The whole theory of modern education is radically unsound. Fortunately in England, at any rate, education produces no effect whatsoever. If it did, it would prove a serious danger to the upper classes, and probably lead to acts of violence in Grosvenor Square. What is your income?

JACK. Between seven and eight thousand a year.

LADY B. [*makes a note in her book*]. In land, or in investments?

JACK. In investments, chiefly.

LADY B. That is satisfactory. What between the duties expected of one during one's life-time, and the duties exacted from one after one's death, land has ceased to be either a profit or a pleasure. It gives one position, and prevents one from keeping it up. That's all that can be said about land.

JACK. I have a country house with some land, of course, attached to it, about fifteen hundred acres, I believe; but I don't depend on that for my real income. In fact, as far as I can make out, the poachers are the only people who make anything out of it.

LADY B. A country house! How many bedrooms? Well, that point can be cleared up afterwards. You have a town house, I hope? A girl with a simple, unspoiled nature, like Gwendolen, could hardly be expected to reside in the country.

JACK. Well, I own a house in Belgrave Square, but it is let by the year to Lady Bloxham. Of course, I can get it back whenever I like, at six months' notice.

LADY B. Lady Bloxham? I don't know her.

JACK. Oh, she goes about very little. She is a lady considerably advanced in years.

LADY B. Ah, now-a-days that is no guarantee of respectability of character. What number in Belgrave Square?

JACK. 149.

LADY B. [*shaking her head*]. The unfashionable side. I thought there was something. However, that could easily be altered.

JACK. Do you mean the fashion, or the side?

LADY B. [*sternly*]. Both, if necessary, I presume. What are your politics?

JACK. Well, I am afraid I really have none. I am a Liberal Unionist.

LADY B. Oh, they count as Tories. They dine with us. Or come in the evening, at any rate. Now to minor matters. Are your parents living?

JACK. I have lost both my parents.

LADY B. Both? . . . That seems like carelessness. Who was your father? He was evidently a man of some wealth. Was he born in what the Radical papers call the purple of commerce, or did he rise from the ranks of the aristocracy?

JACK. I am afraid I really don't know. The fact is, Lady Bracknell, I said I had lost my parents. It would be nearer the truth to say that my parents seem to have lost me. . . . I don't actually know who I am by birth. I was . . . well, I was found.

LADY B. Found!

JACK. The late Mr. Thomas Cardew, an old gentleman of a very charitable and kindly disposition, found me, and gave me the name of Worthing, because he happened to have a first-class ticket for Worthing in his pocket at the time. Worthing is a place in Sussex. It is a seaside resort.

LADY B. Where did the charitable gentleman who had a first-class ticket for this seaside resort find you?

JACK [*gravely*]. In a hand-bag.

LADY B. A hand-bag?

JACK [*very seriously*]. Yes, Lady Bracknell. I was in a hand-bag—a somewhat large, black leather hand-bag, with handles to it—an ordinary hand-bag, in fact.

LADY B. In what locality did this Mr. James, or Thomas, Cardew come across this ordinary hand-bag?

JACK. In the cloak-room at Victoria Station. It was given to him in mistake for his own.

LADY B. The cloak-room at Victoria Station?

JACK. Yes. The Brighton line.

LADY B. The line is immaterial. Mr. Worthing, I confess I feel somewhat bewildered by what you have just told me. To be born, or at any rate, bred, in a hand-bag, whether it had handles or not, seems to me to display a contempt for the ordinary decencies of family life that remind one of the worst excesses of the French Revolution. And I presume you know what that unfortunate movement led to? As for the particular locality in which the hand-bag was found, a cloak-room at a railway station might serve to conceal a social indiscretion—has probably, indeed, been used for that purpose before now—but it could hardly be regarded as an assured basis for a recognized position in good society.

JACK. May I ask you then what you would advise me to do? I need hardly say I would do anything in the world to insure Gwendolen's happiness.

LADY B. I would strongly advise you, Mr. Worthing, to try and acquire some relations as soon as possible, and to make a definite effort to produce at any rate one parent, of either sex, before the season is quite over.

JACK. Well, I don't see how I could possibly manage to do that. I can produce the hand-bag at any moment. It is in my dressing-room at home. I really think that should satisfy you, Lady Bracknell.

LADY B. Me, sir! What has it to do with me? You can hardly imagine that I and Lord Bracknell would dream of allowing our only daughter—a girl brought up with the utmost care—to marry into a cloak-room, and form an alliance with a parcel? Good morning, Mr. Worthing!

[*Lady Bracknell sweeps out in majestic indignation.*]

JACK. Good morning! [*Algernon, from the other room, strikes up the Wedding March. Jack looks perfectly furious, and goes to the door.*] For goodness' sake don't play that ghastly tune, Algy! How idiotic you are! [*The music stops, and Algernon enters cheerily.*]

ALGER. Didn't it go off all right, old boy? You don't mean to say Gwendolen refused you? I know it is a way she has. She is always refusing people. I think it is most ill-natured of her.

JACK. Oh, Gwendolen is as right as a trivet. As far as she is concerned, we are engaged. Her mother is perfectly unbearable. Never met such a Gorgon . . . I don't really know what a Gorgon is like, but I am quite sure that Lady Bracknell is one. In any case, she is a monster, without being a myth, which is rather unfair. . . . I beg your pardon, Algy, I suppose I shouldn't talk about your own aunt in that way before you.

ALGER. My dear boy, I love hearing my relations abused. It is the only thing that makes me put up with them at all. Relations are simply a tedious pack of people who haven't got the remotest knowledge of how to live, nor the smallest instinct about when to die.

JACK. Oh, that is nonsense!

ALGER. It isn't!

JACK. Well, I won't argue about the matter. You always want to argue about things.

ALGER. That is exactly what things were originally made for.

JACK. Upon my word, if I thought that, I'd shoot myself. . . . [*A pause.*] You don't think there is any chance of Gwendolen becoming like her mother in about a hundred and fifty years, do you, Algy?

ALGER. All women become like their mothers. That is their tragedy. No man does. That's his.

JACK. Is that clever?

ALGER. It is perfectly phrased! and quite as true as any observation in civilized life should be.

JACK. I am sick to death of cleverness. Everybody is clever now-a-days. You can't go anywhere without meeting clever people. The thing has become an absolute public nuisance. I wish to goodness we had a few fools left.

ALGER. We have.

JACK. I should extremely like to meet them. What do they talk about?

ALGER. The fools? Oh! about the clever people, of course.

JACK. What fools!

ALGER. By the way, did you tell Gwendolen the truth about your being Ernest in town, and

Jack in the country?

JACK [*in a very patronizing manner*]. My dear fellow, the truth isn't quite the sort of thing one tells to a nice sweet refined girl. What extraordinary ideas you have about the way to behave to a woman!

ALGER. The only way to behave to a woman is to make love to her, if she is pretty, and to someone else if she is plain.

JACK. Oh, that is nonsense.

ALGER. What about your brother? What about the profligate Ernest?

JACK. Oh, before the end of the week I shall have got rid of him. I'll say he died in Paris of apoplexy. Lots of people die of apoplexy, quite suddenly, don't they?

ALGER. Yes, but it's hereditary, my dear fellow. It's a sort of thing that runs in families. You had much better say a severe chill.

JACK. You are sure a severe chill isn't hereditary, or anything of that kind?

ALGER. Of course it isn't!

JACK. Very well, then. My poor brother Ernest is carried off suddenly in Paris, by a severe chill. That gets rid of him.

ALGER. But I thought you said that . . . Miss Cardew was a little too interested in your poor brother Ernest? Won't she feel his loss a good deal?

JACK. Oh, that is all right. Cecily is not a silly, romantic girl, I am glad to say. She has a capital appetite, goes for long walks, and pays no attention at all to her lessons.

ALGER. I would rather like to see Cecily.

JACK. I will take very good care you never do. She is excessively pretty, and she is only just eighteen.

ALGER. Have you told Gwendolen yet that you have an excessively pretty ward who is only just eighteen?

JACK. Oh! one doesn't blurt these things out to people. Cecily and Gwendolen are perfectly certain to be extremely great friends. I'll bet you anything you like that half an hour after they have met, they will be calling each other sister.

ALGER. Women only do that when they have called each other a lot of other things first. Now, my dear boy, if we want to get a good table at Willis's, we really must go and dress. Do you know it is nearly seven?

JACK [*irritably*]. Oh! it always is nearly seven.

ALGER. Well, I'm hungry.

JACK. I never knew you when you weren't. . . .

ALGER. What shall we do after dinner? Go to a theatre?

JACK. Oh, no! I loathe listening.

ALGER. Well, let us go to the Club?

JACK. Oh, no! I hate talking.

ALGER. Well, we might trot round to the Empire at ten?

JACK. Oh, no! I can't bear looking at things. It is so silly.

ALGER. Well, what shall we do?

JACK. Nothing!

ALGER. It is awfully hard work doing nothing. However, I don't mind hard work where there is no definite object of any kind.

[*Enter Lane.*]

LANE. Miss Fairfax.

[*Enter Gwendolen. Lane goes out.*]

ALGER. Gwendolen, upon my word!

GWEND. Algy, kindly turn your back. I have something very particular to say to Mr. Worthing.

ALGER. Really, Gwendolen, I don't think I can allow this at all.

GWEND. Algy, you always adopt a strictly immoral attitude towards life. You are not quite old enough to do that. [*Algernon retires to the fireplace.*]

JACK. My own darling.

GWEND. Ernest, we may never be married. From the expression on mamma's face I fear we never shall. Few parents now-a-days pay any regard to what their children say to them. The old-fashioned respect for the young is fast dying out. Whatever influence I ever had over mamma, I lost at the age of three. But although she may prevent us from becoming man and wife, and I may marry someone else, and marry often, nothing that she can possibly do can alter my eternal devotion to you.

JACK. Dear Gwendolen!

GWEND. The story of your romantic origin, as related to me by mamma with unpleasing comments, has naturally stirred the deeper fibers of my nature. Your Christian name has an irresistible fascination. The simplicity of your character makes you exquisitely incomprehensible to me. Your town address at the Albany I have. What is your address in the country?

JACK. The Manor House, Woolton, Hertfordshire. [*Algernon, who has been carefully listening, smiles to himself, and writes the address on his shirt-cuff. Then picks up the Railway Guide.*]

GWEND. There is a good postal service, I suppose? It may be necessary to do something desperate. That, of course, will require serious consideration. I will communicate with you daily.

JACK. My own one!

GWEND. How long do you remain in town?

JACK. Till Monday.

GWEND. Good! Algy, you may turn round now.

ALGER. Thanks, I've turned round already.

GWEND. You may also ring the bell.

JACK. You will let me see you to your carriage, my own darling?

GWEND. Certainly.

JACK [to Lane, who now enters]. I will see Miss Fairfax out.

LANE. Yes, sir. [Jack and Gwendolen go off. Lane presents several letters on a salver to Algernon. It is to be surmised that they are bills, as Algernon, after looking at the envelopes, tears them up.]

ALGER. A glass of sherry, Lane.

LANE. Yes, sir.

ALGER. Tomorrow, Lane, I'm going Bunburying.

LANE. Yes, sir.

ALGER. I shall probably not be back till Monday. You can put up my dress clothes, my smoking jacket and all the Bunbury suits. . . .

LANE. Yes, sir. [Handing sherry.]

ALGER. I hope tomorrow will be a fine day, Lane.

LANE. It never is, sir.

ALGER. Lane, you're a perfect pessimist.

LANE. I do my best to give satisfaction, sir. [Enter Jack. Lane goes off.]

JACK. There's a sensible, intellectual girl! The only girl I ever cared for in my life. [Algernon is laughing immoderately.] What on earth are you so amused at?

ALGER. Oh, I'm a little anxious about poor Bunbury, that's all.

JACK. If you don't take care, your friend Bunbury will get you into a serious scrape some day.

ALGER. I love scrapes. They are the only things that are never serious.

JACK. Oh, that's nonsense, Algy. You never talk anything but nonsense.

ALGER. Nobody ever does. [Jack looks indignantly at him, and leaves the room. Algernon lights a cigarette, reads his shirt-cuff, and smiles.]

CURTAIN

This act from one of the most brilliant of English comedies illustrates the dramatist's obligation to be swift in communication and clear. A dramatist is forced to reveal everything through the action and the dialogue. He cannot, like the novelist or short-story writer, step in himself and tell the audience about his characters' histories, personalities, abilities, interests, private thoughts and so on. It is to be remarked in *The Importance of Being Earnest* that all these matters are revealed exclusively through the action and dialogue—and the reader of the entire play will find this truth even more powerfully enforced. (It is unfortunately the case that some twentieth-century dramatists behave like novelists and have someone like a Narrator talk directly to the audience and supply the information which ought to be conveyed only through action and dialogue. When they do so, they not only betray their incapacity to master the dramatic form, but also while that Narrator is talking thoroughly destroy all the illusion which is so basic to the theatre. When this clumsy device is used it often has the added inconvenience of pelting us all with more information than we can possibly digest at one time.)

Wilde called his comedy a farce, and in a farce the emphasis is on the complication of incidents rather than on the characterization. But this need not be so in the hands of a master, and is not so here. Algernon is seen from the very start as a flippant, completely irreverent, forever hungry (especially for cucumber sandwiches), sly young man, who lives to be amusing (e.g., his remarks about his playing the piano, his inquiries about the consumption of his champagne—"I ask merely for information," his seizing on the sandwiches, etc.). Lane, the butler, is clearly a very satisfactory one, but a snob ("in married households the champagne is rarely of first-rate quality"). Though Jack, because of the tone of the play, is sometimes witty, he is far less so than Algernon, whose light touch he lacks, and is basically a serious and very romantic young fellow (e.g., his constant objections to Algernon's cleverness as "nonsense," and his method of proposing to Gwendolen).

Almost immediately upon Jack's entrance the plot begins. He is taken aback by Algernon's query about his country residence; "Shropshire is your county, is it not?" When Jack responds, "Eh? Shropshire? Yes, of course," we see that he is lying and suspect at once that he is leading a double life.

The business of the cigarette case, while it could not possibly be more diverting, and may seem to have been invented only for that purpose, is much more than a delightful piece of persiflage. It plays a major role in the plot. It serves many ends: it tells us about little Cecily (who will figure importantly in the next two acts); it tells us that Jack is known as Jack in the country but as Ernest in town (the knowledge of which Algernon is going to use to his own advantage in the next act); it leads to the revelation that Jack has invented a wicked brother named Ernest, whose irresponsibilities give Jack an opportunity to slip now and then into London, where he passes as that same Ernest; it leads as well to the information that if Gwendolen agrees to marry him, Jack intends to kill off this mythical brother Ernest, an act he performs when she does accept him—and when he has "killed off" brother Ernest in the next act, it makes for what is the most hilariously funny scene in Act II. He will there enter in elaborately sombre mourning clothes, announce Ernest's death, but in the meantime Algernon has come on the scene pretending to be that same wicked Ernest, and has been enthusiastically welcomed as such by Cecily, who has fallen in love with him; Jack's lugubrious appearance and assumed stricken expression when everyone knows that "Ernest" is in the house (in the person of Algernon) keeps audiences laughing throughout the passage. Even the apparently trifling matter of Algernon's proving that Jack is Ernest because he possesses a card bearing Ernest's name and address, is going to have important consequences in the next act when Algernon will use the card to pass himself off as Jack's brother Ernest. During this sprightly dialogue we are also told that Jack has no parents and was adopted by Cecily's grandfather; that too is to have important consequences in the play.

Upon the entrance of Lady Bracknell and Gwendolen we have two new interesting characters, both profoundly involved, it will turn out, with the working of the plot. Lady Bracknell, one of the great parts for a skillful comedienne, is a brilliant portrait of a certain kind of aristocrat. Her deliberate lack of heart and her rudeness, which certain Britishers of rank and certain Americans of wealth consider it their right to exhibit wherever possible, are made extremely amusing and also involve a great deal of social satire on Wilde's part. Characteristic of her are her observations, "I think it high time that Mr. Bunbury made up his mind to live or die. This shilly-shallying with the question is absurd," and that at the musicale she is planning she wishes music "that will encourage conversation" while it is being performed. Algernon's flippancy, which has more than a grain of truth in it, is also characteristic: "If one plays good music, people don't listen, and if one plays bad music, people don't talk." The ridiculous prejudices of her time (1895) and class are further revealed in Lady Bracknell's, "French songs I cannot possibly allow. People seem to think they are improper, and either look shocked, which is vulgar, or laugh, which is worse. But German sounds a thoroughly respectable language."

We see, upon her temporary exit, that her daughter, Gwendolen, pays lip service to her mother, but does as she pleases. In the dialogue that follows with Jack, it is evident that she is a flirt and means to capture Jack, who is only too anxious to be caught, but who fumbles badly in his proposal, though Gwndolen, in her elegant way, does everything to help him. But he is dismayed when he discovers that she fell in love with him because his name is Ernest; he protests that it isn't a very charming name. Wouldn't she prefer Jack? No, people with that name are invariably dull and plain, she replies. (The name Ernest will figure largely in the last act.) After her warm encouragement, when Jack speaks of marriage, Gwendolen makes it clear that she will not be cheated of the usual ritual: "Married, Mr. Worthing? . . . I adore you. But you haven't proposed to me yet." When Lady Bracknell returns and learns of the proposal, she cross-examines Jack about his wealth, possessions, etc., and all seems to be going well until she asks about his parents. It is then that we learn that Jack was found as an infant in a hand-bag at the Victoria railroad station's cloak-room by Cecily's grandfather, who bestowed upon him the name of Worthing. Lady Bracknell's class prejudices are now declared with violence: she strongly advises Jack to find at least one parent before the season is over. When he begs her to accept as evidence the hand-bag, she cries: "You can hardly imagine that I and Lord Bracknell would dream of allowing our only daughter ... to marry into a cloak-room, and form an alliance with a parcel?" That hand-bag, when produced in Act III, will turn out to be the climax of the play.

Before the act is over Gwendolen returns to find out Jack's country address so they may keep in touch. Algernon, who is present, makes a note of the address, and will use it in the next act, to the further complication of the plot.

Thus, it is to be noted that, despite all the persiflage, everything done and a great deal of what is said are to be basic to the development of the plot.

We observe, then, that of all literary forms the drama clings closest to the essentials of plot and characterization. The dramatist, we repeat, must be swift and clear: swift, because he must carry his audience along with him; clear, because his audience must understand everything at the moment it is being done or said. Drama, in short, does not allow the audience to deflect its attention for a moment.

This uninterrupted absorption which the performed play demands can be achieved only when the work enables the audience to identify itself to some degree with some character or characters in the story. Some novels have been written with a kind of emotional detachment, so that the reader finds himself holding aloof from all the characters and examining them like specimens in a case or under a microscope. That kind of pure objectivity is impossible in the theatre. A play allows no one a second's reflection, private speculation or withdrawal of attention; to continue to carry his audience along, therefore, the dramatist must manage to compel his spectators to ally themselves with someone or some people in the play in order to participate in what is going on. In a play one is always "for" or "against" certain persons of the drama. In *Hamlet* we are "for" Hamlet, Horatio and Ophelia and "against" the king, the queen and Polonius. In *The Importance of Being Ernest* we are "for" Jack and surely must find Algernon irresistible, and are "against" Lady Bracknell. But since this is a farce our feelings are not heavily called upon.

PLOT: LOGIC, CENTRAL CHARACTER AND CLIMAX

Aristotle declared plot to be the very soul of drama. We deal with plot as the most fundamental of the requirements of drama. Let us consider these passages from *Romeo and Juliet;* they contain what is crucial to the plot of the tragedy:*

DRAMATIS PERSONÆ

ESCALUS, *Prince of Verona.*
PARIS, *a young nobleman, kinsman to the Prince.*
MONTAGUE,
CAPULET, *heads of two houses at variance with each other.*
AN OLD MAN, *of the Capulet family.*
ROMEO, *son to Montague.*

*Here we confronted a vexing difficulty. Considerations of space did not permit reprinting an entire full-length play for the study of plot; the one-act play has neither the importance nor the scope to serve our multiple needs. Moreover, we wished, naturally, to use a great play; but excerpting one is an exercise in defacement. Further, it was natural to prefer a great play by the world's greatest dramatist: in his case the offense of abridgment would be paramount—a point of view unshared by Shakespearean troupes! We at length decided that the best way to mitigate an unavoidable literary sin was to choose a great play, but not one of his greatest —in short, *Romeo and Juliet.* It is Shakespeare's earliest masterpiece, we think, but a masterpiece with flaws. Only a work so profligate of magnificence and beauty could afford so many passages of poor taste. Any Shakespearean scholar would agree that had this play been written ten years later, much that now stands in it would have been omitted. It is the work of a young master who has just begun to find himself. We therefore take some comfort from the thought that although our method necessitates omitting some of the sublimest scenes in the play, it also has involved omitting most of the worst. At any rate, we do not pretend here to be considering *Romeo and Juliet*—only its plot.

MERCUTIO, *kinsman to the Prince, and friend to Romeo.*
BENVOLIO, *nephew to Montague, and friend to Romeo.*
TYBALT, *nephew to Lady Capulet.*
FRIAR LAURENCE, *a Franciscan.*
FRIAR JOHN, *of the same order.*
BALTHASAR, *servant to Romeo.*
SAMPSON,⎫
GREGORY,⎭ *servants to Capulet.*
PETER, *servant to Juliet's nurse.*
ABRAHAM, *servant to Montague.*
AN APOTHECARY.
THREE MUSICIANS.
PAGE *to Paris; another* PAGE; *an* OFFICER.
LADY MONTAGUE, *wife to Montague.*
LADY CAPULET, *wife to Capulet.*
JULIET, *daughter to Capulet.*
NURSE *to Juliet.*
CITIZENS *of Verona:* KINSFOLK *of both houses;* MASKERS, GUARDS, WATCH-
MEN, *and* ATTENDANTS.

SCENE—*Verona; Mantua.*

(Act I, sc. 1) The servants of the Montagues and Capulets half-heartedly try to pick a quarrel with one another, but fight in earnest on the entry of hot-headed Tybalt, Juliet's cousin. Benvolio, a man of moderation, tries to stop the fray. Soon the whole town is taking sides in the fighting, though Montague and Capulet themselves seem more to be keeping up the appearances of a feud than anxious to participate in it:

CAP.   Give me my long sword, ho!
LADY C. A crutch, a crutch! why call you for a sword?
CAP. My sword, I say! Old Montague is come, And flourishes his blade in spite of me.
MONT. Thou villain Capulet!—Hold me not, let me go.
LADY M. Thou shalt not stir one foot to seek a foe.

The Prince enters, orders the contention to cease, and threatens:

On pain of torture, from those bloody hands
Throw your mistempered weapons to the ground
And hear the sentence[1] of your moved prince.
Three civil brawls, bred of an airy word
By thee, old Capulet, and Montague,
Have thrice disturb'd the quiet of our streets
And made Verona's ancient citizens
Cast by their grave beseeming ornaments
To wield old partisans,[2] in hands as old,
Cank'red with peace, to part your cank'red hate.
If ever you disturb our streets again,
Your lives shall pay the forfeit of the peace.[3]
                                                                    —93–104

Romeo arrives and confesses to Benvolio that he is smitten by the beauty of Rosaline, who does not return his love. He seems to luxuriate in his unhappiness:

ROM. Tut, I have lost myself; I am not here; This is not Romeo, he's some other where.

[1]Decree.

[2]Spears with two-edged knives affixed.

[3]I.e., of breaking the peace.

BEN. Tell me in sadness,[4] who is that you love?
ROM. What, shall I groan and tell thee?
BEN.   Groan! why, no; But sadly tell me who.
ROM. Bid a sick man in sadness make his will: Ah, word ill urged to one
that is so ill! In sadness, cousin, I do love a woman.
BEN. I aim'd so near when I supposed you loved.

                                                                    —203–211

We do not feel that Romeo is in love with Rosaline so much as in love with love. (Sc. 2)
Paris, kinsman to the Prince, asks Capulet for the hand of Juliet. Although she is only
fourteen, Capulet consents with the proviso that the girl herself be willing:

> The earth hath swallow'd all my hopes but she,
> She is the hopeful lady of my earth:
> But woo her, gentle Paris, get her heart;
> My will to her consent is but a part;
> An she agree, within her scope of choice
> Lies my consent and fair according voice.

                                                                    —14–19

That night the Capulets are to hold a feast. When Capulet and Paris go out, Romeo, reading
for an illiterate servant of the Capulets a list of guests to be invited to the festivities, discovers
that Rosaline will be there. He and Benvolio decide to attend too, though not invited. (Sc.
3) We meet Juliet, a girl utterly obedient to her parents. Her mother having summoned her,
she enters, saying:

> Madam, I am here. What is your will?

Has Juliet thought of matrimony? her mother asks. No, the girl replies. Lady Capulet
responds:

> Well, think of marriage now

—and tells her of Paris' proposal, urging her to accept him. After praising Paris' accomplishments, she concludes:

> Speak briefly, can you like of Paris' love?

Juliet promises to try, and adds:

> But no more deep will I endart mine eye
> Than your consent gives strength to make it fly.

                                                                    —6, 69, 96, 98–99

(Sc. 4) Romeo, Benvolio and their hot-tempered, witty friend Mercutio are about to join the
Capulet feast. Mercutio ridicules Romeo because of his enslavement to Rosaline. Romeo,
still enjoying the role of a wounded lover, announces that he does not intend to dance, and
speaks of a premonition that some occurrence tragic to him will commence tonight. (Sc. 5)
The three young men, masked, enter among other masked dancers at the Capulet feast.
Romeo and Juliet see each other, and fall in love at first sight:

ROM. [to a Servingman]. What lady's that,   It seems she hangs upon the cheek of night
  which doth enrich the hand   Like a rich jewel in an Ethiop's ear—
Of yonder knight?   Beauty too rich for use, for earth too dear!
  SERV. I know not, sir.   So shows[5] a snowy dove trooping with crows
  ROM. O, she doth teach the torches to burn   As yonder lady o'er her fellows shows.
  bright!   The measure[6] done, I'll watch her place of stand

                                                     [5]Appears.
[4]In all seriousness.   [6]Figure of the dance.

And, touching hers, make blessed my rude hand.
Did my heart love till now? Forswear it, sight!
For I ne'er saw true beauty till this night.
    TYB. This, by his voice, should be a Montague.
Fetch me my rapier, boy. What, dares the slave
Come hither, cover'd with an antic face,[7]
To fleer and scorn at our solemnity?[8]
Now, by the stock and honour of my kin,
To strike him dead I hold it not a sin.
    CAP. Why, how now, kinsman? Wherefore
      storm you so?
    TYB. Uncle, this is a Montague, our foe;
A villain, that is hither come in spite
To scorn at our solemnity this night.
    CAP. Young Romeo is it?
    TYB.   'Tis he, that villain Romeo.
    CAP. Content thee,[9] gentle coz,[10] let him
      alone.
'A bears him like a portly[11] gentleman,
And, to say truth, Verona brags of him
To be a virtuous and well-govern'd youth.
I would not for the wealth of all this town
Here in my house do him disparagement.
Therefore be patient, take no note of him.
It is my will; the which if thou respect,
Show a fair presence and put off these frowns,
An ill-beseeming semblance for a feast.
    TYB. It fits when such a villain is a guest.
I'll not endure him.
    CAP.   He shall be endur'd.
What, goodman boy?[12] I say he shall. Go to![13]
Am I the master here, or you? Go to!
You'll not endure him? God shall mend my
    soul![14]
You'll make a mutiny among my guests!
You will set cock-a-hoop![15] you'll be the man![16]
    TYB. Why, uncle, 'tis a shame.
    CAP.   Go to, go to!
You are a saucy boy. Is't so, indeed?
This trick may chance to scathe[17] you. I know
    what.
You must contrary me! Marry, 'tis time.—

    [7]Grotesque mask.

    [8]Feast.

    [9]Calm yourself.

    [10]Cousin was a word applied generally to any rela-
tive.

    [11]Dignified.

    [12](Addressing Tybalt as though he were an impu-
dent child.)

    [13]I.e., "Get out!"

    [14]I.e., "Bless my soul!"

    [15]You'll be cock of the walk!

    [16]You'll run the show!

    [17]Injure.

Well said, my hearts![18] —You are a princox[19] —
    go!
Be quiet, or—More light, more light!—For
    shame!
I'll make you quiet; what!—Cheerly, my hearts!
    TYB. Patience perforce[20] with wilful choler[21]
    meeting
Makes my flesh tremble in their different greet-
    ing.
I will withdraw; but this intrusion shall,
Now seeming sweet, convert to bitt'rest gall.
[Exit.]
    ROM. If I profane with my unworthiest hand
    This holy shrine,[22] the gentle fine is this:
My lips, two blushing pilgrims, ready stand
    To smooth that rough touch with a tender
    kiss.
    JUL. Good pilgrim, you do wrong your hand
    too much,
Which mannerly devotion shows in this;
For saints have hands that pilgrims' hands do
    touch,
    And palm to palm is holy palmers'[23] kiss.
    ROM. Have not saints lips, and holy palmers
    too?
    JUL. Ay, pilgrim, lips that they must use in
    pray'r.
    ROM. O, then, dear saint, let lips do what
    hands do!
They pray; grant thou, lest faith turn to de-
    spair.
    JUL. Saints do not move, though grant for
    prayers' sake.
    ROM. Then move not while my prayer's
    effect[24] I take.
Thus from my lips, by thine my sin is purg'd.
                   [Kisses her.]
    JUL. Then have my lips the sin that they have
    took.
    ROM. Sin from my lips? O trespass sweetly
    urg'd!
Give me my sin again.   [Kisses her.]
    JUL.   You kiss by th' book.[25]
    NURSE. Madam, your mother craves a word
    with you.

    [18]Capulet turns from Tybalt for a moment to
speak to some of his guests.

    [19]Saucy boy.

    [20]Forced patience.

    [21]Self-willed anger.

    [22]Juliet's hand.

    [23]A palmer was a pilgrim under vow to go from
shrine to shrine.

    [24]Fulfillment.

    [25]According to the rules.

ROM. What is her mother?

NURSE.   Marry, bachelor,[26]
Her mother is the lady of the house.
And a good lady, and a wise and virtuous.
I nurs'd her daughter that you talk'd withal.
I tell you, he that can lay hold of her
Shall have the chinks.[27]

ROM.   Is she a Capulet?
O dear account! my life is my foe's debt.[28]

BEN. Away, be gone; the sport is at the best.

ROM. Ay, so I fear; the more is my unrest.

CAP. Nay, gentlemen, prepare not to be gone;
We have a trifling foolish banquet towards.
Is it e'en so?[29] Why then, I thank you all.
I thank you, honest gentlemen. Good night.
More torches here! Come on then, let's to bed.
Ah, sirrah, by my fay,[30] it waxes late;
I'll to my rest.
    [*Exeunt, all but Juliet and Nurse.*]

JUL. Come hither, nurse. What is yond gentle-
    man?

NURSE. The son and heir of old Tiberio.

JUL. What's he that now is going out of door?

NURSE. Marry,[31] that, I think, be young Pe-
    truchio.

JUL. What's he that follows there, that would
    not dance?

NURSE. I know not.

JUL. Go ask his name.—If he be married,
My grave is like to be my wedding bed.

NURSE. His name is Romeo, and a Montague,
The only son of your great enemy.

JUL. My only love, sprung from my only hate!
Too early seen unknown, and known too late!
Prodigious birth of love it is to me
That I must love a loathed enemy.

NURSE. What's this? what's this?

JUL.   A rhyme I learnt even now
Of one I danc'd withal.
    [*One calls within 'Juliet.'*]

NURSE.   Anon, anon![32]
Come, let's away; the strangers all are gone.
    [*Exeunt.*]

                                —43–146

(Act II, sc. 1) Finding it impossible to leave without seeing Juliet again, Romeo escapes from his friends, and leaps the orchard wall into the Capulet garden. (Sc. 2) In the garden flooded by moonlight, Romeo observes Juliet as she comes out on her balcony:

[*Enter Juliet above at a window.*]
But soft! What light through yonder window
    breaks?
It is the East, and Juliet is the sun!
Arise, fair sun, and kill the envious moon,
Who is already sick and pale with grief
That thou her maid art far more fair than she.
Be not her maid, since she is envious.
Her vestal livery is but sick and green,[33]
And none but fools do wear it. Cast it off.
It is my lady; O, it is my love!
O that she knew she were!
She speaks, yet she says nothing. What of that?
Her eye discourses; I will answer it.
I am too bold; 'tis not to me she speaks.
Two of the fairest stars in all the heaven,
Having some business, do entreat her eyes
To twinkle in their spheres till they return.
What if her eyes were there, they in her head?

The brightness of her cheek would shame those
    stars
As daylight doth a lamp; her eyes in heaven
Would through the airy region stream so bright
That birds would sing and think it were not night.
See how she leans her cheek upon her hand!
O that I were a glove upon that hand,
That I might touch that cheek!

JUL.   Ay me!

ROM.   She speaks.
O, speak again, bright angel! for thou art
As glorious to this night, being o'er my head,
As is a winged messenger of heaven
Unto the white-upturned wond'ring eyes
Of mortals that fall back to gaze on him
When he bestrides the lazy-pacing clouds
And sails upon the bosom of the air.

JUL. O Romeo, Romeo! wherefore art thou
    Romeo?

[26]Young gentleman.
[27]Plenty of money.
[28]Because Juliet is a Capulet.
[29]Must you go?
[30]Faith.

[31](An expletive.)
[32]In a moment!
[33]Sallow.

Deny thy father and refuse thy name!
Or, if thou wilt not, be but sworn my love,
And I'll no longer be a Capulet.

    ROM. Shall I hear more, or shall I speak at
    this?

    JUL. 'Tis but thy name that is my enemy.
Thou art thyself, though not[34] a Montague.
What's Montague? It is nor hand, nor foot,
Nor arm, nor face, nor any other part
Belonging to a man. O, be some other name!
What's in a name? That which we call a rose
By any other name would smell as sweet.
So Romeo would, were he not Romeo call'd,
Retain that dear perfection which he owes[35]
Without that title. Romeo, doff thy name;
And for that name, which is no part of thee,
Take all myself.

    ROM. I take thee at thy word.
Call me but love, and I'll be new baptiz'd;
Henceforth I never will be Romeo.

    JUL. What man art thou that, thus bescreen'd
    in night,
So stumblest on my counsel?[36]

    ROM.   By a name
I know not how to tell thee who I am.
My name, dear saint, is hateful to myself,
Because it is an enemy to thee.
Had I it written, I would tear the word.

    JUL. My ears have yet not drunk a hundred
    words
Of that tongue's utterance, yet I know the sound.
Art thou not Romeo, and a Montague?

    ROM. Neither, fair saint, if either thee dislike.

    JUL. How cam'st thou hither, tell me, and
    wherefore?
The orchard walls are high and hard to climb,
And the place death, considering who thou art,
If any of my kinsmen find thee here.

    ROM. With love's light wings did I o'erperch
    these walls;
For stony limits cannot hold love out,
And what[37] love can do, that dares love attempt.
Therefore thy kinsmen are no let[38] to me.

    JUL. If they do see thee, they will murther
    thee.

    ROM. Alack, there lies more peril in thine eye
Than twenty of their swords! Look thou but
    sweet,
And I am proof against their enmity.

    JUL. I would not for the world they saw thee
    here.

    ROM. I have night's cloak to hide me from
    their sight;
And but[39] thou love me, let them find me here.
My life were better ended by their hate
Than death prorogued,[40] wanting of thy love.

    JUL. By whose direction found'st thou out this
    place?

    ROM. By love, that first did prompt me to en-
    quire.
He lent me counsel, and I lent him eyes.
I am no pilot; yet, wert thou as far
As that vast shore wash'd with the farthest sea,
I would adventure for such merchandise.

    JUL. Thou knowest the mask of night is on my
    face;
Else would a maiden blush bepaint my cheek
For that which thou hast heard me speak to-
    night.
Fain would I dwell on form—fain, fain deny
What I have spoke; but farewell compliment![41]
Dost thou love me? I know thou wilt say 'Ay';
And I will take thy word. Yet, if thou swear'st,
Thou mayst prove false. At lovers' perjuries,
They say Jove laughs. O gentle Romeo,
If thou dost love, pronounce it faithfully.
Or if thou thinkest I am too quickly won,
I'll frown, and be perverse, and say thee nay,
So[42] thou wilt woo; but else, not for the world.
In truth, fair Montague, I am too fond,
And therefore thou mayst think my haviour
    light;[43]
But trust me, gentleman, I'll prove more true
Than those that have more cunning to be
    strange.[44]
I should have been more strange, I must confess,
But that thou overheard'st, ere I was ware,
My true-love passion.[45] Therefore pardon me,
And not impute this yielding to light love,
Which the dark night hath so discovered.

    ROM. Lady, by yonder blessed moon I swear,
That tips with silver all these fruit-tree tops—

    JUL. O, swear not by the moon, th' inconstant
    moon,
That monthly changes in her circled orb,
Lest that thy love prove likewise variable.

[34]Even if you were not.
[35]Owns.
[36]Secrets.
[37]Whatever.
[38]Obstacle.

[39]Unless.
[40]Delayed.
[41]Ceremonious speech.
[42]Provided that.
[43]Immodest.
[44]More distant.
[45]Strong feelings.

ROM. What shall I swear by?

JUL.   Do not swear at all;
Or if thou wilt, swear by thy gracious self,
Which is the god of my idolatry,
And I'll believe thee.

ROM.   If my heart's dear love—

JUL. Well, do not swear. Although I joy in
thee,
I have no joy of this contract to-night.
It is too rash, too unadvis'd, too sudden;
Too like the lightning, which doth cease to be
Ere one can say 'It lightens.' Sweet, good night!
This bud of love, by summer's ripening breath,
May prove a beauteous flow'r when next we meet.
Good night, good night! As sweet repose and rest
Come to thy heart as that within my breast!

ROM. O, wilt thou leave me so unsatisfied?

JUL. What satisfaction canst thou have tonight?

ROM. Th' exchange of thy love's faithful vow
for mine.

JUL. I gave thee mine before thou didst request
it;
And yet I would it were to give again.

ROM. Would'st thou withdraw it? For what
purpose, love?

JUL. But to be frank and give it thee again.
And yet I wish but for the thing I have.
My bounty is as boundless as the sea,
My love as deep; the more I give to thee,
The more I have, for both are infinite.
I hear some noise within. Dear love, adieu!
[Nurse calls within.]
Anon, good nurse! Sweet Montague, be true.
Stay but a little, I will come again.

ROM. O blessed, blessed night! I am afeard,
Being in night, all this is but a dream,
Too flattering-sweet to be substantial.
[Enter Juliet above.]

JUL. Three words, dear Romeo, and good
night indeed.
If that thy bent[46] of love be honourable,
Thy purpose marriage, send me word to-morrow,
By one that I'll procure to come to thee,
Where and what time thou wilt perform the rite;
And all my fortunes at thy foot I'll lay
And follow thee my lord throughout the world.

NURSE [within]. Madam!

JUL. I come, anon.—But if thou meanest not
well,
I do beseech thee—

NURSE [within]. Madam!

JUL.   By-and-by[47] I come.—
To cease thy suit and leave me to my grief.
To-morrow will I send.

ROM.   So thrive my soul—

JUL. A thousand times good night!   [Exit.]

ROM. A thousand times the worse, to want thy
light!
Love goes toward love as schoolboys from their
books;
But love from love, towards school with heavy
looks.
[Enter Juliet again, above.]

JUL. Hist! Romeo, hist! O for a falc'ner's voice
To lure this tassel-gentle[48] back again!
Bondage is hoarse and may not speak aloud;
Else would I tear the cave where Echo lies,
And make her airy tongue more hoarse than mine
With repetition of my Romeo's name.
Romeo!

ROM. It is my soul that calls upon my name.
How silver-sweet sound lovers' tongues by night,
Like softest music to attending ears!

JUL. Romeo!

ROM.   My dear?

JUL.   At what o'clock to-morrow
Shall I send to thee?

ROM.   By the hour of nine.

JUL. I will not fail. 'Tis twenty years till then.
I have forgot why I did call thee back.

ROM. Let me stand here till thou remember it.

JUL. I shall forget, to have thee still stand
there,
Rememb'ring how I love thy company.

ROM. And I'll still stay, to have thee still forget,
Forgetting any other home but this.

JUL. 'Tis almost morning. I would have thee
gone—
And yet no farther than a wanton's[49] bird,
That lets it hop a little from her hand,
Like a poor prisoner in his twisted gyves,[50]
And with a silk thread plucks it back again,
So loving-jealous of his liberty.

ROM. I would I were thy bird.

JUL.   Sweet, so would I.
Yet I should kill thee with much cherishing.
Good night, good night! Parting is such sweet
sorrow,
That I shall say good night till it be morrow.
[Exit.]

---

[46]Aim.
[47]Immediately.

[48]A male hawk.
[49]A child's.
[50]Fetters.

ROM. Sleep dwell upon thine eyes, peace in thy breast!
Would I were sleep and peace, so sweet to rest!

Hence will I to my ghostly[51] father's cell,
His help to crave and my dear hap to tell. [*Exit.*]

—2–191

(Sc. 3) Romeo goes to see his friend and confessor, Friar Laurence, who wonders whether Romeo has been spending the night with Rosaline. The young man behaves as though he had never heard that name before, and confides his hopes to marry Juliet. Believing that such a union might end the family feud, the good Friar agrees to help the lovers. (Sc. 4) Mercutio tells Benvolio of a challenge which Tybalt, whom he loathes, has sent to Romeo. Romeo enters, now in high spirits, and exchanges pleasantries with Mercutio. The Nurse enters, asking to be allowed to speak to Romeo alone. When his friends depart, Romeo sends a message to Juliet, arranging for their marriage:

ROM. Bid her devise
Some means to come to shrift[52] this afternoon;
And there she shall at Friar Laurence' cell
Be shriv'd and married. Here is for thy pains.
    NURSE. No, truly, sir; not a penny.
    ROM. Go to! I say you shall.
    NURSE. This afternoon, sir? Well, she shall be there.
    ROM. And stay, good nurse, behind the abbey wall.
Within this hour my man shall be with thee
And bring thee cords made like a tackled stair,
Which to the high topgallant[53] of my joy
Must be my convoy[54] in the secret night.
Farewell. Be trusty, and I'll quit thy pains.
Farewell. Commend me to thy mistress.   —191–204

(Sc. 5) Juliet impatiently awaits the old woman's return. On her arrival, the Nurse teases the girl and then reveals the meeting place, which is to be at Friar Laurence's cell. (Sc. 6) Romeo and Juliet are at the Friar's cell and ready for the marriage ceremony:

JUL. Good even to my ghostly confessor.
    FRIAR. Romeo shall thank thee, daughter, for us both.
    JUL. As much[55] to him, else is his thanks too much.
    ROM. Ah, Juliet, if the measure of thy joy
Be heap'd like mine, and that thy skill be more
To blazon[56] it, then sweeten with thy breath
This neighbour air, and let rich music's tongue
Unfold the imagin'd happiness that both
Receive in either by this dear encounter.
    JUL. Conceit[57] more rich in matter than in words,
Brags of his substance, not of ornament.
They are but beggars that can count their worth;[58]
But my true love is grown to such excess
I cannot sum up sum of half my wealth.
    FRIAR. Come, come with me, and we will make short work;
For, by your leaves, you shall not stay alone
Till Holy Church incorporate two in one.
    [*Exeunt.*]

—21–37

[51]Spiritual.
[52]Confession.
[53]Summit (literally, the mast above the topmast).
[54]Means of conveyance.

[55](Good even.)
[56]Describe.
[57]Understanding.
[58]Possessions.

(Act III, sc. 1) It is a hot day, and Benvolio advises quitting the streets: this is the kind of day on which one may expect fighting. Mercutio, in a dangerous mood, refuses to leave. Tybalt comes in, looking for Romeo:

[*Enter Tybalt and others.*]

BEN. By my head, here come the Capulets.

MER. By my heel, I care not.

TYB. Follow me close, for I will speak to them. Gentlemen, good den.[59] A word with one of you.

MER. And but one word with one of us? Couple it with something; make it a word and a blow.

TYB. You shall find me apt enough to that, sir, an you will give me occasion.

MER. Could you not take some occasion without giving?

TYB. Mercutio, thou consortest with Romeo.

MER. Consort?[60] What, dost thou make us minstrels? An thou make minstrels of us, look to hear nothing but discords. Here's my fiddle-stick;[61] here's that shall make you dance. Zounds, consort!

BEN. We talk here in the public haunt of men. Either withdraw unto some private place And reason coldly of your grievances, Or else depart. Here all eyes gaze on us.

MER. Men's eyes were made to look, and let them gaze. I will not budge for no man's pleasure, I.

[*Enter Romeo.*]

TYB. Well, peace be with you, sir. Here comes my man.

MER. But I'll be hang'd, sir, if he wear your livery.[62] Marry, go before to field, he'll be your follower! Your worship in that sense may call him man.

TYB. Romeo, the love I bear thee can afford No better term than this: thou art a villain.[63]

ROM. Tybalt, the reason that I have to love thee Doth much excuse the appertaining[64] rage

To such a greeting. Villain am I none. Therefore farewell. I see thou knowest me not.

TYB. Boy, this shall not excuse the injuries That thou hast done me; therefore turn and draw.

ROM. I do protest I never injur'd thee, But love thee better than thou canst devise[65] Till thou shalt know the reason of my love; And so, good Capulet, which name I tender As dearly as mine own, be satisfied.

MER. O calm, dishonourable, vile submission! Alla stoccata[66] carries it away.   [*Draws.*] Tybalt, you ratcatcher,[67] will you walk?

TYB. What wouldst thou have with me?

MER. Good King of Cats, nothing but one of your nine lives. That I mean to make bold withal, and, as you shall use me hereafter, dry-beat the rest of the eight. Will you pluck your sword out of his pilcher[68] by the ears? Make haste, lest mine be about your ears ere it be out.

TYB. I am for you.

ROM. Gentle Mercutio, put thy rapier up.

MER. Come, sir, your passado![69]

ROM. Draw, Benvolio; beat down their weapons. Gentlemen, for shame! forbear this outrage! Tybalt, Mercutio, the Prince expressly hath Forbid this bandying in Verona streets. Hold, Tybalt! Good Mercutio!

[*Tybalt under Romeo's arm thrusts Mercutio in, and flies.*]

MER.   I am hurt. A plague o' both your houses! I am sped.[70] Is he gone and hath nothing?

BEN.   What, art thou hurt?

MER. Ay, ay, a scratch, a scratch. Marry, 'tis enough. Where is my page? Go, villain, fetch a surgeon.

[*Exit Page.*]

---

[59]Good evening.

[60]A company of musicians. Because of their low rank in society, Mercutio by pretending to misunderstand Tybalt feigns that he has been insulted.

[61]I.e., his sword.

[62]Mercutio pretends that Tybalt meant "servant" by "man."

[63]Low fellow.

[64]Fitting.

[65]Guess.

[66]A term from fencing: "at the thrust."

[67]Earlier in the play, Mercutio has been punning on Tybalt's name. Tybert was King of the Cats in the old tale of *Reynard the Fox.*

[68]Outer garment (i.e., scabbard).

[69]Thrust.

[70]Done for.

ROM. Courage, man. The hurt cannot be much.

MER. No, 'tis not so deep as a well, nor so wide as a church door; but 'tis enough, 'twill serve. Ask for me to-morrow, and you shall find me a grave man. I am peppered, I warrant, for this world. A plague o' both your houses! Zounds, a dog, a rat, a mouse, a cat, to scratch a man to death! a braggart, a rogue, a villain, that fights by the book of arithmetic! Why the devil came you between us? I was hurt under your arm.

ROM. I thought all for the best.

MER. Help me into some house, Benvolio, Or I shall faint. A plague o' both your houses! They have made worms' meat of me. I have it, And soundly too. Your houses!

[Exit, supported by Benvolio.]

ROM. This gentleman, the Prince's near ally,[71]
My very friend, hath got this mortal hurt
In my behalf—my reputation stain'd
With Tybalt's slander—Tybalt, that an hour
Hath been my kinsman. O sweet Juliet,
Thy beauty hath made me effeminate
And in my temper soft'ned valour's steel!

[Enter Benvolio.]

BEN. O Romeo, Romeo, brave Mercutio's dead!
That gallant spirit hath aspir'd the clouds,
Which too untimely here did scorn the earth.

ROM. This day's black fate on more days doth depend;
This but begins the woe others must end.

[Enter Tybalt.]

BEN. Here comes the furious Tybalt back again.

ROM. Alive in triumph, and Mercutio slain?
Away to heaven respective lenity,[72]
And fire-ey'd fury be my conduct[73] now!
Now, Tybalt, take the 'villain' back again
That late thou gavest me; for Mercutio's soul
Is but a little way above our heads,
Staying for thine to keep him company.
Either thou or I, or both, must go with him.

TYB. Thou, wretched boy, that didst consort him here,
Shalt with him hence.

ROM.   This shall determine that.

[They fight. Tybalt falls.]

BEN. Romeo, away, be gone!
The citizens are up[74] and Tybalt slain.
Stand not amaz'd. The Prince will doom thee death
If thou art taken. Hence, be gone, away!

ROM. O, I am fortune's fool!

BEN.   Why dost thou stay?

[Exit Romeo.]

—38–141

The townsmen come running in. Soon the Prince arrives. Benvolio gives him an account of the slaying of Mercutio (kinsman to the Prince) and Tybalt, but makes his story highly partial to Romeo. Infuriated, the Prince dooms Romeo:

PRINCE.   And for that offence
Immediately we[75] do exile him hence.
I have an interest in your hate's proceeding,
My blood[76] for your rude brawls doth lie a-bleeding;
But I'll amerce[77] you with so strong a fine
That you shall all repent the loss of mine.
I will be deaf to pleading and excuses;
Nor tears nor prayers shall purchase out abuses.
Therefore use none. Let Romeo hence in haste,
Else, when he is found, that hour is his last.
Bear hence this body, and attend our will.
Mercy but murders, pardoning those that kill.

[Exeunt.]

—191–202

(Sc. 2) Juliet awaits Romeo at night for the consummation of their marriage. The Nurse enters and melodramatically reveals that Romeo has slain Tybalt. When Juliet learns of Romeo's banishment, she declares that she would have preferred to hear of the death of her

[71]Kinsman.
[72]Mildness which is the result of reflection.
[73]Conductor.
[74](In arms.)
[75]Kings and princes use the "royal we" for I.
[76]Mercutio was his kinsman.
[77]Penalize.

whole family. To comfort her in her misery, the Nurse volunteers to find Romeo and bring him to her. (Sc. 3) At his cell, Friar Laurence informs Romeo of the Prince's decree. At the thought of separation from Juliet, Romeo falls to the floor in grief. The Nurse comes in and tells of Juliet's unhappiness:

NURSE. O, she says nothing, sir, but weeps and weeps;
And now falls on her bed; and then starts up,
And Tybalt calls; and then on Romeo cries,
And then down falls again.
ROM.   As if that name,
Shot from the deadly level of a gun,
Did murder her, as that name's cursed hand
Murder'd her kinsman. O, tell me, friar, tell me,
In what vile part of this anatomy
Doth my name lodge? tell me, that I may sack
The hateful mansion.   [*Drawing his sword.*]
FRIAR.   Hold thy desperate hand:
Art thou a man? thy form cries out thou art:
Thy tears are womanish; thy wild acts denote
The unreasonable fury of a beast:
Unseemly woman in a seeming man!
Or ill-beseeming beast in seeming both!
Thou hast amazed me: by my holy order,
I thought thy disposition better temper'd.
Hast thou slain Tybalt? wilt thou slay thyself?
And slay thy lady that in thy life lives,
By doing damned hate upon thyself?

—99–118

The Friar continues to give Romeo a sound scolding for his rash attempt on his own life, and reminds him that since the Prince had earlier promised death for fighting in the streets, Romeo has much to be grateful for. He urges the young man to join his wife:

Go get thee to thy love, as was decreed,
Ascend her chamber, hence and comfort her.
But look thou stay not till the watch be set,
For then thou canst not pass to Mantua,
Where thou shalt live till we can find a time
To blaze[78] your marriage, reconcile your friends,
Beg pardon of the Prince, and call thee back
With twenty hundred thousand times more joy
Than thou went'st forth in lamentation.
Go before, nurse. Commend me to thy lady,
And bid her hasten all the house to bed,
Which heavy sorrow makes them apt unto.
Romeo is coming.
    NURSE. O Lord, I could have stay'd here all
    the night
To hear good counsel. O, what learning is!
My lord, I'll tell my lady you will come.
    ROM. Do so, and bid my sweet prepare to
    chide.

NURSE. Here is a ring she bid me give you, sir.
Hie you, make haste, for it grows very late.
                                            [*Exit.*]
ROM. How well my comfort is reviv'd by this!
FRIAR. Go hence; good night; and here stands
    all your state:[79]
Either be gone before the watch be set,
Or by the break of day disguis'd from hence.
Sojourn in Mantua. I'll find out your man,
And he shall signify from time to time
Every good hap to you that chances here.
Give me thy hand. 'Tis late. Farewell; good night.
    ROM. But that a joy past joy calls out on me,
It were a grief so brief to part with thee.
Farewell.

                                            [*Exeunt.*]

—146–175

[78]Proclaim.   [79]Your affairs.

(Sc. 4) Because his daughter seems too stricken by Tybalt's death to hear Paris' suit, Capulet himself decides that she and Paris shall marry—in fact, within three days. (Sc. 5) After a single night of love, Romeo takes his leave of Juliet. She feels lost and terrified. Lady Capulet comes in to tell her of joyful news: Juliet is soon to marry Paris. Off guard, Juliet angrily declares that she will not marry him. Capulet comes in, and learning of his daughter's stubborn refusal to wed Paris, denounces her and threatens to disown her unless she goes through with the ceremony. Left alone with the Nurse, Juliet in despair asks for guidance. Too worldly, the Nurse counsels Juliet to marry Paris. Romeo in exile, she says, is as good as dead. Horrified at such indecency and betrayal, Juliet pretends to agree. She declares to herself that henceforth she will never take the Nurse into her confidence.

(Act IV, sc. 1) At Friar Laurence's cell, Paris meets Juliet. She is very curt with him, and asks to be allowed to speak with the Friar alone. She tells the old man her fears; he then gives her a potion that will produce the effect of death. After she has drunk it and is thought by her family to be dead, she will be borne to the Capulet vault. The Friar, meanwhile, will have sent for Romeo, and the two may flee Verona together and find their happiness elsewhere. She agrees to the scheme. (Sc. 2) The Capulet household is busy making preparations for the approaching wedding. Juliet, pretending repentance over her rebellion, announces her willingness to marry Paris. (Sc. 3) After bidding her mother and the Nurse goodnight, Juliet knows that she must now take the potion:

JUL. Farewell! God knows when we shall meet again.
I have a faint cold fear thrills through my veins
That almost freezes up the heat of life.
I'll call them back again to comfort me.
Nurse!—What should she do here?
My dismal scene I needs must act alone.
Come, vial.
What if this mixture do not work at all?
Shall I be married then to-morrow morning?
No, no! This shall forbid it. Lie thou there.
[Lays down a dagger.]
What if it be a poison which the friar
Subtilly hath minist'red[80] to have me dead,
Lest in this marriage he should be dishonour'd
Because he married me before to Romeo?
I fear it is; and yet methinks it should not,
For he hath still been tried[81] a holy man.
I will not entertain so bad a thought.
How if, when I am laid into the tomb,
I wake before the time that Romeo
Come to redeem me? There's a fearful point!
Shall I not then be stifled in the vault,
To whose foul mouth no healthsome air breathes in,
And there die strangled ere my Romeo comes?

Or, if I live, is it not very like
The horrible conceit[82] of death and night,
Together with the terror of the place—
As in a vault, an ancient receptacle
Where for this many hundred years the bones
Of all my buried ancestors are pack'd;
Where bloody Tybalt, yet but green[83] in earth,
Lies fest'ring in his shroud; where, as they say,
At some hours in the night spirits resort—
Alack, alack, is it not like that I,
So early waking—what with loathsome smells,
And shrieks like mandrakes[84] torn out of the earth,
That living mortals, hearing them, run mad—
O, if I wake, shall I not be distraught,
Environed with all these hideous fears,
And madly play with my forefathers' joints,
And pluck the mangled Tybalt from his shroud,
And, in this rage, with some great kinsman's bone
As with a club dash out my desp'rate brains?
O, look! methinks I see my cousin's ghost
Seeking out Romeo, that did spit his body
Upon a rapier's point. Stay, Tybalt, stay!
Romeo, I come! this do I drink to thee.
[She falls upon her bed within the curtains.]
—14–59

(Sc. 4) There is much afoot in the Capulet mansion because of the wedding. (Sc. 5) The Nurse enters Juliet's room to awaken her on her marriage morning, and finds her apparently dead.

[80]Provided.
[81]Proved.
[82]Thoughts.
[83]Freshly laid.
[84]The mandrake when uprooted was said to shriek in a manner fatal to the hearer.

Her shrieks bring in Lady Capulet and Capulet. They are overwhelmed with grief. Paris and the Friar enter. Paris is stricken with sorrow at his loss. The Friar speaks words of comfort.

(Act V, sc. 1) In Mantua, the exiled Romeo has been dreaming of Juliet. His servant, Balthasar, enters in haste to tell him the shocking news of Juliet's death:

> BALTHASAR. Her body sleeps in Capel's monument,
> And her immortal part with angels lives.
> I saw her laid low in her kindred's vault,
> And presently took post to tell it you:
> O, pardon me for bringing these ill news,
> Since you did leave it for my office, sir.
> ROM. Is it e'en so? then I defy you, stars!
> Thou know'st my lodging: get me ink and paper,
> And hire post-horses; I will hence to-night.
> BAL. I do beseech you, sir, have patience:
> Your looks are pale and wild, and do import
> Some misadventure.
> ROM. Tush, thou art deceived:
> Leave me, and do the thing I bid thee do.
> Hast thou no letters to me from the friar?
> BAL. No, my good lord.
> ROM.   No matter: get thee gone,
> And hire those horses; I'll be with thee straight.
> [Exit Balthasar.]
> Well, Juliet, I will lie with thee to-night.
> Let's see for means:—O mischief, thou art swift
> To enter in the thoughts of desperate men!
> I do remember an apothecary,
> And hereabouts a' dwells.

—18–38

Romeo knocks at the apothecary's door, and bribes the man to sell him a powerful poison. He hastens away to die by Juliet's side. (Sc. 2) A fellow-friar informs Friar Laurence that the latter's important letter to Romeo has not been delivered. The messenger charged with the delivery has been quarantined in a house because of the plague.

> FRIAR L. Who bare my letter then to Romeo?
> FRIAR JOHN. I could not send it,—here it is again,—
> Nor get a messenger to bring it thee,
> So fearful were they of infection.
> FRIAR L. Unhappy fortune! by my brotherhood,
> The letter was not nice, but full of charge
> Of dear import, and the neglecting it
> May do much danger. Friar John, go hence;
> Get me an iron crow and bring it straight
> Unto my cell.
> FRIAR J. Brother, I'll go and bring it thee. [Exit.]
> FRIAR L. Now must I to the monument alone;
> Within this three hours will fair Juliet wake:
> She will beshrew me much that Romeo
> Hath had no notice of these accidents;
> But I will write again to Mantua,
> And keep her at my cell till Romeo come:
> Poor living corse, closed in a dead man's tomb!
> [Exit.]

—13–30

(Sc. 3) It is night in the cemetery before the Capulet vault:

[*Enter Paris and his Page with flowers and a torch.*]

PAR. Give me thy torch, boy. Hence, and stand aloof.
Yet put it out, for I would not be seen.
Under yond yew tree lay thee all along,
Holding thine ear close to the hollow ground.
So shall no foot upon the churchyard tread,
Being loose, unfirm, with digging up of graves,
But thou shalt hear it. Whistle then to me,
As signal that thou hear'st something approach.
Give me those flowers. Do as I bid thee, go.

PAGE [*aside*]. I am almost afraid to stand alone
Here in the churchyard; yet I will adventure.

PAR. Sweet flower, with flowers thy bridal bed I strew—
O woe! Thy canopy is dust and stones—
Which with sweet water[85] nightly I will dew;
Or, wanting that, with tears distill'd by moans.
The obsequies that I for thee will keep
Nightly shall be to strew thy grave and weep.

[*The Page whistles.*]
The boy gives warning something doth approach.
What cursed foot wanders this way to-night
To cross my obsequies and true love's rite?
What, with a torch? Muffle me, night, awhile.

[*Enter Romeo, and Balthasar with a torch, a mattock,[86] and a crow of iron.*]

ROM. Give me that mattock and the wrenching iron.
Hold, take this letter. Early in the morning
See thou deliver it to my lord and father.
Give me the light. Upon thy life I charge thee,
Whate'er thou hearest or seest, stand all aloof
And do not interrupt me in my course.
Why I descend into this bed of death
Is partly to behold my lady's face,
But chiefly to take thence from her dead finger
A precious ring—a ring that I must use
In dear employment. Therefore hence, be gone.
But if thou, jealous,[87] dost return to pry
In what I farther shall intend to do,
By heaven, I will tear thee joint by joint
And strew this hungry churchyard with thy limbs.
The time and my intents are savage-wild,
More fierce and more inexorable far
Than empty tigers or the roaring sea.

BAL. I will be gone, sir, and not trouble you.

ROM. So shalt thou show me friendship. Take thou that.
Live, and be prosperous; and farewell, good fellow.

BAL. [*aside*]. For all this same, I'll hide me hereabout.
His looks I fear, and his intents I doubt.[88]

ROM. Thou detestable maw, thou womb of death,
Gorg'd with the dearest morsel of the earth,
Thus I enforce thy rotten jaws to open,
And in despite I'll cram thee with more food.

[*Romeo opens the tomb.*]

PAR. This is that banish'd haughty Montague
That murd'red my love's cousin—with which grief
It is supposed the fair creature died—
And here is come to do some villanous shame
To the dead bodies. I will apprehend him.
Stop thy unhallowed toil, vile Montague!
Can vengeance be pursu'd further than death?
Condemned villain, I do apprehend thee.
Obey, and go with me; for thou must die.

ROM. I must indeed; and therefore came I hither.
Good gentle youth, tempt not a desp'rate man.
Fly hence and leave me. Think upon these gone;
Let them affright thee. I beseech thee, youth,
Put not another sin upon my head
By urging me to fury. O, be gone!
By heaven, I love thee better than myself,
For I come hither arm'd against myself.
Stay not, be gone. Live, and hereafter say
A madman's mercy bid thee run away.

PAR. I do defy thy conjuration[89]
And apprehend[90] thee for a felon here.

ROM. Wilt thou provoke me? Then have at thee, boy!

[*They fight.*]

PAGE. O Lord, they fight! I will go call the watch.

[*Exit.*]

PAR. O, I am slain! If thou be merciful,
Open the tomb, lay me with Juliet. [*Dies.*]

ROM. In faith, I will. Let me peruse this face.
Mercutio's kinsman, noble County Paris!
What said my man when my betossed soul
Did not attend him as we rode? I think
He told me Paris should have married Juliet.
Said he not so? or did I dream it so?

[85]Perfume.
[86]A pickaxe.
[87]Suspicious.

[88]Suspect.
[89]Adjuration.
[90]Arrest.

Or am I mad, hearing him talk of Juliet,
To think it was so? O, give me thy hand,
One writ with me in sour misfortune's book!
I'll bury thee in a triumphant grave.
A grave? O, no, a lanthorn,[91] slaught'red youth,
For here lies Juliet, and her beauty makes
This vault a feasting presence[92] full of light.
Death, lie thou there, by a dead man interr'd.
[*Lays him in the tomb.*]
How oft when men are at the point of death
Have they been merry! which their keepers call
A lightning before death. O, how may I
Call this a lightning? O my love! my wife!
Death, that hath suck'd the honey of thy breath,
Hath had no power yet upon thy beauty.
Thou art not conquer'd. Beauty's ensign yet
Is crimson in thy lips and in thy cheeks,
And death's pale flag is not advanced there.
Tybalt, liest thou there in thy bloody sheet?
O, what more favour can I do to thee
Than with that hand that cut thy youth in twain
To sunder his that was thine enemy?
Forgive me, cousin! Ah, dear Juliet,
Why art thou yet so fair? Shall I believe
That unsubstantial Death is amorous,
And that the lean abhorred monster keeps
Thee here in dark to be his paramour?
For fear of that I still[93] will stay with thee
And never from this palace of dim night
Depart again. Here, here will I remain
With worms that are thy chambermaids. O, here
Will I set up my everlasting rest[94]
And shake the yoke of inauspicious stars
From this world-wearied flesh. Eyes, look your
    last!
Arms, take your last embrace! And, lips, O you
The doors of breath, seal with a righteous kiss
A dateless bargain to engrossing[95] death!
Come, bitter conduct;[96] come, unsavoury guide!
Thou desperate pilot, now at once run on
The dashing rocks thy seasick weary bark!
Here's to my love! [*Drinks.*] O true apothecary!
Thy drugs are quick. Thus with a kiss I die.
[*Falls.*]
[*Enter Friar Laurence, with lanthorn, crow,
and spade.*]
    FRIAR. Saint Francis be my speed![97] how oft
        tonight

Have my old feet stumbled at graves! Who's
    there?
    BAL. Here's one, a friend, and one that knows
        you well.
    FRIAR. Bliss be upon you! Tell me, good my
        friend,
What torch is yond that vainly[98] lends his light
To grubs and eyeless skulls? As I discern,
It burneth in the Capels' monument.
    BAL. It doth so, holy sir; and there's my mas-
        ter,
One that you love.
    FRIAR.   Who is it?
    BAL.   Romeo.
    FRIAR. How long hath he been there?
    BAL.   Full half an hour.
    FRIAR. Go with me to the vault.
    BAL.   I dare not, sir.
My master knows not but I am gone hence,
And fearfully did menace me with death
If I did stay to look on his intents.
    FRIAR. Stay then; I'll go alone. Fear comes
        upon me.
O, much I fear some ill unthrifty[99] thing.
    BAL. As I did sleep under this yew tree here,
I dreamt my master and another fought,
And that my master slew him.
    FRIAR.   Romeo!
Alack, alack, what blood is this which stains
The stony entrance of this sepulchre?
What mean these masterless and gory swords
To lie discolour'd by this place of peace?
[*Enters the tomb.*]
Romeo! O, pale! Who else? What, Paris too?
And steep'd in blood? Ah, what an unkind hour
Is guilty of this lamentable chance!
The lady stirs.
[*Juliet rises.*]
    JUL. O comfortable[100] friar! where is my lord?
I do remember well where I should be,
And there I am. Where is my Romeo?
    FRIAR. I hear some noise. Lady, come from
        that nest
Of death, contagion, and unnatural sleep.
A greater power than we can contradict
Hath thwarted our intents. Come, come away.
Thy husband in thy bosom there lies dead;
And Paris too. Come, I'll dispose of thee
Among a sisterhood of holy nuns.
Stay not to question, for the watch is coming.
Come, go, good Juliet. I dare no longer stay.

[91]Lantern.
[92]A chamber where a monarch appears
on state occasions.
[93]Always.
[94]*To set up one's rest* is to resolve firmly.
[95]Seizing all.

[96]Conductor.
[97]Prosper me!
[98]In vain.
[99]Unfortunate.
[100]Bringing comfort.

JUL. Go, get thee hence, for I will not away.
[*Exit Friar.*]
What's here? A cup, clos'd in my true love's
  hand?
Poison, I see, hath been his timeless[101] end.
O churl! drunk all, and left no friendly drop
To help me after? I will kiss thy lips.
Haply[102] some poison yet doth hang on them
To make me die with a restorative.[103]

[*Kisses him.*]
Thy lips are warm!
  CHIEF WATCH [*within*]. Lead, boy. Which
    way?
  JUL. Yea, noise? Then I'll be brief. O happy
    dagger!
This is thy sheath; there rest, and let me die.
[*She stabs herself and falls.*]

—1–170

The two families, arriving too late, now learn of all the mischief their hate has caused. They vow friendship:

  CAP. O brother Montague, give me thy hand:
This is my daughter's jointure,[104] for no more
Can I demand.
    MONT.   But I can give thee more:
For I will raise her statue in pure gold;
That whiles Verona by that name is known,
There shall no figure at such rate be set
As that of true and faithful Juliet.
  CAP. As rich shall Romeo's by his lady's lie;
Poor sacrifices of our enmity!
  PRINCE. A glooming peace this morning with it brings;
The sun for sorrow will not show his head:
Go hence, to have more talk of these sad things;
Some shall be pardon'd and some punished:
For never was a story of more woe
Than this of Juliet and her Romeo.

—296 to end

Let us refresh our memories as to what we have already learned (in Chapter 5) about plot. *Plot,* of course, *is a matter of action*—of the deeds that are done during the course of the story. (Action is a happening which has a consequence; it can be either physical or mental. A violent physical happening which has no consequence does not qualify as dramatic action.) The characters of a play may be moved by subconscious processes which the audience is aware of; and these subconscious processes may lead to important actions. But such motivations are not part of the plot. Plot is made up of action. Thus, a modern writer might conceivably have chosen to explain Romeo's relationship with Juliet as a reaction from his frustration over Rosaline (Shakespeare makes it the result of Romeo's being in love for the first time in his life); that frustration, though a motive for the plot, would not be part of the plot itself.

But action in itself does not necessarily constitute plot. A story detailing the many events occurring in the life of one individual may be totally lacking in plot: for example, a story which traced Romeo's life from birth, through his boyhood adventures, his experiences at school, his first attraction to a woman, his frustration over Rosaline, and so on through the meeting with Juliet and the consequences thereof. Romeo's boyhood adventures, his experiences at school and his frustration over Rosaline do not coordinate into a plot because between these events there exists no logical connection with Romeo's action in the play.

Action which constitutes plot is to be distinguished from a series of unrelated incidents in that *a plot contains a logical unity within itself:* it begins at a certain point; this beginning

[101]Untimely.
[102]Perhaps.
[103](His kiss would, were he alive, have been able to restore the dead to life.)
[104]Marriage portion.

contains the roots of the middle; the middle gives rise to the question which the play must settle; the end answers the question, completing what was begun in the beginning.

In *Romeo and Juliet* what is pertinent to the play in the first act leads to the *beginning of the plot* (Act I, sc. 5):

1. Romeo, member of a family that is at feud with the family of Juliet, meets Juliet and falls in love with her. What follows this happening leads to the *middle of the plot* (Act II, sc. 6):

2. Although their families are at feud, Romeo marries Juliet. This deed immediately raises a question to be answered by the *end* of the play:

3. Will Romeo find happiness or catastrophe in his marriage with Juliet? This being a tragedy, the answer provided by the end is "catastrophe."

From our discussion it has been clear that *a plot always concerns the acts of a central character.* That person is the *doer* of the action. *Romeo and Juliet,* however, might seem uniquely confusing among the world's tragedies in this respect. Are there not two central characters?* Could one have not, just as well, stated the plot above by interchanging Juliet's name with Romeo's (i.e., Juliet, member of a family that is at feud with the family of Romeo, meets Romeo and falls in love with him; and so on to the middle and end)? Moreover, some people might insist that Juliet is perhaps a shade more engrossing as a person than Romeo.† The latter argument is, however, irrelevant.‡ For *plot,* being a matter of action, *is independent of characterization* in its logic, however it may be motivated by it.

The question as to who is the central character can be settled beyond dispute once the climax is identified. *The climax,* an important part of the structure of the plot, *is the moment during which the central character does something which determines the course of the remaining action.* If the question of the play is "Will Romeo find happiness or catastrophe in his marriage with Juliet?" the climax must be an act of Romeo's which will determine the answer to that question; if the question is "Will Juliet find happiness or catastrophe in her marriage with Romeo?" the climax must be an act of Juliet's. Now, what is the moment, once the lovers are married, which dooms them to catastrophe?

For, let us remember, Shakespeare was careful to make it clear that, despite the feud, catastrophe was not at all inevitable for them. When Paris first sues for Juliet's hand (Act I, sc. 2) her father states that his will is but a part "to her consent" and adds that she has her own "scope of choice" for a husband.∫ Later, when Tybalt discovers Romeo at the Capulet feast, and burns to quarrel with him (Act I, sc. 5), Capulet refuses to allow him to do so, speaks of Romeo in terms of great admiration, and declares that not all the wealth of Verona could cause him to do Romeo "disparagement" in their house. This emphatically raises some hope that the young lovers will have a chance of happiness, and perhaps by their

---

*Two central characters are, of course, a contradiction in terms—except in the hypothetical case of two people always acting together and as one person in exactly the same way.

†We are not disposed to agree with this. If it is felt, it is probably due to the fact that actresses have done better by Juliet than actors have by Romeo. In a tragedy, for reasons which we must presently inspect, the central character must also be the most absorbing one. *Romeo and Juliet* gives the impression of having two central characters because the desires of the two lovers remain identical—i.e., to be together. But their *actions* are not at all identical.

‡In plays which are not tragedies it often happens that *the most interesting character may not* at all *be the central one*—see Chekhov's *The Three Sisters.* The central character is central only to the plot.

∫There is no reason to doubt that he means this. To a careless reader he may seem later tyrannical in his fury over Juliet's refusal to go through with the marriage to Paris, but it should be remembered that at that time he not only is ignorant of the fact that his daughter is married to Romeo—he does not even know that the two have ever met. Juliet has consented to marry Paris; now suddenly (Act III, sc. 5), when all arrangements have been made, she refuses for no apparent reason. Her father is not entirely to blame if he regards her change of mind as the willfulness of a spoiled child.

union be the means of restoring peace between the families. Certainly, after the catastrophe, the heads of the rival houses are quick to embrace each other and at once bury their hate (Act V, sc. 3).

With some chances of happiness, then, clearly indicated—what is the act which places the lovers beyond the possibility of felicity? It is Romeo's slaying of Tybalt. That deed, the climax of the tragedy, is the one which determines the course of the remaining action. Not only does it make Romeo's marriage beyond acceptance by the Capulets, but it immediately places his very life in jeopardy. The Prince has ordained death to any further disturbers of the peace (Act I, sc. 1). To emphasize the point, Shakespeare has Romeo remember this while Tybalt and Mercutio are fighting (Act III, sc. 1), for Romeo cries, "The Prince expressly hath forbid this bandying in Verona streets." Yet, a few minutes later he commits his fatal error. Made reckless by his sense of guilt for being responsible for Mercutio's death, he casts aside all thoughts of his future life with Juliet, and challenges Tybalt to a fight to the death, exclaiming: "Either thou or I, or both, must go" with Mercutio. This is the climax, his killing of Tybalt, and it is, as it should be, the act of the central character.*

The climax of a play can also be described in terms of character. At the beginning of a play a certain set of relationships is established between the leading characters. If the play has a plot these relationships are going to be altered during the course of the action. *The climax is the moment at which the greatest dislocation takes place in the relationship between the leading characters as established at the beginning of the play.* At the beginning of our play there is some hope that Romeo will find happiness with Juliet; he has already found means of being with her. When he kills Tybalt, he immediately puts himself under sentence of death and completely annihilates the possibility of being with her; the Prince lightens the sentence to exile, but that too means separation from her.

The deed which forms *the climax should be* (as we have noted in Chapter 5) *an expression of the personal traits of the central character.* How true this is of Romeo we shall presently see.

While we are considering *Romeo and Juliet* it is opportune to discover something about the nature of tragedy. A word concerning the history of tragedy will afford insight into its essentials.

TRAGEDY, ITS ORIGINS AND FUNCTION

Tragedy in the Western world apparently originated in ancient Greece as part of the ceremonies connected with the Festival of Dionysus. This holiday, in one respect, corresponds to the Christian Lent and the Hebrew Day of Atonement; it was the occasion for each individual to achieve an inner purification (in Greek, *katharsis*). During the Golden Age of Athens, when tragedies were first written for a theatre, dramatists participated in a public competition, each contestant submitting a trilogy.† A committee selected the drama-

---

*Juliet, on the other hand, performs no deed that forfeits her chances of happiness with Romeo. Tybalt's slaying of Mercutio is perhaps the most exciting moment of the play. But, as we have already observed (in Chapter 5), the climax is not to be looked for in the most exciting moment. Tybalt is obviously not the central character. His deed, however, provides the *motive* for the climax.

†I.e., three tragedies connected in subject matter. We have surviving one such trilogy by the earliest of the great Athenian dramatists, Aeschylus: his *Agamemnon, Libation-Pourers* and *Eumenides,* dealing, respectively, with Clytemnestra's slaying of her husband, Agamemnon; with Orestes' slaying in vengeance (with the aid of his sister, Electra) his mother, Clytemnestra, and her lover; and with Orestes' atonement for the crime of matricide. (Just as in the chapter on Fiction we had to speak of novels you may not have read, so in this chapter we shall refer to plays that we have no space for, hoping that in time you will have read them all. We take this liberty because fiction and drama are the literary forms most important to the contemporary audience. If we use the triple measure of greatness of accomplishment, historical importance and contemporary appeal, drama easily stands foremost.—Remember that motion pictures and television plays are drama.—Reading the plays we allude to will help you immeasurably in cultivating your taste, in enriching your pleasures.)

tists who had written the most excellent tragedies, and on a succession of days each dramatist was given a day during which his trilogy was presented. At the end of the Festival, one of the playwrights was accorded a prize by public applause.* The audience was made up of the entire citizenry of Athens, who came to the theatre (fulfilling duties partly religious, partly civic) to achieve through *katharsis* a greater inner well-being.

From Aristotle's *Poetics* we take the clue as to how this inner purgation was to be attained. Every normal human being goes about with a certain weight of pity and awe in his bosom. When channeled into the activities of daily living these emotions equip a man with compassion, on the one hand, and, on the other, with a sense of proportion concerning his place in the scheme of things. But the ordinary circumstances of life do not allow him sufficient occasion for healthfully employing this pity and this awe. Unexpressed in action and retained within his bosom, they begin to fester and to damage his spiritual health. An excess of pity degenerates a man into a sentimentalist, a lover of the maudlin, ready to weep over things unworthy of tears;† an excess of awe debases a man into a coward or even a neurotic. The Athenian citizen attending the theatre, by identifying himself with the hero of a tragedy, was able to undergo vicariously the tragic experience of the hero; in this way channeling his own pity and awe, he was able to disburden his bosom of its freight of these emotions. At the close of the tragedy he was chastened into a sober understanding of human destiny and his place in the scheme of things. He could leave the theatre with new perspectives and in a state of better spiritual health.

Dionysus may (or may not!) be dead. But the function of tragedy remains the same—because it meets an all-important human need. We are ever in need of this spiritual cleansing and chastening. Our own lives—luckily—do not partake of the tragic. We are not given the opportunity to expend ourselves on grand or noble issues. However important our own griefs may seem to us privately, when viewed objectively they are more likely to be petty and trivial than magnificent. Thus, we accumulate day by day a sickening store of frustrations and vexations. We go to a tragedy and it achieves the purposes for which tragedy was first created: we identify ourselves with the hero, suffer vicariously with him in his experiences, and are cleansed. We drink with Romeo the poison and feel his death-throes, yet remain physically sound; we dash out our eyes with Oedipus,‡ yet retain their sight; with Othello we plunge the dagger into our breast, yet remain unwounded; with Electra∫ we help direct her brother's sword against their mother, yet remain innocent of the heinous crime of matricide. And we come away saddened but purged of pettiness, chastened but seeing more into the heart of things.

A feeling of exaltation is also part of the awe which we know at the catastrophe suffered by the tragic hero. His downfall involves as well a sort of transfiguration, as though at the moment it occurs it were his role and his privilege to stand as representative of the human race and by his catastrophe expiate its failings. His heedlessness may be only the impetuosity of youth, as with Romeo, or almost criminal, as with Macbeth and Electra, but his sufferings transform him—because he reaps a harvest he has sown—at his downfall into a sacrifice offered for all of us. (This transformation is, of course, true only to the extent to which we can identify ourselves with the tragic hero.) This sense of exaltation in tragic catastrophe has been nobly stated by Richard Strauss in his tone-poem *Death and Transfiguration*.

---

*It is hard to resist the conviction that at that period the general public at Athens had attained a level of taste rarely, if ever, known again in the world. The prize was most often awarded to Aeschylus, their sublimest poet, and next most often to Sophocles, their greatest dramatist.

†E.g., the sentimentalist will sorrow for the hardened murderer awaiting execution but be indifferent to the murderer's innocent victim.

‡In Sophocles' *Oedipus the King.*

∫In Sophocles' *Electra.*

To cleanse the soul and to transfigure our pity and awe—this is the high function to which tragedy is called. It is doubtful that any other exercise of human creativity is higher. It is not surprising therefore that the boundaries of tragedy are austerely marked off; serving such high purposes, it reserves to itself, like a temple of worship, certain holy ground onto which the profane may not intrude. On this territory we may smile a little—even laugh a little, provided the laughter does not shatter the solemnity of the air. But we do not come here to be indignant; nor do we come here to be depressed.

A tragedy must not leave us indignant, or how shall we, while we are inflamed, be purged? It must not leave us depressed, or how shall we be cleansed? Moreover, how shall indignation or depression permit us to identify with the hero? Such emotions are outside the precincts of tragedy. It is not that room is lacking in the theatre for plays which arouse indignation; Ibsen's unrelenting onslaught on human hypocrisy and self-delusion gave the world some of its best plays (*A Doll's House, The Wild Duck, An Enemy of the People*), which rightfully arouse our ire. As for plays which leave us depressed, we confess to be in a critical minority: we cannot understand the use of paying our hard-earned cash for a seat in the theatre with the purpose of leaving in a suicidal mood—no matter how much the playwright's skill is to be admired. However, we are living in times when it is considered indecent to ask whether a work was worth creating at all—times, moreover, in which some of our best minds have demonstrated, by awarding prizes to plays whose object is to depress, that they enjoy being thrust into the dumps. We therefore do not debate the value of that school of dramatic writing. In short, the kind of play which undertakes to make the audience indignant certainly has a place in the theatre; the kind of play which undertakes to depress may or may not have an analogous place—in any case, it exists. But neither sort can be described as a tragedy, since neither undertakes to afford, and neither can afford, a *katharsis*.

This is more than a matter of labels or of the splitting of hairs. For a tragedy, to be effective (i.e., provide a purging), must conform to certain basic principles, which are the very conditions of its existence. *A tragedy must,* as we have seen, *evoke both pity and awe* —a pity which is compassion, and an awe which is a revelation both of man's littleness in the face of the vast complexities through which he must find his way, and of man's greatness of soul in standing up, despite his littleness, against those complexities. (Those complexities may be variously described as God, Nature, Society, or other forces.) Pity without awe is not enough, and too readily deteriorates into bathos (witness the worst of Dickens' novels); it is in the absence of awe that most would-be tragedies fail (e.g., Arthur Miller's *Death of a Salesman*).

THE NATURE OF THE TRAGIC HERO AND HIS EXPERIENCES

Where is the source of pity and awe in a tragedy? Largely, in the character of the hero, for it is with him that the audience must identify itself. Inevitably, therefore, only a certain kind of human being will do as a tragic hero. Such a man must not be too good, for though we should pity his fall, it would make us indignant; if he is too angelic, we cannot identify with him. He must not be too wicked, for then we should not feel pity at his fall but rejoice in it; if he is too bad, he would alienate us, rather than invite our identification with him* —unless, of course, we are psychopathic. He must be a man or woman, essentially good, whose character is marred by a fatal shortcoming—the *tragic flaw* of esthetic discussion— a weakness which proves his undoing.

He must also be a man above average or the commonplace in his qualities (unlike the

*Macbeth, among Shakespeare's great heroes, is a crucial instance. Shakespeare contrives through the magic of his art to retain our sympathies for Macbeth throughout, murderer though he is. We feel that despite his crimes he is essentially a good man foundering in evil. If we ever were made to feel otherwise about him, the play would cease to be a tragedy and deteriorate into melodrama (as does *Richard III*).

central character of *Death of a Salesman*).* We cannot identify with an average or common-place man. We may talk largely about the average man and even smugly boast of our sympathy with him—but we never mean *ourselves* by the expression; the "average man" is always somebody else. Privately no one thinks of himself as commonplace. We are all aware of stately possibilities, ignored by the world; give us the opportunity to play our role in an appropriately noble setting, and everyone should soon see—! No, we may pity the average man, but we cannot also help somewhat looking down on him, for we know ourselves not to be average. For this reason, we do not identify ourselves with him in a play. In him there can be no awe. We can identify only with a hero who is above the average.

By definition a tragedy will show this hero's experiences ending in catastrophe. *The catastrophe will be brought about by the hero's own* fatal weakness, his *tragic flaw*. It cannot be accident which brings about his downfall; accident is beyond logic or explanation, and the audience could not identify itself with an all-determining action which is only an accident. An accident is something which will not happen to us; it is an occurrence which we cannot, and should not (if we are to remain sane) count upon. But being human, we can identify with a deed which is the product of human weakness. We may be made sorrowful by the fall which is brought about by a tragic flaw of the hero, but we are not depressed by it. For there is at least dignity in the catastrophe of which a man is himself somewhat the author.

Let us pause now to take another look at Romeo, and see how he exhibits the character-istic traits of the hero of a tragedy. He is not too good; when we first meet him he is clearly a callow youth in love with love (small wonder that Rosaline does not take him seriously) and rather a trial to listen to; he will unburden his synthetic woes to anyone who will hear him.† He has, moreover, as we shall observe in a moment, a tragic defect of character. He is, of course, not wicked. He is a man full of the potentialities of beauty and magnificence —and these love causes to blossom in him—whose splendor is marred by a fatal weakness. He is, too, a man above the average, for only such a man could love as he loves.

What is his tragic flaw? Love nourishes his finest qualities, and transforms him from a shallow youth to a radiant and mature man. But it also unleashes his fatal weakness, heedlessness. To begin with, having fallen in love with Juliet, he makes no attempt to deal with the family feud; it would not have been too difficult, as we have seen, to win Capulet's consent. It is beside the point that he does not guess this. What is tragic is that he does not even try. But his recklessness is most fatally evident at the climax. Though he warns Tybalt and Mercutio of the Prince's decree against fighting, Mercutio's death converts him into a creature forsaken by his reason. Indeed, when Tybalt reenters (Act III, scene 1) Romeo rejects intelligence, and deliberately embraces a policy of rashness:

> Away to heaven, respective lenity,
> And fire-ey'd fury be my conduct now!

*The "depressing" plays, of which we have spoken, make it their business to have average men as their heroes, mediocrities with whom no one will identify. These works are usually described by their authors as tragedies. No one questions the noble social intentions of these playwrights, but a play does not become a tragedy because it is labeled one, nor because it is "sad." The requirement of being above the average has nothing to do, of course, with social rank. Thomas Hardy's Jude (in *Jude the Obscure*), despite his lowly station, is a truly tragic figure because of the qualities of soul which raise him above the average; Theodore Dreiser's Clyde (in *An American Tragedy*, which, by the way, is no tragedy), coming from an equally lowly origin, is not a tragic figure because his author has intentionally, and successfully, portrayed him as commonplace. The death of a Jude makes the world a poorer place; the death of a Clyde leaves the world much as it was. Of course, exalted social position does not necessarily qualify a man as a tragic hero. A monarch with a petty soul would be no better a candidate than Clyde.

†Shakespeare, who knew everything about human nature, makes an interesting point. When Romeo *thinks* he is in love with Rosaline, the whole world is told about it and is busy discussing it. When he really falls in love, not even his closest friends are aware that he has met Juliet. It never occurs to him to take anyone into his confidence, except Friar Laurence, whose help he needs.

He rushes into the arms of disaster, as though it, not Juliet, were his bride.

In a tragedy the climax results from the hero's tragic flaw. It is the deed which dooms him to catastrophe because of his own shortcomings.

Romeo demonstrates this rashness in many other places. In Friar Laurence's cell (Act III, scene 3) he tries to kill himself. In exile when his servant brings word that Juliet is dead (Act V, scene 1), he at once decides to die too. His servant notes that his wild looks "import some misadventure." Declaring that mischief is ever "swift to enter in the thoughts of desperate men," he loses not a moment in buying the poison at the apothecary. When he reaches Verona again after a wild ride during which his "betossed soul did not attend" anything his servant tried to tell him (concerning Paris and Juliet) (Act V, scene 3), he never thinks of going first to Friar Laurence to find out how matters stand. He is so eager for death that, rather than explain his presence at the tomb, he fights with Paris, whom he rashly regards only as an impediment to his self-destruction. At last, by Juliet's side, his drinking the poison is his final act of recklessness. He is clearly the author of his own doom, and that is why we can identify ourselves with him. All of us are only too likely to be rash, when we should be patient, and to bring down catastrophe upon our own heads because of our heedlessness.

Of course, in life accidents do occur, and tragedy, as a representation of the issues of life, also shows the role played by accident as we work out our destinies. In *Romeo and Juliet* the element of chance is stronger than is usual in Shakespeare's tragedies. The failure of Friar Laurence's letter to be delivered to Romeo certainly powerfully cooperates with the hero's tragic flaw to bring about catastrophe. But Romeo's own recklessness has involved him in disaster long before that. As we have seen, his killing Tybalt made his life at once forfeit. And even after the misfortune of the letter's delay, had Romeo had the wisdom to see Friar Laurence before going to the tomb, his death as well as Juliet's could have been avoided. Thus, accident in a tragedy appears as a force that is likely to make our own folly trebly catastrophic. Our own shortcomings start a landslide; accident may convert that landslide into an avalanche.* Tragedy, thus, reminds us all that, once we give the rein to our own weaknesses, we may expect the chances of life to cooperate in bringing us to grief.

CHARACTERIZATION

Before we leave *Romeo and Juliet* we should like to make some brief comments on the characterizations which may be discerned even in our excerpted passages. Shakespeare is the perfect dramatist in his ability to make us feel that the persons of his plays do what they do because of what they are, and that they are what they are because of what they do. (This superb awareness of what is rare and yet absolutely as it should be in drama, will be found much more remarkably at work in the later tragedies: *Julius Caesar, Hamlet, Othello, Macbeth, Lear, Antony and Cleopatra,* and *Coriolanus*—as well as in the great comedies and histories: *The Merchant of Venice, Much Ado About Nothing, As You Like It, Twelfth Night, Measure for Measure, Henry IV, Parts I* and *II,* and *Henry V.*) This is an ideal to which all dramatists who are cognizant of the laws of their craft aspire, though few of even the best attain. Many otherwise capable playwrights manage their characterizations statically, and take the easier way of allowing various persons of the drama to sketch in other characters by talking about them or discussing them. The greatest masters of the drama depend on such a device very little. For instance, only Friar Laurence in the play—and he but briefly—

---

*It is unlucky that Duncan comes to stay at Macbeth's castle on that particular night, for that is the night Macbeth is prepared to murder; but people do spend the night at a friend's house, and get up quite alive next morning in time for breakfast. It is unlucky that Desdemona loses the handkerchief just when she does; but many faithful wives lose a gift of their husband's without running the risk of being slain. In other words, it is the defect in Macbeth's and in Othello's characters which converts an innocent event into the beginning of their own doom.

comments on Romeo's callowness; no one later points out Romeo's rashness. Before our eyes he is seen by his own behavior to become transformed from a belated adolescent into a highly poetic, strong-willed adult through the alchemy of love. We also observe, with awe, that same alchemy suddenly liberate his innate recklessness. The very nature of drama is that it moves (the word comes from the Greek *dran,* "to do"), and dramatic characterization is at its best when it is revealed through action. Shakespeare, above all others, has an almost uncanny power to make his men and women unfold as human beings, scene by scene. Great portraits like those of Shylock, Portia, Beatrice, Rosalind, Viola, Hamlet, Othello, Iago, Macbeth, and Lady Macbeth are, as it were, being painted throughout the entire course of the play; every time we meet them, we learn new facets of their makeup; and the picture is really not finished until the end of the play.

So, too, we see Juliet grow in quality and richness of personality. At the beginning of the play she is a colorless, obedient child—needing the guidance of her parents and ready to follow it even in the matter of marriage. We see her transformed too by love; the quiet girl becomes a passionate, ecstatic young woman. She too is utterly reckless; no more than Romeo does she attempt to win her parents over, or to take them into her confidence. We see how much easier it is for her in her abandon to drink the Friar's potion (which she fears may be deadly) than to tell her father and mother the truth. We see these things without blaming either lover, for we never forget that they are very young. We can only commiserate with their rashness.

We see first Mercutio's merriment and lightning-like wit in his verbal bouts with his friends. We understand why such a man would naturally loathe Tybalt for living so much according to rules and regulations. We become acquainted with his violence when he tries to provoke Tybalt's anger against himself, and see him whip himself up almost into a frenzy when trying to force Tybalt to fight with him. He prefers to live dangerously and to fling his life away. And even in death there is a jest upon his lips:

> Ask for me tomorrow and you shall find me a grave man.

We see how much Tybalt, equally hot-tempered, is a stickler for family honor and pride, and is sudden to take offense at Romeo's presence at the Capulet feast even though the head of the house feels no harm is being done. What is amazing, considering his nature, is the long time he takes to pick up Mercutio's challenge to fight, despite the latter's repeated insults and provocation. (In those days but one word of insult was enough to precipitate a duel.) But he is out to avenge himself for Romeo's imagined slight, and with that singleness of mind which Mercutio detests in him, he intends to take care of one thing at a time.

Benvolio is throughout the voice of sympathy and moderation. We observe his concern for Romeo's unhappiness over Rosaline and his eagerness to help him recover from it. We hear him urging Mercutio to withdraw before any trouble starts in the streets on that hot day. We watch him try to stop the duel between Mercutio and Tybalt. He is a quiet man, but a true friend and the salt of the earth.

Our omissions of certain passages has diminished the vividness with which the Nurse is depicted in the play: they would show her to be a coarse, worldly, garrulous creature, but utterly devoted to Juliet, for whom alone she seems to live. Friar Laurence, in the full text, will be seen as kind, sympathetic to the yearnings of young people, indulgent with their frailties, but willing to speak home truths when needed—a thoroughly humane priest.

Most dramatists would have been tempted to make of Paris, because he is Romeo's rival, a villain. Shakespeare, wiser, has made him a charming, elegant and sincere young man. Indeed we know nothing to his disparagement. The genuineness of his love for Juliet is seen in the last act when, unknown to anyone else, he comes to mourn her loss at the tomb. Despite the ideality of his character, he emerges not as a tragic figure but only as a pathetic one. It is he, above all others in the play, who is a victim of circumstances. He is innocent of any knowledge of Romeo's claim to Juliet, and is destroyed by forces outside his control.

Since, unlike Romeo, he is not the author of his own doom, though we pity him, we cannot identify with him.

Every one of the traits possessed by these men and women is intimately involved with the happenings in the play. These people do what they do because of what they are, and they seem to be what they are because of what they do. Characterization thus managed becomes integral to the plot, and in the theatre invokes a maximum of audience interest.

COMEDY

So much, then, for tragedy. Let us turn to the larger, earthier province of comedy.

As an introduction to it, here is an extremely skillful one-act play, *Shoptalk*, by the American dramatist Michael Turque (1933–):

DRAMATIS PERSONAE

THE DIRECTOR	MRS. PURVIS
PURVIS	A RECEPTIONIST
BRIGHT	

TIME: *Today.*

SCENE: *The office of the company president in a large industrial plant. Seated behind a wide, brilliantly polished mahogany desk, in the presidential chair, is the Director. He wears a black armband. Behind him hangs the late president's portrait, draped in black.*

[*The Director takes out a pocket watch. He places it on the desk. Then he switches on the intercom.*]

DIRECTOR. Have Mr. Purvis and Mr. Bright arrived?

VOICE. Yes, Sir.

DIRECTOR. Would you ask them to come in, please? [*There is a knock at the door.*] Come in. [*A receptionist is seen opening the door. Enter Purvis and Bright.*] Mr. Purvis—Mr. Bright—won't you come in?

PURVIS AND BRIGHT. Thank you.

DIRECTOR [*indicating chairs*]. Please make yourselves comfortable, gentlemen. [*Both men sit.*] For one of you the memory of today's triumph will be one of life's treasures; the joyous aftertaste of a goal successfully pursued. Something to savor for the rest of your years. For the other, well, it can't be helped.

PURVIS. Excuse me, Director, but—but what precisely will happen to the other?

DIRECTOR. According to the rules, the, ah, unsuccessful aspirant must leave the company in the most discreet way possible. The last one, I can't think of his name, made a clean break. Overdose of phenobarbital, I think.

BRIGHT. Did he give the Old Man, that is, J. P.—did he give him much of a fight?

DIRECTOR. The contest was epic.

BRIGHT. J. P. was probably icewater.

DIRECTOR. He was a man of amazing control.

PURVIS. They say he could make his rage work for him more effectively than any president in the history of the company.

BRIGHT [*pointing to the portrait*]. Just look at that head. The strength of the jaw—the fire of integrity at once illuminating the eyes and casting an iron shadow of resolution across the brow. Moses couldn't have looked more the patriarch. No wonder J. P. was such an effective liar.

PURVIS. Yes, and the texture of his voice; vibrant yet subdued. Oracular. Who could disbelieve the word of such a man?

DIRECTOR. But deception was only one of the qualities that pushed him to the top. The thing that distinguished him as a man among men was his deep devotion to the company. It was his life. He had a feeling for the company that is difficult, impossible, fully to describe. The company was his mother and father. It was the flesh of his flesh. If a subsidiary was in trouble, he could sense it. When our Portland distributors were being picketed by strikers, he complained of a tightness in his chest. The doctors told him it was his heart. When the strike was settled, the tightness disappeared and they could find no trace of cardiac disturbance.

BRIGHT. That's a beautiful story.

PURVIS. But didn't he have any outside interests—a hobby—a wife?

BRIGHT. He was married, wasn't he?

DIRECTOR. Well, yes, he was. But it was nothing serious. It happened in his youth. He was in college at the time. It was a question then of not really knowing what he wanted.

PURVIS. But what happened to her? Was she at his funeral? I didn't see her.

DIRECTOR. She was institutionalized some years ago. A weak, sickly type. Some sort of breakdown.

PURVIS. Oh.

DIRECTOR. But it's getting late, gentlemen, and you know, time is money. Let us turn our attention to the inquiry. [*Bright draws his chair closer to the Director's desk.*] The rules are very simple. They are the rules we all live by from day to day. The cardinal precept of the—er—game is that each man pursue his advantage to the best of his ability.

BRIGHT. Why, then there's no mystery at all.

DIRECTOR. What do you mean, Mr. Bright?

BRIGHT. Well, Sir, you know this procedure of the company's for selecting a successor to the presidency has grown through the years into a sizeable legend.

DIRECTOR. Yes, that's natural enough. But surely, gentlemen, you weren't taken in by this mystical claptrap. Because if you were, the company has made a grave mistake about you.

BRIGHT. No, of course not. It was just office gossip. I'm sure neither of us took it seriously. [*He turns to Purvis.*] You were joking before when you mentioned something about a fire ritual, weren't you, Purvis?

PURVIS. I never said anything of the kind. What are you talking about, Bright?

DIRECTOR. Ha ha, I see. Very good, Mr. Bright, but we haven't really begun yet. Now there is one more thing. I want to warn you both that if you make any accusations you can't substantiate, it will count very heavily against you. You understand that? [*Both men nod.*] Well then, gentlemen, I think you may begin.

BRIGHT. First of all, Director, I'd like to point out a serious breach of company policy. Not to impugn Mr. Purvis' ancestry, or to blame him for something over which he had no control, it is nevertheless true that he doesn't belong to the Church Of The True Faith. Now while our charter doesn't expressly forbid it, it's certainly against all tradition to consider an outsider for the presidency.

DIRECTOR. Good, Mr. Bright. You've been doing your homework. Yes, that's true. The Fathers did feel that an unconventional religious affiliation might be damaging to the company. But as you say, it isn't actually forbidden by the charter. And in Purvis' case I felt there was no danger, and that the precedent could be safely broken.

PURVIS. Thank you, Director. May I present my opening remarks?

[*Bright chuckles.*]

DIRECTOR. Please do, Mr. Purvis.

PURVIS. First, I would like to enter as evidence in my own behalf, [*to the Director*] if that is the proper expression . . .

BRIGHT. Oh, get on with it, Purvis.

PURVIS. I would first point to my record of service with the company. [*He lays several documents on the desk.*] As you can see, Sir, I have a perfect record of attendance, except for a three-week leave some years ago when I was operated on for double hernia.

BRIGHT. Double? Very prudent, Purvis, to have so economically managed your time.

[*The Director smiles at Bright, who is feeling very confident.*]

PURVIS. Also, I may say I feel a certain pride in the fact, recorded by our official timekeeper, that in twenty years I have never been tardy.

DIRECTOR [*good-humoredly*]. True, true.

BRIGHT. I must admit that tardy-wise my record doesn't approach yours, Purvis. In fact, Director, if the truth be known, just this morning I punched in thirty-seven minutes late. But let's get down to cases.

DIRECTOR. Good.

BRIGHT. I've been working here for five years. In that short time I've made more money for the company than Purvis has in twenty.

PURVIS. May I point out that for seventeen of my twenty years of service I was an accountant? I was hardly in a position to benefit the company financially. It's only in the last three years that I've had anything to do with shaping company policy; and furthermore, in that short time I've made proportionately more for the firm than you, Mr. Bright.

BRIGHT. If I can unscramble your words, Mr. Purvis, you claim that you've made more for the company during your service than I?

DIRECTOR. Only proportionately, Mr. Bright. But of course that's highly theoretical. After all, Mr. Purvis, the company employed you only because it felt that you would make a profit for it, even in your capacity as chief accountant. The company's motive in its selection of personnel as well as in its larger operations is always profit.

BRIGHT. Exactly. Thank you, Director.

DIRECTOR. Don't thank me, Mr. Bright. You should have made that point yourself, instead of purposely misconstruing Mr. Purvis' words.

[*Bright looks unhappy.*]

PURVIS. You see, Bright, honesty may sometimes be the best policy.

[*Director chuckles.*]

BRIGHT. Too bad your wife doesn't hold your view.

[*Director shifts attentively in his seat. Purvis stiffens.*]

PURVIS. What do you mean by that?

BRIGHT. Director, I suggest that a man who can't manage his own business is unfit to manage the company's.

DIRECTOR. Be more specific, Mr. Bright. Are you making an accusation?

BRIGHT. Director, I accuse Purvis of being ignorant of the fact that his wife is an adulteress.

[*Purvis starts toward Bright belligerently.*]

DIRECTOR [*with authority*]. Purvis!

[*Purvis stops.*]

PURVIS [*softly*]. You're a liar.

DIRECTOR. You know, Mr. Bright, that a false accusation will seriously damage your chances.

BRIGHT. I let my accusation stand.

DIRECTOR. According to the rules of procedure as laid down by the charter, you, Mr. Purvis, may demand that Mr. Bright substantiate his accusation. But understand, you aren't obliged to ask for proof.

PURVIS. Yes.

DIRECTOR. Let me outline the consequences of your alternatives. If you don't contest the charge, it will mean that you are willing to let it stand as evidence against you. I will then assume that you have been aware of your wife's alleged indiscretion, and that, for whatever personal reason, you have chosen to do nothing about it. Furthermore, I will assume that your indignation just before was no more than an observation of propriety. Now this kind of evidence is serious. But it isn't necessarily damning.

PURVIS. I'm not sure I follow you.

DIRECTOR. For example, it was well known that our late president was married in name only; that he and his wife made their separate—ah—arrangements years ago. Most people think of this behavior as being very sophisticated—mature is the word they use. Two people prove they can be adult about an unfortunate marriage—you see what I'm driving at, Mr. Purvis?

PURVIS. I see. I can, if I choose, accept the accusation, and play it down. It may even redound to my credit.

DIRECTOR. Precisely. Now as to the consequence of your other alternative: If Mr. Bright were unable to supply proof for his accusation on demand, he would, to all intents and purposes, be disqualified. On the other hand, if he were able to prove his contention, you would look very foolish indeed.

PURVIS. How would it affect my candidacy?

DIRECTOR. Very gravely, I'm afraid. You see, it would be evidence of an oversight. The company cannot afford a careless president.

PURVIS. I see.

BRIGHT. Come now, Purvis, what's it going to be? Surely you want to know the truth. A man can't spend his life with a woman he's not absolutely sure of. If you have the smallest suspicion, it will eat you alive. Every day it will grow a little, like a tumor. You'll never feel easy again.

PURVIS. Can't you keep quiet!

DIRECTOR [*benignly*]. Let Mr. Purvis make his own decision, Mr. Bright.

BRIGHT. But I'm trying to help. Look—even if you never completely believe she's been unfaithful—just that small edge of doubt, getting sharper every day—razor-sharp, till every thought you have of her brushes up against it and bleeds—

PURVIS [*pauses; then*]. I want proof.

BRIGHT. Good!

DIRECTOR. All right, Mr. Bright. It's your move.

BRIGHT. I asked Mrs. Purvis to make herself available this morning; [*to Purvis*] she's very obliging that way— [*to the Director*] Just in case she was needed. Unless I'm mistaken, she's waiting in the outer office.

DIRECTOR [*switching on the intercom*]. Is Mrs. Purvis in the building?

VOICE. She's sitting right here, Sir.

DIRECTOR. Please ask her to come in.

VOICE. Yes, Sir.

[*There is a pause. Then, a knock at the door.*]

DIRECTOR. Please come in.

[*The door is opened by a receptionist. Enter Mrs. Purvis. She is a pretty, well-dressed woman in her late thirties. She looks enquiringly to Bright, then to her husband.*]

DIRECTOR. Good morning, Mrs. Purvis. Very good of you to give up your morning for us.

MRS. PURVIS. Good morning, Director. I'm happy to lend any assistance. [*To her husband*] Hello, John.

DIRECTOR [*watching her very carefully*]. You know Mr. Bright, our assistant manager?

MRS. PURVIS. Certainly. It's always a pleasure to see you, Mr. Bright.

BRIGHT. Hello, Mrs. Purvis.

MRS. PURVIS. Wasn't it last Christmas that you were out to our house? You've been very sparing with your attentions. You must come visit us again, very soon.

BRIGHT [*smiling*]. That will be my pleasure.

PURVIS. After you hear why the Director called you in, you'll think twice about your invitation, Helen.

MRS. PURVIS. What do you mean, John?

PURVIS. When Bright asked you to come here this morning, why didn't you tell me?

MRS. PURVIS. As a matter of fact, Mr. Bright called half an hour after you left.

BRIGHT. If you weren't always so punctual, you'd have known about my call.

MRS. PURVIS. What's happened? I wish someone would explain.

PURVIS. Here, Helen. [*Purvis leads her to a*

chair.] Sit down. [*Mrs. Purvis sits.*] You know, Helen, these presidential contests can be very lurid.

MRS. PURVIS. Yes?

PURVIS. Bright here has made an accusation against me. It involves you. [*Mrs. Purvis looks anxiously to Bright.*] He says . . . that is . . . he accuses me of harboring an adulteress.

MRS. PURVIS. Adulteress—

BRIGHT. It's all right, Helen. I explained to you that I might have to use this as evidence. You can forget about looking shocked. Just tell them the truth.

MRS. PURVIS. It's true.

PURVIS. True? What? What are you saying?

MRS. PURVIS. Don't sound more of a fool than you are, John. Yes, I've been unfaithful.

PURVIS [*apparently broken*]. Why, Helen? Why?

MRS. PURVIS. Really, what could you expect? For the past twenty years your every waking hour has been devoted to the company. Every thought fixed on your career. Even during the first days of our marriage. Coming home every night after one. No letup.

PURVIS. But it was for you, Helen—for you as well as for me.

MRS. PURVIS. In the beginning I used to wait for you at night; wait to hear your car grind up the gravel drive. But you were always so tired. After a while I pretended I was asleep. Our marriage became nothing more than an arrangement —a mutual convenience. I kept your house; you kept me. Our marriage degenerated into one of those clever arrangements—

PURVIS [*looking at Mrs. Purvis' fur coat*]. Not an unprofitable one for you.

MRS. PURVIS. Oh, no. After you became an executive, there were plenty of parties, automobiles, fur coats; plenty of everything, including loneliness.

PURVIS. Very moving. Really, Helen, you're quite an actress. But let's stick to the facts. [*To the Director.*] My wife would have you believe that overweening ambition was the cause of my downfall. That's a laugh. You're married, aren't you, Director?

DIRECTOR. Why, yes.

PURVIS. Then you know that married men have an opportunity rarely enjoyed by bachelors; the opportunity of apprehending those facets of female psychology that are completely hidden to everyone but the husband. Some of these revelations are really astonishing. For instance—you wouldn't suspect that my wife—that demure and most correct paragon of an executive helpmate—

you would never in a million years suspect that she nurtured an ambition so pernicious, that to see it in its raw and palpitating state would make your blood run cold.

MRS. PURVIS. Why, John, you've a considerable flair for the dramatic, yourself.

PURVIS. Yes, you never really did take the trouble to know me, did you, Helen? But then, you were always so completely wrapped up in yourself. That was your mistake. [*To the Director*] Do you remember, Director, when you raised me to my first executive position?

DIRECTOR. Why, yes, Mr. Purvis—that was some three years ago, wasn't it?

PURVIS. Three years, two months, seven days.

DIRECTOR [*smiling*]. Quite.

PURVIS. If you'll recall, there was another man, Charlie Haberman, a colleague of mine in the accounting department. You were also considering him for the job.

DIRECTOR. That's true.

PURVIS. And do you remember why you finally decided to give me the promotion?

DIRECTOR. Well, let me see . . . oh, yes. Of course I felt you were really the man I wanted all along—but something happened that finally settled the matter for me. At the office Christmas party—this man, Haberman, became very drunk —very abusive.

PURVIS. Do you remember who was the object of his abuse?

DIRECTOR. Hmm. Why, it was your wife— Mrs. Purvis. That's right! . . . He accused her of . . . of leading him on, making him think she cared, and then laughing in his face—or some such nonsense. Some men can't handle liquor at all. He showed very poor judgment, drinking as much as he did. A Christmas party was no excuse.

PURVIS. Exactly. Everyone knew that poor Charlie made a fool of himself on two scotch-and-sodas. Everyone, including my lovely wife.

BRIGHT [*worried*]. Is this true?

MRS. PURVIS. What if it is? Don't you be a fool.

PURVIS. You see, working in the same department, Charlie and I were rather friendly. He was out to our place almost every weekend. He and Mrs. Purvis got to know each other very well.

BRIGHT [*sardonically*]. I underestimated you, Helen.

PURVIS. Poor Charlie. Whenever a man acts strangely out of character, look to his wife—or his mistress. Now, Helen, for the record, who is your current source of consolation and comfort?

MRS. PURVIS. Apparently you're having your

little game, John, although considering your position, it's beyond me why you should choose cat and mouse. But, just for the record then, I'm in love with Mr. Bright, and as soon as we've dissolved our marriage, or rather, as soon as you've dissolved it, I'm going to marry him.

PURVIS. Forgive the obtuseness, Helen. A matter of form. [*Mrs. Purvis nods.*] You felt that the smart money was on Bright's candidacy, and you acted accordingly—correct?

MRS. PURVIS. Your insinuations are revolting.

BRIGHT. Look, Purvis. I gave Helen what you never took the trouble, or were never able, to give her—that's all. She loves me. Why not let it go at that?

DIRECTOR [*clearing his throat*]. Well, the case seems clear, Mr. Purvis. It's a strange and unhappy tale you've told, but Mr. Bright does seem to have put one over on you. In the absence of any further accusations, charges, or countercharges, I will adjourn the meeting and give you my verdict after lunch.

BRIGHT. You must make an effort to be sporting, Purvis. After all, business is business.

PURVIS. Yes, and all's fair in love and war, I know. I couldn't agree with you more, Mr. Bright. Therefore, I have one further piece of evidence to submit. [*Purvis reaches into his coat pocket and draws a small revolver.*] Director, you've just heard my wife and her lover freely admit their illicit relation. [*He points the gun so that it covers both Bright and his wife.*]

DIRECTOR. Unquestionably.

BRIGHT. Don't be a fool, Purvis, put away that gun. You're likely to hurt someone.

PURVIS. Don't concern yourself, Bright. There won't be any accidents. I'm really quite expert with firearms. Ask Helen. She'll tell you. I even have a little target range in my basement. One of the few diversions I allow myself.

DIRECTOR [*with renewed interest in Purvis*]. What do you propose to do, Mr. Purvis?

PURVIS. I think you'll admit I've been provoked to the limit of self-restraint?

DIRECTOR. You have been badly used.

PURVIS. People in my situation have been known to behave very rashly indeed.

DIRECTOR. True.

MRS. PURVIS. He's mad!

PURVIS. In fact, just recently there was a case similar to mine. *Ex parte Hoffman, Supreme Court,* to be specific. They called it justifiable homicide. Remarkably similar. It seems the wife and her lover, not content with tasting the forbidden fruit, added spice to the dish by flaunting their affair in the husband's face. The outraged husband supplied a condiment of his own by peppering both of them with a twelve-gauge shotgun. He got off scot-free. Unqualified acquittal. Every man on the jury shook his hand.

DIRECTOR. I see you've been doing your homework, too, Mr. Purvis.

PURVIS. After company hours.

DIRECTOR. Of course.

PURVIS. Here is the situation, Director. Although I hesitate to put you to any inconvenience, I'm afraid I shall have to call upon you to testify in my behalf before a grand jury. Of course, the results of this hearing are assured.

DIRECTOR. Diabolical! This is extraordinary. Now understand, Mr. Purvis, what you suggest is unprecedented. [*To himself*] Frightening to think how it will affect future elections. Who could have thought it would come to this? Hmm. [*To Purvis*] On the other hand, as you pointed out, you would be perfectly justified in exercising your righteous indignation.

BRIGHT. For God's sake, Director, don't let him do it!

[*The telephone rings.*]

DIRECTOR [*answering the phone*]. Hello . . . oh yes, dear. . . . How are the children? Good . . . yes, I'll meet you at the restaurant in ten minutes. Right. Good-bye, dear. [*He hangs up.*] Mr. Purvis, [*pointing to the gun*] I'm in no position to argue with you. You'll have to do as your conscience and your judgment dictate.

MRS. PURVIS [*crying*]. No!

DIRECTOR [*looking at his watch*]. I'll have to hurry. My wife is meeting me for lunch. You know how they fuss when you're late. I'll be back in an hour. I assume that by then all the evidence will have been presented. [*The Director looks at Purvis, nods.*] Good! I'll give you my verdict after lunch. The final deliberation in serious matters should always be made over a glass of port.

MRS. PURVIS [*her hands over her eyes*]. Horrible . . . horrible!

DIRECTOR [*affably*]. Nice seeing you again, Mrs. Purvis. Your visits are much too rare. I know . . . perhaps we can all get together some evening for a drink. And, I promise you, Mrs. Purvis, no shoptalk. Well, good-bye for now.

[*As the Director leaves, Purvis still aiming the gun, the curtain descends.*]

At the close of Plato's *Symposium* Socrates is busy advancing to the sleepy guests the theory "that the genius of comedy was the same with that of tragedy, and that the true artist in tragedy was an artist in comedy also." Certainly comedy and tragedy are not totally dissimilar. Both spring from our knowledge that we ought to live with a sense of perspective —a clear notion of our own limitations and shortcomings, and of our place in the scheme of things. Comedy and tragedy both deal with human beings who have either lost this perspective or else have never possessed it. (Romeo and Juliet lose theirs; Purvis, Bright and the Director seem never to have had any.)

Comedy, too, had its origins in the celebration of Dionysus. He was the god of procreation and fertility, and anciently it was the custom for the celebrants to disguise themselves as birds, horses and other animals while singing chants of fertility with many ribald sexual allusions. Instead of the katharsis of tragedy these embryonic comedies offered the euphoria of laughter.

Eventually, at Athens, comedy was accorded an honorable place during the Festival of Dionysus too. The great practitioner of the art of comedy was Aristophanes (?448–?380 B.C.), who flourished at the time of the heyday of Greek tragedy. But Aristophanic comedy did not establish the traditions in which later comedy has been written. It tends to be fantastic or grotesque rather than realistic. It was too deliberately meant for its own times. Loose in structure, full of ribald contemporary allusion and comment, it contained much horseplay and buffoonery. Its aim was to provoke the release of laughter and to castigate certain citizens. Here and there, by exception, some few modern writers have created in the Aristophanic spirit—a notable example (without the ribaldry) being the libretti which Sir William S. Gilbert (1836–1911) composed for the music of Sir Arthur Sullivan.

Comic tradition dates, rather, from the days of Menander (c. 342–292 B.C.), leading dramatist of the Athenian school of the so-called New Comedy. His plays were imitated by the two leading Roman dramatists Plautus and Terence. The people in these plays are more or less ordinary human beings, and the plot evokes our interest and mirth chiefly by the ingenuity of its complications. These traditional traits comedy has always since maintained.

During the Middle Ages the word "comedy" was loosely applied to any writing, including the most serious, whose ending was happy. (It is for this reason that Dante called his great poem *The Divine Comedy*.) The medieval connotation of the word persists in many plays (like Shakespeare's *Twelfth Night*) where the plot is essentially serious and the resolution is a happy one.

The difference between comedy and tragedy is that tragedy deals with aberrations that are deeply moving, awe-inspiring, and worthy of compassion; comedy deals with aberrations that are amusing, absurd, or contemptible. Tragedy is, in consequence, largely intuitive and emotional in its apprehension of life; comedy, on the other hand, is largely critical and intellectual. The world, said Horace Walpole, is a comedy to those who think and a tragedy to those who feel. And since we all both think and feel, comedy and tragedy satisfy different and important aspects of human needs.

Romeo and Juliet inspire us with wonder at their magnificence, intensity of love, and utter recklessness in surrendering to it; their very abandon is a testimony to their greatness of soul. The characters in *Shoptalk* amaze us too—not with awe, however, but with the strange twists and perversions of their common humanity. We are diverted by their ingenuity, but they inspire us more with contempt than respect. No less than characters in a tragedy are they busy compounding mischief—we feel that all three men are living on the edge of a volcano—but we view their machinations not with compassion but with amused derision.

Tragedy concerns itself with individuals, their soul-states, and the doom they bring upon themselves. Comedy has always been more concerned with the social group, the foibles of the time, the absurdities of social relationships. Its focus, therefore, is less on what is universal in man's soul than on what is typical in his conduct. Unlike those of tragedy, its characters are not idealizations of the quintessences of human nature, but people whose behavior is more like that of ordinary people—and even of people below the level of ordinary conduct. This is not to say that comedy excludes from its casts of characters superior individuals. But when such people are present in a comedy, either the comic emphasis is not on their superiority but on their all-too-human frailties (as with Beatrice and Benedick in *Much Ado About Nothing,* and with Jack and Gwendolen in *The Importance of Being Earnest*) or else we look elsewhere than at them (as elsewhere than at Shylock in *The Merchant of Venice* and Isabella in *Measure for Measure*) for the comic revelation of weaknesses. Any comedy, taken as a whole, does not especially concern itself with what is divine in man. Rather, it turns a questioning eye upon the vagaries, follies and pretenses of contemporary manners. Comedy reveals man in his rather silly or thoroughly absurd side.

Shoptalk, for instance, presents three men typical of the sort shaped by the ruthlessness of modern industry. They are, from a human point of view, monsters; but they are monsters just because they have abandoned the values that tie one to common humanity. We cannot reject the essential truth with which the dramatist has conceived them; the play is clear-eyed, if devastating, in demonstrating the logic underlying the philosophy of ruthless competition (summed up in the catchphrase, "business is business"). By general consent the world of business is another world from that of personal relationships; here Christian ethics are asked not to intrude. It is these values—or rather, the lack of values—which the author is satirizing.

Although comedy does tend to devote itself to the contemporary, it does not follow that it therefore becomes dated with the passage of time. It is interesting, for example, to know that the author of *Shoptalk* has stated that when he began to plan this comedy, he first thought of writing about an episode connected with the Trojan War: the quarrel of Ajax and Odysseus over the armor of Achilles. He then decided to transfer his theme to a modern setting, and proceeded to make all the necessary adjustments in character and story thereby required. What is worthwhile noting is that, set before Troy or in an industrial plant, the theme is a timeless one, as it should be in a work of art. Comedy can find timeless themes because human nature does not change much. On the other hand, it is safe to assume that had the playwright chosen the ancient setting, his characters would have spoken as members of the modern world. That is the way of comedy. No matter what their historical period, the characters in a comedy talk and behave as though they were contemporaries of the audience for which they were first created. There would be little point in a dramatist's castigating or ridiculing customs or values already obsolete. Thus, one of our own contemporaries could conceivably place his attack on religious hypocrisy in the era when Jupiter, Juno, Minerva, Venus and Mars were the gods to be worshipped; but the things said and done would have to be applicable to religious worship in our own time.

The province of comedy is a wide one, and many comedies are not so sharply satirical as *Shoptalk.* It is the function of comedy to amuse us but that does not imply that it is required to make us laugh outright. Some of the world's best comedies are more likely to make us smile (e.g., Molière's *The Misanthrope*). Some contain too much bitter truth to allow us more than a faint smile—perhaps a sardonic one (e.g., Shakespeare's *Measure for Measure*). Some contain truth so grim that we cannot smile at all (e.g., Ibsen's *The Wild Duck*). Some comedies are frankly boisterous in their fun (e.g., Shakespeare's *The Comedy of Errors*). Some are irresistibly gay and lighthearted (e.g., Wilde's *The Importance of Being Earnest*). Some are kindly in their exhibition of human folly (e.g., Goldsmith's *She Stoops to Conquer*). Some are vitriolic in their attack on human depravity (e.g., Jonson's *Volpone*). Some writers of comedy merely shake their heads whimsically at the spectacle of human frailty; some apply a lash to it.*

---

*Our discussion in this chapter takes cognizance of five basic types of drama:
1. Tragedy
2. Comedy

The mirth we anticipate from comedy comes in varying degrees from humor (the situations) and wit (the manipulation of language). Both wit and humor emanate from the presentation of the incongruous and the shock of the unexpected. Everything in the situation of *Shoptalk* is rooted in incongruity with normal human values. The reactions of Purvis, Bright and the Director constantly shock us with what is little to be anticipated in the reactions of normal human beings. This is the very stuff of comedy.

Comedy, no less than tragedy, it should be superfluous to state, depends for its success upon soundness of plot (herein differing from farce). Indeed, far more than tragedy, does comedy invoke interest through the complications of the action. A strong plot holds such complications in a coordinated whole.

In *Shoptalk* the plot revolves about Purvis. All three men are almost of equal interest, but Purvis is the doer of the action. The beginning of the plot may thus be stated:

1. Purvis, who understands the rigid qualifications for the presidency of the company, is competing with Bright according to the rules (which stipulate that a false accusation will be damning), and he is accused by Bright of being ignorant of his wife's adultery. And the middle:

2. Although, if Purvis does not demand proof, his domestic arrangements (however poisonous privately) may redound to his credit—and if, to show the accusation false, he does demand proof and the proof is established, it could destroy his chances—he does demand proof of Bright, and is ready to play the dangerous game.

This move of his raises the question which the end of the play must answer:

3. Will Purvis be able to play the game skillfully enough against Bright to win the presidency or will he kill his own chances?

The answer provided by the conclusion is, He wins.

The climax of the play is the moment when Purvis takes out his gun and aims it at his wife and her lover. This deed makes the conclusion inevitable. Quoting the Hoffman case, he fortifies his position as the sudden aggressor, and makes it clear that he more than meets the qualifications for the late J. P.'s office—icy control, effective rage, devotion to the company. In fact he proves himself J. P.'s superior; while the late president had merely managed to suffer through his marriage within the constrictions of outward respectability, Purvis' moves are such as not only to avenge him on his wife and her lover but also make their murder the means of his ascendancy to office. His devilish cleverness is so effective that the Director has no choice but to be enlisted in his aid, his future eminence is assured

The three men, although they are alike in the traits nurtured by their occupation, are nevertheless distinguished from one another as people. The Director is a man of diabolical aloofness—until his brief telephone conversation near the end gives another dimension to his character. Bright is nimble-witted, ruthless, living only for his ambition; him we dislike

---

3. The play "of grave experience."
4. Melodrama
5. Farce

It is clear from our examples that we consider satirical drama to be within the precincts of comedy. Some critics would not agree, on the grounds that there are satirical plays (like *The Wild Duck*) whose tone is utterly devoid of all but the grimmest mirth. They would also point out that in some serious plays which are clearly not tragedy or comedy (#3 above) there may be present strong satirical elements—as, for example, O'Casey's brilliant *Juno and the Paycock*. Such critics prefer to think the satirical a sixth type of drama. We are not so much interested in nomenclature as in dramatic principles and the aspects of drama, and therefore are of no mind to quarrel over the matter. We agree that while the definitions of tragedy, melodrama and farce may be stated clearly, that is not the case with the other two types. But conceiving comedy to be as spacious in its realm as we do, we think that, laughter aside, a play whose prevailing tone is satirical must be classed as a comedy. When satire is strongly present in our third type of play but does not capture the tone of the whole, we prefer to think of the satirical as only an element in a play "of grave experience."

very early in the play. Our sympathies are at the same time aroused for Purvis as the underdog; it is only after the play is over that we realize that his is a character with concealed depths, and that this man might, under sufficient provocation, turn out to be the most dangerous of them all.

THE ONE-ACT PLAY

While we are considering *Shoptalk,* let us briefly examine the characteristics of the one-act play. Like the short story, it is an elaboration of a single, significant incident.* (Its playing time in the theatre varies from approximately twenty minutes to a little over an hour.)

It must be obvious that in such a play a dramatist cannot achieve the richness of characterization possible in a full-length play. The multiplicity of incidents in *Romeo and Juliet* enables the playwright to allow his characters to expand as the play progresses. We have seen how both Romeo and Juliet achieve growth before our eyes—how every time we meet them anew we become acquainted with other facets of their personalities. This growth is also true of some minor characters like Mercutio and Paris. Indeed, in Shakespeare's greatest plays the leading figures emerge with such full-rounded reality that we feel we know them rather better than members of our own family. In the case of the latter, experience teaches us that it would be hazardous to predict their behavior in a new situation. But, once familiar with Beatrice,† we know how differently from Desdemona she would behave if she were married to Othello: she would laugh him out of his misconception long before he allowed himself to be engulfed by it, and have him on his knees apologizing for his folly. If Portia‡ were the beloved of Hamlet instead of Ophelia, he would not have had new miseries piled upon his head because of her, but a wise and capable counselor to share his problems. Desdemona,ʃ had she been King Lear's youngest daughter, would have managed, we are certain, better than Cordelia to be honest with her father's demands without driving him into disastrous rage.

The dramatization of a single significant incident does not permit the author of the one-act play to realize human beings in this full dimension which makes characters in great full-length plays more real to us than people we meet every day. There is not time enough for the playwright to acquaint us with more concerning his characters than the single incident demands that we know. If, for example, Mrs. Purvis is less vividly depicted than the three men and is a more shadowy figure, that is as it should be. She is only an instrument of the plot. To know more about her would only diminish the prominence given to Purvis and Bright, the two most important characters. As for the Director, he remains, as he is required to be, a man of dehumanized impersonality; only at the end does the little telephone conversation give us a fleeting glimpse which modifies just enough the impression he has created.

One is likely to find a small cast of characters in the one-act play; there is, again, not time enough during the course of its action for the audience to become familiar with more than a few.

Finally, it is rare for a dramatist to attempt tragedy within the limits of this form; there is not scope enough for him to scale the heights. Consequently, when he prefers to write in

---

*There are a few plays which have been miscalled one-acters. These deal with two or more incidents, in token whereof there is a curtain (or blackout) called for once, twice, or more often, before the play is over (e.g., Clifford Odets' *Waiting for Lefty*). If we are to keep our notions straight, such plays should be considered abbreviated forms of the full-length play. They are to the full-length play as the novelette is to the novel.

†Of *Much Ado About Nothing.*

‡Of *The Merchant of Venice.*

ʃOf *Othello.*

a serious, rather than a comic, mood he will probably choose the territory bordering tragedy —a region over which some of the atmosphere of the tragic is breathed, but where awe and purgation are not to be experienced.

A term is seriously needed to distinguish the kind of play which, having no intention to inspire or to achieve purgation, is neither tragedy nor comedy. A scrutiny of the best plays written in the twentieth century will reveal that, among a few expert comedies (e.g., Garson Kanin's *Born Yesterday*) and even fewer tragedies (e.g., Peter Shaffer's *Five Finger Exercise* or *The Royal Hunt of the Sun*), the majority have been dramas that occupy this middle ground.* Without any ambition that our phrase gain wide currency, but only to find a phrase practical for our own purposes, we shall designate such a play as one "of grave experience."

It is interesting to speculate upon the reasons why pure comedy is scarce in our time, and tragedy scarcer. Tragedy cannot blossom in an atmosphere of skepticism, not to say, cynicism. The eighteenth century was such an age too, and produced no tragedies in our language worthy of the name. Skepticism and cynicism are likely to look upon the sublime with jaded eyes; for tragedy a public philosophy not uncongenial to the sublime is necessary. Moreover, the concepts of right and wrong are basic to tragedy, and in our time these concepts have been under attack from many quarters, such as psychology, anthropology, the economic interpretation of history. We are taught that there is no such thing as an absolute right or an absolute wrong, that good and evil are relative to time, place, environmental influences. In a relativistic climate tragedy cannot thrive. Most noxious of all to the tragic concept: we have been accustomed to explain away evil as owing to forces outside individual responsibility. If a young man forces an arsenic cocktail down his doting parents' throats in his haste to inherit their fortune, we say, "Naturally, poor boy! They ruined him by being too good to him." If the parents in the case had been neglectful of him, we would say instead: "Naturally, poor boy! Did they realize how they were thwarting his childhood that time they refused to buy him a bicycle? This consequence could have been foreseen then." If a group of hoodlums makes a sport of throwing old men into the harbor, we explain, "After all, these boys were raised in the slums!"† The hero deprived of personal responsibility for his deeds can never be a tragic hero.

As for comedy, the history of our time has been such a tale of nightmare and horror, it may very well be that we have almost forgotten how to laugh. Since the late 1930s people old enough to think have been living in an atmosphere of unremitting tension. There has always been either a major war or the threat of one in the air. We have been forced to digest as realities the incredible atrocities of genocide; ovens into which thousands of human beings were thrust; concentration camps whose function has been to degrade and dehumanize men, women and children; slave-labor armies recruited from highly civilized men and women; countries overrun without warning by foreign powers who machine-gun liberty out of existence. All of us have, intermittently, been threatened with either the extinction of everything that gives meaning to life, or the annihilation of humanity itself. It may be true that under these circumstances the comic spirit is more needed than ever. But it is also understandable that under them playwrights might feel either ashamed to indulge it or else unequal to embrace it.

*A subdivision of this category is the so-called *problem play,* a term much used since the days of Ibsen (1828–1906). The *problem play* is one that deals with a social problem; e.g., John Galsworthy's (1867–1933) *Justice,* which investigates the problem of legal justice.

†And we are thereby careful to forget children who have returned love for love, children who have returned love for neglect, as well as children raised in the most wretched of circumstances—in the same tenements, in fact, as the hoodlums—who become not criminals but ornaments of civilized society.

LIMITATIONS OF THE ONE-ACT PLAY

We may pause to note once more that *the one-act play is an elaboration of a single incident, and* to note too that it *no further delineates the persons of the drama than the action requires,* as in *Shoptalk.*

From *Shoptalk* we may deduce one more trait of the one-act play. Because its form is so limiting, the one-act play is likely to be more sensational, more "theatrical" than the dramatic full-length play. There is not time or space to prepare a richly full, noble, or deeply moving conclusion. (For this reason the one-act play, despite the quality of a number of one-acters, has not achieved the importance in literature or on the stage comparable to the importance in letters of the short story. There was a time when dramatists expressed considerable interest in the form; this interest seems to have been recently renewed. There were companies devoted to their presentation, and the public was interested in attending the theatre to see a group of one-act plays performed. The restriction to a single incident, the sketchiness of characterization demanded, will explain why to writers it has become more of an excellent discipline* for the creation of more ambitious works than an important literary or dramatic form in itself.) To compensate for the difficulty of managing a noble or deeply moving conclusion, the one-act play often terminates in a scene which contains a certain element of shock.

MELODRAMA AND FARCE

A word remains to be said concerning two kinds of work the entire aim of which is, in some degree, to shock: the melodrama and the farce. Melodrama sets out to play upon our nerves by use of the sensational and the unexpected (e.g., Bram Stoker's *Dracula;* Agatha Christie's *Witness for the Prosecution*). Farce sets out to shock us by any device it can summon, the chief device being, again, the unexpected (e.g., Thornton Wilder's *The Matchmaker*). Melodrama and farce trouble themselves little about principles of dramatic composition, plot or characterization. Their business is to keep things moving, as diverting situation follows diverting situation—no matter how inconsequentially strung together. Melodrama is more concerned with a suspenseful story in which violence or the threat of violence is present, and farce with a hilarious one, than is either with the inner logic of cause and effect provided by a sound plot. While melodrama and farce keep us on edge or provoke us to laughter, they need make no apologies. They sometimes provide an entertaining evening in the theatre, and claim to do no more than that. They rarely make a serious bid for consideration as literature. But, on occasion, a dramatist may so load his work with significance of meaning that even in these forms he may achieve literary height. Pirandello's melodrama *Six Characters in Search of an Author* is one of the most thoughtful plays of our century; and France's farce *The Man Who Married a Dumb Wife* is a timeless satire on the medical and legal professions.

---

*Which is the reason why, with the limitations of space imposed upon *us,* it has served us so well in this chapter.

VERSE
TECHNIQUES
7

THERE IS no question that the best way to develop taste and understanding in any of the arts is to expose oneself over a period of time to the works of the great creators. In music, for instance, anyone, without being able to identify an F# or syncopated four-quarter time or a diminished seventh, can nevertheless learn to be aware of melodies, rhythms and harmonies by listening attentively to the works of the great composers and thus come into close contact with the creator's meaning. So too in poetry, anyone, without stopping to identify the technicalities of versemaking, can learn to be aware of the effects contributed by rhythm, rhyme, assonance and verse forms and thus come into close contact with the poet's meaning. But it is also true that one procures a great deal more out of music when one does know something about its technicalities—such as the structure of a sonata or symphony, or of an individual movement; instrumentation; counterpoint; modulation—and that the more one knows of these matters the more one procures of the composer's meaning. Just so in poetry, if one does stop to identify and analyze the formal aspects of a poem, the more one procures of the poet's intentions and the poem's meaning. For with these matters the poet himself perforce came to grips.

In Chapter 4 we attempted to provide an understanding for all readers of the basic aspects of verse technique, without going into the science of versemaking. But we know too that there are many readers who wish to know something about the latter. Having already covered the fundamentals of rhythm and rhyme, we now proceed to their more technical aspects.

STRESSED AND LONG SYLLABLES

It is a deplorable fact that although there have been many writings on versification, a considerable portion of them are of little use because of false analogies drawn between English and Latin versemaking. In Latin the basis of verse was the length and shortness of syllables; in English the basis of verse is the stressed syllable. In Latin it was always possible to equate two short syllables with one long syllable, and therefore to substitute two short syllables where a long one belonged. But in the English system we cannot substitute two weak syllables for a stressed one; no number of weak syllables will be equivalent to a stressed syllable.*

This confusion between long and strong, short and weak, has needlessly complicated the whole discussion of English versification. A great many phenomena which theorists have pretended to find in our verse are indeed there in theory only. What follows in these pages,

---

*As we have seen in Chapter 4, the time element in English verse provides much of its subtle music. But the time element is not at the basis of the verse; it is a force that does indeed add dimension to our poetry, though it is not, like stress, of *prime* consideration. In Latin poetry, the situation was precisely the other way round.

without hoping to be exhaustive, should make clear all that is essential in English versification. *What we have to say, naturally, is applicable only to the English language.* We are utterly ignorant of the Chinese.

FOOT AND METER

The unit of meter is known as the *foot.*

A foot is a group of syllables (or one syllable) containing one and only one stress. (We employ from here on the sign of the ictus, é, to indicate the stressed syllable.) Thus:

kéttle contains one foot.
Pópocátepétl contains three feet.

The two words which begin the line

In the áge that was gólden

do not constitute a foot because they contain no stress. Those six words contain two feet because there are two stressed syllables.

In English poetry we find almost exclusively only four kinds of feet. In combinations of two syllables:

1. The *iambic* (as in the word *delíght*),* a weak syllable followed by a stressed syllable—

When Éve/ upón/ the fírst/ of mén/
The áp/ple préssed/ with spé/cious cánt/,
Ohl whát/ a thóu/sand píl/ies lhén/
That Ád/am wás/ not ád/amánt/.
—"A Reflection" by THOMAS HOOD

2. The *trochaic* (as in the word *fáther*),* a stressed syllable followed by a weak syllable—

Háil to/ thée, blithe/Spírit!
—from "To a Skylark" by PERCY BYSSHE SHELLEY

There are no other combinations of two syllables possible. Two weak syllables would not constitute *a* foot because of the absence of a stressed syllable. Two stressed syllables would, by our definition, constitute *two* feet. (In Latin, two *long* syllables constitute what is called a *spondee.* In English we do not have such a foot, though, as we shall see in a moment, we can produce the effect of one.) A *foot of only one syllable* (stressed, of course) *is* simply *a variant of the iambic or trochaic,* with the weak syllable missing:

A bróther's múrder. Práy cán I nót

In this line from *Hamlet* (III/iii/38) the weak syllable before *can* is missing, and that word therefore is a complete foot, a variant of the iambic, like all the other feet in the line. The conjunction of two stressed syllables in *Pray* and *can* gives the *effect* of a spondee; but we have, as we have seen, two feet here, not one foot.

In combinations of three syllables:

3. The *anapestic* (as in the first three syllables of the word *anapést/ic*),* two weak

---

*To make things easier, in our definition of each of the four feet we have illustrated with "as in the word . . ." But it should be remembered that a foot does not necessarily begin with the beginning of a word. The word *ápple,* for instance, might have been used to illustrate a trochee; but in the example we cite from Thomas Hood it appears (line 2) in an iambic line. Here the stressed syllable, *áp,* terminates the foot; it could also be used in a trochaic line to begin the foot:

Ápple,/ ápple,/ ón the/ boúgh.

It could equally well terminate an anapest if preceded by two weak syllables:

For an áp/ple a dáy/.
Keeps the dóc/tor awáy/.

Or it could begin a dactyl if the whole word were followed by another weak syllable:

Ápples won't/grów on a/ múlberry/ trée/.

syllables followed by a stressed syllable—

> In the áge/ that was góld/en, the hál/cyon tíme/,
>   All the bíl/lows were bálm/y and bréez/es were blánd/.
> Then the pó/et was név/er hard úp/ for a rhýme/,
> Then the mílk/and the hón/ey flew frée/and were príme/,
>   And the vóice/ of the túr/tle was héard/ in the lánd/.
>
> In the tímes/ that are guílt/y the wínds/ are pervérse/,
>   Blowing fáir/ for the shárp/er and fóul/ for the dúpe/.
> Now the pó/et's condí/tion could scárce/ly be wórse/,
> Now the mílk/ and hón/ey are stráined/ through the púrse/,
>   And the vóice/ of the túr/tle is déad/ in the sóup/.
>   —from "Pessimism" by NEWTON MACKINTOSH

4. The *dactylic* (as in the word *sérious*),* a stressed syllable followed by two weak
   syllables—

> Scíntillate/, scíntillate/, glóbule aur/ífic/,
> Fáin would I/ fáthom thy/ náture's spe/cífic/,
> Lóftily/ póised in the/ éther ca/pácious/,
> Stróngly re/sémbling a/ gém carbo/náceous/.
>   —ANONYMOUS

It will be noted that in the last example, the final weak syllable, as is often the case, is omitted at the end of the line.

Theoretically, another foot consisting of three syllables ought to exist in English as it does in Latin, the *amphibrach,* which in classical verse consisted of a long syllable between two short ones. But in English we do not in actuality have a foot consisting of a stressed syllable between two weak ones (as the word *forgótten* would presumably illustrate). Though in an isolated word like *forgotten,* we might seem to have an example of the amphibrach, the foot cannot maintain itself as an amphibrach in a complete line of any length: our ears will not maintain the stressed syllable *between* two weak syllables, and rapidly we unconsciously convert such a line into either anapests or dactyls. For instance, let us take the following line from Swinburne's "Hesperia," which has been cited by handbooks, in their desperate search for this imaginary foot, as being written in amphibrachs:

> Thy líps cannot láugh and thine éyes cannot wéep; thou art pále as a róse is.

If we could hear amphibrachs as such we should have to hear the line this way:

> Thy líps can/not láugh and/ thine éyes can/not wéep; thou/ art pále as/ a róse
>   is/.

But it is manifestly impossible to hear the line that way. After a few syllables the ear will arrange the line either as anapestic:

> Thy líps/ cannot láugh/ and thine éyes/ cannot wéep;/ thou art pále/ as a róse
>   is/

(in which case we have a weak syllable missing at the beginning of the line and, to rhyme later with *encloses,* an extra weak syllable at the end); or as dactylic:

> Thy líps cannot/ láugh and thine/ éyes cannot/ wéep; thou art/ pále as a/ róse
>   is/

(in which case we have an extra weak syllable at the beginning of the line and one missing at the end). Our ear's choice of anapestic or dactylic would be conditioned by the other lines in the poem.

It is clear from this example that before deciding the pattern from the first foot only, we must examine the entire line. Thus:

> The wáys

might seem to be iambic; but when we read the entire line (from Swinburne's "March"):

> The wáys of the wóodlands are fáirer and stránger than dréams that fulfíll us
> in sléep with delíght

we hear that the line is written in feet of three syllables; we therefore will hear the line either as anapestic:

> The wáys/ of the wóod/lands are fáir/er and strán/ger than dréams/ that
> fulfíll/ us in sléep/ with delíght/

or as dactylic:

> The wáys of the/ wóodlands are/ fáirer and/ stránger than/ dréams that
> ful/fíll us in/ sléep with de/líght/

If we hear the line as anapests, the first foot is varied by the omission of a weak syllable; if we hear it as dactyls, the first foot is varied by the addition of a weak syllable and the last foot is varied by the omission of the final two weak syllables (i.e., a masculine ending).

And now we must introduce some modification of an earlier suggestion. In Chapter 4 we remarked that if one maintains the normal accent in words of two or more syllables and is also careful to stress the important monosyllables, scanning a line will more or less take care of itself. But with anapests and dactyls (as well as with "accentual verse"—see page 245, below) that does not always apply. In the line from "Hesperia," above, the normal accent in *cannot* is twice deliberately undervalued for the sake of the meter. So, too, in the amusing "Pessimism," quoted above, we undervalued the normal accent in the word *blowing*. We can do this because the intervention of two weak syllables between stresses in an anapestic or dactylic line makes the stresses rather heavier than in iambic or trochaic lines. This undervaluing of normal accent occurs only now and then in poems with anapestic or dactylic lines because of the vast number of monosyllables in English. (There is only one such instance in "Pessimism.")

Before we proceed, it would be well to warn the reader again not to confuse, as theorists so often have done, a *stressed* syllable with a *long* syllable. In the opening lines of Milton's "On His Blindness":

> When Í consíder hów my líght is spént,
> Ere hálf my dáys in thís dark wórld and wíde

dark is a long syllable, which adds a wonderful dimension to the rhythm. Unhappily, some theorists, recognizing that *dark* is an important word in the line, yet failing to understand the time element in verse, would suggest we read the line as:

> Ere hálf my dáys in thís dárk wórld and wíde

which utterly ruins the rhythm of the poem as a whole.

Again, this confusion between a long monosyllable and a stressed monosyllable has been responsible for suggestions that we read the opening of Shelley's "Ode to the West Wind":

> O wíld West Wínd, thou bréath of Áutumn's béing
> Ó wíld Wést Wínd thou bréath of Áutumn's béing ...

—a clumsy chaos, ill-fitting the sweep of the subject. If we remember to give *O* and *West* (as well as, for that matter, *thou*) their due length, the line takes on the intended breadth without violating the basic rhythm.

Importance in meaning, then, can be conveyed by the *length* of a monosyllable even when the word appears in an unstressed position.

These then are the four feet to be found in English poetry—the iambic, the trochaic, the anapestic and the dactylic. Because as it is spoken our language roughly falls into the iambic pattern (our sentences usually begin with a weak syllable followed by a stress—e.g., The dáy I sáw, etc.; I thínk we óught, etc.), the iambic is by far the most common of all four.

The *number* of feet in a line makes the *meter.*

> A line of 1 foot is in *monometer.*
> A line of 2 feet is in *dimeter.*
> A line of 3 feet is in *trimeter.*
> A line of 4 feet is in *tetrameter.*
> A line of 5 feet is in *pentameter.*
> A line of 6 feet is in *hexameter.*
> A line of 7 feet is in *heptameter.*
> A line of 8 feet is in *octameter.*

The most common meter in English is the pentameter. Brilliant deduction: the most common line in English is the iambic pentameter.

By this time it should be obvious that it is unwise to speak of the *number of syllables* in an English line. It is the *number of stresses* which is significant. Thus, it would be idle to define any form as requiring, let us say, ten syllables to the line. Ten syllables could constitute totally different meters:

1. Iambic pentameter—When Í/ consí/der hów/ my líght/ is spént/
2. Dactylic tetrameter—Párdoned in/ héaven the/ fírst by the/ thróne . . .
3. Anapestic trimeter—With no líght/ but the twí/light of tér/ror

By definition an iambic pentameter line might seem to require exactly ten syllables, but it often contains eleven because of an additional weak syllable. A dactylic tetrameter line might seem to call for twelve syllables, but by the omission of one or two weak syllables it often has ten or eleven. (See 2 above.) An anapestic trimeter line might seem to call for nine syllables, but by the addition of one or two weak syllables it often has ten or eleven. (See 3 above.)

We may study a variety of lines in the following poem:

Fair dáffodíls, we wéep to sée	(tetrameter)
You háste awáy so sóon;	(trimeter)
As yét the éarly-rísing sún	(tetrameter)
Has nót attáined his nóon.	(trimeter)
Stay, stáy	(monometer)
Untíl the hásting dáy	(trimeter)
Has rún	(monometer)
Bút to the évensóng;	(trimeter)
And, háving práyed togéther, wé	(tetrameter)
Will gó with yóu alóng.	(trimeter)
We háve short tíme to stáy, as yóu,	(tetrameter)
We háve as shórt a spríng;	(trimeter)
As quíck a grówth to méet decáy,	(tetrameter)
As yóu or ánythíng.	(trimeter)
We díe	(monometer)

10

As yóur hours dó, and drý   (trimeter)
　　　　Awáy   (monometer)
　　Líke to the súmmer's ráin;   (trimeter)
Ór as the péarls of mórning's déw, (tetrameter)
　　Né'er to be fóund agáin.   (trimeter)   20
　　　　　　　—"To Daffodils" by ROBERT HERRICK

The verse throughout this poem is iambic, though it is to be noted that in the eighth line of the first stanza and the last three lines of the second stanza, Herrick begins with a stressed syllable, possibly because this variation lends a note of gravity to his conclusion. We may also observe, in passing, that having set up a metrical arrangement in the first stanza, he adheres to it in the second. This gives shape to the poem as a whole.

We have already had instances of the variations common in the last foot of a line:

And Í have lóved the Óctopús,   (iambic tetrameter)
Since wé were bóys togéther;   (iambic trimeter)
I lóve the Vúlture ánd the   (iambic tetrameter)
　　　　Shárk,
I éven lóve the wéather.   (iambic trimeter)
　　　　—from "The Oneness of the Philosopher
　　　　with Nature" by G. K. CHESTERTON

The first and third lines are normal iambic lines. But the second and fourth lines have an extra weak syllable at the end. *An iambic or anapestic line ending in a weak syllable has* what is called *a feminine ending*. (Trochaic and dactylic lines *normally* end with a weak syllable.)

Táke her up ténderly,   (dactyllic dimeter)
Líft her with cáre;   (dactyllic dimeter)
Fáshioned so slénderly,   (dactyllic dimeter)
Yóung, and so fáir!   (dactyllic dimeter)
　　　　—from "The Bridge of Sighs" by THOMAS HOOD

The first and third lines are normal dactylic lines. But the second and fourth lines lack the two final weak syllables, and thus end with a stress. *A trochaic or dactylic line ending in a stressed syllable has* what is called *a masculine ending*.

ACCENTUAL VERSE

We have already observed that Anglo-Saxon poetry involved none of the four feet we have identified but was based exclusively on the stresses in a line without regard to the arrangement of the weak syllables. (See pp. 123–124.) Some modern poets have revived this way of writing verse.

Ís the níght chílly and dárk?
The níght is chílly, but nót dárk.
The thín gray clóud is spréad on hígh,
It cóvers bút not hídes the ský.
The móon is behínd, and át the fúll;
And yét she lóoks both smáll and dúll.
The níght is chíll, the clóud is gráy:
'Tis a mónth befóre the mónth of Máy,
And the Spríng comes slówly úp this wáy.
　　　　　　　—from "Christabel"
　　　　　　　by SAMUEL TAYLOR COLERIDGE

In his preface to "Christabel" Coleridge himself thus described the meter: "... The metre of 'Christabel' is not, properly speaking, irregular, though it may seem so from its being founded on a new principle:* namely, that of counting in each line the accents, not the syllables. Though the latter may vary from seven to twelve, yet in each line the accents will be found to be only four. Nevertheless, this occasional variation in number of syllables is not introduced wantonly, or for the mere ends of convenience, but in correspondence with some transition in the nature of the imagery or passion."

Such verse is often called *accentual verse*. Other poets have employed it since.

> Únder yonder béech-tree síngle on the gréen-sward,
>   Cóuched with her árms behínd her golden héad,
> Knées and tresses fólded to slíp and ripple ídly,
>   Líes my young lóve sleeping in the sháde.
> Hád I the héart to slíde an arm benéath her,
>   Préss her parting líps as her wáist I gather slów,
> Wáking in amázement she cóuld not but embráce me:
>   Thén would she hóld me and néver let me gó? . . .
>   —from "Love in the Valley"
>   by GEORGE MEREDITH

"Love in the Valley" makes clear that the stricture we made above (see pp. 242–243) concerning anapests and dactyls is likely to be even more often applicable to accentual verse. If one read Meredith's poem:

> Únder yónder béech-trée síngle on the gréen-swárd,
>   Cóuched with her árms behínd her gólden héad,
> Knées and trésses fólded to slíp and rípple ídly,
>   Líes my yóung lóve sléeping in the sháde . . .

there would be no basic rhythm at all, though we should be following either the normal accent of the two-syllabled words or the stress involved in the meaning. Here again, as with anapests and dactyls, we may be called upon to *undervalue the normal stress in favor of the stronger stress called for* in the pattern of the line. After a few lines read haphazardly, one is easily directed to the correct stresses in a well-written poem in accentual verse. Of course, in this type of verse wherever the stresses do fall, they are always on a normally stressed syllable or monosyllabic word, as the stanza from "Love in the Valley" demonstrates.

The poet Gerard Manley Hopkins (1844–1889) also wrote a considerable body of accentual verse. He called his system of versemaking, *sprung rhythm*. (The word *sprung*, he said, connoted for him "something like *abrupt*.") He defined sprung rhythm as "scanning by accents or stresses alone, without any account of the number of syllables." He further remarked, "The essence of sprung rhythm [is]: *one stress makes one foot.*" (We have so little quarrel with this definition that we have maintained that in *any* English meter, one stress makes one foot.)

> Márgarét, are you gríeving
> Over Goldengrove unleaving?
> Léaves, líke the things of man, you
> With your fresh thoughts care for, can you?
>   —from "Spring and Fall"
>   by GERARD MANLEY HOPKINS

The most notable departure of Hopkins in many of his poems is that for the music of his sprung rhythm he will direct us (by an accent mark over the syllables concerned) to stress certain syllables when we might be tempted to pass over them as not strong enough to call

---

*Coleridge was not familiar with the Anglo-Saxon system of versification, and hence innocently thought his principle "new."

for a stress. His music, in short, is often deliberately contrived by ignoring the natural tendency in English to avoid the juxtaposition of two stresses (e.g., *leaves* and *like*). His bold originality has produced some magnificent results.

VERSE FORMS

BLANK VERSE

Anglo-Saxon poetry, as we have remarked, for centuries contained no rhyme. One of the most important verse techniques in English has been a line, *blank verse,* which is in *unrhymed iambic pentameter:*

> But sóft! What líght through yónder wíndow bréaks?
> It ís the Éast, and Júliet ís the sún!
> Aríse, fair sún, and kíll the énvious móon.
> —*Romeo and Juliet,* II/ii/3–5

Blank verse is the medium in which some of our greatest poetry has been written: Shakespeare's plays, Milton's *Paradise Lost,* and some of the most important works of Wordsworth, Shelley, Keats, Tennyson, Browning and many others.

Blank verse is of three types:

1. *End-stopped, in which the thought requires a pause at the end of the line.* The example quoted above, from *Romeo and Juliet,* is end-stopped.

2. *Verse with enjambment, in which the thought runs on to the next line without a pause:*

> If music be the food of love, play on,
> Give me excess of it; that, surfeiting,
> The appetite may sicken and so die.
> That strain again—it had a dying fall.
> O, it came o'er my ear, like the sweet sound
> That breathes upon a bank of violets.
> —*Twelfth Night,* I/i/1 seq.

The second and fifth lines have enjambment; the other lines are end-stopped.

3. *Run-on, in which the verse pours on for several lines without a significant pause:*

> Never, Iago. Like to the Pontic sea,
> Whose icy current and compulsive course
> Ne'er feels retiring ebb, but keeps due on
> To the Propontic, and the Hellespont,
> Even so my bloody thoughts with violent pace
> Shall ne'er look back, ne'er ebb to humble love
> Till that a capable and wide revenge
> Swallow them up.
> —*Othello,* III/iii/453 seq.

A good actor would probably not pause except briefly at "Hellespont" while delivering these lines, the irresistible sweep of which powerfully expresses the wave of violence which is engulfing Othello at that moment of the drama.

THE COUPLET

Two successive rhyming lines in the same meter are called *a couplet.*

> Why the warning finger-tip
> Pressed for ever on thy lip?

To remind the pilgrim Sound
That it moves on holy ground,
In a breathing-space to be
Hushed for all eternity.
                        —"To Silence" by JOHN BANISTER TABB

This poem was written in three tetrameter couplets. Many epigrams are written as couplets, because of the neatness thus imparted to the satire:

Here lies my wife: here let her lie!
Now she's at rest and so am I.
                        —"Epitaph Intended for His Wife"
                        by JOHN DRYDEN

THE HEROIC COUPLET

Particularly favored in the satires of the late seventeenth and the eighteenth centuries, *heroic couplets are a series of rhymed iambic pentameter couplets, in which a complete thought is contained in each couplet:*

Has Heaven reserved, in pity to the poor,
No pathless waste, or undiscovered shore?
No secret island in the boundless main?
No peaceful desert yet unclaimed by Spain?
Quick, let us rise, the happy seats explore,
And bear oppression's insolence no more.
This mournful truth is everywhere confessed:
Slow rises worth by poverty depressed.
                        —from "London" by SAMUEL JOHNSON

THE TERCET

The tercet is a stanza of three lines, in which all the lines are in rhyme:

Whenas in silks my Julia goes,   (a)
Then, then, methinks, how sweetly flows   (a)
The liquefaction of her clothes.   (a)

Next, when I cast mine eyes, and see   (b)
That brave vibration, each way free,   (b)
O, how that glittering taketh me!   (b)
                        —"Upon Julia's Clothes" by ROBERT HERRICK

This poem is written in two tercets.

TERZA RIMA

When a poem is written in *terza rima* it *is* written in *stanzas of three lines, which rhyme aba, bcb, cdc, ded and so forth:*

But knowing now that they would have her speak,   (a)
She threw her wet hair backward from her brow,   (b)
Her hand close to her mouth touching her cheek,   (a)

As though she had had there a shameful blow,   (b)
And feeling it shameful to feel aught but shame   (c)
All through her heart, yet felt her cheek burned so,   (b)

She must a little touch it; like one lame   (c)
She walked away from Gauwaine, with her head   (d)
Still lifted up; and on her cheek of flame   (c)

The tears dried quick; she stooped at last and said: (d)
"O knights and lords, it seems but little skill   (e)
To talk of well-known things past now and dead . . ."   (d)
                                   —from "The Defence of Guenevere"
                                   by WILLIAM MORRIS

The model for *terza rima* has been Dante's masterwork, *The Divine Comedy.*

THE QUATRAIN

The quatrain is a stanza of four lines:

"Farewell!" into the lover's soul   (a)
    You see Fate plunge the fatal iron.   (b)
All poets use it. It's the whole   (a)
    Of Byron.   (b)

"I only feel—farewell!" said he;
    And always fearful was the telling—
Lord Byron was eternally
    Farewelling.

"Farewell!" A dismal word, 'tis true
    (And why not tell the truth about it!);
But what on earth would poets do
    Without it?
                        —from "Farewell" by BERT LESTON TAYLOR

Some quatrains rhyme only in the second and fourth lines:

O my Luve's like a red, red rose
    That's newly sprung in June;
O my Luve's like the melodie
    That's sweetly played in tune! . . .
                                   —from "A Red, Red Rose"
                                   by ROBERT BURNS

Some rhyme *aabb:*

A Sensitive Plant in a garden grew,   (a)
And the young winds fed it with silver dew,   (a)
And it opened its fan-like leaves to the light,   (b)
And closed them beneath the kisses of night.   (b)
                                   —from "The Sensitive Plant"
                                   by PERCY BYSSHE SHELLEY

Some rhyme *abba:*

Ring out the old, ring in the new,   (a)
    Ring, happy bells, across the snow: (b)
    The year is going, let him go;   (b)
Ring out the false, ring in the true.   (a)
                                   —from "In Memoriam"
                                   by ALFRED, LORD TENNYSON

And in some quatrains the first, second and fourth lines rhyme:

> I sometimes think that never blows so red   (a)
> The Rose as where some buried Caesar bled;   (a)
> That every Hyacinth the Garden wears   (x)
> Dropt in her Lap from some once lovely Head.   (a)
> > —from the *Rubáiyát of Omar Khayyám*
> > by EDWARD FITZGERALD

THE BALLAD STANZA

The folk ballads of the Middle Ages were often written in quatrains of alternating tetrameters and trimeters, in which only the trimeters are in rhyme:

> The kíng síts in Dúmferling tóune   3
> Drínking the blúde-reid wíne,   (a)
> "O whár will Í get gúid sáilor[1]
> To sáil this schíp of míne?"   (a)
> > —from "Sir Patrick Spens" (ANONYMOUS)

RIME ROYAL

The rime royal is a stanza of seven iambic pentameter lines rhyming ababbcc:

> O lady myn that called art Cleo,[1]   (a)
> Thow be my speed fro this forth, and my
> > Muse,   (b)
> To ryme wel this book, til I have do;   (a)
> Me nedeth here noon othere art to use.   (b)
> Forwhi[2] to every lovere I me excuse,   (b)
> That of no sentement I this endite,   (c)
> But out of Latyn in my tonge it write.   (c)
> > —from *Troilus and Criseyde*
> > by GEOFFREY CHAUCER

OTTAVA RIMA

The ottava rima is a stanza of eight iambic pentameter lines rhyming abababcc:

> Oh, Hesperus![1] thou bringest all good things—   (a)
> Home to the weary, to the hungry cheer,   (b)
> To the young bird the parent's brooding wings,   (a)
> The welcome stall to the o'erlabored steer;   (b)
> Whate'er of peace about our hearthstone clings,   (a)
> Whate'er our household gods protect of dear,   (b)
> Are gathered round us by thy look of rest;   (c)
> Thou bring'st the child, too, to the mother's breast. (c)
> > —from *Don Juan*
> > by GEORGE GORDON, LORD BYRON

THE SPENSERIAN STANZA

Invented by Edmund Spenser (1552?–1599) for his epic, *The Faerie Queene, the Spenserian stanza* has proved one of the most important of stanzas in the hands of later English

---

[1]Some prefer: *sailór.*   [2]Therefore.

[1]Clio, muse of history.   [1]The evening star.

poets such as Burns, Byron, Shelley and Keats. It *is a nine-line stanza, of which the first eight lines are in iambic pentameter and the ninth line in iambic hexameter, the rhyme scheme being ababbcbcc:*

The One remains, the many change and pass;	(a)
Heaven's light for ever shines, Earth's shadows fly;	(b)
Life, like a dome of many-colored glass,	(a)
Stains the white radiance of Eternity,	(b)
Until Death tramples it to fragments.—Die,	(b)
If thou wouldst be with that which thou dost seek!	(c)
Follow where all is fled!—Rome's azure sky,	(b)
Flowers, ruins, statues, music, words, are weak	(c)
The glory they transfuse with fitting truth to speak.	(c)

—from "Adonais" by PERCY BYSSHE SHELLEY

THE SONNET

The sonnet is certainly one of the chief poetic forms in English literature. *A sonnet is a poem written in fourteen lines of iambic pentameter, according to the Italian, the English, or the Mason manner.*

Italian sonnet. Sometimes called *the Petrarchan sonnet,* because of the brilliant sonnets which the Italian poet Petrarch wrote in this form, the Italian sonnet *is made up of an octave* (a unit of eight lines) *and a sestet* (a unit of six lines). (See the sonnet sequence, "Their Critical Summer," by Anne Marx, Chapter 3.) *The octave rhymes abbaabba; the sestet rhymes one of four ways: cdecde:*

What is a sonnet? 'Tis the pearly shell	(a)
That murmurs of the far-off murmuring sea;	(b)
A precious jewel carved most curiously;	(b)
It is a little picture painted well.	(a)
What is a sonnet? 'Tis the tear that fell	(a)
From a great poet's hidden ecstasy;	(b)
A two-edged sword, a star, a song—ah me!	(b)
Sometimes a heavy-tolling funeral bell.	(a)
This was the flame that shook with Dante's breath;	(c)
The solemn organ whereon Milton played,	(d)
And the clear glass where Shakespeare's shadow falls:	(e)
A sea this is—beware who ventureth!	(c)
For like a fiord the narrow floor is laid	(d)
Mid-ocean deep sheer to the mountain walls.	(e)

10

—"The Sonnet" by RICHARD WATSON GILDER

or *cdeedc:*

The curtains were half drawn, the floor was	
swept	(a)
And strewn with rushes, rosemary and may	(b)
Lay thick upon the bed on which I lay,	(b)
Where through the lattice ivy-shadows	
crept.	(a)
He leaned above me, thinking that I slept	(a)
And could not hear him; but I heard him	
say:	(b)
"Poor child, poor child"; and as he turned	
away	(b)
Came a deep silence, and I knew he wept.	(a)
He did not touch the shroud, or raise the fold	(c)
That hid my face, or take my hand in his,	(d)
Or ruffle the smooth pillows for my head:	(e)
He did not love me living; but once dead	(e)
He pitied me; and very sweet it is	(d)
To know he still is warm though I am cold.	(c)

10

—"After Death" by CHRISTINA ROSSETTI

or *cdcdcd:*

The world is too much with us: late and soon,	(a)
Getting and spending, we lay waste our powers.	(b)
Little we see in nature that is ours;	(b)
We have given our hearts away, a sordid boon!	(a)
This sea that bares her bosom to the moon,	(a)
The winds that will be howling at all hours,	(b)
And are up-gathered now like sleeping flowers;	(b)
For this, for everything, we are out of tune;	(a)
It moves us not.—Great God! I'd rather be	(c)
A pagan suckled in a creed outworn;	(d)
So might I, standing on this pleasant lea,	(c)
Have glimpses that would make me less forlorn;	(d)
Have sight of Proteus rising from the sea;	(c)
Or hear old Triton blow his wreathèd horn.	(d)

10

—"The World Is Too Much with Us"
by WILLIAM WORDSWORTH

or *cdcdee:*

Mysterious Night! when our first parent knew	(a)
Thee from report divine, and heard thy name,	(b)
Did he not tremble for this lovely frame,	(b)
This glorious canopy of light and blue?	(a)
Yet 'neath a curtain of translucent dew,	(a)
Bathed in the rays of the great setting flame,	(b)
Hesperus with the host of heaven came,	(b)
And lo! creation widened in man's view.	(a)
Who could have thought such darkness lay concealed	(c)
Within thy beams, O Sun! or who could find,	(d)
Whilst fly, and leaf, and insect stood revealed,	(c)
That to such countless orbs thou mad'st us blind?	(d)

10

Why do we, then, shun death with anxious strife?   (e)
If light can thus deceive, wherefore not life?   (e)
                —"To Night" by JOSEPH BLANCO WHITE

It should be noted that the basic characteristic of the Italian sonnet is not so much the rhyme scheme as the thought division at the end of the eighth line. (Milton sometimes prefers to break the thought in the middle of the eighth line.)

English sonnet. Sometimes called *the Shakespearean sonnet,* because of the great sonnets Shakespeare wrote in this form, the English sonnet *is made up of a unit of twelve lines (usually,* though not always, *consisting of three quatrains) and a concluding couplet, rhyming ababcdcdefefgg. The apartness* from the preceding twelve lines *of the concluding couplet is the distinguishing mark of the English sonnet.* In other words, the major thought division is at the end of the twelfth line.

Since there's no help, come let us kiss and part,—   (a)
Nay I have done, you get no more of me;   (b)
And I am glad, yea, glad with all my heart,   (a)
That thus so cleanly I myself can free.   (b)
Shake hands for ever, cancel all our vows,   (c)
And when we meet at any time again,   (d)
Be it not seen in either of our brows   (c)
That we one jot of former love retain!   (d)
Now at the last gasp of Love's latest breath,   (e)
When his pulse failing, Passion speechless lies,   (f)   10
When Faith is kneeling by his bed of death,   (e)
And Innocence is closing up his eyes,   (f)
—Now if thou would'st, when all have given him over,   (g)
From death to life thou might'st him yet recover!   (g)
                —Sonnet from *Idea* by MICHAEL DRAYTON

Drayton's sonnet shows the tendency of the twelve-line unit to be divided into three quatrains. Shakespeare's sonnets usually follow this procedure, but sometimes he prefers to keep the twelve lines intact without any break—as do other sonneteers:

Tired with all these, for restful death I cry,—   (a)
As, to behold desert a beggar born,   (b)
And needy nothing trimm'd in jollity,   (a)
And purest faith unhappily forsworn,   (b)
And gilded honor shamefully misplaced,   (c)
And maiden virtue rudely strumpeted,   (d)
And right perfection wrongfully disgraced,   (c)
And strength by limping sway disablèd,   (d)
And art made tongue-tied by authority,   (e)
And folly doctor-like controlling skill,   (f)   10
And simple truth miscall'd simplicity,[1]   (e)
And captive good attending captain ill: (f)
    Tired with all these, from these would I
        be gone,   (g)
    Save that, to die, I leave my love alone.   (g)
                —"Sonnet LXVI" by SHAKESPEARE

[1]Stupidity.

In the earlier days of sonnet writing in England, before the two forms—Italian and English—were quite established, there was a certain amount of fluidity in the rhyme patterns, as this sonnet (XXXIV) from Spenser's *Amoretti* illustrates:

> Lyke as a ship, that through the Ocean wyde,
> By conduct of some star doth make her way;
> Whenas a storme hath dimd her trusty guyde,
> Out of her course doth wander far astray!
> So I, whose star, that wont with her bright ray
> Me to direct with cloudes is over cast,
> Doe wander now, in darknesse and dismay,
> Through hidden perils round about me plast.
> Yet hope I well that, when this storme is past,
> My Helice,[1] the lodestar of my lyfe,   10
> Will shine again, and looke on me at last,
> With lovely light to cleare my cloudy grief.
> Till then I wander carefull, comfortlesse,
> In secret sorrow, and sad pensiveness.

Sixteen-line sonnet. Before the form of the sonnet was set in English, some early sonneteers wrote their works occasionally in sixteen, rather than fourteen, lines. The sixteen-line sonnet was revived by the great Victorian poet George Meredith (1828–1909) in a sonnet sequence, *Modern Love:*

> By this he knew she wept with waking eyes:
> That, at his hand's light quiver by her head,
> The strange low sobs that shook their common bed,
> Were called into her with a sharp surprise,
> And strangled mute, like little gaping snakes,
> Dreadfully venomous to him. She lay
> Stone-still, and the long darkness flowed away
> With muffled pulses. Then, as midnight makes
> Her giant heart of Memory and Tears
> Drink the pale drug of silence, and so beat   10
> Sleep's heavy measure, they from head to feet
> Were moveless, looking through their dead black years,
> By vain regret scrawled over the blank wall.
> Like sculptured effigies they might be seen
> Upon their marriage-tomb, the sword between;
> Each wishing for the sword that severs all.
>
> —"Sonnet I" from *Modern Love*
> by GEORGE MEREDITH

But sixteen-line sonnets are still very rare.

The "pure" rhyme schemes of both Italian and English sonnets allow a poet considerable freedom of choice. Each has its own rightness as a poetic form. Since these forms have been set some writers have used other rhyme schemes for the sonnet, hybrids showing characteristics of this or that "pure" form—sometimes using the *abbaabba* rhyme of the Italian in the English twelve-and-two division of the thought, for example. Some critics feel that however satisfying in other respects the piece may be as a poem, a "hybrid" sonnet fails to afford the pleasure peculiar to the sonnet, or that pleasure which mastered form can give the cultivated reader.

The sonnet provides a good occasion to enforce the truth that the form of a work of art is inseparable from the idea embodied. How different are the Italian and the English sonnet forms from each other! The Italian is calmer, more adapted to reflective moods, its rhyme scheme everywhere making for symmetry and balance. It is the concluding couplet

---

[1]Ursa Minor, a constellation including the North Star.

which makes the English sonnet more dramatic, sharper, and more exciting, and its rhyme scheme lends a certain air of greater freedom and lyricism. The choice of the one or the other, therefore, would depend upon the poet's material, whether for instance it lends itself to reflection or to dramatic effect.

Mason Sonnet. The American poet Madeline Mason (1913–   ), in her volume, *At the Ninth Hour: A Sonnet Sequence in a New Form* (1958), introduced what is now known as the Mason sonnet, an innovation that has inspired a number of fine poets to employ it in their poems. The rhyme scheme is *abc abc cbd badda.* The rhyme scheme does *not* imply that the sonnet is written in three pairs of three lines and a concluding passage of five. The charms of the Mason sonnet will be found in the harmonious design into which the sequence of repeated rhymes falls, as well as in the recurrence of the opening rhyme in the last line.

As I would hunt for clover, one fourleaf	(a)
Somewhere concealed among the crowding grass,	(b)
And push the blades aside that all spring back	(c)
Against my hands and eyes, my wild belief	(a)
In luck still findable, so I'd unmass	(b)
All these not you, their sameness unstack	(c)
To see, unique, your gold against their black.	(c)
I shall not find, and if I did, you'd pass	(b)
As any stranger would, not mine to know.	(d)
Sun-grafted so, the image on mind's glass,	(b)
The everlasting glory of the brief.	(a)
I see again that sharp, once-only glow,	(d)
A woodland all unleafed, against its snow	(d)
The darkening gold of one wind-laid oakleaf.	(a)

—"The Oakleaf" by MADELINE MASON

It would be possible to see this sonnet as unbroken in thought for all its fourteen lines; nevertheless, there are slight subdivisions ending with the seventh, eleventh and fourteenth lines. It is to be remarked that the last line repeats deliberately the same *word* as the first line in the rhyme scheme. Such is, however, not always the case, and Miss Mason often employs another word to rhyme with the first line.

Here is an example of a Mason sonnet in which the last line does not repeat the word at the end of the first line:

Battling a midnight storm for notice, she	(a)
was blacker than the dark outside our door—	(b)
a comely little cat with golden eyes.	(c)
She pleaded then to share the ecstasy	(a)
of food and warmth, stood suppliant before	(b)
our house and broke our hearts with her lost cries.	(c)
And finally, so that we'd realize	(c)
she never meant to leave us any more,	(b)
she flung herself against our windowpane.	(d)
Who could resist her longer? We adore	(b)
each sable paw. Safe from catastrophe,	(a)
she is locked in with us. The sound of rain	(d)
tonight is mingled with her voice again.	(d)
Now, she is begging us to set her free.	(a)

—"Angelique" by SARAH LOCKWOOD

Here there are definitely divisions at the end of lines nine, thirteen and fourteen. Thus we see that the Mason sonnet is capable of a variety of structure divisions or may be conceived as a fourteen-line unit. In all cases the chime of the rhyme scheme holds the work together, whatever the divisions or if there be no division at all.

Here follows another Mason sonnet in which there is no break in the thought from beginning to end:

Mad!—with desk-tasks waiting for me still—	(a)
to stretch upon the grass in Maytime's light	(b)
without in cranium one thought profound!—	(c)
rather, busy tracing every frill	(a)
the filmy clouds are making in their flight.	(b)
I snatch a dandelion deep from the ground;	(c)
the catbird's call (unconvincing sound)	(c)
could tempt what dog? The cardinal's crest too bright	(b)
for sun, I edge between my teeth blade-grass;	(d)
a squirrel flees a hound in pretended fright,	(b)
two frantic sparrows decide to mock with will	(a)
a baptism in the dust. With sudden pass	(d)
a thrush soars up a gaping oak's crevasse,	(d)
demanding world's attention to his trill.	(a)

—"May Afternoon" by BERNARD GREBANIER

THE ODE

An ode is a lyrical poem of exalted emotion. Such a poem usually is fairly extensive rather than brief.

In English we have the regular Pindaric ode, the irregular ode, the regular stanzaic ode, and the choral ode.

The regular Pindaric ode. The regular Pindaric ode consists of three larger sections, each section having three stanzas called *a strophe, an antistrophe, and an epode,* respectively. In each of these larger sections, *the antistrophe exactly matches* the meter and rhyme scheme of *the strophe.* But from section to section each new strophe and antistrophe may set up a new design of meter and rhyme scheme. The epodes have their own pattern.

I. 1

"Ruin seize thee, ruthless King!
Confusion on thy banners wait,
Tho' fann'd by Conquest's crimson wing
They mock the air with idle state.
Helm, nor Hauberk's twisted mail,
Nor even thy virtues, Tyrant, shall avail
To save thy secret soul from nightly fears,
From Cambria's[1] curse, from Cambria's tears!"
   Such were the sounds, that o'er the crested
      pride
Of the first Edward[2] scatter'd wild dismay, 10
As down the steep of Snowdon's[3] shaggy side
He wound with toilsome march his long array.
Stout Glo'ster stood aghast in speechless trance;
To arms! cried Mortimer,[4] and couch'd his quiv-
   ring lance.

I. 2

   On a rock, whose haughty brow
Frowns o'er old Conway's[5] foaming flood,
Robed in the sable garb of woe,
With haggard eyes the Poet stood;
(Loose his beard, and hoary hair
Stream'd, like a meteor, to the troubled air) 20
And with a Master's hand, and Prophet's fire,
Struck the deep sorrows of his lyre:
   "Hark, how each giant-oak, and desert cave,
Sighs to the torrent's awful voice beneath!
O'er thee, O King! their hundred arms they wave,
Revenge on thee in hoarser murmurs breathe;
Vocal no more, since Cambria's fatal day,
To high-born Hoel's harp,[6] or soft Llewellyn's
   lay.

[1]Wales.

[2]Edward I of England.

[3]Highest of mountains in Wales.

[4]Mortimer and Gloucester were the chiefs in Edward's conquering army as it proceeded through Wales.

[5]A river in Wales.

[6]Hoel and the names following are Welsh bards, some of whom are historical, some created by the poet's fancy.

I. 3

"Cold is Cadwallo's tongue,
That hush'd the stormy main;   30
Brave Urien sleeps upon his craggy bed:
Mountains, ye mourn in vain
Modred, whose magic song
Made huge Plinlimmon[7] bow his cloud-topp'd
    head.
On dreary Arvon's shore[8] they lie,
Smear'd with gore, and ghastly pale:
Far, far aloof th' affrighted ravens sail;
The famish'd Eagle screams, and passes by.
    Dear lost companions of my tuneful art,
Dear, as the light that visits these sad eyes,   40
Dear, as the ruddy drops that warm my heart,
Ye died amidst your dying country's cries—
    No more I weep. They do not sleep.
On yonder cliffs, a grisly band,
I see them sit, they linger yet,
Avengers of their native land:
With me in dreadful harmony they join,
And weave with bloody hands the tissue of thy
    line:—

II. 1

    " 'Weave the warp, and weave the woof,
The winding sheet of Edward's race.   50
Give ample room, and verge enough
The characters of hell to trace.
Mark the year, and mark the night,
When Severn shall re-echo with affright
The shrieks of death, thro' Berkeley's roofs that
    ring,
Shrieks of an agonising King![9]
She-Wolf of France,[10] with unrelenting fangs,
That tear'st the bowels of thy mangled Mate,
From thee be born, who o'er thy country hangs
The scourge of Heav'n. What Terrors round him
    wait!   60
Amazement in his van, with Flight combined,
And Sorrow's faded form, and Solitude behind.

II. 2

    " 'Mighty Victor, mighty Lord,[11]
Low on his funeral couch he lies!
No pitying heart, no eye, afford
A tear to grace his obsequies.
    Is the sable Warrior fled?[12]
Thy son is gone. He rests among the Dead.
The Swarm, that in thy noon-tide beam were
    born?
Gone to salute the rising Morn.   70
Fair laughs the Morn, and soft the Zephyr
    blows,[13]
While proudly riding o'er the azure realm
In gallant trim the gilded Vessel goes;
Youth on the prow, and Pleasure at the helm;
Regardless of the sweeping Whirlwind's sway,
That, hush'd in grim repose, expects his evening
    prey.

II. 3

    " 'Fill high the sparkling bowl,
The rich repast prepare;
Reft of a crown, he yet may share the feast.
Close by the regal chair   80
Fell Thirst and Famine scowl
A baleful smile upon their baffled Guest.
    Heard ye the din of battle bray,
Lance to lance, and horse to horse?
Long Years of havoc[14] urge their destined course,
And thro' the kindred squadrons mow their way.
Ye Towers of Julius,[15] London's lasting shame,
With many a foul and midnight murther fed,
Revere his Consort's faith, his Father's fame,
And spare the meek Usurper's holy head.[16]   90
Above, below, the rose of snow,
Twined with her blushing foe,[17] we spread:
The bristled Boar[18] in infant-gore
Wallows beneath the thorny shade.
Now, brothers, bending o'er the accursed loom
Stamp we our vengeance deep, and ratify his
    doom.

[7]A mountain in Wales.

[8]The coast opposite the isle of Anglesey.

[9]Edward II (1307–1327), murdered in Berkeley Castle.

[10]Edward II's wife, Isabella, "she-wolf of France," who conspired against her husband.

[11]Edward III (1327–1377).

[12]The Black Prince, Edward III's son, hero of the Hundred Years' War. He predeceased his father.

[13]The corrupt reign of Richard II (1377–1400). See Shakespeare's play *Richard II.*

[14]The War of the Roses.

[15]The Tower of London, the building of which was by legend attributed to Julius Caesar.

[16]Henry VI.

[17]The white rose of York and the red rose of Lancaster.

[18]Richard III's insignia.

III. 1

" 'Edward, lo! to sudden fate
(Weave we the woof. The thread is spun)
Half of thy heart we consecrate.
(The web is wove. The work is done.)'—   100
     Stay, oh stay! nor thus forlorn
Leave me unbless'd, unpitied, here to mourn!
In yon bright track, that fires the western skies,
They melt, they vanish from my eyes.
     But oh! what solemn scenes on Snowdon's
          height
Descending slow their glitt'ring skirts unroll?
Visions of glory, spare my aching sight,
Ye unborn Ages, crowd not on my soul!
No more our long-lost Arthur[19] we bewail.   110
All-hail, ye genuine Kings, Britannia's Issue,[20]
     hail!

III. 2

"Girt with many a baron bold
Sublime their starry fronts they rear;
And gorgeous Dames, and Statesmen old
In bearded majesty, appear.
In the midst a Form divine![21]
Her eye proclaims her of the Briton-Line;
Her lion-port, her awe-commanding face,
Attemper'd sweet to virgin-grace.
What strings symphonious tremble in the air,
What strains of vocal transport round her play![120]
Hear from the grave, great Taliessin,[22] hear;

They breathe a soul to animate thy clay.
Bright Rapture calls, and soaring, as she sings,
Waves in the eye of Heav'n her many-color'd
     wings.

III. 3

"The verse adorn again
Fierce War and faithful Love,
And Truth severe, by fairy Fiction drest.[23]
In buskin'd[24] measures move
Pale Grief, and pleasing Pain,
With Horror, Tyrant of the throbbing breast.[130]
A Voice, as of the Cherub-Choir,
Gales from blooming Eden bear;[25]
And distant warblings lessen on my ear,
That lost in long futurity expire.
     Fond impious Man, think'st thou, yon san-
          guine cloud,
Rais'd by thy breath, has quench'd the Orb of
     day?
To-morrow he repairs the golden flood,
And warms the nations with redoubled ray.
     Enough for me: With joy I see
The different doom our Fates assign.   140
Be thine Despair, and scept'red Care,
To triumph, and to die, are mine."—
     He spoke, and headlong from the moun-
          tain's height
Deep in the roaring tide he plung'd to endless
     night.
                    —"The Bard" by THOMAS GRAY

It would be hard for a poet to achieve more symmetry than Gray achieves in this poem. The subject is neatly divided into each of the three sections. In I, the Bard stops Edward I, at the head of his conquering army, in the mountain passes of Wales, and bids him hearken. In II, the Bard curses him. In III, the Welsh return triumphant with the Tudor family. Each of these three sections has its own strophe, antistrophe and epode (I, 1, 2, 3; II, 1, 2, 3; III, 1, 2, 3); in each section the strophe and antistrophe match in meter and rhyme scheme. And in the very final couplet, the old bewhiskered Bard, the business of the poem being over, appropriately jumps off the mountain's height into the roaring tide. (The trouble with this poem is that there is too much disparity between the cold elegance of its form and the wild romanticism of its subject.) Samuel Johnson's comment was: "He has a kind of strutting dignity, and is tall by walking on tiptoe."

[19]Welsh legend promised that Arthur would return to rule once more over Britain.

[20]Henry VII, first of the Tudors, who came to the throne in 1485, was of a Welsh family.

[21]Elizabeth I.

[22]A Welsh bard.

[23]A reference to Spenser's *The Faerie Queene.*

[24]A reference to the greatness of Elizabethan tragedy (the buskin was worn by actors of tragedy in ancient Greece).

[25]A reference to Milton's *Paradise Lost.*

The irregular ode. In the irregular ode the stanzas vary in meter and length.

I

Pindar[1] is imitable by none;
    The phoenix Pindar is a vast species alone.
Whoe'er but Daedalus with waxen wings could
    fly
And neither sink too low nor soar too high?
      What could he who followed claim
But of vain boldness the unhappy fame,
      And by his fall a sea to name?
    Pindar's unnavigable song,
Like a swollen flood from some steep mountain,
      pours along;
    The ocean meets with such a voice   10
From his enlarged mouth as drowns the ocean's
    noise.

II

So Pindar does new words and figures roll
Down his impetuous dithyrambic tide,
    Which in no channel deigns to abide,
    Which neither banks nor dikes control.
    Whether the immortal gods he sings
    In a no less immortal strain,
Or the great acts of god-descended kings,
Who in his numbers still survive and reign,
    Each rich embroidered line,   20
    Which their triumphant brows around
    By his sacred hand is bound,
Does all their starry diadems outshine.

III

Whether at Pisa's race[2] he please
To carve in polished verse the conquerors' im-
    ages,
Whether the swift, the skilful, or the strong
Be crownèd in his nimble, artful, vigorous song,
Whether some brave young man's untimely fate
In words worth dying for he celebrate,
    Such mournful and such pleasing words 30
As joy to his mother's and his mistress' grief
    affords,
    He bids him live and grow in fame;
    Among the stars he sticks his name;
The grave can but the dross of him devour,

So small is death's, so great the poet's power.
Lo, how the obsequious wind and swelling air
    The Theban swan does upwards bear
Into the walks of clouds, where he does play,
And with extended wings opens his liquid way,
    Whilst, alas, my timorous Muse   40
    Unambitious tracks pursues;
    Does, with weak, unballast wings,
    About the mossy brooks and springs,
    About the trees' new-blossomed heads,
    About the gardens' painted beds,
    About the fields and flowery meads,
    And all inferior beauteous things,
      Like the laborious bee,
      For little drops of honey flee,   50
And there with humble sweets contents her in-
    dustry.
    —"The Praise of Pindar" by ABRAHAM COWLEY

It will be noted that in this kind of ode there is no attempt to repeat the design of the first stanza in the second.

    Regular stanzaic ode. The regular stanzaic ode is an ode written in regular stanzas; usually, though not always, the stanza is made up of both long and short lines (as in the Pindaric and irregular ode).

    It is done!
      Clang of bell and roar of gun
Send the tidings up and down.
      How the belfries rock and reel!
      How the great guns, peal on peal,
Fling the joy from town to town!

    Ring, O bells!
      Every stroke exulting tells
Of the burial hour of crime.
      Loud and long, that all may hear,   10
      Ring for every listening ear
Of Eternity and Time!

    Let us kneel:
      God's own voice is in that peal,
And this spot is holy ground.
      Lord, forgive us! What are we,
      That our eyes this glory see,
That our ears have heard the sound!

    For the Lord
      On the whirlwind is abroad;   20
In the earthquake He has spoken:
      He has smitten with this thunder
      The iron walls asunder,
And the gates of brass are broken!

[1]Great lyric poet of ancient Greece, in honor of whose odes the Pindaric ode is named.
[2]Pisa was near Olympia, the scene of the Olympic Games, which Pindar's *Odes* celebrate.

Loud and long
Lift the old exulting song;
Sing with Miriam by the sea,
He has cast the mighty down;
Horse and rider sink and drown;
"He hath triumphed gloriously!"   30

Did we dare,
In our agony of prayer,
Ask for more than He has done?
When was ever his right hand
Over any time or land
Stretched as now beneath the sun?

How they pale,
Ancient myth and song and tale,
In this wonder of our days,
When the cruel rod of war   40
Blossoms white with righteous law
And the wrath of man is praise!

Blotted out!
All within and all about
Shall a fresher life begin;
Freer breathe the universe
As it rolls its heavy curse
On the dead and buried sin!

It is done!
In the circuit of the sun   50
Shall the sound thereof go forth.
It shall bid the sad rejoice,
It shall give the dumb a voice,
It shall belt with joy the earth!

Ring and swing,
Bells of joy! On morning's wing
Send the song of praise abroad!
With a sound of broken chains
Tell the nations that He reigns,
Who alone is Lord and God!   60
—"Laus Deo!" by JOHN GREENLEAF WHITTIER*

What distinguishes such an ode from other regular stanzaic poems is the exaltation or rhapsodic tone in which it is written.

The choral ode. Written in imitation of the odes sung by the Chorus in ancient Greek drama, our choral ode *is utterly free in its form,* each line being in whatever design the poet chooses for it.

The lyre's voice is lovely everywhere;
In the court of gods, in the city of men,
And in the lonely rock-strewn mountain-glen,
In the still mountain air.
Only to Typho[1] it sounds hatefully,—
To Typho only, the rebel o'erthrown,
Through whose heart Etna drives her roots of stone,
To embed them in the sea.
Wherefore dost thou groan so loud?
Wherefore do thy nostrils flash,   10
Through the dark night, suddenly,
Typho, such red jets of flame?
Is thy tortured heart still proud?
Is thy fire-scathed arm still rash?
Still alert thy stone-crushed frame?
Doth thy fierce soul still deplore
Thine ancient rout by the Cilician hills,
And that curst treachery on the Mount of Gore?

Do thy bloodshot eyes still weep
The fight which crowned thine ills,   20
Thy last mischance on this Sicilian deep?
Hast thou sworn, in thy sad lair,
Where erst the strong sea-currents sucked thee down,
Never to cease to writhe, and try to rest,
Letting the sea-stream wander through thy hair?
That thy groans, like thunder prest,
Begin to roll, almost drown
The sweet notes whose lulling spell
Gods and the race of mortals love so well,
When through thy caves thou hearest music swell?   30
But an awful pleasure bland
Spreading o'er the Thunderer's[2] face,
When the sound climbs near his seat,
The Olympian council[3] sees;
As he lets his lax right hand,

*This poem was written while the bells were ringing and the cannons booming in celebration of the passage of the Constitutional Amendment abolishing slavery (1865).

[1] A giant or monster of ancient Greek mythology, having a hundred heads and breathing out flame. Wanting sovereignty over gods and men, he was, after a terrifying struggle, subdued by Jove's thunderbolts. He was buried under Mount Etna in Sicily.

[2] Jove's.

[3] The company of the gods on Olympus.

Which the lightnings doth embrace,
Sink upon his mighty knees.
And the eagle,[4] at the beck
Of the appeasing, gracious harmony,
Droops all his sheeny, brown, deep-feathered
    neck,   40
Nestling nearer to Jove's feet;
While o'er his sovran eye
The curtains of the blue films slowly meet.
And the white Olympus-peaks
Rosily brighten, and the soothed gods smile

At one another from their golden chairs,
And no one round the charmed circle speaks.
Only the loved Hebe[5] bears
The cup about, whose draughts beguile
Pain and care, with a dark store   50
Of fresh-pulled violets wreathed and nodding
    o'er;
And her flushed feet glow on the marble floor.
       —from Act II of *Empedocles on Etna*
       by MATTHEW ARNOLD

FRENCH FORMS

Certain forms imported from France—chiefly the ballade, the rondel, the rondeau, the sestina, the villanelle, and the triolet—have proved inviting to English poets on occasion. Highly artificial, they are a challenge to a poet's skill and it takes considerable technical dexterity to manage any of them. As an example of the artifice of such forms we offer a villanelle.

The villanelle is written in nineteen lines, five stanzas of three lines and one of four lines, with only two rhymes; as refrain *the first line reappears as the sixth, twelfth and eighteenth lines,* and *the third line reappears as the ninth, fifteenth and nineteenth lines.* The three-line stanzas rhyme *aba;* the last stanza *abaa:*

    "A little, passionately, not at all?"
    She casts the snow petals on the air:
And what care we how many petals fall!

    Nay, wherefore seek the Seasons to forestall?
    It is but playing, and she will not care,
A little, passionately, not at all!

    She would not answer us if we should call
    Across the years: her visions are too fair;
And what care we how many petals fall?

    She knows us not, nor recks if she enthrall   10
    With voice and eyes and fashion of her hair,
A little, passionately, not at all!

    Knee-deep she goes in meadow grasses tall,
    Kissed by the daisies that her fingers tear:
And what care we how many petals fall!

    We pass and go: but she shall not recall
    What men we were, nor all she made us bear:
    "A little, passionately, not at all!"
And what care we how many petals fall!
       —"A Villanelle of Marguerites"[1]
       by ERNEST DOWSON

---

[4]The bird sacred to Jove.
[5]Cupbearer to the gods.

---

[1]Marguerite is the French word for daisy.

FREE VERSE

Free verse is verse written without the discipline of meter. Free verse worthy of the name is not simply prose broken up into lines; it rejects meter because it requires for each line its own subtleties of rhythm. In free verse every line must justify its own rhythm in terms of the thought-content of that line.

There was a child went forth every day,
And the first object he look'd upon, that object he
    became,
And that object became part of him for the day
    or a certain part of the day,
Or for many years or stretching cycles of years.

The early lilacs became part of this child,
And grass and white and red morning-glories,
    and white and red clover, and the song of the
    phœbe-bird,
And the Third-month lambs and the sow's pink-
    faint litter, and the mare's foal and the cow's
    calf,
And the noisy brood of the barnyard or by the
    mire of the pond-side,
And the fish suspending themselves so curiously
    below there, and the beautiful curious liquid,
And the water-plants with their graceful flat
    heads, all became part of him.   10

The field-sprouts of Fourth-month and Fifth-
    month became part of him,
Winter-grain sprouts and those of the light-yel-
    low corn, and the esculent roots of the gar-
    den,
And the apple-trees cover'd with blossoms and
    the fruit afterward, and wood-berries, and
    the commonest weeds by the road,
And the old drunkard staggering home from the
    outhouse of the tavern whence he had lately
    risen,
And the schoolmistress that pass'd on her way to
    the school,
And the friendly boys that pass'd, and the quar-
    relsome boys,
And the tidy and fresh-cheek'd girls, and the
    barefoot Negro boy and girl,
And all the changes of city and country wherever
    he went.
His own parents, he that had father'd him and
    she that had conceiv'd him in her womb and
    birth'd him,
They gave this child more of themselves than
    that,   20

They gave him afterward every day, they became
    part of him.

The mother at home quietly placing the dishes on
    the supper-table,
The mother with mild words, clean her cap and
    gown, a wholesome odor falling off her per-
    son and clothes as she walks by,
The father, strong, self-sufficient, manly, mean,
    anger'd, unjust,
The blow, the quick loud word, the tight bargain,
    the crafty lure,
The family usages, the language, the company,
    the furniture, the yearning and swelling
    heart,
Nor plann'd and built one thing after another as
    an architect plans and builds a house.

I do not think seventy years is the time of a man
    or woman,
Nor that seventy millions of years is the time of
    a man or woman,
Nor that years will ever stop the existence of me,
    or any one else.   30
Is it wonderful that I should be immortal? as
    every one is immortal;
I know it is wonderful, but my eyesight is equally
    wonderful, and how I was conceived in my
    mother's womb is equally wonderful,
And pass'd from a babe in the creeping trance of
    a couple of summers and winters to articu-
    late and walk—all this is equally wonderful.

And that my soul embraces you this hour, and we
    affect each other without ever seeing each
    other, and never perhaps to see each other,
    is every bit as wonderful.

And that I can think such thoughts as these is just
    as wonderful,
And that I can remind you, and you think them
    and know them to be true, is just as wonder-
    ful.
           —"There Was a Child Went Forth"
           by WALT WHITMAN

It would be more accurate to say of some of our best *free-verse* poets, not that their verse is written without the discipline of meter, but that it *is verse in which the meter is constantly changing in the lines.*

Hark! ah, the Nightingale!
The tawny-throated!
Hark! from that moonlit cedar what a burst!
What triumph! hark—what pain!
O Wanderer from a Grecian shore,[1]
Still, after many years, in distant lands,
Still nourishing in thy bewilder'd brain
That wild, unquench'd, deep-sunken, old-world
    pain—

    Say, will it never heal?
And can this fragrant lawn   10
With its cool trees, and night,
And the sweet, tranquil Thames,
And moonshine, and the dew,
To thy rack'd heart and brain
    Afford no balm?
    Dost thou to-night behold
Here, through the moonlight on this English
    grass,
The unfriendly palace in the Thracian wild?[2]
    Dost thou again peruse
With hot cheeks and sear'd eyes   20
The too clear web, and thy dumb Sister's shame?
    Dost thou once more assay
Thy flight, and feel come over thee,
Poor Fugitive, the feathery change
Once more, and once more seem to make resound
With love and hate, triumph and agony,
Lone Daulis, and the high Cephissian vale?[3]
    Listen, Eugenia—
How thick the bursts come crowding through the
    leaves!
    Again—thou hearest!   30
Eternal Passion!
Eternal Pain!

          —"Philomela" by MATTHEW ARNOLD

It will be seen here that the base of the verse is essentially iambic—which is often the case in free verse—not surprisingly in a language which is essentially iambic as spoken. Many critics have been of the opinion that there are very few excellent free verse poems in existence. Certainly it is the most difficult of all media to handle well, because its success depends upon the most delicate kind of dependence upon rhythm. There is nothing more appalling than bad free verse—i.e., prose masquerading as poetry, and a great many of our most capable poets have preferred to avoid free verse altogether. This much is a matter of record: its high priest, Walt Whitman, turned to it only after considerable experience with metrical verse. And that has been the case with most of its brilliant practitioners.

A great deal of free verse has been written in the twentieth century. But the tendency now is away from it and toward stricter forms.

[1]Arnold uses this version of a Greek story: King Tereus of Phocis, who was married to Philomela, dishonored her sister Procne and, to prevent her from speaking, cut out her tongue. Procne wove the story into a shawl-like garment. After serving the flesh of Tereus' son to him in a dish, the sisters fled. Tereus pursued. Answering their prayer for deliverance, the gods changed Procne to a swallow and Philomela to a nightingale.

[2]Tereus is often called the King of Thrace.

[3]Daulis was Tereus' city in Phocis—"lone" Daulis because it was on a lofty hill; the Cephissus was a river in Phocis.

GLOSSARY
OF ENGLISH LITERARY TERMS

ABSTRACT LANGUAGE, language which expresses a concept apart from any particular or material instance (as in *beauty, loyalty*): See Howells' "Criticism and Fiction," page 51.

ACCENTUAL VERSE, meter based exclusively upon the stresses in a line without regard to the number of weak syllables: See Coleridge's "Christabel," page 245.

ALLEGORY, a literary form in which symbolic actions are tied together to make a narrative: See *Everyman*, page 74.

ALLITERATION, the proximity of words beginning with the same consonantal sound, or with any vowel sound: *concealed craft; open avowal.*

AMBIGUITY, a verbal nuance which permits alternative reactions to the same piece of language: See Shakespeare's "Sonnet LXXIII," page 64.

ANAPEST, a foot of three syllables of which the last one is stressed: *reacquáint.*

ANECDOTE, the relation of an interesting or amusing incident, reported as being true: See page 146.

ANTISTROPHE, the second stanza in each group of three stanzas which constitute a Pindaric ode; it exactly matches in meter and rhyme scheme the *strophe* (first stanza) of its group: See Gray's "The Bard," I,2; II,2; III,2, page 256

ANTITHESIS, the balancing of contrasted expressions: See the opening of Dickens' *A Tale of Two Cities*, page 119.

APOSIOPESIS, leaving it to the hearer or the reader to finish the expression or sentence:

> BEATRICE. But what is he [Benedick] to a lord?
>
> MESSENGER. A lord to a lord, a man to a man, stuffed with all honorable virtues.
>
> BEATRICE. It is so indeed, he is no less

than a stuffed man; *but as for the stuffing—*
Well, we are all mortal.
> —*Much Ado About Nothing*, I/i/56 seq.

APOSTROPHE, a sudden address to someone or something not present:

> Return, O holy Dove, return . . .
> —Cowper's "Walking with God"

ASSONANCE, a coinciding of sounds. See below.

ASSONANCE, CONSONANTAL, a coinciding of the consonants in the final stressed syllable and of all the sounds following that syllable, the stressed vowel differing: *groined, groaned.*

ASSONANCE, VOCALIC, a coinciding of the final stressed vowel, the sounds following that vowel differing: *pronounced, doubt.*

AUBADE, a song for the dawn:

> It was the lark, the herald of the morn,
> No nightingale. Look, love, what envious streaks
> Do lace the severing clouds in yonder east.
> Night's candles are burnt out, and jocund day
> Stands tiptoe on the misty mountain tops . . .
> —*Romeo and Juliet*, III/v/6 seq

BALLAD, a narrative in verse: See *Ballad, Art* and *Ballad, Folk* below.

BALLAD, ART, a ballad written by a given poet in the traditions of the old folk ballad: See Sitwell's "The Ballad of Sister Anne," page 91.

BALLAD, FOLK, a ballad of the people, of unknown authorship: See "Edward," page 90.

BALLAD STANZA, a quatrain of alternating tetrameters and trimeters; usually only the trimeters are in rhyme: See "Sir Patrick Spens," page 250.

BALLADE, a lyrical poem in three stanzas and an envoy; the stanzas are usually of eight lines and the envoy usually of four; the eight lines rhyme *ababbcbc*, the envoy *bcbc*, the rhymes in all stanzas remain the same; each stanza and the envoy end with the identical line by way of refrain.

BLANK VERSE, unrhymed iambic pentameter:

> Nor less when spring had warmed the cultured Vale,
> Moved we as plunderers where the mother-bird
> Had in high places built her lodge . . .
> —Wordsworth's *The Prelude*

CLASSIC, writing devoted to order, clarity and moderation as the chief virtues: See Addison, page 17.

CLIMAX, the moment in a plot during which the central character does something that determines the course of the remaining action of the story; e.g., Romeo's killing of Tybalt.

CLOSET DRAMA, a work written in a succession of acts or scenes, the whole being arranged in speeches assigned to various characters—without any intention of its being presented in a theatre; e.g., Shelley's *Prometheus Unbound.*

COMEDY, a play the chief end of which is to amuse; e.g., Wilde's *The Importance of Being Earnest.*

CONCEIT, an elaborate figure of speech which provides an involved analogy:

> They have left thee naked, O Lord; O that they had!
> This garment too I would they had denied.
> Thee with thyself they have too richly clad,
> Opening the purple wardrobe in thy side.
>
> O never could there be garment too good
> For thee to wear, but this, of thine own blood.

—Crashaw's "Upon the Body of Our Blessed Lord, Naked and Bloody"

CONCRETE LANGUAGE, language which designates a thing or class of things which can be perceived by our senses (as in *tree, Charles*): See the selection from Darwin's *The Descent of Man,* page 52.

CONNOTATIVE LANGUAGE, language used for its associational values:

> Out, out, brief candle!
> —*Macbeth,* V/v/23

COUPLET, two successive rhyming lines in the same meter:

> Life is a jest, and all things show it;
> I thought so once, but now I know it.
> —Gay's "My Own Epitaph"

CYNICISM, a contemptuous disbelief in human decency, expressed with seemingly ruthless candor.

DACTYL, a foot of three syllables of which the first one is stressed: géneral.

DENOTATIVE LANGUAGE, language used in its basic dictionary meaning:

> My pictures blacken in their frames
> As night comes on . . .
> —Landor's "Death of the Day"

DIMETER, a line of two feet:

> With ravished ears
> The monarch hears . . .
> —Dryden's "Alexander's Feast"

DRAMA, a story of human conflict written for the stage.

ELEGY, a poem of lament for someone dead: See Browne's "On the Countess Dowager of Pembroke," page 38.

ELLIPSIS, the omission of a word or words necessary for complete grammatical construction:

> Favors to none, to all she smiles extends.
> —Pope's *The Rape of the Lock*

END-STOPPED LINE, a line in which the thought causes a pause at the end of a line:

> The quality of mercy is not strain'd.
> —*Merchant of Venice,* IV/i/184

ENJAMBMENT, a linking of the lines so that the thought continues without pause from the end of a line into the next:

> It droppeth as the gentle rain from heaven
> Upon the place beneath. . . .
> —*Merchant of Venice,* IV/i/185–186

ENVOY, the dedication at the end of a ballade, usually in four lines: See *Ballade,* above.

EPIC, a long narrative poem celebrating the deeds of a hero.

EPIC, ART, an epic modeled on Homer's epics, and employing certain Epic Conventions (see below); e.g., Milton's *Paradise Lost.*

EPIC CONVENTIONS, certain poetic apparatus found in Homer, and imitated by later epic poets, beginning with Virgil: announcement of the subject of the poem, an appeal to the Muse, plunging into the middle of the story, an enumeration of the opposing hosts, long epic speeches, epic similes, a descent into Hell; e.g., Milton's *Paradise Lost.*

EPIC, FOLK, an epic celebrating the deeds of a hero of the race, of folk authorship; e.g., *Beowulf.*

EPIC SIMILE, an extensive simile, common to Art Epics:

As bees
In springtime, when the sun with Taurus rides,
Pour forth their populous youth about the hive
In clusters; they among fresh dews and flowers
Fly to and fro, or on the smoothèd plank,
The suburb of their straw-built citadel,
New rubbed with balm, expatiate, and confer
Their state affairs; so thick the aëry crowd
Swarmed and were straitened. . . .
—*Paradise Lost,* I, 768 seq.

EPIGRAM, a brief and pointed poem:

Swans sing before they die—'twere no bad thing
Should certain persons die before they sing.
—Coleridge's "An Epigram"

EPITAPH, an inscription memorializing the dead:

Here a pretty baby lies
Sung asleep with lullabies;
Pray be silent, and not stir
Th' easy earth that covers her.
—Herrick's "Upon a Child"

EPITHET, an expression used to characterize someone or something:
deep-browed Homer.
—Keats's "On First Looking into Chapman's Homer"

EPODE, the third stanza in each group of three stanzas in a Pindaric ode; it does not match the first two stanzas in either meter or rhyme scheme: See Gray's "The Bard," I,3; II,3; III,3, page 256.

EUPHEMISM, coating an unpleasantness with sweetness: he passed away (for "he died").

EUPHONY, the pleasant effect resulting from a combination of lovely sounds:
And daffadillies fill their cups with tears . . .
—Milton's "Lycidas"

EUPHUISM, an elaborately artificial style (popularized by John Lyly in his *Euphues*) characterized by rhythms heavily marked through the use of balance, antithesis, alliteration, and preciosity of imagery:

This is that good pelican, that to feed her people spareth not to rend her own person
. . .
—Lyly on Queen Elizabeth I

FARCE, a type of play whose action is loosely strung together, without much attention to plot or characterization; its chief end is to provoke laughter through incongruous situations: e.g., Thornton Wilder's *The Matchmaker.*

FEMININE ENDING, the end of an iambic or anapestic line containing one or more extra weak syllables in the last foot:

Our God's forgotten, and our soldiers slighted . . .
—Quarles' "Of Common Devotion"

FIGURATIVE IMAGERY, imagery so employed that the meaning of the expression is an extension of the image:

To see the world in a grain of sand . . .
—Blake's *Auguries of Innocence*

FIGURE OF SPEECH, the use of words in a nonliteral sense, so that the meaning is to be found in an extension of the image:

Put out the light, and then *put out the light.*
—*Othello,* V/ii/7

FOOT, a group of syllables (or one syllable) containing one and only one stress: begín.

FREE VERSE, verse written without the discipline of meter or in which the meter is constantly changing: See Arnold's "Philomela," page 263.

HENDIADYS, a figure of speech in which one idea is split into two equal parts by the use of two nouns connected by *and:* of wisdom and of reach (for *far-reaching wisdom*).

HEPTAMETER, a line of seven feet:
Rejóice, of Énglish héarts, rejóice! rejóice, oh, lóvers déar!
—Beaumont and Fletcher's *The Knight of the Burning Pestle*

HEROIC COUPLET, two rhyming lines of iambic pentameter in which a complete unit of thought is contained:
What cannot praise effect in mighty minds,
When flattery soothes, and when ambition blinds!
—Dryden's *Absalom and Achitophel*

HEXAMETER, a line of six feet:

Thée I behóld as a bírd borne ín with the wínd from the wést.
—Swinburne's "Hesperia"

HUMOR, the revelation of human traits in an amusing situation.

HYPERBOLE, an exaggeration for effect: as old as the hills.

HYSTERON-PROTERON, defined by Laurence Sterne as "putting the cart before the horse": I put on my shoes and stockings.

IAMB, a foot of two syllables of which the second one is stressed: prefér.

IDYL, a poem describing rural or domestic life; the term is frequently used interchangeably with "pastoral"; e.g., Spenser's *The Shepherd's Calendar.*

INVECTIVE, a denunciation to discredit someone or something with an array of facts: See page 30.

INVERSION, transposing the normal order of words: Of thee I sing.

INVOCATION, an appeal to the Muse or to God for inspiration:

Sing, heavenly Muse, that on the secret top
Of Oreb, or of Sinai, did'st inspire
That shepherd who first taught the chosen seed,
In the beginning, how the heavens and earth
Rose out of chaos . . .
                        —*Paradise Lost,* I, 6 seq.

IRONY, a meaning opposite to the literal meaning of the words employed: See Swift's *A Modest Proposal,* page 72.

KATHARSIS, an inner purgation achieved by the audience through witnessing or reading a tragedy.

KENNING, a metaphorical name: *foamy fields* for "sea."

LITERAL IMAGERY, images so employed that the meaning of the expression lies in their literal or strict denotation: naked savages bedaubed with paint.

LITOTES, a rhetorical device in which an idea is conveyed by a negation of its opposite: *not the least* of my woes (for "one of the greatest of my woes").

LYRIC, a poem of song-like quality (e.g., song, ode, elegy): See Keats's "Ode to a Nightingale," page 106.

LYRICAL WORK, a work written with strong emotional expression: See Thomas Wolfe's "From Death to Morning," page 108.

MASCULINE ENDING, the ending of a trochaic or dactylic line in which the last foot, lacking the usual weak syllable (or syllables), ends on a stress:

Why the warning finger-tip . . .
                        —Tabb's "To Silence"

MELODRAMA, a type of play whose action is loosely strung together, without much attention to plot or characterization; its chief end is to play upon the nerves of the audience through tense situations; e.g., Bram Stoker's *Dracula.*

METAPHOR, a figure of speech which identifies one person or thing by another:

All the world's a stage . . .
                        —*As You Like It,* II/vii/139

METER, the number of feet in a line of verse; e.g., monometer, dimeter, etc.

METONYMY, the use of a word for another which it suggests; the effect for the cause, the sign for the thing signified, etc.: See FitzGerald's *Rubáiyát,* page 61.

MOCK HEROIC, the employing, for the sake of humor, all the serious conventions of an epic poem (see *Epic Conventions,* above) in dealing with a light subject; e.g., Pope's *The Rape of the Lock.*

MONOMETER, a line of verse containing only one foot:

I am
A clam . . .
                        —Anon., "Nirvana"

NARRATIVE, an account of happenings (as history, tale, story).

NONSENSE, a kind of satire which indulges in fun for its own sake: See Johnson's "If the Man Who Turnip Cries," page 29.

NOVEL, a relatively long piece of prose fiction, with a more or less complex plot; e.g., Melville's *Moby Dick.*

NOVELETTE, a short novel; e.g., Willa Cather's *My Mortal Enemy.*

OBJECTIVE APPROACH, that of a writer who deals with his material not from the limitations of his own experience, but from what he has observed of the world at large; e.g., Hawthorne's *The Scarlet Letter.*

OCTAMETER, a line of eight feet:
Cómrades, léave me hére a líttle, whíle as yét 'tis éarly mórn.
                        —Tennyson's *Locksley Hall*

OCTAVE, the first section of eight lines in an Italian sonnet: See Gilder's "The Sonnet," page 251.

ODE, a lyrical poem of exalted emotions: See Keats's "Ode to a Nightingale," page 106.

ODE, CHORAL, an ode, free in form, written in imitation of the odes sung in ancient Greek drama by the Chorus: See Arnold's *Empedocles on Etna,* page 260.

ODE, IRREGULAR (sometimes called the *Irregular Pindaric*), an ode in which the stanzas vary in length and meter: See Cowley's "The Praise of Pindar," page 259.

ODE, PINDARIC, an ode consisting of three larger sections, each of these sections having three stanzas called a *strophe,* an *antistrophe* and *epode;* in each of these larger sections the antistrophe exactly matches the strophe in meter and rhyme scheme: See Gray's "The Bard," page 256.

ODE, REGULAR STANZAIC, an ode written in regular stanzas: See Whittier's "Laus Deo," page 259.

ONOMATOPOEIA, sound imitative of the meaning of a word: whir, clang.

OTTAVA RIMA, a stanza of eight iambic pentameter lines rhyming *abababcc.*

PARADOX, an assertion or an attitude apparently contradictory or opposed to common sense: See Donne's "Holy Sonnet XIV," page 63.

PARALLELISM, the casting of similar ideas in similar forms of expression:

government of the people, by the people, for the people . . .
—Lincoln's "Gettysburg Address"

PASTORAL, a literary work dealing with rural life and scenes, shepherds, shepherdesses, flocks, etc.; e.g., Shelley's "Adonais."

PENTAMETER, a line of five feet:

Look off, dear Love, across the sallow sands . . .
—Lanier's "Evening Song"

PERIODIC SENTENCE, a sentence in which the essential meaning is not completed until the end of the sentence:

I should not have affixed so comprehensive a title to these few remarks, necessarily wanting in any completeness upon a subject the full consideration of which would carry us far, did I not seem to discover a pretext for my temerity in the interesting pamphlet lately published under this name by Mr. Walter Besant . . .
—Henry James's *The Art of Fiction*

PERSONIFICATION, the ascribing of personality to the inanimate or to the abstract:

Grief made the young Spring wild, and she threw down
Her kindling buds, as if she Autumn were. . . .
Shelley's "Adonais"

PLAY, a work written to be presented in a theatre by actors before an audience.

PLOT, the organization of the action of a story into a beginning, a middle, and an end; the roots of the middle are in the beginning; the roots of the end are in the middle; the end must make complete what was begun in the beginning.

PROSE, straightforward discourse (as distinguished from poetry).

PROSODY, the science of making verses.

PUN, the juxtaposition or identifying of words which sound alike but have different meanings:

KING. How is it that the clouds still hang on you?

HAMLET. Not so, my lord; I am too much i' the sun. (i.e., *o' the son*)
—*Hamlet,* I/ii/66–67

QUATRAIN, a stanza of four lines:

Stand close around, ye Stygian set,
With Dirce in one boat conveyed,
Or Charon, seeing, may forget
That he is old and she a shade.
—Landor's "Dirce"

QUIBBLE, a play upon words:

I wish he would explain his explanation. . . .
—Byron's *Don Juan*

REALISTIC WRITING, writing creating a sense of everyday reality: See Millay's "The Return from Town," page 11.

REFLECTIVE, primarily meditative, with structure following either a logical or associational presentation of ideas: See Chesterton's "A Piece of Chalk," page 103.

REFRAIN, a phrase or a line repeated at intervals in a poem: See "Back and Side Go Bare," page 27.

RHETORICAL QUESTION, a question put for rhetorical effect, no answer to it being expected:

Heaven and earth,
Must I remember? Why she would hang on him
As if increase of appetite had grown
By what it fed on. . . .
—*Hamlet,* I/ii/142 seq.

RHYME, the coinciding in the final stressed vowel and in all the sounds following that vowel, the preceding consonant (if any) being different: stone, atone; clowning, frowning; ache, take.

RHYME SCHEME, an arranged pattern of rhymes in a poem; e.g., the first, fourth, fifth and eighth lines rhyming together and the second, third, sixth and seventh rhyming together in an Italian sonnet, *abbaabba.*

RHYTHM, the coinciding and failure to coincide of the line's arrangement of stresses and weak syllables with the basic rhythm of the line: the arrangement of:

> Whén tŏ thĕ séssiŏns ŏf swéet sílĕnt thóught

coinciding and failing to coincide with:

∪´∪´∪´∪´∪´—i.e., iambic pentameter.

RIME ROYAL, a stanza of seven iambic pentameter lines rhyming *ababbcc:* See Chaucer's *Troilus and Criseyde.*

ROMANTIC WRITING, writing creating a sense of life unconnected with everyday reality: See Scott's *The Bride of Lammermoor,* page 13.

RONDEAU, a lyrical poem in thirteen lines containing only two rhymes, and an unrhymed refrain after the eighth line and at the end; the refrain is made up of the opening words of the poem; the rhyme scheme is *aabbaaab* (Refrain), *aabba* (Refrain).

RONDEL, a lyrical poem in fourteen lines with only two rhymes; the first two lines are repeated as a refrain in the seventh and eighth and in the thirteenth and fourteenth lines; the rhyme scheme is either *ababba* (line 1) (line 2), *abab* (line 1) (line 2) or *abbaab* (line 1) (line 2), *abba* (line 1) (line 2).

RUN-ON LINES, verse in which there is no significant pause for several consecutive lines: See *Othello* III/iii/453 seq., page 247.

SARCASM, an inversion of the facts made with the purpose of wounding: See page 29.

SARDONIC, THE, a pessimistic expression for the purpose of self-relief in adversity: See page 30.

SATIRE, an attack on an individual or an institution or manners: See Swift's "A Modest Proposal," page 72.

SESTET, the concluding six lines of an Italian sonnet; it may be rhymed *cdecde* or *cdeedc* or *cdcdcd* or *cdcdee:* See Gilder's "The Sonnet," page 251. C. Rossetti's "After Death," page 252, Wordsworth's "The World Is Too Much with Us," page 252, White's "To Night," page 252.

SESTINA, a lyrical poem, usually of six stanzas containing six lines each, plus a tercet as the conclusion; there is no rhyme, but each of the six stanzas contains the same end-words for the lines, but arranged in a different order for each stanza; in the tercet three of these words are in the middle of the lines and three are at the ends.

SHORT STORY, a comparatively short piece of prose fiction, whose plot deals with one significant incident: See Woolf's "The New Dress," page 68.

SIMILE, a figure of speech which compares one person or thing with another:

> Like a dog he hunts in dreams . . .
> —Tennyson's "Locksley Hall"

SONNET, a poem in fourteen lines of iambic pentameter, written according to the English, the Italian or Mason style; see below.

SONNET, ENGLISH (sometimes called the "Shakespearean"), a sonnet made up of a unit of twelve lines rhyming *ababcdcdefef* and a couplet rhyming *gg;* the twelve lines are often divided into three quatrains: See Drayton's "Idea," page 253.

SONNET, ITALIAN (sometimes called the "Petrarchan"), a sonnet made up of an octave (a unit of eight lines) and a scstct (a unit of six lines); the octave rhymes *abbaabba;* the sestet rhymes *cdecde* or *cdeedc* or *cdcdcd* or *cdcdee:* See Gilder's "The Sonnet," page 251, C. Rossetti's "After Death," page 252. Wordsworth's "The World Is Too Much with Us," page 252, White's "To Night," page 252.

SONNET, MASON, a sonnet whose rhyme scheme is *abc abc cbd badda,* which may be written as one unit or with subtle divisions of two, three or four. Sometimes the word at the end of the first line is repeated as the last word in the sonnet. See Mason's "The Oakleaf," Lockwood's "Angelique" and Grebanier's "May Afternoon," page 256.

SPENSERIAN STANZA, a nine-line stanza, of which the first eight are in iambic pentameter and the ninth in iambic hexameter; the rhyme scheme is *ababbcbcc:* See Shelley's "Adonais," page 251.

SPRUNG RHYTHM, "scanning by accents or stresses alone, without any account of the number of syllables" (G. M. Hopkins): See Hopkins, page 246.

STANZA, a succession of lines forming a unit of grouping in the poem.

STROPHE, the first stanza in each group of three stanzas in a Pindaric ode; it sets up a pattern of meter and rhyme scheme which is matched in the second stanza (the *anti-*

strophe): See Gray's "The Bard," I,1; II,1; and III,1, page 256.

SUBJECTIVE APPROACH, that of a writer who deals with material drawn and viewed from his own experience: See Poe's "A Dream within a Dream," page 5.

SYMBOL, something used to stand for something else: the lion (symbol of courage).

SYMBOLISM, the recurrent use of the same symbol in a work: See Woolf's "The New Dress," page 68.

SYNECDOCHE, the substituting of the part for the whole or the whole for the part: that victorious *brow*. —Arnold's "Shakespeare"

TALE, a story narrating a series of incidents not organized into a plot: See "A Doctor of the Laws," page 148.

TERCET, a stanza of three lines; they often are all in rhyme: See Herrick's "Upon Julia's Clothes," page 248.

TERZA RIMA, a stanzaic arrangement for a poem of some length, in which the stanzas are of three lines rhyming *aba, bcb, cdc, ded, efe,* etc.: See Morris's "The Defence of Guenevere," page 248.

TETRAMETER, a line of four feet:

I stóod, and sáw my místress dánce . . .
    —Shirley's "Upon His Mistress Dancing"

TONE, the author's attitude manifested in his work as satirical, compassionate, witty, reflective, playful, cold and so forth.

TRAGEDY, a play which undertakes, in tracing the catastrophic career of its hero, to provide an inner purging of the audience through the agency of pity and awe; e.g., *Hamlet.*

TRAGIC FLAW, the character defect in a tragic hero which brings about his downfall; e.g., the rashness of Romeo.

TRILOGY, three plays connected in subject matter; e.g., *Agamemnon, The Libation Pourers,* and *The Eumenides* of Aeschylus.

TRIMETER, a line of three feet:

The skíes they were áshen and sóber . . .
    —Poe's "Ulalume"

TRIOLET, a lyrical poem in eight lines with only two rhymes; the first line reappears as the fourth and again as the seventh; the second line reappears as the eighth; the rhyme scheme is *aba* (line 1) *ab* (line 1) (line 2).

TROCHEE, a foot of two syllables of which the first one is stressed: wánder.

TROPE, the use of figurative language; a figure of speech.

VERS LIBRE, free verse.

VILLANELLE, a lyrical poem in nineteen lines; five stanzas are of three lines and the last of four lines, with only two rhymes; the first line reappears as the sixth, twelfth and eighteenth lines; the third line reappears as the ninth, fifteenth and nineteenth lines; the three-line stanzas all rhyme *aba;* the last stanza rhymes *abaa:* See Dowson's "A Villanelle of Marguerites," page 261.

WIT, a manipulation of words that surprises, for the purpose of throwing light on ideas: See page 30.

INDEX